# The Emerging Lesbian

WORLDS OF DESIRE:
THE CHICAGO SERIES ON SEXUALITY, GENDER, AND CULTURE
EDITED BY GILBERT HERDT

**Also in the series:**
*American Gay*
by Stephen O. Murray

*Out in Force: Sexual Orientation and
the Military*
edited by Gregory M. Herek,
Jared B. Jobe, and Ralph M. Carney

*Queer Forster*
edited by Robert K. Martin
and George Piggford

*The Cassowary's Revenge:
The Life and Death of Masculinity
in a New Guinea Society*
by Donald Tuzin

*Mema's House, Mexico City:
On Transvestites, Queens, and Machos*
by Annick Prieur

*Travesti: Sex, Gender, and Culture among
Brazilian Transgendered Prostitutes*
by Don Kulick

*Sambia Sexual Culture:
Essays from the Field*
by Gilbert Herdt

*Gay Men's Friendships:
Invincible Communities*
by Peter M. Nardi

*No Place Like Home: Relationships and
Family Life among Lesbians and Gay Men*
by Christopher Carrington

*Beyond Carnival: Male Homosexuality
in Twentieth-Century Brazil*
by James N. Green

*A Plague of Paradoxes: AIDS, Culture,
and Demography in Northern Tanzania*
by Philip W. Setel

*The Course of Gay and Lesbian Lives:
Social and Psychoanalytic Perspectives*
by Bertram J. Cohler
and Robert M. Galatzer-Levy

*Homosexualities*
by Stephen O. Murray

*The Bedtrick: Tales of Sex
and Masquerade*
by Wendy Doniger

*Money, Myths, and Change: The Economic
Lives of Lesbians and Gay Men*
by M. V. Lee Badgett

*The Night Is Young: Sexuality in Mexico
in the Time of AIDS*
by Héctor Carrillo

Tze-lan D. Sang

# THE EMERGING LESBIAN
## Female Same-Sex Desire in Modern China

THE UNIVERSITY OF CHICAGO PRESS

CHICAGO AND LONDON

**Tze-lan D. Sang** is assistant professor of Chinese literature at the University of Oregon.

The University of Chicago Press, Chicago 60637
The University of Chicago Press, Ltd., London
© 2003 by The University of Chicago
All rights reserved. Published 2003
Printed in the United States of America

12 11 10 09 08 07 06 05 04 03      1 2 3 4 5

ISBN: 0-226-73478-1 (cloth)
ISBN: 0-226-73480-3 (paper)

The publisher gratefully acknowledges a Subsidy for Publication from the Chiang Ching-Kuo Foundation for International Scholarly Exchange.

Library of Congress Cataloging-in-Publication Data

Sang, Tze-lan D.
  The emerging lesbian : female same-sex desire in modern China / Tze-lan D. Sang.
    p. cm. — (Worlds of desire)
  Includes bibliographical references and index.
  ISBN 0-226-73478-1 (alk. paper) — ISBN 0-226-73480-3 (pbk. : alk. paper)
  1. Lesbians—China.  I. Title.  II. Series.
  HQ75.6.C6 S25   2003
  305.48′9664′0951—dc21

                                              2002013302

*For my parents and my grandmother*

# CONTENTS

# ILLUSTRATIONS

# ACKNOWLEDGMENTS

This project was originally undertaken as a doctoral dissertation in the Department of Comparative Literature at the University of California at Berkeley. I am indebted to its initial readers, Lydia Liu, Michael Lucey, Samuel Hung-nin Cheung, Elizabeth Abel, and the late William Nestrick, for their skillful guidance.

Over the years I have benefited from the advice or encouragement of many other scholars, including Stephen West, David Der-wei Wang, Hsiao-yen Peng, Carolyn Dinshaw, Judith Zeitlin, Mayfair Yang, Judith Butler, Wen-hsin Yeh, Gail Hershatter, Hua Wei, Michelle Yeh, Sung-sheng Yvonne Chang, Theodore Huters, Lisa Rofel, Shu-mei Shih, Andrew Jones, Sylvia Li-chun Lin, Dorothy Ko, Siao-chen Hu, Giovanni Vitiello, Susan Glosser, Jerlian Tsao, Paola Zamperini, Sophie Volpp, Chien-ming Yu, Cynthia Brokaw, Wendy Larson, Bryna Goodman, Maram Epstein, Sebastian Liao, and Haun Saussy. Carol Wang, Jien-mei Lee, Ping-ying Chang, and Tamara Chin inspired me with their friendship and insights.

Interviews with Chen Ran and Lin Bai were essential for my reconceptualization of the book. I am grateful to the two writers for sharing their views on art and creativity with me and to Shen Rui for her wonderful assistance.

Parts of chapters 3, 7, and 8 were presented at the University of California at Santa Barbara, Stanford University, the University of California at Berkeley, San Francisco State University, Columbia University, the University of Chicago, and the University of Oregon. Stimulating questions prompted me to reconsider several arguments.

The anonymous readers for the University of Chicago Press pointed out errors in the manuscript and suggested valuable sources that helped to redress them. Gilbert Herdt, the general editor of the Worlds of Desire series, and Douglas Mitchell at the University of Chicago Press gave me unswerving support as they patiently waited for the day that I would part with the manuscript. Their encouragement and wise counsel were indispensable to the completion of the book.

Research at various stages was sponsored by two dissertation fellowships from the Chiang Ching-kuo Foundation and the Mellon Foundation as well as by faculty research grants from the Center for the Study of Women in Society and the College of Arts and Sciences at the University of Oregon. The Department of East Asian Languages and Literatures at the University of Oregon and the Department of Asian Languages at Stanford University both provided time off from teaching that facilitated my writing. A generous publication subsidy from the Chiang Ching-kuo Foundation defrayed some of the production expenses.

Last but not least, my parents and family have lavished their affection on me, which has made my scholarly pursuit a joyful endeavor.

# INTRODUCTION

## A Century of Transformation

Sitting in a dimly lit library room one afternoon, and leafing though the inaugural issue of the early Chinese women's literary magazine *Meiyu* (The words of eyebrows), I stumbled on a set of photographs with the caption "Chinese beauties' activities of leisure [*Zhongguo meiren zhi xianqing*]."[1] There were altogether four photographs, representing, respectively, "a long uninterrupted chat [*xuyu*]," "waiting for the moon [*daiyue*]," "reading a poem [*dushi*]," and "a competition in makeup [*douzhuang*]" (see fig. 1).[2] Among these images (published in Shanghai in 1914) was a picture of two young women dressed in the style of the late Qing and early Republican era and sitting together in a wooden chair. More precisely, one was sitting in the other's lap, her arm around her friend's shoulder, her friend's arm around her waist. That these women would embrace each other in a chair while having an intimate and drawn-out conversation was obviously meant neither to shock nor to titillate. The venue for the photograph was a respectable magazine featuring romantic fiction in simple, classical language and edited by and especially for gentry-class literary

美 人 閒 之 情

讀 詩

絮 語

鬥 妝

待 月

FIGURE 1 "Chinese beauties' activities of leisure" (*clockwise from upper right*): "a long uninterrupted chat"; "waiting for the moon"; "a competition in makeup"; and "reading a poem." (*Meiyu*, no. 1 [1914]: 4)

women (*caiyuan*).³ The magazine, which had a traditional bent and would look conservative a few years later compared with May Fourth literary magazines published in the modern, Europeanized vernacular, presented the girls as fine specimens of the Chinese gentlewoman.⁴ They were engaging in a laudable pastime, like reading a poem or basking in moonlight in a garden, that was suitable for ladies of superior beauty and sentiment. However, to a Chinese female reader—me—looking at this image at the end of the twentieth century, such an unrestrained public display of physical affection has come to seem quaint and startling.⁵

This image, randomly salvaged from the disintegrating pages of an old magazine, is just one of the many indications that much has changed since the early twentieth century in the Chinese social conception of women's proper relations and intimacy with one another. The point is not necessarily that physical affection has become statistically rare among female friends in Chinese societies but that to exhibit such physical affection in public has come to involve, increasingly, new frameworks of signification and perception that depart from the venerable notions of friendship and sisterhood. Compare the tête-à-tête on display in *Meiyu* with the lesbian (*nü tongzhi*) intimacy staged for the camera in two commercial magazines, *G&L: Re'ai zazhi* (G&L: Love magazine) and *Tugo* (Together), both of which catered to gay and lesbian readerships in late-twentieth-century Taiwan and Hong Kong.⁶ The extent of bodily contact visible in the lesbian mise-en-scènes in *G&L* and *Tugo* rarely exceeds that in "Chinese beauties' activities of leisure" in *Meiyu* (see figs. 2–4).⁷ Yet the contextualizations and, as a result, the significations of publicly *visible* female-female physical contact differ dramatically.

There is now a considerable fraction—if not yet the majority—of the population in Taiwan, Hong Kong, and the cosmopolitan cities of mainland China sufficiently sensitized by agents such as the mass media to the notion of female homosexuality and the controversy surrounding it to detect in the enthusiastic exhibit in *Meiyu* of two women locked in each other's arms the unknowing innocence of a bygone era. That innocence is similar, in a way, to that of the male author Chen Sen, who crafted an elaborate novel, *Pinhua baojian* (A precious mirror for classifying flowers), in the mid-nineteenth century to exalt the romantic love between male literati patrons and boy actors specializing in female roles in the Beijing theater. Commenting on the novel in 1918, Hu Shi, one of the chief architects of the May Fourth New Culture Movement, excused Chen from blame, that is, declared him innocent because, unlike the moderns, he "did not know that a man's love of beautiful boys was a bad thing [*bu zhi*

FIGURE 2
The lesbian chic?
(*Tugo*, no. 5
[1998]: 8)

FIGURE 3
Sisterhood and
recipes. (*Tugo*,
no. 3 [1998]: 116)

FIGURE 4 The happy ending of "Mulans" (a photographic story). (*G&L: Re'ai zazhi,* no. 15 [1998]: 136)

*nanse wei eshi*]."[8] There is one significant difference between Chen's unabashed praise for male-male erotic love and *Meiyu*'s lack of embarrassment about female-female intimacy, however. While one man's love for another—particularly the desire of the literatus when aroused by the beauty of an actor—was celebrated by Chen as an exquisite, rapturous passion (which can be quasi-egalitarian among some of his characters),[9] intimacy between female friends was evidently not recognized by *Meiyu* as love of the same significance and magnitude. Instead of being recognized as erotic desire (*se*), female-female intimacy belonged in much more general categories, such as the feelings (*qing*) among sisters (*jiemei*) and friends (*you*).

Certainly, the change from innocence to a sensitivity about female-female intimacy was not universal in Chinese societies; nor did the transformation occur overnight. As a matter of fact, it is probably even the case that there have been periods of recess, relapse, redirection, and divergence. But the initial ripples of change had begun and were felt in the forward-looking, modernity-enamored stratum of the urban Chinese population in the 1910s and 1920s. Although the Republican period (1912–49), especially the May Fourth decade (1915–27), has been frequently noted by China scholars of today for its major changes in gender and sexual conceptions, practices, and politics—such as the binary definitions of gender introduced by Western biology, the imbrication of women's emancipation in the projects of nation building and modernization, or the brand-new urban images of the modern girl and the femme fatale, bold in desire and adventurous in love with men—female same-sex relations during the Republican era have tended not to draw attention from present-day researchers.[10] The oversight has been remedied to a significant extent in the last decade, by literary critics in particular.[11] Major critics in China, Taiwan, and the United States, including Meng Yue, Dai Jinhua, Hsiao-yen Peng, Tani Barlow, Lydia Liu, David Der-wei Wang, Ying-ying Chien, and Wendy Larson, have all commented on the romantic feelings between women depicted in the short stories of certain May Fourth female authors, especially Lu Yin and Ding Ling.[12] However, beyond identifying the presence of women's homoerotic feelings in select literary texts, much of the context in which these fictional representations surfaced remains to be reconstructed. In truth, there was an unprecedented debate over female same-sex love forming in the May Fourth era, replete with medical categorizations in sex-education pamphlets, intellectual discussions in feminist and education magazines, a cluster of fictional representations by male and female authors besides Lu Yin and Ding Ling, and commentaries from self-styled psychoanalytic critics such as Zhao Jingshen and Pan Guangdan and social historians such as Chen Dongyuan. Why was female same-sex love a public issue? How did it suddenly become so? What did the debate do to the previously respectable public sight of female-female intimacy as in "a long uninterrupted chat"?

This book attempts to answer some of these questions. It complements previous research on the transformation in gender and sexual ideals in the May Fourth era. It also grew out of a discontentment with prior studies positing major changes in Chinese attitudes toward same-sex sexuality in the course of Westernization, studies that have discussed predominantly male-male sexuality.[13] In this regard, this study is the first to attempt to shed light on the transition from premodern to modern Chinese conceptions of same-sex relations in the early twentieth century by taking a female-centered perspective, that is, by focusing on female-female relations. As I demonstrate in the first half of the book, a historical transition took place in the early twentieth century whereby female same-sex desire became a problematic issue requiring public discussion in Chinese society. Female-female intimacy, formerly negligible and insignificant in the patriarchal familial organization of traditional China, became distinctively associated with feminism, on the one hand, and psychobiological abnormality, on the other. The growing visibility, or increasing discursive production, of female same-sex desire in modern Chinese culture in the 1910s and 1920s reflected Chinese women's changing economic, social, and political status—above all, upper- and middle-class women's entrance into wage labor, women's unprecedented participation in public life, and women's relative economic independence from the patriarchal family. The social significance of women's same-sex relations, be it positive or negative, intensified with women's increased social, economic, and political strength. In a manner paralleling the rise of "sexuality" in the West (at least according to Foucault),[14] a system deploying sexuality—one that classifies and evaluates the types and intensities of bodily sensations, emotional attachments, and personal characteristics—became a powerful supplement to kinship—the system of alliance—as social control in modernizing China.

Another major impetus behind this study is the resurgence of female homoerotic literature in the People's Republic of China (PRC) in the 1990s, not to mention the blossoming of a female homoerotic literature in Taiwan, which coincides with a burgeoning lesbian identity politics. Granted that the recent female homoerotic literatures written in Chinese across the Taiwan Strait appear to be counterdiscourses that combat regulative forces in the local environment, I see important commonalities between them. They openly resist the modern sexological abnormalization of same-sex intimacy, which has occurred in many Asian societies as well as in Europe and America since the early twentieth century. In many instances, they are examples of a "reverse discourse," in which "homosexuality [begins] to speak in its own behalf, to demand that its legitimacy and 'naturality' be acknowledged, often in the same vocabulary, using the same categories by which it was medically disqualified."[15] They challenge, moreover, dominant definitions of femininity, and their critiques of the gender strictures fostered by the patriarchal family, the state, and the capitalist economy are among the most incisive in their respective local contexts. In other words, these literatures deserve consideration, first, as local engagements with globally influential discourses of sexuality and, second, as radical feminist politics stemming from same-sex desire and/or lesbian subjectivity.

While recent critics and theorists writing on the lesbian literatures and cultures of the West have raised the issue of whether lesbian studies should "come out of feminism,"[16] I contend that gender analysis is the most effective and appropriate means for understanding the importance of female homoerotic writing in the current Chinese-speaking world. Among other reasons, "sexuality is a key site of the construction of gender differences and of the hierarchies inscribed in them," as Harriet Evans maintains in her study of the dominant discourses of sexuality in the PRC since 1949.[17] Upholding gender as an overarching analytic category does not mean that I desexualize female homoeroticism. In fact, as my readings of specific texts will show, I often ask pointed questions about the representability of female-female lust in a particular time and place. Moreover, my conception of feminism does not presume that there is an essential femininity unifying all women. Rather, I understand feminism as a commitment to furthering girls' and women's freedom from subordination, discrimination, violence, and deprivation arising from biological sex difference. And I am interested in the subversion of gender norms and identities as much as in the overall empowerment of girls and women.

In subsequent sections of this introductory chapter, I delineate how my interests in gender and sexuality intersect with a number of current debates: the discussion of transnational sexuality in queer studies; China scholars' research on a shift in the Chinese gender system during China's transition from empire to modernity; and contemporary public discussions of the category *woman,* of feminism, and of female homoeroticism in post-Mao China and post–martial law Taiwan. Along the way, I sketch out the main narrative presented in this book and conclude with a critical reflection on the fraught issue of terminology.

## Thinking Sexuality Transnationally

Issues of transnationality and globalization have recently become prominent in the study of sexuality in the West. In the introduction to a recent collection of essays published in *GLQ,* the guest editors, Elizabeth Povinelli and George Chauncey, announce the arrival of a "transnational turn" in lesbian and gay studies and urge their fellow queer theorists to stop taking the nation-state as the privileged and self-evident unit or site for investigation.[18] Ironically, this well-intentioned and sophisticated injunction to all to take culture as circulatorially rather than territorially based evinces yet again American hegemony and the extent to which queer theorists of rich Anglophone countries can unwittingly erase the ineluctable conditions involved in the studies of Third World nations and cultures. Certainly, thinking transnationally is something that researchers of Third World cultures in modernity have been doing all along, for how can they avoid it? As Lydia Liu argues so cogently in her study of early-twentieth-century Chinese literature and national culture, Chinese modernity is a translated modernity.[19] Although Liu does complicate the notion of translation to argue that meanings are locally reconfigured rather than transposed in a forthright and self-identical fashion from the metropolitan West to the peripheries, the question of Western influence is never far from any investigation of modern developments in the Third World. The complexity of translated modernity in the non-West means that, even when a particular non-Western space for inquiry is ostensibly identified as the nation, it is always already shot through with colonial, imperial, transnational, cosmopolitan, global—whatever we call it—presence and valence. In short, it has been an absolutely rudimentary task for scholars studying Third World nation-states to take cognizance of the transnational links and circulations between "local" formations and the hegemonic West. These transnational linkages and movements confront scholars at every turn because of the ravages of colonialism and the acceleration of globalization since the end of the cold war. The injunction to think sexuality transnationally, therefore, is a reminder more useful to queer theorists who are preoccupied with Western sexualities and currently confine themselves to local and national interpretive frameworks than to scholars studying sexuality in modern Third World nations.

Indeed, the selection of articles made by Povinelli and Chauncey speaks as much about the unequal degrees to which transnationality has (already) been factored into scholarly narratives about the sexualities of the West and the rest. The six essays on transnational sexualities are about China, Indonesia, Puerto Rico, Brazil, South Africa, and Taiwan. Not a single piece, for instance, overtly addresses how a transnational perspective might complicate the stories of North American sexualities—despite Povinelli and Chauncey's professed dissatisfaction with the predominantly local and national frameworks in Americanist histories of sexuality.[20]

Among the essays in this transnational collection, one of the shared themes is how theorists may move discussions of non-Western gay, lesbian, and queer identities away from reductive conclusions about their sameness with or difference from Western, especially American, sexual identities. Tom Boellstorff taps into the rich theory of postcolonial subjectivity and complicates the binarisms of sameness versus difference. He asserts, "The issue is not the world's becoming more the same or more different under globalization . . . but the transformation of the very yardsticks by which one decides whether something is the same or different in the first place, that is, the reconfiguration of the grid of similitude and differ-ence."[21] Lisa Rofel, in a different manner, disturbs the local/global binary by calling attention to the fact that "the local and global are both acts of positioning, perspectives rather than mere locales, used as signifiers of difference." She argues that seeing the local and the global as both dis-cursively produced in contexts rather than transparent "might help us move beyond invocations of similitude and difference in our discussions of cosmopolitan gay identities outside the West. . . . To comprehend sex-ual identities in places outside the United States . . . entails examining how they articulate with discursive productions of culture and place."[22]

Specifically examining cosmopolitan gay male identities emerging in postsocialist China at the close of the twentieth century, Rofel argues that cultural citizenship, or the desire for belonging in China, has become a chief technique of normalization in the matters of sex. She explains: "Cul-tural citizenship is a rubric or trope I use to convey novel processes of subjectification, new modes of inclusion and exclusion, and new forms of governmentality." Put in mundane and simplified terms, she suggests that the sense of legitimacy among young, middle-class, and Beijing-based gay male subjects hinges critically on whether they can live in "harmony" with family and society in China; their activism has, as a result, tended to avoid confrontation and opt for other tactics. Rofel makes a valid point, but the presence of a desire for cultural belonging does not, it seems to me, rule out the possibility that there are other forms of governmentality that overlap or intersect with the discourse of cultural citizenship. Rofel ar-gues, "Cultural citizenship, rather than legal subjectivity or psychological personality, establishes proper and improper sex in postsocialist China."[23] This downplaying of other forms of governmentality that regulate and define sex in postsocialist China is uncalled for and is contradicted in fact by the details of gender, class, and legal inclusions/exclusions that punc-tuate Rofel's own analysis.

Rofel's dismissal of the possibility of a psychologized gay subjectivity in China, in particular, is inconclusive since, in the gay salon in Beijing where she conducted fieldwork, it might be easier for gay persons to dis-cuss issues such as their relations to family and foreign gays than to di-vulge the details of their psychological turmoil or the pangs of love and self-recognition in front of a dozen strangers. If one's encounter with these gay persons is mediated through their private letters, creative writing, or autobiographical narratives, for instance, one might form a very different picture of the extent to which the psyche figures in the construction of cosmopolitan gay identities in China.[24] The overconfidence of Rofel's formulation of cultural citizenship as the central issue in cosmopolitan Chinese gay subjectivity is brought into sharp relief especially when her theoretical lens is diverted from a predetermined focus on gay men to take gender difference into account. Rofel notes that gay men in China continue to be affected by the parental imperative to marry and produce offspring in order to continue the patrilineal family line in fulfillment of their filial duty and that this imperative affects gay men perhaps more than it does gay women. Although Rofel chooses not to pursue the question of gender difference further, what has come through vividly in this detail is the persistent disciplinary force of the gender orthodoxy and its differential effects on those who form their primary emotional and sexual bonds with the same sex.[25] In other words, gender and other techniques of normalization, including medical, legal, and class ones, remain necessary categories of analysis and cannot be lightly displaced by a consideration of cultural citizenship and cosmopolitanism.

In brief, I welcome Povinelli and Chauncey's call for nuanced transnational frameworks in thinking lesbian, gay, and queer sexualities inside and outside the West, and I admire Rofel's brilliant explication of the simultaneous existence of gay cosmopolitanism and cultural citizenship in a non-Western metropolis such as Beijing. But it is worth remarking that what is conspicuously missing in current discussions of transnational gay identities in China is an understanding of the temporal depth of transnational processes. The encounter between Chinese subjects and Western sexual discourses and the anxieties that such an encounter provoked about Chinese culture did not begin in the 1990s. As Rofel notes, "Invocations of culture at [the gay] salon tend to be ahistorical—or rather, as in China at large, tend to disavow history and thus reveal its own historicity."[26] If this is true, then elite researchers have an even greater responsibility to resist this collective disavowal and to provide a long view of the transnationalization of sex in China.

The reintegration of China into the international arena, set in motion by the redevelopment of a market economy during the last two decades, merely, to borrow Chris Berry's words, "further hybridizes an already hybridized space."[27] And, for better or worse, in order to look at the lengthy, uneven, and at times intermittent process of hybridization, taking the nation as a provisional geographic unit may be one of the more efficacious organizational strategies. To date, there are few serious investigations (in any language) of Chinese sexualities prior to the present era that are comparable, in terms of density of description, to historians' research on sex in Euro-American history.[28] This meagerness in itself requires serious reflection. The scarcity cannot be entirely attributed to a general neglect of the question of sex among the historians of China. The lack tells, in fact, of a decimated desire for national and local histories among the educated elite as well as the masses of China because the national past has long been presumed worthless.[29] In this case, unthinkingly to privilege the globe over the nation or the local place as the most legitimate, the most sophisticated, and the ultimate framework for studying sexuality may all too easily deflect intellectual curiosity away from the periphery back to the West again and, thus, unwittingly reinscribe the all-too-obvious inequalities between the West and the rest in the current transnational production and circulation of sexual knowledge and identities.

For these reasons, whereas I recognize the global circulation of sexual discourses in the modern world as a fact, and while I acknowledge the central roles that global cities play in the formation of a transnational sexual economy and culture, this study will not completely do away with the nation as a structure. I do not, in the main, discuss sex on a global scale.[30] Rather, I see my task, first and foremost, as that of discovering as many local details as possible—whether they are the details of premodern Chinese literary depictions of female-female love and eroticism, the particulars of the initial translations of European and Japanese sexology into Chinese in the early twentieth century, or the details of female homoerotic texts by May Fourth and post-Mao Chinese women writers. Only after a careful accumulation of details can one know with some certainty the specific features of transnational sexuality in twentieth-century China.

### Discourse

The geographic locus for this study is what is called *China* in common-sense language. However, China is by no means a self-same territorial entity through time.[31] In some sense, the materials for my study are linked to one another by language rather than by location. What I am interested in are discourses in Chinese rather than a fixed physical space. In the case of premodern China, I examine sources primarily from the late-imperial era (ca. 1600–1911) without distinguishing among regions. In comparison, the sources from Republican China that are pertinent to my study show a clear pattern of having been published in the cities, chief among which are Beijing and Shanghai. When it comes to the late twentieth century, I am drawn to the discourses from the two descendant nation-states of Republican China—the PRC on the mainland and the Republic of China (ROC) on Taiwan. And, again, the discourses have radiated predominantly from the metropolises, especially Beijing and Taipei. My choice of the PRC and Taiwan, instead of Hong Kong or any other Chinese place, for study at the turn of the millennium is dictated by the quantity and the quality of mainland Chinese and Taiwanese female homoerotic literatures in the last decade. If one were to disregard elite literary representation altogether and to examine instead lesbian communities, then Hong Kong may be appropriate for fieldwork, as other researchers have suggested.[32]

My choice to emphasize elite literature as a subject matter is deliberate. Literature has been a particularly important forum in which Chinese publics have openly debated at various moments of the twentieth century the matters of gender and sexuality, in a manner that is relatively (but not absolutely) independent from the state and capitalist interests. Here, I make an underlying assumption, one that concurs with Mayfair Yang's recent contention that one can meaningfully speak of the existence of "public spheres" at certain moments in twentieth-century Chinese history.[33] Yang's formulation of the public sphere is a critical revision of Jürgen Habermas's seminal concept of the bourgeois public sphere in Western Europe. According to Habermas, with the development of capitalism and the modern state in the seventeenth and eighteen centuries, private people came together to debate issues of common concern and compel public authority to legitimate itself before public opinion. This idealized image of the bourgeois public sphere is then pitted, by Habermas, against the public sphere as it exists in the late nineteenth century and the twentieth, where certain features of advanced capitalism—such as the concentration of capital into very large, mighty corporations, the monopolistic power of the media to mold "public opinion," and a pervasive commodification of culture—have fundamentally transformed the structure of the public sphere and threatened to undermine its rationality.[34]

Historians have disagreed over whether Habermas's theory, formulated in the context of Western Europe, can be successfully reworked to shed light on certain activities of the gentry and merchant classes in the late-imperial era and on the modern period in China.[35] However, the intensified commercialization and urbanization that occurred in China in the late nineteenth and early twentieth centuries, including the development of certain social institutions such as the mass printing industry and the journalistic press, suggest that it is both plausible and unavoidable for researchers to examine the possibilities of public spheres and their features during this period.[36] Leo Lee and Andrew Nathan, for instance, have argued that the phenomenal growth of the periodical press and fiction publishing at the end of the Qing (1644–1911) gave rise to an initial urban mass culture and provided a new forum for political discussion and action.[37] And, as Bryna Goodman observes, "In the early Republican period, as in the last years of the Qing dynasty, there was an expansion in notions of public space, public print, and the numbers of people who constituted 'the public.' . . . In their associational behavior and discursive practices, urban residents intensified their engagement with the twin modern imperatives of being public and representing *the* public." Analyzing the steps that native-place associations in Shanghai took to reform their structures, Goodman maintains that the catalyst for public practices in the early years of the Republic was "the broadly perceived absence of an effective state in a modern world-system. The constitution of the public was envisioned as a popular remedy for this lack, as if the act of embodying the ideal state in local associational practices could conjure forth such a state at the national level."[38] With regard to the PRC of the late twentieth century, Xudong Zhang identifies Chinese intellectuals' lively discussion of culture (the so-called Culture Fever) in the mid- and late 1980s as the first instance of an emergent "public culture" outside the state apparatus in the history of the PRC, or at least "a Chinese 'public sphere' heralded by its cultural constitution."[39] Although other China scholars do not necessarily use the terminology of Habermas's public-sphere theory, many have put forth observations about the opening up of an unofficial social space in China during the 1980s and early 1990s.[40] The possibility to examine specific developments such as these gives credence to Mayfair Yang's assertion that the pressing question is, "not whether a Western category [i.e., the public sphere] fits traditional Chinese culture, but how a modern global category would work itself out in the particular modernity of China."[41]

That elite literature functions in Chinese societies as a forum for vibrant, serious discussion of gender and sexuality is especially true during the May Fourth era and in the late twentieth century. Elite literature, in other words, has been a potential place for critical exchange in modern Chinese public spheres, even as it is also a discursive site where questions of power are never far away. Here, I am aware of the tension between a Foucauldian notion of discourse and a Habermasian concept of the public sphere. Foucault's understanding of discourse links it intimately to power, which seems to contradict Habermas's utopian belief in the possibility of rational communication. However, I believe that the power relations effected through discourse do not necessarily preclude an element of critical exchange in the process, and vice versa. And, while a perfectly critical, rational, and open public sphere may be a utopian ideal that has never been fully realized anywhere, this does not hinder us from "call[ing] for an examination of the ways by which public spheres can establish and maintain their independence from three institutional forces that dominate modern societies: the logic and interests of the state, the market, and evolving forms of patriarchal kinship and family modalities," as Mayfair Yang maintains.[42]

In a nutshell, this study reconstructs the process in which female homoeroticism became a significant object of discussion and contention in the Chinese public arena. In particular, it explicates the crucial role that artistic literature has played in the overall discursive formation. In asking questions about discourse, I share Tani Barlow's conviction (expressed in a different context) that examining discursive construction allows us to "move away from the mythology of the indivisible, bounded, essential subject."[43] What interests me, in other words, is not simply reconstructing a genealogy of the Chinese lesbian. Rather, a more basic and urgent task is, in my view, to investigate the shifting terms of the representations of female-female relations through time and their varied constructive and/or regulatory effects.[44] And, since language enables/precludes subject positions, the discursive "is also always social," as Barlow claims.[45]

In her writing, Barlow has shed crucial light on a major shift from late-imperial kin-inflected categories of female subject positions such as *nü* (daughter) and *fu* (wife) to a biological category of woman—*nüxing*—introduced by May Fourth Chinese translators of European physiology, sexology, and social theory.[46] According to Barlow, along with the Victorian sex binary, May Fourth intellectuals also introduced "notions of female passivity, biological inferiority, intellectual inability, organic sexuality, and social absence." Furthermore, "the most shocking of all Chinese feminism's arguments substituted sexual desire for reproductive service to *jia* [family] as the foundation of human identity."[47]

Barlow astutely senses that May Fourth intellectuals, especially male feminists, were attracted to something in the European texts—what Foucault has termed *sexuality*. Although she does not elaborate the implications of her insight, here I would like to carry the inquiry further. I contend that, in an ironic and yet unsurprising way, the liberalization of opposite-sex courtship and premarital romantic relationships among the urban Chinese upper and middle classes under the banner of modernization during the May Fourth era was in itself a regimentation of desire. The normalization of opposite-sex romantic love was achieved in part through the abjection of same-sex love, which was decontextualized from China's long-standing homosocial and homoerotic practices and reclassified as a newly identified psychological perversion that was at once naive, unnatural, abnormal, ill, and depraved.[48] The scientism of Western-oriented May Fourth intellectuals was assisted by their anxiety over the weakness and regression of the Chinese race, which made them susceptible to the sway of late-nineteenth- and early-twentieth-century European sexology, which claimed to discover hereditary degeneracy, male effeminacy, and female masculinity in homosexuality. The most extreme among the key advocates of heterosexual normalcy was perhaps "Dr. Sex," Zhang Jingsheng, a France-returned professor of philosophy and self-styled sexologist. Zhang was keen on improving Chinese racial strength by promoting techniques for achieving heterosexual orgasm; tellingly, he chastised, in a heavy-handed manner verging on racial self-loathing, the Chinese people's signs of androgyny, gender reversal, sexual incompetence, and homosexuality.[49]

More important, amid the influence of sexology and the May Fourth intellectuals' push toward a binary gender system, the reading public's negative perceptions of women's same-sex love were shaped in particular by male intellectuals' anxiety about women's new opportunities: they could receive formal education, they could enter the professions, they were no longer confined to the home and enjoyed greater physical freedom and mobility, they could refuse offers of marriage, and they could even practice separatism. Male intellectuals' warnings against women's same-sex love as damaging to health loomed large as a diffused form of patriarchal control that obscured male power. Contemporaneous with this process of abjection, however, dissenting voices were audible. In the 1920s, Chinese translations of the English social thinker Edward Carpenter's defense of homogenic love sought to forestall the impending pathologization and moral condemnation of same-sex love in the Chinese context. Among female intellectuals, Lu Yin's fiction resisted the societal denigration of female same-sex love by idealizing it as a lifestyle that was an alternative to and more fulfilling than marriage. Voices like hers ought to be brought back—as some researchers have begun to do—to serve as examples of female subjectivity and subaltern resistance.

It cannot at this point be overemphasized that my goal in identifying the genesis of an unprecedented discourse of female same-sex love in China during the early twentieth century does not equal arguing that this discourse revolutionized consciousness once and for all and overturned all habits of thinking that had come before. The daring assertions that Foucault made in volume 1 of the *History of Sexuality* about a radical rupture in sexual epistème ushered in by the discipline of psychopathology capture some dimensions of the transformation here, but they are insufficient to provide a precise understanding of the change in question.[50] Rather than the succession of one distinct discursive paradigm by another resulting in a break with the past, the transformation in May Fourth China was first and foremost a matter of discursive proliferation and diversification. Prior to the formation of the category *female same-sex love* in the 1910s and 1920s, there had not existed in Chinese a general category of wide currency comparable to *nanse* (male-male eroticism) demarcating a particular set of female-female relations. Strong romantic feelings between women fell under the broad rubrics *sisterhood, friendship,* and *emotion,* which lacked specificity. Although Ming and Qing erotica flaunted scenes of sex between women, the sex acts were not construed as constituting an independent erotic mode (*feng, dao*) or a personal taste (*pi*), as was male-male eroticism.[51] At the end of the Qing, some male commentators criticized some women for having formed tightly woven women's communities that were at odds with male-female relations, such as the *zishu nü* (women who vowed spinsterhood) in Canton or the man-despising *mo jing dang* (mirror-rubbing gang) in Shanghai. However, such practices were isolated local phenomena, and the appellations used to describe them were not extended and applied to women in other places. Missing, in short, was a well-rounded, integrated category for female-female relations on a par with male-male eroticism.

The May Fourth neologism *female same-sex love* created a hypothetical symmetry between female and male homosexualities and, thus, filled in a gap left open by previous Chinese terms bestowing limited significance on female-female intimate relations. This did not, however, amount to a complete displacement of one set of words by the other. The new taxonomy of *female same-sex love* did not simply supplant existing concepts such as *friendship* or *sisterhood* (see figs. 5 and 6). Rather, the neologism merely enriched the symbolic domain and increased the number of systems of meanings available. Unquestionably, some Chinese speakers preferred, and still prefer, to abide by the traditional categories of *friendship* and *sisterhood* instead of adopting *same-sex love* as a lens through which to observe intimate relations between women.[52]

Even if we observe that the sexological neologisms acquired considerable prestige and popularity among the urban Chinese educated class

FIGURE 5 Sisterhood (or women's friendship) was a popular motif in the advertisement paintings on calendar posters of the Republican era. To see the paintings in a catalog, see, e.g., Zhang, *Lao yuefenpai guanggao hua.*

FIGURE 6 *Top:* "Sisters Appreciating Flowers," an advertisement painting of the Republican era. *Bottom:* Two other Republican-era advertisements with similar compositions.

during the 1920s, that popularity must be qualified by what Foucault use-fully maintains in *The Archaeology of Knowledge:*

> To say that one discursive formation is substituted for another is not to say that a whole world of absolutely new objects, enunciations, concepts, and theoretical choices emerges fully armed and fully organized in a text that will place that world once and for all; it is to say that a general transforma-tion of relations has occurred, but that it does not necessarily alter all the elements; it is to say that statements are governed by new rules of formation, it is not to say that all objects or concepts, all enunciations or all theoretical choices disappear. On the contrary, one can, on the basis of these new rules, describe and analyse phenomena of continuity, return, and repetition.[53]

In the May Fourth era, precisely because each of the Chinese words used earlier to describe female-female relations had a limited semantic scope and specific focus (designating either feelings, or sex acts, or local com-munities), none of them could contradict the seemingly all-encompassing biological category *female same-sex love.* Instead, the former categories could easily be absorbed and become part of the meaning of this new cate-gory. For instance, although male intellectuals such as Chen Dongyuan and Pan Guangdan adopted *female same-sex love* and implicitly rejected older terms as inadequate, what they did was not so much eliminate the older categories as superimpose the newer on the older.[54] In no time, they started to use *female same-sex love* to discuss phenomena in the past such as *bai xiangzhi* (women taking a vow to become bosom friends) and *guizhong niyou* (intimate friends in the inner chambers).[55] They began, in other words, to move swiftly between discourses and translate from one discourse into another as if there existed equivalencies instead of sheer incommensurability between the two.

### The Shifting Equilibrium of Power

In identifying the genesis of an unprecedented psychobiological dis-course of female same-sex love in May Fourth China, my purpose is not simply to romanticize a traditional past in which female-female intimacy appeared unregulated. Of far greater interest to me are the seeming con-tradictions between strictures and latitude and the particular equilibrium of power that was struck.

Until the twentieth century, female-female eroticism—unlike male-male eroticism—appeared only infrequently in both the elite and the popular writing (such as history, law, poetry, personal essays, drama, and fiction) produced by men, writing that dominated the "outer," social sphere, which was distinct from the "inner," domestic sphere.[56] As Giovanni Vitiello keenly observes, "Female homosexuality is encountered far less often in [traditional] Chinese literature than male homosexuality. *Qing shi* (The anatomy of love), for instance, includes chapters on love between plants and stones, but ignores love between women."[57] When women's same-sex attraction did surface in men's writings, it was figured as the insignificant, the laughable, the naughty, and, on rare occasions, the anomalous. Basically, female-female eroticism was dismissed to a gray zone of amorality rather than demonized as a vice. Female-female emotional and physical intimacies were not an object of moral admonition. Confucian tenets of female chastity were concerned exclusively with female-male congress, and women's adultery and promiscuity by definition involved males. In a similar fashion, traditional legal codes did not criminalize female-female behavior (neither, for that matter, do modern codes); in fact, they did not mention female-female desire at all. The complete absence of female-female eroticism from traditional Chinese moral and legal codes suggests that it did not constitute a significant source of anxiety for men.

Literature further shows that men often trivialized female-female intimacy rather than treating it punitively or prohibiting it. In fiction, drama, autobiography, and the notation books known as *biji,* the late-imperial male authors who touched on women's sexual intimacy were in general so phallocentric as not to acknowledge female-female sex as authentic sex.[58] Typically in their writing, female-female affection enjoys legitimacy as sisterhood, and female-female intercourse is viewed as a secondary, substitutive practice that does not exclude conventional marriage or cross-sex activity. Mutual longings and pleasures among women are rendered harmless by the male polygamous imagination, appropriated either to enhance or to collaborate with male desire for female bodies. Even in male homoerotic literature, which occasionally does associate the intercourse between women with male-male eroticism, female-female attraction is subsumed under the male mode and deemed inferior.[59] In late-imperial literati writing, it is only when certain women commit themselves to other women *and* resist men/marriage that women's love is portrayed as extraordinary and strange, and such odd women are reprimanded or exorcised/banished from the human community through a variety of writing strategies. A limited number of individual literati did have the insight that some women could be unusually attracted and committed to female friends. In representations, these women's choice of same-sex friendship and self-development over marriage, which entails subordination to a man, leads them to religious practice. Not unusually, such women assume a supernatural aura or status because of their unworldly nonconformity. Similar nonconformist female figures may be encountered in elite women's verse narratives (*tanci*) and dramatic works from the late Ming and the Qing. However, most women's texts, including those that boldly create cross-dressing and career-seeking heroines, ultimately refeminize their heroines to obtain closure and refrain from causing a permanent breach of the gender norm.

Confronted with the pattern of neglect instead of condemnation in literati writings, one may well be tempted to see the past in a rosy light. However, we do so at our own peril, for, while there were no explicit prohibitions on female-female intimacy, there were many other strictures on women's lives. To give the most obvious example, didactic literature for women was in high demand and was used in elite families in the late-imperial era to mold women's habits.[60] To give another example, local officials were during the high Qing (1683–1839) keen on stamping out what they viewed as dangerous religious activities among laywomen, as Susan Mann notes.[61] In other words, in the late-imperial system, besides attempting to construct what it considered the proper womanhood, the ruling male elite also took definite measures to inhibit women's practices that it perceived as threatening the social order. That female-female intimacy was ignored does not mean that women had unlimited liberty. It simply means that it was not perceived as threatening by men.

The fact that there was not a biological thinking in the late-imperial era pronouncing female-female intimacy unnatural further indicates that the familial/social imperative on women's marrying, domesticity, and reproduction required no argument about women's bodily nature to justify its own operation or to impose itself on women. Footbinding, which was practiced among the elite and gained some popularity among the nonelite in the late-imperial era, provides an extreme but perhaps useful illustration of my point. The natural female body had to be broken and sculpted so that culture could be created. What mattered was culture, not nature. *Li* (ritual, rites), the source of social power, was the purview of literate males. Yet, although women were precluded from performing the rites, the rule of *li* was predicated on the discipline of women. As Angela Zito eloquently observes:

> We might . . . be tempted to take a pessimistic view of women as doubly negated. Rarely literate, they could only approximate the fulfillment of filial

duty due to their own ancestors, whom they left behind to join another family. Yet they were necessary to this particular discursive production in dauntingly material ways. They wove the silk upon which men wrote and bore the sons who venerated their husbands. These disciplined relinquishments of mobility, of participation in circulation, insured and justified the control of their produced value. But it is important to note that "discipline" has a very Foucauldian ring. In this case it also denotes a kind of participation, a learning of a skill and the knowledge of a position—the skill of being feminine, of embodying a certain and necessarily absolutely (if shifting) different place within the whole.[62]

Femininity was fully understood as an acquired skill. Hence, late-imperial society, especially the elite, placed a high premium on the education and training of women according to detailed protocols. Meanwhile, given women's utter divestiture of power in social, economic, and political terms, there was simply no necessity for men to justify such disciplining of women except to say that it fulfilled a part in the magnificent totality of a morally superior culture.

In this light, the emergence in the May Fourth era of a psychobiological discourse propagated by men and concerning the unhealthy, abnormal, and unnatural character of love/desire between women signaled precisely an attempt to legitimate the marriage imperative at a moment when the traditional codes of decorum, or the Confucian vision of culture, no longer seemed natural and were breaking down. European biology was invoked by iconoclasts in the first place to attack traditional dictates, and biology was invoked even more after traditional rules lost ground. In a world dominated by men, the female body liberated from tradition had to be reconstituted and reinscribed into marriage and the family. The psychobiological discourse of cross-sex love, a theory about women's inherent need for men if they were to attain emotional and sexual fulfillment, was the logical tool that male intellectuals found.

Thus, in the early twentieth century, the traditional, predominantly dismissive views of female same-sex eroticism held by Chinese men underwent dramatic transformation. Because of the massive Westernization of China on many fronts, including a widespread agitation for women's liberation, female-female desire in modern Chinese public discourse acquired the status of the sexual and at the same time that of depravity. The term *homosexuality* was first translated from late-nineteenth- and early-twentieth-century European sexology—often mediated through Japanese sources—into Chinese during the 1910s and 1920s. From the very beginning, the category's fascination and usefulness for May Fourth Chinese intellectuals lay largely in its ability to place the passion between women under a common rubric with the passion between men and to make female same-sex love a tangible, substantive entity open to description and evaluation. In both urban journals devoted to women's issues and sex-education pamphlets, intellectuals depended on such medical neologisms as *nüzi tongxing lian'ai* (female homosexuality), *qingyu zhi diandao* (sexual inversion), *yichang* (abnormality), and *biantai* (perversion) for talking about women's, especially middle-class New Women's, autonomous sexuality, such as female students and teachers' passionate friendships in schools.[63] Inherent in the modern authoritarian project initiated by European doctors such as Richard von Krafft-Ebing and Havelock Ellis, which was later adopted by May Fourth intellectuals, mostly men, was the attempt to grasp, contain, and regulate female sexuality conceptually in the face of women's growing access to education and professions as well as their increasing economic independence from the patriarchal family.[64] In other words, female-female desire did not become men's anxiety and fear in China until some women were gaining recognition as persons with integrity—as individuated *grown-ups,* just as men were.[65] Prior to women's gaining men's recognition of their demand and potential for independence, women's sex meant but the miming games of child-like slaves in bondage, women's romantic affection the commiseration among slaves.

During the 1920s and early 1930s, it became common knowledge among the educated urban Chinese class that women's "same-sex love" (*tongxing lian'ai, tongxing ai, tongxing lian*) was a psychological or sexual perversion according to "modern science." The medical division between normality and aberration categorically relegates women's same-sex desire to a defective and morbid status. As a form of control, "sexual psychology" is more insidious than moralism and more expansive than legislative criminalization.[66] Beginning in the Republican period, "sexual science" established itself as the chief rationale for the discrimination against female as well as male homoeroticism in modern Chinese culture. During the Republican period, two views of female homosexuality became popular in urban Chinese print media and medical sources, largely owing to the influence of Havelock Ellis. Ellis attributes women's same-sex desire to "sexual inversion," or the inversion of gender. He asserts, "The chief characteristic of the sexually inverted woman is a certain degree of masculinity."[67] Operating with a rigid, conservative definition of *sexual difference,* prescribing what either femininity or masculinity is, this theory of sexual inversion conflates erotic object choice with gender identity. Being phallocentric, Ellis regards all desire for women as masculine.[68] Meanwhile, Ellis, like other specialists in his time, believes that many female homoerotic feelings, behaviors, and relations are "pseudo"-homosexuality. Above all, he asserts that girls' romantic friendships prevalent in all-girl schools—incidentally a matter of grave concern for Republican Chinese intellectuals—are inconsequential sex play. According to him, since most girls do not lack femininity, their desires are not really inverted. In love with their own sex, schoolgirls are merely exercising their sentimental and occasionally sexual faculties in rehearsal for opposite-sex love later in life.[69] A typical response to Ellis's theory came from Pan Guangdan, one of Ellis's Chinese translators. For Pan as well as many other Republican intellectuals, same-sex love or homosexuality is an intersubjective relation the possibility of which is widespread among the population, rather than a peculiar essence localized in a small number of individuals. Pan believes that, despite the prevalence of same-sex love in women's schools, most schoolgirls change their minds on graduation. They willingly follow the path of heterosexual marriage and family life.[70]

It was in Republican discourse that female-female love first gained an equal footing with male-male love, attracting even more public attention and curiosity than male homoeroticism did. Perhaps some Chinese New Women at the time were comforted by the fact that they could call their love by that name—*same-sex love* on a par with *cross-sex love.* Nonetheless, the meaning of female-female love was deeply contentious in public discourse. In the time when the urban Chinese middle class learned about the "scientific" theories of women's abnormal sexual inversion and temporary homosexuality, fiction writers of the May Fourth generation depicted many New Women who had romantic, erotic relationships with one another as students or teachers in boarding schools. This corpus of representations by such novelists as Lu Yin, Ling Shuhua, Ding Ling, Yu Dafu, and Zhang Yiping allows us glimpses into female authors' homoerotic desire and male authors' voyeurism and fantasy as well as the limited cultural legitimacy of female same-sex desire. In female writers' works, the reader can encounter female lovers aspiring to establish alternative families and lifestyles in a time of social change. Men's representations, by contrast, exploit the physical excitement that sex between women, as a sight of double female flesh, may stimulate in the male spectator/reader.

Despite the differences, whether authored by men or by women, May Fourth fictional representations of New Women's same-sex love share a common limitation. They fail to assert the legitimacy of female-female lust. The representations sever female same-sex friendship from physical desire, with the result that women's intimate same-sex relations appear to be either aesthetic, platonic unions or vacuous, depraved lust. Female writers' inability to present a perfect synthesis of love and lust between women is an especially alarming indicator that intellectuals' advocacy of "free love" during the May Fourth New Culture Movement was predicated on the idealization of heterosexuality and the denigration of same-sex intimacy. The cultural reform that liberalized opposite-sex socialization, courtship, and marriage in the 1920s involved transposing the center of many Chinese youths' affection from a same-sex to a cross-sex axis. It elevated opposite-sex love as able to "unite two people in body and soul" (*lingrou he yi*) despite the fact that there were considerable intellectual and emotional differences between men and women, ancient rules of propriety having separated the sexes for centuries. Male intellectuals' liberation of women's sexuality, in particular, held up erotic relationships with men as what women should desire and pursue. The seemingly liberatory discourse succeeded in inculcating a rejection of same-sex passion as either naive or base in some of the period's most radical women. Only by a resistant reading strategy can we now locate the missing link between women's feelings (*qing*) and their lust (*yu*) for their own sex in May Fourth New Women's writing. The female friendships in Lu Yin's work, for example, reveal an undercurrent of sensuality and physical longing.

### Contestations in the Late Twentieth Century

In the May Fourth era, despite the fact that female same-sex love had only limited legitimacy in discourse, there was nonetheless open discussion of the subject among intellectuals, who felt free to disagree with each other. In the 1930s and 1940s, the public sphere for such debate dwindled for a number of reasons: the deepening national crisis, the onset of the Sino-Japanese War, the political conservatism of the Nationalist government, and the Nazis' persecution of homosexuals and destruction of sexological research in 1930s Europe, among others. Total silence regarding homosexuality did not fall on China, however, until after Mao's takeover. After the Communist Revolution of 1949, the Republican discourse on homosexuality was largely erased from the public arena. Literature and the arts avoided the category *homosexuality* for several decades, for there are practically no artistic representations touching on it from the 1950s, 1960s, and 1970s.[71] Nor did the official sex-advice material make any mention of homosexuality.[72] The PRC's official dictionary of the modern

Chinese language, first published in 1973, includes the Republican neologism for homosexuality, *tongxing lian'ai,* tersely defined as "the love relationship that takes place between men or between women, a form of psychological perversion."[73] However, details of outdated medical theories of homosexuality as gender inversion and psychic pathology did not resurface in the urban popular consciousness until a multitude of publications about sex emerged in the 1980s and 1990s, with the reintroduction of a capitalist economy and Western culture.

The post-Mao era bears many superficial similarities to the May Fourth era in terms of the discovery of *sexual difference* as a category. Not only has an essentialist sex binarism arisen partly in reaction against the masculinization of women during the Maoist era, but Western feminism has also been reintroduced (if to a limited extent) in China. What is more, there has been a rapid heterosexualization of culture, which ostensibly counteracts the Maoist taboo on romantic love between unmarried men and women, which was denounced as bourgeois, individualistic, and politically reactionary. Thus, in post-Mao China, women scholars have, on the one hand, spontaneously set up research centers for women's studies and embarked on a quest for a "female consciousness" rescued from the Maoist erasure of women's gender awareness, the Communist Party's denial of the achievements of May Fourth liberal feminists, and so forth. On the other hand, unemployment among women rises at a staggering rate, prostitution and the trafficking in women return en masse, the working conditions of the female labor force are horrendously exploitative, and a new consumer economy blatantly propagates gender differentiation and hierarchy in everyday life.[74]

In this time of many contradictions, the representations of female homoeroticism by serious women writers such as Chen Ran and Lin Bai are caught in a whirlwind of competing interpretations. While feminist literary critics (including some seemingly liberal male critics) in the PRC extol the authentic "female consciousness" and the portrayal of "sisterhood" in their works, conservative male readers accuse them of a whole gamut of crimes ranging from the neglect of women's duty as the loving mothers of mankind to solipsism, self-indulgence, and intellectual pettiness. Furthermore, profit-oriented publishers package their works as food for the masses' voyeuristic consumption. In the second half of this book, then, I examine the local interpretations of their works and explore alternative readings. I argue that Lin Bai's interest in female homoeroticism motivates her to criticize the Maoist patriarchal state's incursion into women's private lives. She also punctures the myth of the heterosexual romance and questions/denaturalizes the sexological discourse that has produced homophobia in women like her protagonists. Chen Ran's homoerotic inscription is not as haunted by the ghost of sexological discourse and homophobia as Lin's. Rather, Chen takes an innovative stance to theorize female same-sex love in terms of "gender-transcendent consciousness." She frankly despises the post-Mao consumerist production of gender essentialism and heterosexuality as pleasure. Although there are moments when she discusses gender in terms of biological difference and social construction, her desire to transcend gender is refreshingly critical of hierarchical gender norms and plainly challenges the current refeminization and debasement of women and the reification of heterosexual normalcy in post-Mao China.

Interestingly, however, at a time when post-Mao society as a whole, including elite women scholars, is primarily interested in the discovery of *woman* as a category rather than the deconstruction of it, Chen's position has often been swept under the nebulous rubric *female consciousness*.[75] Fundamentally, female homoeroticism is not commonly recognized by either literary critics or the general public as external to femininity. On the contrary, female same-sex intimacy is understood as part and parcel of the essence of the mysterious other—woman. The prejudices that critics express against Chen's and Lin's representations of female homoeroticism, therefore, are often couched in arguments that fault the narrowness of female consciousness rather than same-sex desire per se.

Meanwhile, in Taiwan, the social energy released by the lifting of martial law in 1987 has erupted into a number of new, identity-based social movements, including a lesbian movement that increasingly distinguishes itself from an already-established women's movement. The emergence of an avant-garde literature about lesbian and other queer desires in 1990s Taiwan, then, is directly fueled by the birth of lesbian activism and the battle cries of academic feminist and queer theorists. This does not mean, however, that lesbians' fight to define themselves in positive terms and gain public legitimacy has been completed. Many difficulties remain, and the battle continues on multiple fronts, against the patriarchal family, the state, and a capitalist economy dominated by men.

In a milieu in which identity has become a new principle for the understanding of the self and for group formation, the writer Qiu Miaojin's autobiographical fiction is interesting on many levels. On the most superficial level, she constructs a lesbian identity through narration, and she appropriates sexological clichés about homosexuality to ascribe her own homosexual orientation to nature. However, even as she builds up a lesbian identity, she hacks it away with cruelty. Her self-conscious reflection on the process of autobiographical writing calls into question the reliability of memory and, hence, the authenticity of self-representation. She is also unique among an entire generation of new queer writers in that she is extremely critical of the failures of the public sphere in Taiwan after martial law. Her satire unflinchingly exposes the takeover of the public sphere by hyperreal media simulacra. Because the mass media has saturated everyday life, and because the fervor for identity politics runs amok in society, public communication has become pitifully irrational and partisan. The public sphere has turned into a circus, populated by a surplus of sensational media effects and spectacles. By reflecting critically on the (im)possibility of truthful lesbian representation in Taiwan's public arena, then, Qiu not only confronts homophobia but also identifies a structural problem in the advanced capitalist public sphere.

Issues explored by Qiu through satirical allegory have been discussed explicitly by female activists in lesbian and feminist organizations. These activists are similarly wary of the dominance of the mass media in the public sphere, and they have also asked difficult questions about identity. By examining a series of debates between feminists and lesbian activists, I show that the development of identity politics has forced feminists and lesbian activists to rethink the boundaries of their respective identities as well as their overlap. Through these open discussions, a lesbian feminist identity that sets itself apart from mainstream feminism has emerged clearly into public view. Many lesbian activists still mark themselves as feminists—however, a different type of feminist. They challenge many technologies of gender, but with a redoubled sense of urgency they attack one in particular—compulsory heterosexuality.[76] Their feminist position is a militant one. Such a confrontational feminist stance is to date barely visible in the PRC, where the differences in gender ideologies among women, including feminists, are as yet largely unexamined and rarely articulated.[77]

However, although the lesbian feminist is now a recognizable personage in Taiwan, at least in print, having such a radical identity has its price. Whereas, in writing, Taiwanese lesbian feminists are extremely daring and adamant in attacking patriarchy and the heterosexual mainstream society, very few of them can come out as such in everyday life. The lesbian feminist identity, then, is a self-marginalizing identity precisely because of its uncompromising militancy. This mode of minority identity politics forms a stark contrast to the situation in the PRC, where Chen Ran and Lin Bai, two intellectual female writers who are critical of the heterosexual romance, clearly want to keep labels of sexual identity at bay. And it is only in the last few years that a cosmopolitan lesbian identity has begun to form among certain younger women in metropolitan Beijing and other major cities. However, these cosmopolitan lesbians currently in their early twenties have shown very little interest in antagonizing mainstream society.[78] One might argue that the English identity category *lesbian*, which has had a close connection to radical feminism in recent Western history, finds its closest counterpart in Taiwan rather than in China.

### Translating across Time, across Space

This brings me to the issue of terminology. In writing this book, I have been wary of the historicity of words. However, historicity can be honored only within limits. If I were to use a completely historicized vocabulary, this work would be unreadable, if not impossible to write in the first place, since it would then be full of Chinese terms that are never fully translatable—across time, across languages.

It is perhaps a cliché by now that, just like *the homosexual, the invert, the gay,* or *the queer, the lesbian* is an identity construct that has its specific history and cultural context. Above all, the word *lesbian* embodies a certain affirming perception of the self and community that has become possible only recently in the West. Some might even go so far as to assert that the word does not stand for an identity; it *is* that identity. With volume 1 of *The History of Sexuality,* Michel Foucault single-handedly called the attention of a generation of scholars to the invention of the homosexual personage by the discipline of *psychopathia sexualis* as it formed itself in nineteenth-century Europe. Thus, David Halperin, for instance, insists that there have been only one hundred years of homosexuality.[79] As Gert Hekma points out, the term *homosexual* was coined in 1869–70 by the novelist Karl Maria Kertbeny, who was himself a follower of the lawyer Karl Heinrich Ulrichs's innovative theory of the Uranian as "a female soul enclosed in a male body."[80] Ulrichs's theory became fashionable among psychiatric physicians, and the categories *homosexual* and *invert* were popularized by widely circulated books by later sexologists such as Richard von Krafft-Ebing and Havelock Ellis. The word *gay,* by contrast, deliberately affirms the fact of homosexual object choice, and, as Halperin elucidates, the gay identity is implicitly abandoned by the even more recent *queer,* which "does not name some natural kind or refer to some determinate object; it acquires its meaning from its oppositional relation to the norm."[81]

As these identities, one after another, have all been historicized, it is not surprising that Judith Halberstam recently reminds us: "Within a Foucauldian history of sexuality, 'lesbian' constitutes a term for same-sex desire produced in the mid to late twentieth century within the highly politicized context of the rise of feminism and the development of what Foucault calls a homosexual 'reverse discourse'; if this is so, then 'lesbian' cannot be the transhistorical label for all same-sex activity between women."[82] It would seem that, even when we use *lesbian* as an adjective rather than a noun, it still invokes the history of that identity formation and the subculture in connotation. Can such a word, heavy with culture- and period-specific meanings, be appropriated to describe practices, relations, persons, and communities in a non-Western culture? Furthermore, is it possible to resignify the word through a non-Western culture and thus complicate the meaning of *lesbian* in the Euro-American context?

The assumption of this book is that such resignification is necessary and unavoidable. Just as the word *lesbian* has been stretched many times in Europe and America in recent decades to include diverse communities of women-loving women, there is little to stop contemporary women in a non-Western culture from desiring that label and calling themselves *lesbian*. Presently translated as *nü tongxinglian, nü tongzhi,* or *tongnü* or simply transliterated by pronunciation, the word *lesbian* has in Chinese been claimed and identified with by contemporary women in Taiwan, Hong Kong, and, to a lesser but increasing extent, mainland China. Perhaps the specific local subcultures do not completely correspond to what is commonly seen in North America; nevertheless, contemporary women in transnational China have not been deterred from taking possession of *lesbian,* reinventing it in their own contexts, and giving it new significance.

Such is the nature of globalization: not only is the hegemonic culture taken to be a model by the peripheral, but peripheral forms may also contest, enter, and hybridize the hegemonic form. Explicating the translation of one culture into another language, Lydia Liu asserts that underlying the trope of linguistic equivalence is a complex politics in which "a non-European host language may violate, displace, and usurp the authority of the guest language in the process of translation as well as be transformed by it or be in complicity with it."[83] In other words, Liu foregrounds the shifting allegiance to and departure from Western modernity in Chinese translation and translingual practice. Similarly, observing the persistent formation of cultural difference in the Third World's aspirations to and projects of modernity has led Lisa Rofel to propose the term *other modernities* to describe Third World nation-states in general and post-socialist China in particular. She maintains, "Modernity enfolds and explodes by means of global capitalist forms of domination in conjunction with state techniques for normalizing its citizens. Along with these specific practices, modernity exists as a narrated imaginary: it is a story people tell themselves about themselves in relation to others."[84]

The lesbian identity is, as part of modernity, no exception. By using the translingual Chinese equivalents of the word *lesbian*, women in Taiwan and the PRC at the turn of the millennium are creating stories about themselves in relation to others—about the imagined contemporaneity between Asia and the West and the affinities between their own selves and the lesbians in advanced capitalist countries. The equivalence is phantasmatic because the Taiwanese or Chinese interpretations of what it means to be lesbian may well diverge from common Euro-American beliefs.

It is this understanding of the cross-cultural and translingual contestation inherent in the expansion of the international imagined community of lesbians in the global era that has compelled me to delineate the inventions of *female same-sex love* and *lesbianism* in twentieth-century China for an English-speaking audience. In translating the Chinese *nü tongxinglian, nü tongzhi, tongnü,* and a number of other words (back) into English, there is of course the danger of simplifying and streamlining them in the process, but there is also the possibility that they will gain the rare opportunity to directly challenge and shake up certain dominant North American ways of signifying female same-sex desire and the lesbian.

For an honestly historicist approach to words ought to acknowledge not only the original context of a word but also its instability and the varied signifying effects across space and time that are brought about by performative speech acts. And a certain amount of self-reflexivity or self-irony may be desirable in the historicist approach. Given Halberstam's quickness to historicize the word *lesbian* and to restrict its usage to its original context in the contemporary West, it is surprising that, in the passage from her work quoted earlier, *same-sex activity* is unquestioningly substituted as the transhistorical umbrella term. Surely, if a historicist approach is consistently pushed to the extreme, then, not only are the taxonomies *female homosexual* and *lesbian* of distinctively modern origins, but even such prosaic phrases as *female same-sex activity* and *female same-sex desire,* which do not imply sexual orientation and identity, must be understood as modern inventions as well. Among other reasons, the very notion of sex is shaped by discourse, not least by that of modern biology and medicine. In other words, sex is subject to revision, and it is susceptible to historicization. In *Making Sex,* Thomas Laqueur maintains that the Western belief in a profound physiological difference between males and females demonstrable by biology is relatively recent. In a similar vein, one might argue that the traditional Chinese conception of the sexed body was fundamentally different from the dichotomous approach of modern anatomy. Using Chinese medical tracts from the Song to the Ming periods (960–1644) as evidence, Charlotte Furth has argued that, although in diagnostic practice traditional Chinese physicians paid exact attention to women's difference and created, among other things, *fuke* (medicine for women) to deal with disorders that they regarded as specific to women, in therapeutic theory the body was configured as androgynous. Health in each individual was defined as a balance between yin and yang, and the bodies of males and females were understood not in terms of opposites but rather, according to Furth, as "homologous along a shifting continuum of mixed and interpenetrating substances and energies." Thus, Furth points out, "in any individual, whether male or female, the imbalances that so often tinged male bodies with disproportionate yang heat or female ones with intensified yin cold were in fact potential vulnerabilities, departures from the androgynous ideal of health." [85]

If Laqueur is correct about the short history of the paradigm of two biological sexes in the West, and if Furth is accurate to imply the even shorter career of the paradigm in China, then it is inappropriate to use *same-sex activity* or *same-sex desire* as transhistorical analytic terms. What, however, can replace them? *Same-gender activity* certainly will not do away with all problems. For one, premodern Chinese texts depicting female-female (or male-male) relations often involve opposite-gender role-playing or transgender performance; as a result, *same-gender activity* would be a misnomer for such relations. For another, the modern sexological taxonomy *homosexuality* presumes the sameness of persons' biological sex and not necessarily their gender embodiment, so it is problematic, as well, to paraphrase it as *same-gender activity.* There is, moreover, no limit to such doubting and questioning since the words that we use in modern English to paraphrase or translate words/texts from other languages (or prior English) are bound to fail when it comes to completely reproducing their meanings in the original settings. Ultimately, in this study I have resorted frequently to unwieldy phrases such as *female-female intimacy, female-female relations, female-female love and eroticism,* and similar variants as relatively transhistorical analytic tools, knowing that such phrases are imperfect, if necessary, provisions. Admitting our own situatedness in the present moment may be the ultimate acknowledgment of historical difference.

Finally, while the nature and aim of this project is precisely to bring out the competing and shifting meanings of female-female relations in Chinese sources, part of which is tracing the formation of modern hegemonic terms and how they have been signified by different people, there will be times when I speak in my own voice with my own assumptions about words. To close this introductory chapter, I shall try to reflect on my own definition of certain terminology. I take the word *lesbianism* to be the equivalent of *female same-sex love, female same-sex desire, female homosexuality,* and *female homoeroticism.*[86] It is my belief that *lesbianism* as a category of eroticism covers all possible aspects of eroticism, ranging from longing, idealization, infatuation, worship, attachment, protectiveness, jealousy, and passion to the physical sex act in various forms. I do not privilege either emotional investment or physical sex as the staple of lesbianism. Nor do I maintain that an intersubjective relation must have both spiritual and carnal elements to deserve the rubric *lesbianism. Lesbianism* defined as such does not necessarily preclude opposite-sex eroticism. A woman can have multiple emotional and physical relationships with both sexes at the same time or in succession, and I may use *lesbianism* to name her relationships with women. *The lesbian* as a personal identity, however, postulates a woman's preference for same-sex eroticism over opposite-sex eroticism. A woman may have a preference or an orientation in her fantasies, her physical behavior, or her political identification. While her preferences on various levels may not always correlate, I would maintain that, the more these different levels do correlate, the more coherent and distinctive a lesbian identity there is. To the extent that human subjectivity is often changeable and self-contradictory, I do not necessarily argue that a fixed personal identity, and, in this case, a fixed homogeneous identity defined by eroticism, is desirable. Nevertheless, I devote this study to investigating the conditions that enable the emergence of a distinctive lesbian identity in modern literature in Chinese as well as the political stakes entailed by the public visibility of this identity for women in general in transnational China in the twenty-first century.

ONE :: **PREMODERN CHINA**

# REVISITING PREMODERN CHINESE FEMALE-FEMALE RELATIONS

## Different Approaches to the Past

One of the fundamental questions in contemporary North American and Western European queer studies has been how to deal with the past. Is there a hidden gay and lesbian legacy to be uncovered, as the title of Martin Duberman, Martha Vicinus, and George Chauncey's influential anthology *Hidden from History* suggests? And, if so, on whose terms can it be claimed?[1]

Considering the widespread fascination in the West with histories of sexuality, non-Western as well as Western, it is hardly surprising that, as soon as the modern "sexual science" describing homosexuality and other phenomena was introduced to China from Europe (often by way of Japan) in the early twentieth century, some Chinese intellectuals immediately set about searching for the history of homosexuality in China. The search revealed an inherent belief in the unique value of the national homosexual past and, ironically, also fulfilled an ahistorical desire to project the Chinese onto the world map of universal sexuality. The most emblematic example of such dual tendencies—particularist and globalist views—

during the Republican period was the work done by the sociologist and eugenicist Pan Guangdan, who during the early 1940s wrote an appendix—"Zhongguo wenxian zhong tongxing lian juli" (Examples of homosexuality in Chinese documents)—to accompany his translation of Havelock Ellis's one-volume textbook on sexology, *The Psychology of Sex*.[2] Similar efforts to find and identify instances of homosexuality in premodern Chinese sources recurred later in the twentieth century, especially in two works that appeared in Hong Kong (the port city under British rule to which many Chinese intellectuals migrated on the Communists' takeover of the mainland in 1949): Weixing shiguan zhaizhu's *Zhongguo tongxinglian mishi* (The secret history of homosexuality in China, 1964) and Xiaomingxiong's *Zhongguo tongxing'ai shilu* (The history of homosexuality in China, 1984). The latter inspired, furthermore, a similar work in English, Bret Hinsch's *Passions of the Cut Sleeve*.[3]

In these pioneering texts, the primary impetus was to show that the phenomena of homosexuality, transvestitism, hermaphroditism, and so forth were widely observable in premodern Chinese writings. Detailed investigation of individual authors, local cultures, and time periods, including the differences among them, was minimal. As a result, although these general surveys provided many useful references on which to build further research, they could hardly serve as adequate models for either rigorous documentation or in-depth textual interpretation.

It was during the 1990s that the research into the Chinese sexual past grew more sophisticated. Partly owing to accelerated globalization since the end of the cold war, the capitalist West's lesbian and gay subcultures, discussions of the AIDS epidemic, queer activism, and lesbigay and transgender studies became widely disseminated around the world, and they have been localized in Hong Kong, Taiwan, and mainland China to various degrees by agents such as the mass media, health organizations, academics, creative writers, filmmakers, newly formed lesbian and gay organizations, and users of the Internet. Indeed, what Dennis Altman detects as the internationalization of Western, especially American, gay and lesbian sexual identities certainly did not halt at the borders of Chinese territories.[4] These recent economic and cultural developments in the sexual sphere in the tripartite Greater China region (the mainland, Hong Kong, and Taiwan) gave rise to a new round of debates over what was, and was not, part of the traditional Chinese sexual culture. Unfortunately, participants, including queer activists, often argued in the dark because the existing secondary sources on premodern Chinese same-sex practices were few and lacking in precision.[5]

Globalization gave new urgency to the attempt to produce more thorough and more carefully argued studies of Chinese same-sex sexuality not only of the present era but also of precontemporary and premodern times. Knowledge of the Chinese history of sexuality is valued by many in rapidly transforming Chinese societies in Asia today, evincing an irrepressible yearning for "cultural citizenship" in China (which is an imagined transhistorical entity)—to borrow Lisa Rofel's description of the cosmopolitan gay men in Beijing in the late 1990s.[6] The relevance of the past was, along with the meteoric rise of sexuality studies and queer theory in North America and Western Europe in the 1980s and 1990s, probably a key factor that inspired some specialists in the fields of premodern Chinese literature and history to explore the question of homosexuality. Among others, Matthew Sommer, who works on the representation of illicit sex in late-imperial Chinese law, has analyzed Qing court cases involving rape and related feuds among the marginalized males in settler peasant communities. He finds a strong stigma attached to the penetrated male during the Qing period, which prompted Qing jurists to be particularly concerned about protecting adolescent males of free commoner status from predatory "rootless rascals" (*guang gun*) and the symbolic feminization inflicted by forced anal intercourse (*jijian*).[7] Sophie Volpp, a specialist in late-imperial Chinese literature, examines late Ming and Qing notation books, vernacular fiction, and drama to reveal the complexity of the late-imperial concept of *nanse yi dao* (the way of male love), reconstructing, in particular, the literati libertines' discourse about the superiority of femininity in boy actors during the seventeenth century.[8] Likewise, Giovanni Vitiello, another specialist in late-imperial literature, illuminates the many variations on the theme of *nanse* (male love) in late Ming homoerotica.[9] While directing their inquiries to different materials, these recent studies share one thing: they have begun to historicize eras carefully and to be specific about the literary or legal discourses that they study, procedures not seriously attempted by the general surveys of premodern Chinese homosexuality that appeared prior to the 1990s.

From the perspective of the present study, the most exciting development since the 1990s is that the relatively marginalized question of female same-sex relations has also surfaced in some specialized discussions, particularly studies of previously underresearched literature by late-imperial Chinese women. In her monograph on seventeenth-century elite women in the affluent Yangzi Delta, for example, Dorothy Ko points out the not uncommon expression of same-sex attraction among literary women, especially in the poems exchanged between female relatives and friends.[10]

Researching the lengthy novels in verse (literary *tanci*) by elite women of the Qing, Siao-chen Hu notices the recurring plot of female cross-dressing and female-female love involving gender misrecognition.[11] In her pioneering study of the female dramatists of the late Ming and the Qing, Hua Wei tackles the fact that at least four female playwrights represented themselves through either male characters or cross-dressing female characters. What is more, the playwrights' cross-gendered self-dramatizations often coincided with their expressions of affection and physical attraction for other women.[12]

It is noteworthy that none of these recent studies present themselves as searches for protolesbians in premodern Chinese sources so as to claim a useful genealogy for ethnic Chinese lesbians at the turn of the millennium. Instead, Ko is primarily intrigued by the fact that the attraction between women appeared to be consistent with literary propriety and the gender system in late-imperial China, at least among the gentry class and high-class courtesans. Hu and Hua are similarly concerned with historically specific issues, such as talented elite women's dissatisfaction with their restricted lives, their anxiety about (or discontentment with) marriage by parental arrangement to unsympathetic men, and their fantasies about forming affectionate unions with other women. In other words, Ko, Hu, and Hua have avoided the simple gesture of "sighting" and "recuperating" useful ancestors for late-twentieth-century Chinese lesbians. They focus, rather, on period- and class-specific gender norms and power relations to shed light on the ambitious literary women's desire to appropriate men's prerogatives, including public careers and the love of talented, beautiful, and supportive wives. Hua, in particular, explicitly stresses that the feelings expressed by certain Ming-Qing women dramatists for their female companions are more appropriately dubbed *tongxing zhi lian* (love between members of the same sex) than *tongxinglian* (homosexuality). She explains, "The word *homosexual* as we use it today usually denotes a person's 'sexual orientation' and 'identity,' whereas the phrase *love between members of the same sex* has only a literal meaning, that is, the strong feelings between persons of the same sex, which do not necessarily have anything to do with sexual orientation and identity."[13]

It is highly salutary that these specialized studies of premodern Chinese women's writings show a keen awareness of the historicity of sexual categories and caution against our imposing modern categories on the past. Nonetheless, there are issues to be raised. Among other things, the conclusion that the female-female relations of the past differ from those of modern times seems to be inevitable if, from the outset, difference, instead of similarity, has been sought after and given more weight by the observer. More troubling is the fact that, no matter how sincere modern researchers may be in trying to reconstruct the past in its own terms, they may in fact not be able to tell just how many different points of view existed in the past. What if the particular point of view soliciting the understanding of the moderns across hundreds of years was precisely something that was marginalized in its own time and could articulate itself only through dense metaphors and ambiguous plots? The past may be not single but multilayered. So, even when modern researchers have the best intentions and mean to reconstruct the past in its own terms, they can in fact never be sure whether they are not reinforcing the hegemonic values of the past and further marginalizing some downtrodden, disenfranchised, and disfigured part of the past in the process.

Therefore, it may be that "finding" and "recovering" what may have been hidden in the past are interpretive tactics as necessary as strict respect for the dominant signifying practices of the past. For this reason, I am compelled to employ a hybrid mix of what Nietzsche might call *critical* and *antiquarian* approaches in revisiting late-imperial Chinese female same-sex relations.[14] In the antiquarian mode, rather than search in premodern China for precursors of modern lesbians, I examine the ways in which previous social structures and female same-sex relations may have been mutually defining and constitutive. The assumption here is not that former forms of female same-sex bonding were merely the passive product of major social institutions. Rather, by *mutually constitutive,* I mean some degree of interdependence between the two. At the same time, to understand the exact extent of their mutual determination and reinforcement, it is necessary to pose the question, What kinds of female same-sex relations were preempted by dominant social structures? What might have been pushed into the realm of the infeasible? How might we be critical of that movement of expulsion, see the abjected, and lend it a voice now—anachronistic though it may be?

Such double vision—the ability to see flickering and shadowy ghosts in addition to the literal, surface, and established meanings of things—is desirable.[15] At the same time, it cannot be overemphasized that this exercise should not be reduced to a simplistic naming or "outing" practice. Ultimately, a sincere effort to understand the place and function of female same-sex relations in a prior social order may yield more insights than do quick pronouncements about what could or could not count as *lesbian* in the modern sense.[16] I am interested, then, in pursuing a topography of social tolerance and circumscription that describes the status of female-female relations in premodern China. By using the word *topography*, I submit that one can map the premodern Chinese social landscape using the theme of female same-sex relations, detailing not only the sites and distributions of these relations but also their forms, their intensities, and their interactions with their environs. Such mapping activity can proceed only on the basis of existing documents; therefore, what is being mapped is in fact the remnants of multiple and overlapping representations from the past. Recently, Gregory Pflugfelder eloquently compared the discourses of sexuality to "cartographies of desire." He argued that desire involves constant cognitive mapping and remapping and that the task of a historian of sexuality is, therefore, to provide a map of others' maps.[17]

Pflugfelder's metaphor works well for the various popular, legal, and medical discourses of his subject—male-male sexuality in Japan from the Edo to the early twentieth century. However, while I find Pflugfelder's spatial metaphor compelling, the topographic approach that I have in mind differs in some ways from his. In China prior to the introduction of Western sexology in the early twentieth century, there were indeed sizable historical, literary, and legal discourses concerning male-male sexuality (*nanse, jijian,* etc.), and one can certainly map the multiple cartographies of male-male sexuality. However, very few pre-twentieth-century Chinese texts, other than pornography, explicitly depicted sex between women. There was an absence of the discourse of female-female sexuality if sex is a prerequisite. Far more significant categories of female-female bonds were *sisterhood* and *friendship.* Therefore, in considering premodern Chinese representations, what I am interested in mapping is much broader than a narrowly defined discourse of sex between women. I am drawn, rather, to a wide range of questions about feelings, fantasy, longing, physical familiarity, intimacy, commitment, and gender subordination. This is, needless to say, a major task that requires research involving a multitude of materials and deserves several volumes of its own, and I cannot possibly hope to do justice to it in a small subdivision of a book concerned predominantly with twentieth-century formations. Nevertheless, because to date no one else has undertaken the task of providing an overview of premodern Chinese female same-sex relations in any breadth and depth, it may be appropriate that I fill in some gaps here. For, without some grounded knowledge of premodern Chinese female same-sex relations, it would be impossible to discern the continuities and ruptures between traditional and modern Chinese understandings of love and desire between women.

And any assertions about the effect of Western sexual cultures, episte-mologies, and identities on modern Chinese societies would ring hollow, if not gender blind.

From the perspective of this study—which concerns itself with gender and sexuality—Chinese culture first exhibited a radical instantiation of "modernity" in major Chinese cities during the May Fourth/New Culture era (1915–27).[18] Although modernization, in the form of Westernization, is an inevitably uneven geographic development, I use the adjective *modern* in this study frequently as a device for periodization, referring to the time since the toppling of the Chinese dynastic system and the founding of the Republic in 1911. Although I have chosen a significant political date as an effective device for periodizing cultural development, it is important to note that the epoch immediately preceding the founding of the Republic—the late Qing from the mid-nineteenth century to 1911—already witnessed many initiatives to introduce in China Western mili-tary technology, industry, political systems, communications, trade, edu-cation, literature, natural science, and so forth. The last fifteen years of the Qing, in particular, saw serious elite agitation for Westernization. By par-ticipation in reform politics and publishing in the new mass (print) media in the formative urban public sphere, intellectuals such as Liang Qichao advocated China's modernization through emulation of the West.[19] Tradi-tional womanhood came under attack in both male intellectuals' writings and the women's press as one of the hallmarks of traditional Chinese cul-ture and a symbol of national weakness.[20] As a consequence, the Chinese gentry began to establish schools for girls modeled after Western mis-sionary schools, and a new vogue developed among elite families of send-ing their daughters to the cities or even abroad to be formally educated.[21] This climate of change at the end of the Qing signaled the beginning of the proliferation of new identities for women—the new women.[22] And, although there were practically no public discussions about female same-sex relations through the end of the Qing, the growing numbers of new women eventually helped spawn certain new meanings for female same-sex relations, besides inciting visible public anxiety over them, in the early Republican period, particularly during the May Fourth era.

Of China's long imperial past prior to Republican modernity, the late-imperial period (consisting of the late Ming, from the late sixteenth cen-tury to 1644, and the Qing, from 1644 to 1911) is commonly acknowledged as the segment that left behind the richest materials about women's lives and cultures.[23] Therefore, in investigating premodern/traditional Chinese female-female relations, my observations necessarily pertain principally to the late-imperial period. Significantly, the late-imperial sources relevant to the question of female same-sex relations—sources that others have pointed out or that I have discovered—all fall into certain categories of minor literature (to be explained later). In comparison, non-literary sources such as the law, Confucian teachings on female propriety, and traditional medicine—discourses that observers from a twentieth-century perspective might imagine as having taken an interest in regulating female-female relations—simply ignored the matter.

Late-imperial literature depicted the attraction between women as consistent with the norms of femininity; however, a female identity that is defined by a combination of same-sex preference and the rejection of opposite-sex marriage had difficulty coming into existence and was practically unimaginable. The patterns of circumscribed freedom, co-optation, and abjection constitute the representational terrain that I navigate in what follows.

### The Sources and the Disagreement

How female same-sex love/desire was conceived of and treated in premodern Chinese society is a question to which only tentative and highly speculative answers have been ventured. The uncertainty has extended, in part, from an alleged scarcity of sources. Among late-imperial documents, medical treatises and the law do not discuss the issue at all. Charlotte Furth points out that no sexual behavior was singled out as unhealthy or unnatural in traditional Chinese medicine, which was preoccupied solely with reproductive issues in its treatment of sex.[24] Mathew Sommer, who studies the "illicit sex" section of the Qing legal code and related court cases, finds "not a single mention, let alone prohibition, of female homosexual acts in any Qing or earlier legal source."[25] Similarly, Confucian teachings on female propriety showed no concern about love and intimacy among women, the didactic texts for women not even mentioning the topic. In short, romantic love and desire between women surfaced only in very specific representational sites in late-imperial China. Their appearance was confined to certain genres of minor literature, besides erotic art. By *minor literature* I mean the varieties of writings traditionally deemed insignificant as opposed to the canon of writings comprising the Confucian classics, history, philosophy, and major literati's poetry and essays. The insignificant genres ranged from fiction by men (*xiaoshuo,* in either the vernacular or the classical language, including pornography), to the literati's casual jottings in notation books (*biji*), to elite women's poetry, fictional narratives in verse (*tanci*), and dramatic works. But, even among these, few texts are known for elaborating female-female love and desire as their primary theme.

Among twentieth-century scholars interested in premodern Chinese sexual culture, there have been divided responses to the phenomenal lack of materials, and divergent opinions have been offered on the possible status of female-female love/desire in traditional Chinese society. Although some of the arguments are unsubstantiated and seriously flawed, they have nonetheless enjoyed wide circulation among nonscholarly audiences in Asia and the West.[26] Their popularity and influence require that I address their shortcomings directly rather than simply ignoring them. On the one hand, there is the assertion that, fundamentally, women had very little autonomy in traditional China and, therefore, few opportunities to take a female lover. Bret Hinsch maintains, "[The] lack [of references to lesbianism in traditional sources] was partly due to the relative absence of personal freedom accorded to women. Bound to their husbands economically and often forced into seclusion in the home, many women were denied the opportunities to form close bonds with women outside their household."[27] It is implied that female same-sex bonds were formed only infrequently and considered a violation of proper femininity, which involved cloistered isolation and bondage to men. However, Hinsch does not produce any evidence illustrating such a discouraging attitude in traditional China toward "close bonds" between women.

Hinsch's formulation of the problem is, furthermore, weak in two respects. First, it is unclear why he should insist that, to form love bonds, women had to be able to have liaisons outside their households. Surely, cousins, sisters, sisters-in-law, maids, or concubines belonging to the same household could very well have been lovers. Second, his claim that traditional Chinese women had few chances to form close bonds with women outside their households has only limited validity. In recent research on women's culture in late-imperial China, Dorothy Ko convincingly demonstrates that "traditional Chinese women" were far from a unified group and that their living circumstances and social power must be historicized. In *Teachers of the Inner Chambers,* Ko shows that, in seventeenth-century Jiangnan (roughly the prosperous Yangzi Delta), certain opportunities, such as becoming published authors or itinerant teachers or forging friendships with other women of different families in all-female poetry clubs, were available to some Chinese women of the gentry class, depending on age and locale. Were same-sex relations then especially possible and permissible for such socially privileged women in a specific urban culture? The answer—which Ko seems inclined to give in the affirmative—simply cannot be deduced from any general assumption about Chinese patriarchy but rather demands nuanced thinking and localized research.[28]

Whereas Hinsch suggests that enslavement under patriarchy made lesbianism difficult for traditional Chinese women, other scholars have had the tendency to exclude the question of preference from the consideration of female-female intimacy. They maintain, as a result, that traditional Chinese society was not phobic about lesbianism because it must have been quite tolerant of sex between women. This latter type of opinion has garnered a larger following than the former (i.e., Hinsch's) among scholars. What is more, similar thinking has led to the popularity of a certain "postcolonial" argument propounded in recent years by some Chinese queer activists in Asia, chief among whom is the Hong Kong activist/sociologist Chou Wah-shan. The postcolonial argument idealizes the extent of social tolerance for same-sex relations in traditional China, which is cast as the exact antithesis of the homophobia of modern Chinese societies under the influence of the West.[29] The insight as well as the limitation of such arguments urgently need to be addressed.

The reason offered by twentieth-century commentators for the alleged tolerance of sex between women in traditional China is that female-female eroticism fit nicely into the polygamous marriage system. It is asserted, moreover, that sex between women was probably considered a natural product of the culture of separate male (outer) and female (inner) spheres. An exemplary proponent of this position is Robert van Gulik. In his influential study *Sexual Life in Ancient China* (first published in 1961), van Gulik maintains—on the basis of little evidence—that "sapphism" was tolerated and sometimes even encouraged in the traditional Chinese polygamous household. He believes that sex between women was considered (1) physically harmless because women were said to have an unlimited supply of yin essence (vaginal secretions) and (2) inevitable since it was common that multiple women were obliged to live constantly in close proximity sharing only one legitimate male sex partner.[30] Van Gulik muses that, from a Chinese husband's perspective, sapphism must have appeared useful for preventing adultery or cuckoldry as well as the husband's physical exhaustion from excessive sex.[31] It is maintained that, in traditional China, sapphism was regarded neither as a disease, nor as a crime or an evil, but rather as something natural and positively functional.

Much is clearly missing from van Gulik's consideration. Primarily, is it adequate to understand sapphism in traditional China only in terms of circumstantial necessity (i.e., as a substitute for male-female intercourse) and never in terms of preference or choice? Was there tolerance for sapphism that could not be accommodated by the polygamous arrangement? What happened when sapphists refused to be accommodated by male-centered polygamy? It is significant that such questions do not even arise as van Gulik tries to understand the attitude taken toward female-female eroticism in traditional Chinese sexual culture. He shows tremendous indifference to radically unconventional forms of female sexuality and agency.

Here, a troubling question persists, that is, whether van Gulik's tendency to see female-female eroticism as no more than imitative, circumstantial, and substitute pleasure mirrors certain traditional Chinese construals of the desire between women. In other words, the phallocentric dismissal of the possibility of choice or preference from an understanding and imagining of female same-sex desire may be a feature shared by some traditional Chinese writings and van Gulik's speculation. Therefore, despite his blind spot, van Gulik may in fact have productively sketched a direction in which we can explore how female same-sex desire was represented or discursively constructed in premodern China.

While van Gulik's remarks focus on genital sexual practices between women, similar opinions have been put forth about female-female sensual desire in general. For instance, on the basis of her research on the poetic exchange between gentry women and courtesans in seventeenth-century Jiangnan, Dorothy Ko declares that "attraction between women itself was acceptable in the gender system of seventeenth-century China."[32] In her erudite monograph on Chinese women of the eighteenth century, Susan Mann maintains that sex between man and wife was not necessarily private and could require assistance from the female servants; conceivably, there were constant flows of desire between mistress and maid in such a multipartied situation.[33]

More generally, in 1942, the Chinese sociologist Pan Guangdan claimed: "In traditional Chinese society, women lived in the inner chambers and seldom went out. They did not interact with the general society, and they had little opportunity to be in contact with the opposite sex. Therefore, it was especially easy for homosexual tendencies to develop in women. Between the so-called intimate friends in the females' quarters [*guizhong niyou*] there was commonly a homosexual element. However, we seldom find it recorded. The reason is that it was difficult for outsiders to peep into the inner chambers."[34] Several arguments are made here. First, it is because of the doctrine of separate spheres that Chinese women tended and were allowed to be very intimate with each other. Second, such close bonds were essentially little different from what we understand as homosexuality in "Western sexual psychology" (which, for Pan, means the work of Havelock Ellis). Third, although we can seldom find written records of them, female homosexual relationships were common in traditional China. It is noteworthy that Pan's arguments depend heavily on the inner chamber's seclusion and opacity.

As Pan's argument never moves beyond broad generalizations, certain issues are not raised. If the "intimate friendship in the females' quarters" was shielded from the outsider's prying eyes, did the inner chamber then function as a closet? Were female lovers secretive in order to evade societal punishment and censure? Or was their love known but quietly permitted by the patriarch or, more likely, the matriarch on whom the patriarchal authority to police the inner chambers was conferred? If tolerated by household authorities, was sex between women considered ignominious and so kept unknown beyond the household? If tolerated, could the close bond between women be granted the integrity of passion, romance, or same-sex union? Or was it as a rule perceived as either asexual friendship or nonserious erotic flirtation—a passing youthful phase, a vicarious desire borrowed from men, a substitute for real satisfaction? In short, at what price was tolerance purchased?

While some of these questions cannot be answered and we may never know with certainty what went on among women in the inner chambers, it is relatively easy to tell that the protean possibilities of intimacy in the females' quarters were often construed by late-imperial male writers as laughable, devoid of threatening power, and easy to manage and contain. The assumption about the compatibility between female-female love (whatever the mix of the sentimental and the carnal) and polygamy, or between it and sexual segregation, in traditional China is not exactly something that twentieth-century scholars have conjured out of thin air. Nor is it simply the result of the idealization and exoticization of the cultural other, as a reading of van Gulik's remarks on Chinese sapphism might suggest. The idealization of the function of female-female love/desire in polygamy and the culture of separate spheres is in fact the fantasy of quite a few Chinese literary texts from the late-imperial period. The twentieth-century claims accord with a certain late-imperial phantasmatic scenario.

Before I describe that scenario, one note on the relation between history and literature is necessary. Without corroboration from historical sources, it is problematic to make any claims about the connection between the Ming-Qing literary scenario that I am about to describe and actual practices in Ming-Qing times. Yet, granted that some careful distinction must be drawn between creative texts and social and individual practices in real life, creative literature does important cultural work.[35] In order to understand the social attitude taken toward female same-sex desire in history, it is crucial that we investigate what kinds of desires and fantasies have been allowed in creative literature.

## The Literary Fantasy of Utopian Polygamy

The recurrent Ming-Qing literary fantasy of utopian polygamy has the following basic logic: Because there is love between two women, there is no jealousy between them when they are united with the same man, and, because there is no jealous rivalry between the wives, the marriage is happier than usual. The husband, in particular, enjoys the pleasures that multiple women provide without risking the peace and harmony of his household. The women in love with each other can stay together all their lives by serving the same man; therefore, they are also satisfied. In short, in a polygamous arrangement, the union of a husband with wives who love each other is ideal. Desire between women can function as a superb social lubricant, smoothing the operation of a male-headed, polygamous family.

For example, we find this structure in the comedy *Lian xiang ban* (Women in love) by Li Yu (1611–80), a play usually alluded or referred to (e.g., by Shen Fu in his autobiography dated to the early Qing and by van Gulik in *Sexual Life*) as a text exemplifying the fit between polygamy and female-female love. In the play, the main female characters (Miss Cui and Miss Cao), who are in love, go through much ado to be married to the same man despite Miss Cao's father's refusal to let his daughter become Miss Cui's husband's second wife (concubine). For the reader, doubt is momentarily cast over the viability of bigamy as a practical solution for gentry women's mutual passion and adoration, as Cao's father's objection to his daughter's becoming a mere concubine indicates. But this objection to bigamy is overcome by the strong love between the female protagonists, their resourcefulness in outwitting Cao's father, and their willingness to be of equal status in marriage. Cui's husband, moreover, is portrayed as an agreeable being who is talented, upright, and, above all, gentle and respectful toward women.[36]

The love triangle of three equal parties—a man and two women who attract each other—is a common structure in many late-imperial genres. For example, in the seventeenth-century representative collection of classical tales (i.e., tales in the classical language) *Liaozhai zhiyi* (Liao-zhai's records of the strange) by Pu Songling (1640–1715), at least a dozen stories feature two women who find each other sympathetic, enviable, and admirable united with the same man.[37] Bigamy blessed by the affection between the wives appears in many vernacular "beauty-scholar" (*caizi jiaren*) romances of the early Qing.[38] That a wife might follow her own sensibility to procure a girl of her fancy for her husband even plays an important role in the account of married life given in *Fusheng liu ji* (Six records of a floating life) by Shen Fu (1763–?), an unusually original and candid autobiography by an otherwise obscure writer. The triangle, moreover, surfaces in literary genres in which women excel. In Qing women's *tanci* fiction (narratives in verse sometimes performed and accompanied by a stringed instrument), the combination of intimate female-female friendship and utopian polygamy is a stereotypical situation.[39]

To be precise, there is some difference among the works mentioned above, which constitute a spectrum. At one end of that spectrum, opposite-sex romance is the focus of a story, and the friendship between women occupies a secondary, subservient position. At the opposite end, a story features romantic female lovers who resort to polygyny as an expedient solution, and the female-female attachment and eroticism are hardly offset by the opposite-sex union.

Nevertheless, the fact remains that the idealized intimacy between women in a polygamous context could be readily assimilated to a regulative discourse produced by men on women's jealousy. Dorothy Ko, among others, has pointed out that, in the late Ming and early Qing, jealous wives gained topical prominence in popular literature as well as in didactic literature for women. Plays had satirical titles such as *The Jealousy-Curing Soup,* and instructions on feminine propriety warned that jealousy was the first of the seven reasons that entitled a man to divorce his wife.[40] Given such predominant cultural pressure against women's jealousy, it seems no surprise then that the seventeenth-century male writers Li Yu and Pu Songling conceived of the love between women in a polygamous setting as positive.

Pu Songling, who either invented or elaborated a number of folktales of the blissful union of a man with two women endeared to each other, explicitly celebrated women's tolerance in the strangely sadomasochistic story "Shao nü" ("Miss Shao"), about how a brutal, jealous shrew is transformed into an affectionate sister by her husband's masochistic third concubine, the previous two concubines having been tortured to death by the shrew. In a similar manner, Li Yu was concerned about jealous women.

He lamented the aggravated state of women's jealousy of his day in *Xian-qing ouji* (Casual notes of idle feelings): "In the past, the most that a jealous wife would do to subdue her husband was to force him to kneel, to forbid him to sleep, to have him hold the lamp or fetch water, or to strike him. But recently, there are jealous and ill-tempered women who lock themselves up and go on hunger strikes. Trying to shift their anger onto others, they make their family feel guilty by having them watch their dying acts."[41]

It is no coincidence, then, that Li opens his comedy *Women in Love* with the following encapsulating moral:

> A true beauty is never jealous of another beauty.
> And only true talent is capable of sympathizing with talent.
> Birds not of the same feather are suspicious of each other.
> Such is the way of the world.
> We find the most intense jealousy in women. However,
> Infatuation is also women's forte.
> If a woman transforms the tumor of jealousy into the
> Embryo of passion,
> It will be no ordinary infatuation.[42]

Li Yu philosophizes that, if two women are really alike in that they are both beautiful and talented, they will not be jealous of each other but rather admire each other. According to him, then, female-female infatuation originates in likeness. At the same time, his philosophy serves a practical purpose for polygamous men; it teaches women to replace competitiveness with mutual passion so that they do not cause family strife.

The literary motif of a polygamous marriage successfully containing romantic female same-sex relations expresses primarily the interests of men, namely, a man's happiness in polygamy. However, such an arrangement is also presented as the ideal solution for inordinate female same-sex attraction. What we have, then, is a paradox. At the risk of putting it crudely in late twentieth-century terms: On the one hand, women who strongly desire men—jealous wives and spiteful concubines—are bidden to adopt men's erotic interests, that is, to become relatively bisexual in their sensibility, thereby ameliorating their relationships with other women vying for the favor of men. On the other hand, women romantically committed to each other must curb their passion. They too are forced to be bisexual, but for a different reason. As women, they are the captives of a social system that requires that their bodies be sex objects accessible to men. As a result, women who love and are committed to other women must either accept the polygamous solution or pursue self-destruction. The only other option is to enter celibate, religious environments, renouncing not only marriage but desires of every kind.[43] Yet, as Susan Mann notes of real life in the eighteenth century, the choice of a religious life was not available to all: "Monastic Buddhism offered an alternative to Confucian family life, but Buddhist monasteries recruited nuns almost exclusively from the poorest families or among abandoned or orphaned girls. . . . 'Getting to a nunnery' . . . was not an appropriate choice for a young woman of elite status."[44]

## Beyond Utopian Polygamy

Beyond the world of literary imagination, men's control of women as sex objects was probably effective and practically total in most parts of China in late-imperial times. And it is for this reason that modern Chinese commentators since the May Fourth era have been repeatedly drawn to certain outlandish marriage customs in late-nineteenth- and early-twentieth-century Canton (also known as the Pearl River Delta) and probed them as either an extraordinary product of female homosexuality or a hotbed for it. In other words, the disproportionate amount of intellectual curiosity that these marriage customs have drawn suggests that, until the May Fourth era at least, rarely did women's resistance to marriage and female-female life arrangements become established practices.

In 1926 and 1927, the male intellectuals Kai Shi and Chen Dongyuan debated in the Shanghai feminist magazine *Xin nüxing* (New woman) the origins of two unusual customs (*qite de fengsu*)—*bu luojia* (the bride's delayed transfer after marriage) and *zishu* (sworn spinsterhood)—that were reputedly widely practiced in Canton at the time. Kai Shi maintained that the brides in Canton preferred to remain with their natal families and female companions for as long as possible mainly for two reasons: first, because "the marriage institution was defective [*hunyin zhidu bu liang*]" and imposed too much hardship on women; second, because women "acquired intimate friends with whom they practiced homosexual love [*jie tongxing ai de niyou*]."[45] In response, Chen Dongyuan pointed out that delayed-transfer marriage had existed in the area for over two hundred years, presumably a remnant of the practices of ethnic minority cultures. Nonetheless, like Kai Shi, Chen also applied the neologism of homosexuality in his interpretation. He speculated that the main motive behind women's reluctance to settle down in their husbands' homes or their chosen spinsterhood was homosexuality ("ci su de neimu, ju wo kan guanyu tongxing lian yi fangmian duo xie"), and he asserted that a defective marriage system was the result of homosexuality, not its cause.[46] More than a decade later, when Pan Guangdan surveyed homosexuality in traditional Chinese documents, the unusual Cantonese customs were mentioned again. In a discussion providing otherwise vague evidence of female homosexual relations in traditional Chinese society, Pan referred to the practices as an example of women's homosexual relations reaching the status of a local custom (*fengqi*) in certain times and places. Citing a Qing writer's travelogue, Pan described certain ceremonies—*jinlan hui* (the union of sisters) and *bai xiangzhi* (bonding with an understanding friend)—that women in Canton could perform to bond with their bosom friends. Those who underwent these rituals might even refuse ever to marry men. Most important, Pan attributed the origins of these customs to the fact that, after the (early Qing) ban on maritime trade was lifted, Canton was the first port to come into constant contact with the outside world; as a result, women there were the first among Chinese women to gain professional freedom and economic independence.[47]

More recent sociological and anthropological writers have continued to be fascinated with the related but different customs of delayed-transfer marriage and voluntary spinsterhood. Janice Stockard, not unlike Pan Guangdan, attributes the customs in Canton largely to economic development. She claims that marriage resistance, in particular, emerged in the nineteenth century when women had economic autonomy and power because they had better job opportunities in the silk factories set up by foreign investment than did men.[48] In other words, economic autonomy appears to have been an essential enabling factor in women's self-determination as spinsters and even lifelong companions. The matter is complicated, however, by the fact that, over the centuries, there had been hybridization between the Han Chinese culture and the indigenous minority culture in the Pearl River Delta. Helen Siu, for instance, locates the root of delayed-transfer marriage and women's marriage resistance in the compromise between Han Confucian ideology and the culture of the local ethnic minority and the way in which upwardly mobile families used the local marriage custom to elevate their symbolic status.[49] Despite the disagreement between Siu and Stockard on the question of women's agency, their interpretations concur in identifying these local customs as anomalous. The delayed-transfer marriage found in the Canton Delta was an exception to an otherwise universal pattern of marriage for women in traditional Chinese society.[50] Further historical or anthropological research may reveal lesser-known local customs and institutions similarly hospitable to marriage resistance and female-female lifestyles. However, it is safe to assume that they could exist on only a very limited geographic scale.[51]

Given the atypical and exotic character of such practices, the extent to which they can serve as an inspiration for ethnic Chinese lesbians in the twenty-first century, the majority of whom live outside the areas in which these practices were found, can be determined only on a case-by-case basis. Yet this much is certain: if the sworn spinsterhood and sister unions found in Canton a century ago are inspiring to some lesbians in Taipei or Beijing now, it is probably not because of any simple sense of cultural continuity between past and present or any simple homogeneity between Canton and other parts of China. The felt connection would have to be understood as translocal and transcultural sympathy. Such legacies—for example, sisterly bonding and all-female performance traditions—as China has to bestow on women who consider themselves lesbians are dubious at best.[52] It is not coincidental that the first few issues of the first lesbian community newsletter in Beijing, *Tiankong* (Sky), are littered with Western lesbian images and the trivia of Western lesbian history, such as the legend of Sappho of Lesbos, while making absolutely no mention of any female same-sex practices in China in the past. *Tiankong* does not hide its desire to graft itself onto the history of Western lesbian sexuality and claim a Western genealogy. In this regard, it is somewhat ironic that in Taiwan—the island that aspires to openly declare political independence from China—the local lesbian community magazines have occasionally, if rarely, invoked and appropriated a historical connection with China— for example, female same-sex bonds in the Canton and Huian (in Fujian) of a century ago and in cosmopolitan Shanghai of the 1920s and 1930s (see figs. 7–9).[53] Such efforts, however, are largely overwhelmed by and lost among the constant references to the United States and other parts of the West—for example, the countless photographs of Western lesbians— that seem meant to provide inspiration and a sense of community. The sense of not having a usable Chinese past distinguishes the experience of many ethnic Chinese lesbians from that of the many gay men who cling to the fantasy of belonging to a great homosexual tradition in China.[54]

One can very well imagine the stark contrast between the experiences of (certain) men-preferring men and those of (all) women-preferring women on entering conventional marriage during the late-imperial period in most parts of China, with possible exceptions like Canton. As Matthew Sommer's study of Qing court cases shows, although the penetrated male bore a strong stigma in Qing society, and although only males in the mean

FIGURE 7 A Taiwanese lesbian magazine juxtaposes an advertisement painting of Chinese women dancing in 1930s Shanghai with images of lesbians in the West. (*Ai bao*, no. 2 [1994]: 21)

professions (such as servants and actors) were willing openly to assume the passive role in male-male sexual relations, the penetrating male was apparently not the object of society's contempt.[55] A male's penetration of other males was consistent with normative masculinity in late-imperial China. That is to say, there was no concept akin to *same-sex desire* that universally stigmatized everyone involved in male-male behavior. The immunity from shame was enjoyed, in particular, by elite and/or wealthy men who had a special taste for beautiful boys, a fact well illustrated by the relationships between literati libertines and boy actors of the seventeenth century analyzed by Sophie Volpp.[56] Even if elite men with a taste

愛福好報 / 福自在

1993年12月1日創刊‧復刊以每届台灣字菜第9卷1號‧第三期：Boo：台北郵政83-113號信箱

愛上女子也很自在‧福氣啦

我想有個家　一個不需要多大的地方
在我疲倦的時候　可以讓我依靠它
誰不想有個家　可是就有人沒有它
我只能孤單地尋找自己的家

FIGURE 8 The cover of *Ai bao,* no. 3 (n.d.): "I want a home."

for boys were duty bound to marry women, they were not necessarily obliged to care about their wives and could very well neglect them once they had produced children. In his classic essay on Chinese homosexuality, Pan Guangdan names example after example of emperor and male literatus obsessed with male beauty and passionate in his praise of the male erotic object, without ever bothering to mention whether any was inconvenienced by marriage to a woman. The unspoken assumption shared by Pan and his assumed readers was that, while marriage was the norm, it need not hinder the pursuit and enjoyment of passive male sex objects. Gender inequality, in conjunction with class hierarchy, ensured elite men's sexual freedom in every regard, allowing them to penetrate lower-class men as well as women, in or outside marriage.

By contrast, the marriage imperative meant subordination to strange men for women-preferring women. Staggering physical and emotional

FIGURE 9 Sisterhood and childrearing in the advertisement paintings of the Republican era. One of the paintings inspired "I want a home" (fig. 8 above).

suffering could result, but women had few alternatives. In the stories, legends, and presumably truthful accounts in late-imperial male literati's *biji,* we find scattered examples that impart a vivid sense of how difficult it was for women to form relationships with other women that were lasting and uncompromised by marriage and domination by men. In some, women chose self-destruction over marriage. Theirs may be considered stories of *lesbian martyrdom.* The adjective *lesbian* is, of course, an anachronism, but I use it deliberately here to invoke a connection between those who today have the freedom to identify as lesbian and those who in the past took their own lives precisely because such an identity was unrealizable. One such example is the legend of Xiaoqing of the late Ming.[57] After engaging in what Pan Guangdan maintains was a homosexual relationship with her friend Madame Yang, Xiaoqing fell sick—partly because her husband's principal wife was jealous and marriage disenchanted her, but largely because she and Madame Yang were separated when the latter was forced to follow her husband to a different city—and, succumbing to melancholia, eventually died.[58]

Pan also mentions another example, a story that originally appeared in *Mingzhai xiaoshi* (Short notes from a bright studio, printed 1811), by Zhu Huixiang. The full text is as follows:

### Two Women Committed Double Suicide

There was a Mr. Zhu in the Haiyan county. When he was appointed to head the Shanghai college, he took his favorite concubine along with him. Near their residence there was a girl who was not yet married who was gentle, exquisite, and very good at poetry and embroidery. She and Mr. Zhu's concubine became close friends. Then the girl got married. She did not get along with her husband. She would sleep alone at night and held fast to the rules of chastity. She became a vegetarian and a pious Buddhist. When she had spare time, she visited the Zhu family. She would talk with Mr. Zhu's concubine deep into the night rather than sleep. One night in September, these two women suddenly opened the door and left the house together, and they were nowhere to be found. At dawn their bodies surfaced in the river, and they were still locked in each other's embrace. Subsequently, Qu Ziye (Qu Yingshao) wrote an account of it with details. His language is ingenious, beautiful, and very refreshing.[59]

This account indicates that, if a woman who loved another woman could not adapt to conventional marriage, suicide and religious asceticism were the only options available to her. Only through double suicide could a female couple openly declare and thereby secure acknowledgment of their love. However, that acknowledgment might not be as dignifying as they had hoped. After quoting the story, Pan Guangdan comments: "In the hands of the male literati, such incidents merely supplied a fresh topic for extravagant composition. If we want careful observation and accurate details from them, it is impossible."[60]

Another story ending in suicide—in this case group suicide—is *Wu nü yuan* (The affinity between five young women) by Jiangzhu Nüshi (The crimson pearl female scholar). To defy approaching marriage and separation from one another, five teenage girls who have lived happily together drown themselves. According to Tan Zhengbi, this novel was adapted from an account in the Qing literatus Yang Xunji's *biji Menglan suobi* (At the end of dreams, tiny bits from the pen).[61]

That the formation of intimate bonds between adolescent girls must be no more than a phase is scripted by another Qing male literatus, Changbai Haogezi, in his *biji Yingchuang yicao* (Unusual grass by the firefly window). In the section entitled "Tai yi" (Aberrant birth), intercourse between two young women is ridiculed as an inferior copy of the real thing, a pastime that girls must outgrow. Changbai Haogezi reports the following incident: The adolescent daughter of some eastern Guangdong gentleman got pregnant and gave birth before she was married. Her parents were puzzled and ashamed. Her fiancé's family believed that she had given her virginity to a man. But her sworn sisters protested her honor in the county court. On examination, she proved to be still a virgin. The mystery was solved by an erudite high-ranking official. Judging from the facts that the girl would sleep with one of her sworn sisters in the same bed and that the thing to which she gave birth was like a human slouch—a skin sac shaped like a human but totally empty—he guessed the truth. He announced, "The girl was old enough to know about sex, so she mimed intercourse with her girlfriend. Even though they were both females, owing to the circulation of authentic *qi* [life force] from one to the other she got pregnant. Still, what they had fell short of sex; it was not real sex. Therefore, although it resulted in fruit, the fruit was like a plum whose seed had been drilled out." Her name cleared, the young lady got married. She gave birth to several children. "These babies," Changbai Haogezi tells us, "were healthy with bone and flesh, unlike the fake baby without substance."[62] If we believe that the author's biases determined the way in which he crafted this supernatural and highly unlikely story, we find him implying that sex between women is insubstantial, futile, and unproductive and that a relationship between girls is a phase easily superseded/surpassed by marriage. Moreover, the fact that he frames the whole female homoerotic affair as a mystery indicates the need for secrecy. It is also telling that the gentleman's daughter is forgiven because her hymen is intact—because she is still marriageable.

## Women's Limited Expressions

To recapitulate, female-female relations lack dignity in the representations that they are given by the male elite of late-imperial China.[63] Such relations are either effortlessly incorporated into utopian polygamy in fancifully plotted fiction and drama or recorded as resulting in futile and self-destructive resistance to marriage in semitruthful accounts. Occasionally, female-female desire is described as a passing adolescent phase, one that disappears on marriage. Rarely do these male authors explore the subjective meanings for women of these relationships. If we turn elsewhere, however, and look at elite women's literary expressions during the same era, it is possible to gain a fuller sense of the depth of women's feelings for their female companions at home and friends far away. Indeed, that emotional and sensual depth is one of the subjects explored by the readings of late-imperial women's literature offered by Dorothy Ko and Hua Wei, among others. However, even though tender feelings for and sensual attraction to the same sex abound in late-imperial women's literature, there are obvious limits to the feelings and situations that can be expressed. Writers do not touch on sexual passion between women. And fantasies of cross-gender adventures and same-sex unions are constantly compromised to achieve a socially acceptable closure.

One of the female writers who has caught the attention of modern critics is Wu Zao (1799?–1862?). Consider her *ci* lyric "Zeng Wumen Qinglin jiaoshu" (To the courtesan Qinglin of Suzhou):

> On your slender body
> Your jade and coral girdle ornaments chime
> Like those of a celestial companion
> Come from the Green Jade City of Heaven.
> One smile from you when we meet,
> And I become speechless and forget every word.
> For too long you have gathered flowers,
> And leaned against the bamboos,
> Your green sleeves growing cold,
> In your deserted valley:
> I can visualize you all alone,
> A girl harboring her cryptic thoughts.
> You glow like a perfumed lamp

In the gathering shadows.
We play wine games
And recite each other poems.
Then you sing "Remembering South of the River"
With its heart-breaking verses.
We both are talents who paint our eyebrows.
Unconventional as I am,
I want to possess the promised heart of a beautiful woman like you.
It is spring.
Vast mists cover the Five Lakes.
My dear, let me buy a red painted boat
And carry you away.[64]

The poem is full of fetishistic praise of the courtesan's body parts, clothes, and adornments. Because of its sensual and unabashedly possessive tone, both Ling Chung and Hua Wei have read it in terms of lesbian eroticism. Hua reminds us, furthermore, that masculine identification and discontentment with confinement are the themes animating another work by Wu Zao: the one-act play *Qiao ying* (The disguised image). In the play, the female protagonist, Xie Xucai, laments being caged like a sick crane (*bing he*) instead of being allowed to fly above the clouds like a powerful roc (*fei peng*). She is sorrowful that her literary talents and ambitions are frustrated simply because she is a woman. In her studio, after drinking and imagining herself living the life of a male scholar, Xie expresses her longing to have a beautiful female companion to spend the evening with her.[65]

Both poem and play indicate that Wu Zao's sensual feelings for other women are contiguous with her audacious (*qingkuang*) masculine identification. Through the persona of Xie Xucai, she likens her own literary gift and free spirit to those of Li Bo and Qu Yuan, two ancient male poets of the highest caliber. She also presents her own appreciation for beautiful women as on a par with men's.

Lu Qingzi (dates uncertain), a late Ming writer to whom Dorothy Ko has paid particular attention, is another fascinating example of the literary woman who repeatedly expresses attraction to other women. The following is one of the ten poems addressed by Lu Qingzi to Xu Yuan (1560–1620) on the eve of Xu's trip to a faraway province:

Your face a dazzling crimson,
My hair, a desolate white.
I want to pursue the pleasure of my lifetime,
But the vehicles crowding the road cannot bring me there.[66]

According to Ko, because Lu and Xu were about the same age, Lu's "contrast of Xu's youthfulness with her own fatigued looks is likely to signify her emotional distress at parting instead of a gap in biological age."[67] Overpowered by the fear of separation, Lu unreservedly declares her yearning to follow and be with her friend—the pleasure of her lifetime.

One might wonder why late-imperial literary women like Lu Qingzi could indulge themselves in creating such exuberant expressions of attachment to their female friends and, moreover, succeed in having the poems published. Regarding this issue, Ko asserts: "The spectrum of love and friendship pursued by Xu Yuan and Lu Qingzi was hardly surprising. In a society that upheld the doctrine of separate spheres as the ideal, women were left with much leeway to pursue affective bonds of their own without men's interference. However circumscribed this freedom turned out to be, its heartfelt meaning to the women concerned cannot be denied."[68] This insight is well taken, and the last thing I want is to belittle such romantic bonds as a mere opiate for poor imprisoned souls. However, the frequent motifs of longing and sadness on parting in late-imperial women's poetry should alert us to the physical constraints and lack of mobility that women experienced in real life. The ideal of separate spheres left tangible interfering and constricting traces on women's experience and literary creation. What is more, regardless of what gentry women's actual same-sex practices were, their acute awareness of men's power kept their inscriptions of same-sex possibilities within bounds. For instance, daring as Wu Zao may seem in her identification with male poets of the highest caliber, her expressions of desire for other women did not move beyond subtle, metaphoric sensuality to reveal heated passion or pleasure. Her expressions were not brazenly different from those of other gentry women who might write poems to extol their female friends' and relatives' facial features and ornamented beauty.[69] It was not unusual for female poets to express envy of the men who would marry their beautiful female friends or relatives in the future, but that envy rarely seemed so intense as to suggest jealousy or pain. Not even Wu Zao, who professed to want to monopolize a courtesan's attention, could explicitly describe her own *qingkuang* (audacious, unconventional, gallant) behavior; rather, she had to stop short and articulate her erotic interest as merely a wish.

Similarly, Ming and Qing women's dramatic works and *tanci* novels commonly play with ambiguous same-sex eroticism, usually in cross-dressing plots—a woman dresses up as a man, and another woman falls in love with her. However, the eroticism hinges on illusion and is never physically consummated. To borrow Siao-chen Hu's apt analysis, the sex scene is "endlessly deferred."[70] Furthermore, order usually returns at the end of such plots. The cross-dresser reverts to her female identity, and the women marry men, sometimes the same man. The women cannot defy the imperative of domesticity even though they may regard their "simulated love union" (*jia feng xu huang*) as more enjoyable than the "real" one—marriage with a man.

These representational patterns in late-imperial women's literature suggest that women writers operated on the basis of a keen, if unspoken, awareness of how far they could carry their fantasies without incurring censure. They send their heroines into the wide, wide world to pursue men's careers in the public realm and the love of beautiful and talented women, but only to such an extent that the heroines' adventures can be rationalized in the end as a temporary release from the established gender order. To do otherwise would constitute a serious breach of gender norms. As Siao-chen Hu observes, it is likely that Chen Duansheng (1751?– 96?)—the female creator of *Zai sheng yuan* (The destiny of another lifetime), the most remarkable *tanci* novel with a heroine in men's guise—left her life's work unfinished because she resisted how all stories of women's adventure must end: the heroine must undergo a ritual of refeminization and return to domesticity.[71] Yet, other than the existing gender system's successful reabsorption of her heroine, Meng Lijun, there was no acceptable ending that Chen could write. So she left it open-ended.

## Conclusion: Trivialization and Containment

Late-imperial Chinese women's literary creations of same-sex relations and cross-gender adventures were constrained by their understanding of the male-female hierarchy and the necessity not to cause a permanent breach of gender norms. To grasp the social circumstances that women-loving women faced in life and had little power to change even in fictional writing, one must confront men's attitudes and examine how they were articulated. It is for this reason that, in revisiting premodern Chinese female-female relations, I have brooded over the perspectives in texts written by men. Female same-sex relations were belittled by male authors in numerous ways. At times, female-female romance was ridiculed and turned into comedy salvaged by wise men. At others, it was lamented as a tragedy, but the women were offered no real hope of escape. It is therefore high time that we leave behind the myth that traditional Chinese society was tolerant of female same-sex relations. Such relations lived on borrowed liberty; their existence was premised on men's control and domestic containment. The suffering was far from trivial for those women-loving women who could not adapt themselves to male-headed marriage and men's sexual demands.

Rather than affirm what has been asserted time and again (by certain Sinologists as well as influential queer activists in Hong Kong)—that the prohibition on same-sex love/desire came from the West to China in the twentieth century—I have taken issue with such claims because of their gender blindness and their totalizing tendencies generally. I argue that, in the case of female-female relations, premodern Chinese texts delineated serious social priorities that circumscribed and constrained women's love for other women. At the same time, I suggest that the meaning of a prohibition on female same-sex desire is culturally and historically specific: what it means in late-imperial Chinese texts is different from what it means in Christian or modern medical discourses. Late-imperial Chinese sources never expressed, as did the Christian West, a tangible abomination specifically for the sex act between women as unclean, unnatural, a sin, or a crime.[72] The reason may be that the ancient yin-yang cosmology shaped a biological thinking in which "there was nothing fixed and immutable about male and female as aspects of yin and yang," as Charlotte Furth maintains. Furth argues specifically that "this natural philosophy would seem to lend itself to a broad and tolerant view of variation in sexual behavior and gender roles." However, even Furth admits that, in Ming medical writings, "serious anomaly began with barrenness in the functionally normal, and extended to those with reproductively 'useless bodies.'"[73] In other words, although no sex act was singled out by late-imperial medicine as inherently unnatural, reproductive success was used to draw important distinctions between normal and anomalous bodies.

In effect, reproduction was nothing less than a duty, besides being the yardstick of biological health, for all married women (and most men except those at the lowest levels of society, who could not afford to marry) regardless of their sexual practices. More fundamentally, as the matter concerned female-female relations, the marriage imperative reigned supreme in late-imperial sources. Male-authored fiction and drama routinely subjected female-female relations to participation by men and rejected the possibility that emotional commitments between women might lead to marriage resistance. We can, therefore, conclude only that men's confidence in women's inability to make exclusive romantic commitments to one another had much to do with women's dire lack of social, economic, and political means in premodern Chinese society. Exactly what kind of parameters functioned in late-imperial society to trivialize, prohibit, channel, or produce female same-sex love/desire cannot be adequately reconstructed and substantiated without a thorough investigation of written documents in all genres. Such an immense project is beyond the scope of the present study. (This is a project that, I might note, would not be worth undertaking unless one is prepared to find a broad spectrum of individual attitudes.) My aim has been very modest and very specific: to begin the task by pointing out a visible tendency in late-imperial male-authored texts, especially in imaginative genres such as fiction and drama, that reduced female same-sex desire to a trivial status so long as it remained within men's reach and under men's management.

Meanwhile, although the majority of the late-imperial Chinese male authors who touched on female same-sex intimacy contained it within an idealized domestic structure instead of demonizing and denouncing it, a few male literati did nevertheless show insight into the strength of the love between certain women and their absolute disdain for men. The next chapter takes, therefore, a closer look at such rare instances through an exercise in close reading. In the tales of the strange by the early Qing literatus Pu Songling, phallocentrism is brought into crisis, and men's confidence verges on fear. Tellingly, these stories about resilient and castrating female-female bonds tend to cast (at least some of) the female characters as supernatural beings, such as immortals and transformational spirits. Their superhuman dimensions might have been emblematic of the untenability of women's self-determination and marriage resistance in reality.

# ODD GIRLS IN PU SONGLING'S
# TALES OF THE STRANGE

Late-imperial Chinese men's writings on female-female relations were scattered rather than neatly organized into a system of signification like a body of philosophical teachings, a religion, or a scientific discipline. However, insofar as common motifs and plots can be identified among them (as I have demonstrated in chap. 2), these individual statements have a cumulative effect *like* that of a discourse. After all, a discourse in the Foucauldian sense is precisely something that has seeming unity but is in fact rent by silences and discontinuities.[1] Perhaps no discourse can ever thoroughly do away with self-contradiction and fragmentation. Neither can a discourse completely monopolize the field of meaning making. So, although the majority of late-imperial Chinese men's texts touching on the desire between women either trivialized it as an inferior, imitative play or appropriated it as a harmless dynamic that could smooth the operation of polygamous households, even among these writings can one find stories that unexpectedly defied men's expectations of women's docility. Chapter 2 has already related a few of the anecdotes recorded in the notation books (*biji*) of literati in which women with strong bonds with each other resorted to religious asceticism or even self-destruction in order to opt out of conventional marriage completely. In this chapter, a seventeenth-century literati writer's fantastic tales, long admired for their vivid imagination and elegant classical style, will be scrutinized because of the unusual range of female characters in them. In Pu Songling's *Liaozhai zhiyi* (Liaozhai's tales of the strange), a collection best known to the common Chinese reader today for bringing to life male scholars' wildest sexual fantasies, one finds the cryptic images of certain women who desire only other women and adamantly reject men.[2]

In Pu's tales, the attraction between women is on occasion even chastised as perilous and warned against as futile and having no future. However, although such authorial admonition against serious female-female love is barely hidden, it has seldom been recognized and commented on by modern readers. A preliminary analysis reveals that a lack of research coupled with heterosexual worldviews may have led many modern readers to miss the complexity of certain premodern Chinese representations of women's friendships, such as those in *Liaozhai*. To say the least, a woman's absolute preference for female companionship over sexual domination by a man is manifest in a minority of late-imperial Chinese texts. These texts usually shy away from explicitly indicating the occurrence of full-blown genital sex acts between women. Such acts are found on graphic display only in Ming-Qing pornography, where pleasure instead of love is the subject matter, and where sex is unambiguously phallocentric—sex between women is merely a temporary substitute for or a prelude to sex with a man.[3] Since the concern of the more polite texts is primarily with love (*qing*) instead of organ pleasure, I do not submit that their visions of certain women's same-sex preference are enough to define a clearly sexual lesbian identity in the modern (Western) sense. (Not that female-female genital sexual experience alone is necessarily sufficient to define the modern lesbian identity.) Nevertheless, to the extent that even some self-identified lesbians of the late twentieth century and the early twenty-first consider their preference for women a matter determined more by emotional connection and less by physical sex, the coy late-imperial Chinese texts may be viewed as exploring an important domain of affectivity that is significant even to modern lesbian subjectivities.[4]

Pu Songling wrote many stories that depict close sisterly bonds, but only a handful of these bonds are specifically relations between a woman-preferring woman and her companion—a girlfriend, sister-in-law, or neighbor. Although the stories in this latter group constitute only a small fraction of the nearly five hundred tales (mostly about fantastic beings and strange happenings) in *Liaozhai,* they are nonetheless enough to suggest the author's recurring and ambivalent fascination with female-female love.[5] Together, they indicate that stories of female-female love that turn out well, such as Li Yu's play *Lian xiang ban* (Women in love), provide a lopsided picture of late-imperial Chinese attitudes toward female-female relations—an overly optimistic and benevolent picture, to be precise. Such stories merely concentrate on the ways in which female-female love may fit into an ideal marriage structure.[6] Left vastly unthinkable are women who are attracted only to other women and who resist compromise—compulsory marriage to men.[7] In Pu's work, a woman's preference for women, short of suicidal martyrdom but more determined than polygamy can effortlessly co-opt, appears as an object causing cognitive evasion as well as fascination. On the one hand, there is acknowledgment of the unconventional independence and fundamental difference of a woman who loves only other women; on the other hand, such a woman's difference cannot be directly admitted as such but must be articulated through displacements so that a psychic cushion is provided for the ordinary mind against her shocking qualities and outright naming and censure are unnecessary.

What Pu's stories show is that, since she does not belong to the dominant matrimonial matrix that defines culture, a woman-preferring woman forfeits her right to be considered a woman. In fact, she is not even human. She acquires either a superhuman or a subhuman status, but not quite human. If such an untenable subject position—that of the woman-preferring woman—(re)enters from the realm of abjection into the field of symbolic inscription, she can be nothing except the figure of strangeness, anomaly, the uncanny. However, what is uncanny is unsettling, not *in itself,* but only because it has been measured against a rule of fictive normalcy. The uncanny attribute is invested in an object by a cold masculine gaze that rejects anything deviating from its idealization as inferiority, lack, degeneration, imitation, and, paradoxically, also a horror that brings to one's consciousness the possibility of lack in oneself.

To safeguard himself from the castrating threat of the uncanny, Pu must establish a fundamental distance between himself and the uncanny, fetishize the difference, and hold fast to the difference in his belief. In Freud's conception of *das Unheimliche,* the uncanny is first identified in the doll or the automaton (an imitation), which lacks humanity but is so human-like that it suddenly comes to life.[8] The female fox spirit, parrot fairy, and immortal in Pu's stories of female-female desire are assigned the place of the uncanny—they are asserted to be human-like but essentially different and deeply insufficient. Judith Zeitlin has argued that, in the face of the strange, no horror, only wonder, is expressed in Pu's *Liaozhai*.[9] I would argue that, in the case of Pu's representations of female-female love, this is because the horror has already been worked into a safe distance. The impossibility of the different kind blending in completely or *passing* as a human being for eternity is installed in the mechanism of these specific texts.[10] The lack is kept away from the "ordinary" human world as the difference between species is fetishized.

Fetishism, in Freud's view, involves disavowal and displacement: fetishism ensues from men's denial of women's state of castration. In Lacanian terms, women become the phallus—the supreme object of men's desire—even though women themselves do not have the phallus.[11] It can be noted that, in theorizing about women's lack and the fetishization that disguises that lack, neither Freud nor Lacan is particularly concerned about the difference among women. In this regard, what is intriguing about Pu is precisely his hypothesis of such difference. The woman-preferring woman is assigned by Pu an excessive lack—a preordained nonhumanity—that is exceptional even among women. That excessive lack threatens to expose all women as unable to be the desirable phallus, hence rendering it difficult for the man to make good his own lack by possessing the woman as phallus. What is more, Pu's texts cover up the excessive lack of the uncanny woman-preferring woman through fetishization, but only in such a way that she becomes a transcendental and miraculous entity that simply cannot remain within the economy of desire in the human world.

The representative text in this group of tales is "Feng Sanniang" (The third daughter of the Feng family). As the details of this story make clear, the woman who prefers women and refuses sexual involvement with men has a literal nonhumanity, and similar configurations may be found in a number of other tales. To some, the reading exercise that follows will undoubtedly seem guilty of overpsychologization in that certain linguistic signifiers are probed as if they were real persons with hidden interior depths. I apply an extraordinary amount of pressure to Pu's economical text to yield more information than it may appear to contain. However, these reading strategies are necessary. For, short of close reading and an active pursuit of hidden shades of meaning, we may never move beyond the habit of taking certain anomalous figures at face value and dismissing them offhand as inscrutable random occurrences.

## A Close Reading of "Feng Sanniang"

The story of the third daughter of the Feng family begins with a chance encounter.[12] Fan Shiyiniang, an exquisite beauty and prodigious poet, meets another stunning teenage girl, Feng Sanniang, on Zhongyuan Day in a Buddhist nunnery.[13] Immediately they become enamored of each other. They exchange tokens of friendship on parting, and Shiyiniang invites Feng to visit her home. Day after day Shiyiniang expects Feng, but she never comes.

On Double-Ninth Day, Feng suddenly appears. She climbs over the wall surrounding the garden of the Fan residence to come to Shiyiniang, who is sick and languid from missing her friend. Feng and Shiyiniang live secretly together as sisters in Shiyiniang's chamber for six months until one evening Feng is accosted and insulted by Shiyiniang's brother. Feng then leaves the Fan residence, and Shiyiniang grieves as if she had lost her spouse.

At their reunion some months later, Feng whispers to Shiyiniang as they lie together in bed that she has found an ideal husband for Shiyiniang. The man is Meng Anren, an eighteen-year-old scholar who is handsome and gifted. Feng asks Shiyiniang for a personal object as a token of betrothal to give Meng. Knowing that Meng is poor, Shiyiniang adamantly refuses. Feng, confident that Meng will be successful in the future, visits Meng and confers on him the golden phoenix hairpin that Shiyiniang had once given her, pretending that it is Shiyiniang's token of love to him.

Meng, overjoyed, asks his neighbor to see Madame Fan to propose marriage to Shiyiniang. Madame Fan turns him down because of his poverty. Furthermore, Sir Fan decides to marry Shiyiniang into a powerful gentry family. Shiyiniang, upset at both Feng and her parents, hangs herself on the eve of the wedding planned by her parents so as to honor her engagement to Meng.

After Shiyiniang is buried, Feng makes Meng exhume Shiyiniang's body from the tomb, and she revives Shiyiniang with an elixir. All three flee from Shiyiniang's town. Shiyiniang and Meng are married, and Feng lives in an adjacent house. When Shiyiniang proposes that Feng marry her husband as well so that she and Feng can stay together forever, Feng refuses, claiming that she prefers practicing longevity techniques to marriage. Incredulous, Shiyiniang conspires with Meng against Feng. She makes Feng drunk and has Meng rape Feng, believing that this will make her yield to bigamy. On waking, the indignant Feng takes leave of Shiyiniang. When entreated by Shiyiniang to stay, Feng confesses that she is in reality a fox. She was enchanted by Shiyiniang's beauty at first sight and cannot help loving her. If she stays, love will simply tighten its grip. Bidding Shiyiniang to take care, Feng disappears. A year later, Meng succeeds in the exams for office, and Shiyiniang is able to visit her parents. The story ends.

After reviewing much of the *Liaozhai* criticism published in Chinese in the twentieth century, I discovered that, while the collection as a whole is considered a masterpiece of Chinese literature, "Feng Sanniang" is not particularly well-known or appreciated. And, while many of the individual stories in *Liaozhai* have been the focus of numerous studies, "Feng Sanniang" is seldom mentioned, much less worked on. On the rare occasions when it is mentioned, it is only in passing, and the comments made are unvarying: scholars extol Feng's ability to recognize a man's true value despite his poverty, her steadfast friendship for Shiyiniang, and Shiyiniang's courage in rejecting a marriage arranged by her parents in pursuit of individual happiness.[14] The only exception that I have found so far to the prevalent blindness to the female-female desire in the story is a terse and oblique complaint made by the mainland critic Lei Qunming in 1990: "Pu Songling's creation of a love affair between two women in the first part of the tale and a rape in the second half is not worthy of emulation [*shi buzu weixun de bimo*]."[15]

Qing commentators, however, were somewhat more attentive to the love affair between the two women. Feng Zhenluan, for example, comments on Feng's and Shiyiniang's first encounter: "It is normal for men to fall in love with each other. If a woman falls in love with another woman, to the extent of infatuation, she is constricting herself in a cocoon." And He Shouqi notes: "It is impermissible for a female fox spirit to love a woman. It would be even more inappropriate if they were both women."[16] Both commentaries were meant to elucidate Pu's authorial disapproval of the love affair. Compared to their Qing precursors, modern Chinese critics have been curiously reticent about "Feng Sanniang," avoiding discussion of the female-female desire, if in fact they noticed it. Is, say, the scholarship on *Liaozhai* in the English language better in this regard? Certainly, none of the many partial translations in English include "Feng Sanniang" (and there is no complete English translation). Did these translators consciously observe certain rules of propriety by leaving out a story about young women's mutual crushes? Or did they miss the eros and pathos in the story and so find it pointless, defective, not worth translating?[17] Among academic writers, Judith Zeitlin declares that "Feng Sanniang" is a "unique story of a lesbian love affair"—without going into detail.[18] This suggests that, even when the lesbianism of "Feng Sanniang" is acknowledged by the most perceptive *Liaozhai* specialists, it is considered too isolated an incident for analysis.

Yet, one might wonder, in what sense is "Feng Sanniang" a lesbian love story? Can we judge so simply as to say that the majority of mainstream, or academic, critics have been too heterosexist to notice it?[19] Is it possible that the ambiguous responses to the intense female friendship in the story—ranging from indifference, blindness, and denial to explicit antagonism or acceptance—mirror a certain equivocation in the narrative? After all, the reader finds contradictory things in Pu Songling's text. In the first half of the narrative, Shiyiniang and Feng are totally charmed by each other. In the second half, Feng turns into a matchmaker, and Shiyiniang has little problem, emotionally or physically, acquiring a husband. Perhaps the narrative is equivocal not in the sense that a certain truth about historical lesbian identity has been obfuscated, or censored, by Pu's act of writing. What demands our attention is this: equivocation may be the condition of the experience and existence represented here. What has been at once concealed and revealed in the figure of Feng Sanniang, I argue, is a lesbian identity before it can be named as such. Our inaugural act of naming the *lesbian* in the text, therefore, would be as much violation as redress. On a somewhat different level, "Feng Sanniang" is unique in that it challenges certain twentieth-century assumptions about traditional Chinese latitude on the issue of female-female desire. The text delineates the limits of social tolerance for female-female relations and a marriage imperative for women. The love triangle in the text, moreover, offers a complicated discourse on mimetic desire, the phallus, and the odd woman's self-abnegation and masochism that finds echoes, not only in other *Liaozhai* stories and twentieth-century Chinese lesbian literature, but also in modern Western literary representations of lesbianism.[20]

### The Nunnery as Women's Cruising Ground

On what grounds do we declare "Feng Sanniang" a female-female love story? It may be appropriate that we begin by pondering the evidence of love. For all its subtle phallocentrism (a point to be unfolded gradually), "Feng Sanniang" is a carefully crafted piece about attraction between women. It begins with a description of Fan Shiyiniang's desirable qualities and her constant rejection of young men who propose marriage. It suggests that she has much self-confidence as a young woman. She does not crave men's attention and affirmation of her value. She seems even physically aloof to men's appeal.

It should not be concluded from this that Shiyiniang is uninitiated to desire, however. At the Buddhist nunnery, an intense exchange of looks, or the gaze, between Shiyiniang and Feng takes place. The gaze is loaded with admiration and longing. Feng is pulled by Shiyiniang's charm, following at her heels, wanting but hesitating to speak to her. Shiyiniang is distant and guarded at first—she examines or scrutinizes Feng's appearance. Then, on finding Feng a ravishing beauty, Shiyiniang changes her attitude. Her coldness is replaced by an enthusiasm that reciprocates Feng's adoration and expectancy. Perhaps it was a certain preponderant dependence on visual stimuli in the author's masculine sexuality that motivated him to create the scene of the gaze.[21] However, there is no good reason for us to presume that a more truthful representation of female sexuality would necessarily downplay the importance of visual pleasure in an initial stage of attraction. What attracts both women is beauty, and each falls under the other's spell instantly. Fascination with beauty motivates both to discourse on various topics and to learn about each other's life history. Later on, Shiyiniang misses Feng so much that she falls sick. Her lovesickness forms a stark contrast to the aloofness toward men that she displays in the opening section of the story.

The girls first encounter each other in a Buddhist temple run by nuns. Perhaps it is not too far-fetched if we liken this event to the activity of cruising in an all-female bar. The exchange of looks and desire between Shiyiniang and Feng has similar qualities to modern cruising—people eye each other to decide whether they want to talk and get to know each other. Moreover, the Buddhist nunnery during the Zhongyuan Festival is a festive and essentially all-female locale like an all-female, or simply lesbian, bar. In late-imperial times, women of the gentry class were as a rule confined to the inner quarters of their houses and could go out only on rare occasions, such as for the Qingming Festival (Tomb-Sweeping Day) or when making visits to temples. As a result, the Buddhist nunnery was one of the rare public places where women from respectable families could by chance become acquainted with unrelated women. In "Feng Sanniang," this possibility is pushed to the extreme—the nunnery is portrayed as a locale hospitable to female-female desire, where women appreciative of femininity can fall passionately in love with other women at first sight.

For similar historical circumstances, another text with a female-female love affair as its central theme—*Women in Love* by Li Yu—also contains a scene in which the two main female characters meet and fall in love in a Buddhist nunnery. The scene can be summarized as follows. Miss Cui, who has been married for a month, goes to a Buddhist nunnery to thank the Buddha for giving her an agreeable husband. On the same day, Miss Cao, who, together with her father, has stayed in the nunnery for two days, is scheduled to depart. As Cui exchanges greetings with the nun in charge, Cao watches her from behind a screen and admires her beauty. In the meantime, Cui notices a "beauty's scent" in the air, a scent emanating in fact from Cao's body. After the nun introduces the women to each other, Cui composes a poem in praise of the "beauty's scent," saying that it comes neither from perfumed clothes, nor from the incense of the temple, but "from within [Cao's] layers of clothing." Then Cao composes a poem to praise Cui's poetic talent, saying, "The scent of a woman is no match for the fragrance of ink and poetic expression." Both women thus fall for the other's beauty and poetic talent, and each longs to be constantly in the other's company.[22]

Interestingly, the nun behaves like a mediator in this scene. Not only does she assist Miss Cao and Miss Cui in their exchange of poems of adoration, but, later on, when Cao and Cui are at their wits' end as to how to meet again, she also offers to let them use her nunnery for their rendezvous. The nun, if asexual and therefore not desiring women herself, shows sympathy for an intense female-female relationship. The connection that Li Yu makes here between an all-female ascetic establishment and female-female desire is provocative. It seems that, since the nun is herself outside the matrix of cross-sex marriage and desire, she does not necessarily hold the opinion that the union between man and woman is superior to female-female ties. To her it is clear that the latter relationship represents a powerful "attachment" or "spell of emotion."[23] Therefore, the nun, with a little mercy for others' worldly attachments, can function as an existing social resource to which the two female lovers may turn.

### The Closet of Class

A deep anxiety over the propriety of Shiyiniang and Feng's relationship taints the world of "Feng Sanniang" from the outset. The cause for anxiety is defined, for the most part, as difference in socioeconomic status. When Shiyiniang and Feng become acquainted, Feng hesitates to accept Shiyiniang's invitation to her house. She says to Shiyiniang, "Your family is rich and significant. Since I am not related to your family in the slightest, I am worried about people's contempt. They will sneer at me." Two months later, when Feng appears at Shiyiniang's house and is scolded by Shiyiniang for not fulfilling sooner her promise to visit, Feng reiterates her uneasiness about crossing class borders: "After we parted, I missed you and suffered. However, we humble and poor people are not carefree when we make friends with the wealthy and noble. The prospect of being despised by the nobles' servants intimidates and shames one before one even sets foot in the door. That's what kept me from coming." Later, deciding to stay with Shiyiniang, Feng requests, "That I am here with you must be kept secret. I cannot bear the rumors that gossips might fabricate and spread" (5.611). The apparent cause for Feng's unusual request to keep their friendship unknown beyond Shiyiniang's chamber and personal attendants seems to be always the disparity in their social and economic class.

This being the case, we notice that Feng's attitude toward class boundary is, in fact, ambiguous. At first glance, she shows doubt neither about her own intrinsic worth nor about her and Shiyiniang's mutual attraction. She personally does not consider the mixing of different classes improper, and her anxiety revolves around how third parties (such as servants) might look on their relationship. Yet, on closer examination, her refraining from visiting Shiyiniang for two months and talk about "shame" suggest self-denial and the internalization of others' discrimination on the basis of class. If we push this line of reasoning further, we find that, fundamentally, we do not know whether the discriminating, slandering others who patrol class borders are real or imaginary—whether all of this is not just Feng's paranoid, self-denying fantasy about the importance of class.

Feng's advice to Shiyiniang on how to choose an ideal husband is similarly ambivalent about wealth and power. On the one hand, Feng maintains that a person's abilities are more important than his class; on the other, she would not recommend Meng were she not sure that he will move up in the social hierarchy eventually. It is difficult to determine whether an ideology valorizing nobility and wealth is imposed on Feng and resisted by her or actively subscribed to by her. We witness a kind of double consciousness in her.

What vexes the issue even further is that, essentially, we are left in the dark as to what kind of libel Feng apprehends. Is the transgression of class taboo the real source of her discomfort and fear? What kind of female-female bonding would generate social anxiety around the issue of class? Can class be a screen onto which Feng's repressed anxieties are projected and displaced? Can her double consciousness—the mixture of shame and pride—result from some other self-attribute than her class? Is class a mere excuse for secrecy? What, exactly, we might ask, makes Feng want to hide with Shiyiniang in the closet—Shiyiniang's chamber?

Suppose that class is simply a convenient excuse; then there may not exist any necessary link between the class taboo and the unidentifiable phantom taboo. The two types of taboos that define deviant relations may be completely independent of each other. However, if the issues of class discrimination, alliances, and transgression are not merely excuses but rather touch on or factor into the creation of the phantom pressure that causes Feng's anxiety, then what we have is the intersection of two vectors of power previously thought to parallel each other. The question then becomes how different regulatory ideologies (in this case, class and phantom) that legitimize certain intersubjective relations over others collaborate with or work against each other.

In the case of "Feng Sanniang," I argue that class taboo is more than a screen covering an unspeakable phantom taboo. The questions of property and family lineage, which are central to the definition of class, do not exhaust the phantom issue, but they do motivate it, at least in part. The phantom taboo that works against the union between Feng and Shiyiniang is partly a question of property. Further, insofar as Feng *imagines* her own relationship to Shiyiniang as capable of posing a threat to the usual traffic of property, she reveals the personal meaning that she secretly confers on their relationship.

Six months after Feng's request for secrecy and Shiyiniang's consent, disclosure takes place: "One day, as the girls were playing chess, Madame Fan came into the room unexpectedly. She stared at Feng and exclaimed, 'Indeed my child has a friend!' Then she said to Shiyiniang, 'It pleases us that you have a good female friend at home. Why didn't you tell us earlier?' Shiyiniang told her mother about Feng's fears. Madame Fan looked at Feng and said, 'We are very happy that a nice girl keeps our daughter company. Why did you hide from us?' Feng's face turned crimson. She played with her skirt bands without a murmur" (5.612).

Madame Fan takes no offense at Feng's lower-class status. She considers Feng neither presumptuous nor a threat to Shiyiniang and the Fan family. In contrast, Madame Fan will later strongly object to and attempt to prohibit the connection between Meng Anren and Shiyiniang on the ground of unequal social and financial status. The reason, as can be imagined, is that the institution of marriage entails the exchange of property and the alignment of social power between two families. If Shiyiniang is married to Meng, her person, her dowry, and the Fan connections will become the possessions of Meng, who has little to give in return to reinforce the Fans' social network and wealth. Unlike marriage, the alliance between Shiyiniang and another woman is incapable of effecting such traffic in property and power. Put bluntly, from a dominant perspective, neither Shiyiniang nor Feng has the right to hold property; under patriarchy, they themselves are possessions.[24] Hence, Shiyiniang's parents have no reason to feel that they are giving Shiyiniang away for naught when Shiyiniang befriends Feng. On the contrary, because of Feng's lower socioeconomic status, they believe that they gain a companion, a servant of sorts, for their daughter. In short, anxiety over a bond between women would need to be expressed around the issue of class only if it were imagined possible for a woman of low socioeconomic status to claim a woman of higher standing as a possession.

The people from whom Feng wishes to hide, we thus realize, are none other than Shiyiniang's parents. Her secrecy is overdetermined. Perhaps she has too much self-respect to let them treat her like a servant. Perhaps she fears that the parents—who are currently in possession of Shiyiniang—will force Shiyiniang to end the relationship. However, in reality, Madame Fan accepts the intimate bonding between them as innocent friendship. She regards it as a necessary, harmless form of companionship precisely because she does not suspect the possibility of erotic desire and possessive exclusivity between two girls and the resistance that such bonding may pose to Shiyiniang's future marriage to a man. In contrast to Madame Fan's unsuspecting puzzlement, Feng's blush seems proof of better knowledge and "guilt." She alone is aware of what lies beyond her fear of class discrimination; her magical hold on Shiyiniang must shun parental inspection. Only Feng can tell whether she and her friend cross the thin line between "pure" love and "impure," insane passion. What Feng must closet away from policing forces is, not only that she passes into a household above her class, but also that she dares to possess and be possessed by a valuable object of her own sex.

Feng perceives her clandestine relationship as trespassing both sexual and class taboos. And it is only because she has an unorthodox understanding of female-female relations that she feels anxious about class impropriety. For society in general, the traffic in women does involve important rules and taboos that make sexual and class issues converge.[25] But social authorities (who are represented by Shiyiniang's parents) are concerned only with the transfer of women from one patrilineal family to another, not with ties between women, let alone with whether such ties cross class lines. Although Feng's attraction to Shiyiniang's beauty instantly effects a transgression of class distinctions, it is not a serious transgression in the eyes of society. Feng's anxiety about violating the class taboo both closets a deeper "guilt" and discloses that, for her, a same-sex relationship is, by all measures, comparable to (and, in fact, stronger than) cross-sex marriage.

### The Sexiness and Politics of Indirection

At this point, a voyeuristic reader of Pu's text must ask herself what exactly happens in Shiyiniang's chamber. Is there sensory (tactile etc.) titillation, or genital contact, between the girls, contact that is closeted away from the reader? The narrator relates that these girls chat arm in arm, sleep in the same bed, exchange clothing, and play chess and presumably other games to entertain themselves. What function do these cursory descriptions have? Why does the reader receive an array of opaque textual details? Indeed, what is the task that Pu sets himself—an exposition on the comparability of romance between two women and that between a man and a woman or an essay on the different quality of the two kinds of romance, especially around the issue of carnal desire and genital sexuality?

To answer these questions, one can begin by comparing Pu Songling and Li Yu. Li's emphasis on scent in *Women in Love* heightens the reader's awareness of the corporeal basis for Miss Cao and Miss Cui's mutual attraction. Theirs is not only love at first sight but also love at first smell. Pu and Li are similar in that both bring out the sensuous quality of the connection between two women, the former through sight, the latter through scent. Both authors construct a discourse on the sensuous pleasures shared between women, emphasizing the dimension of aesthetic delight, but refraining from delving into sexual fantasy and intercourse—the typical topos that follows the delights of beauty in the plots of cross-sex attraction. The usual progression from aesthetic appreciation to pleasurable sex is blocked in both authors' stories of female-female love affairs.

Yet there is a difference between Li's approach and Pu's. In *Women in Love,* the withholding of female homoeroticism of a physical nature from conceptualization and representation is, in fact, superficial. Three years and many vicissitudes after Cao and Cui's "mock" marriage ceremony in the nunnery, Cui succeeds in entering Cao's house to be her poetic companion. Cui speaks the last line in their reunion scene: "This will be the first night that I share the pillow and cover with you."[26] Although the wording does not refer to sex explicitly, it suggests physical intimacy long overdue. Throughout the play, it is also clear that Cao's fantasies about Cui in a man's guise and Cui's tender, chivalrous attitude toward Cao exceed "sisterly" affection, embodying sexual interest.

In contrast, in "Feng Sanniang" Pu forecloses on physical eroticism between women. About Feng and Shiyiniang's happy cohabitation for six months, no tales of "immodest acts" between them are ever told. Only after their cohabitation is over does the narrator suggest that the girls' relationship is comparable to that of a married couple—when Shiyiniang cries bitterly on the bed for Feng "as if she had lost her spouse." This analogy does not automatically imply that they are like spouses prior to their separation since it may be only through "deferred action," what Freud calls Nachträglichkeit, that Shiyiniang realizes what Feng has been to her. Still less can the analogy indicate that they have indulged in carnal pleasures. The dark and prudish "Feng Sanniang" strikes one almost as a conscious revision of the upbeat and unabashed Women in Love.[27]

With his opaque style, Pu is either denying the reader a voyeuristic privilege or indicating the absence of sex between the female protagonists. The erotic dimension to their love returns only through substitution. It is as though the female lovers channeled, consciously or unconsciously, their physical desire for each other into some socially inoffensive outlet. Pu effects this displacement by instituting a third term, Meng Anren. Through Meng, the phallus is introduced—both physically and culturally—into the female-female love scene. On this point I will have more to say later.

For the moment, let us take a different approach to the signification of eroticism in "Feng Sanniang"—via other Liaozhai stories. In "Yingning" (Yingning the laughing girl), a story about girlish innocence and compulsive laughter, Pu has Wang Zifu explain to the girl of his dreams, Yingning, that what distinguishes the relationship between husband and wife from other kinds of love is that they "share the pillow and mat at night" (2.153). How a reader takes this little definition of the conjugal relationship will have some bearing on her understanding of Feng and Shiyiniang's bed fellowship. Certainly, Wang's pronouncement may be no more than a prudish euphemism: instead of delineating the sex act, he uses a broad, loose description to refer to an activity that is, in fact, more particular and demands discrete categorizing or naming. Alternatively, it may be argued that, by dint of a speech act, Wang redefines sharing the pillow and mat at night as an activity performed exclusively by married couples. Thus, a husband and wife's sharing the bed at night becomes the prototype of all occasions of sharing the bed. The activity sleeping together carries conjugal love as its kernel of truth, as it were. Insofar as Feng and Shiyiniang sleep together at night, their love is conjugal; they are like husband and wife.

In reply to Wang, Yingning reverses the peculiar signification that he assigns bed sharing; she forecloses its eroticism by exclaiming, "I am not used to sleeping together with strangers!" (2.153). She returns to *sleeping together* the innocence (feigned or not) of literal meaning: sleep is implied to be peaceful, quiet, distanced from excitement. What makes a good bedfellow is no more than familiarity. No component of pleasure is imagined. It is inconvenience that comes to her mind as the probable consequence of her sharing the bed with someone. In short, Yingning categorically desexualizes *sleeping together at night.*

What does it mean, then, for two girls to share a bed? Is the situation sexual, or is it innocent? Perhaps what the words *sharing the pillow and mat* represent is the tension between sex and nonsex, excitement and banality. If so, what Pu exploits in his description of Feng and Shiyiniang sleeping together is precisely the ambiguity of the situation.

Pu's attitude toward sex is interestingly put in his comments at the end of another story, "Jiaonuo" (The fox fairy Jiaonuo). He writes, "I envy Scholar Kong not because he found a ravishing wife but because he found a bosom friend. Looking at the face of such a friend can make one forget hunger; listening to her voice can bring a smile. Giving her one's soul over a meal and conversation brings one greater ecstasy than that of 'untying the dress'" (1.65). Pu declares that spiritual communion is more precious than physical copulation. The comment sheds a special light on "Feng Sanniang." Shiyiniang and Feng repose together—unguarded, they are able to relax and rest side by side. Whether they have sex before falling asleep must, then, be dismissed as a minor issue, almost beside the point. Abundant beauty and intimacy are found in their ability to slumber side by side.

Still, "Feng Sanniang" is a coy text that invites the reader to reflect on the nature of desire and erotic pleasure. If desire is for what is missing, and if fantasy is indispensable to sexuality (as the psychoanalysts Laplanche and Pontalis maintain), then it is only logical to believe that, where there is no physical act, there is most desire, most fantastical pleasure, and, thus, most sexuality.[28] What is more, one may obtain extreme sexual pleasure from conversation, self-sacrifice, finding the surrogate, and so forth. Although it is never indicated that the love between Shiyiniang and Feng is physically consummated, is this love, as a result, any less able to produce sensual transport?

Pu keeps the female homoeroticism of his story perfectly liminal. A textual detail such as "Feng moved over to share the same pillow with Shiyiniang" is seductive but perhaps no more than that. Its erotic charge—

the specter of a kiss or an embrace—can be either taken up or dismissed by the reader. The detail is a delicate sign open to different ideological appropriations. In Pu's polite and subtle text, one finds no graphic descriptions of orgasmic sex between women, as one sometimes does in late Ming and Qing pornography. Whatever female-female erotic pleasure one gains from Pu's text must be wrested from it, with the aid of fantasy.

For example, with imagination one may read the female-male-female triangle in Pu's text as a mechanism for fending off the "threat" of female homoerotic contact and, at the same time, bolstering female homosocial bonding and achieving mediated eros.[29] It is as though a wish for genital consummation were expressed by Feng's attempt to arrange marriage between a man of her choice and Shiyiniang. Meng becomes Feng's double—she delegates to him her desire—when she transfers to him the golden phoenix hairpin—a token of commitment and union—that Shiyiniang has presented to her. This striking detail conflates the meaning of same-sex friendship and cross-sex marriage, calling into question the difference between the two. Meng's entry into the game is for Feng a moment of both abjection and vicarious gratification. By the same token, Shiyiniang obtains vicarious pleasure from making Meng deflower Feng. Erotic exchange is carried out between the two women through Meng Anren. Such triangulation of desire is a female counterpart of the male homosocial (male-female-male) erotic paradigm that Eve Sedgwick illuminates in the tradition of English literature.[30]

However, one must be wary of idealizing such obscure, mediated, and wildly phantasmatic lesbian eros, for it is fraught with questions of women's agency and men's supremacy. Can Meng Anren, the man, simply be turned into a mediating element, no longer an independent agent? Does he not usurp the authority of the origin, claiming spontaneity and self-referentiality? Although the women may intend to employ Meng as a transferable phallus (or, shall we say, a two-pronged dildo?) that gains its meaning from the women's desire for each other, within a patriarchal cultural frame it is nevertheless all too possible that the phallus will simply efface its own transferability when attached to the man and become the fixed reference point for every other desire.[31] It is as though during the process of triangulation Pu asserted that the male phallus is indispensable to erotic pleasure. In concrete terms, it is difficult for us to distinguish Feng's matchmaking from the self-sacrifice and obedience to male desire that are systematically required of women. Similarly, although Shiyiniang's intentions are good when she orchestrates Meng's rape of Feng, that rape in fact constitutes betrayal. At best, what little satisfaction the women may gain from mediated eros is masochistic—the pleasure of inflicting punishment on oneself and of subordination. Yet the pleasure of masochism is never safe. As Sacher-Masoch demonstrates in his "Venus in Furs," what one would like to think of as self-inflicted, contractual humiliation may turn out to be unexpected abuse from an alien and vulgar other.[32] The man, the supposedly mediating term between Shiyiniang and Feng, can easily mutate into an unruly figure who pursues his own desires, goals, and conquests, defeating whatever agency Feng and Shiyiniang may imagine themselves to possess. The rape of Feng is a vivid trope for such a turn in power relations.

### Silencing the Woman-Preferring Woman: Her Loss of Performative Force

In "Feng Sanniang," certain instances of women's speech acts, such as refusal and the declaration of one's oddity, fail to elicit the desired response in the hearer. These utterances are deprived of their performative force.[33] Sometimes it is because the hearer purposely acts against the female speaker's intention as expressed in her request or rejection. But what I am interested in is an even more obnoxious form of performative deprivation. When a woman says something, the utterance, even though it registers with the hearer, is not recognized as seriously meaning exactly what it says. It does not count. The utterer's position is like that of an actor who cries "fire" in the theater and means it but who is perceived by the audience as not to be taken seriously. In an essay on J. L. Austin's speech act theory and Catharine A. MacKinnon's antipornography arguments, Rae Langton has isolated this phenomenon and labeled it *illocutionary disablement*.[34]

In "Feng Sanniang," illocutionary disablement is most apparent in Feng's rejection of sexual relations with men. Somehow, the role that Feng occupies as a woman in society makes it impossible for her to make utterances that effectively reject marriage proposals or declare her own nonconforming life choices. When Shiyiniang asks her to marry Meng Anren, Feng rejects the proposal by saying that she wants to practice longevity techniques and, hence, does not wish to marry. Shiyiniang hears Feng's words but fails to take them seriously. Instead, she smiles as if incredulous. When Shiyiniang later devises Meng's rape of Feng, therefore, it does not strike us that she understands herself to be purposefully contradicting Feng's will. The case is rather that Shiyiniang believes that she is carrying out what Feng secretly desires but is too shy or hypocritical to admit wanting. In other words, the "no" that Feng says to Shiyiniang fails not only on the perlocutionary level (i.e., it fails to make Shiyiniang abandon the idea of bigamy) but also on the illocutionary level (i.e., it fails to constitute itself as a genuine refusal).

There is of course the question to what extent Feng's declaration of the longevity project is rhetorical. But, even if her speech about longevity is a pretext, the effect that she sincerely desires may be to dissuade her friend. In the first place, her use of a pretext may be why her refusal sounds feigned to Shiyiniang, and consequently the refusal results in both illocutionary and perlocutionary failures. If this is the case, how might Feng have rejected the marriage proposal in a more straightforward manner? Do social circumstances allow her to make a truthful account of her feelings? If she can never voice the true grounds for her refusal of men but must always give a socially acceptable excuse for that refusal, then there is silencing at a very basic level. She is intimidated, or she believes that nobody will understand, so she does not even try to voice her genuine antipathy toward marriage. Swallowing her words, she does not even perform the locutionary act.

Thus, we find Feng subjected to threefold silencing—on the locutionary, illocutionary, and perlocutionary levels. It is not until she has decided to leave human society altogether that she disregards silencing social forces to declare her love for Shiyiniang. She says to Shiyiniang: "I must now tell you the truth—I am a fox. By chance I saw your beautiful face. At first sight I fell in love with you. I let love hold me in its grip, like a silkworm tying itself up in a cocoon. That's why a mistake like today's could happen. It was destined to happen because I was enchanted with love. My undoing was not caused by human efforts. If I stay, the spell over my emotions will multiply without end. You have a prosperous life ahead of you. Take care" (5.616).

Once Feng performs the locutionary act of uttering her painful passion for Shiyiniang, it becomes possible for some of her hearers, namely, the readers of Pu's text, to recognize the seriousness of her refusal of a man's sexual advances and the queer subtext that subtends that refusal. Not all readers, however, have picked up on her speech as a serious declaration of one woman's love for another. As a speech act declaring queerness, it fails ever so often on the illocutionary and perlocutionary levels, for "Feng Sanniang" is remembered, time and again, as a story about selecting a husband, about how a farsighted girl helps her friend choose the right man to marry.

A question may arise at this point as to why one should believe that queer desire is the fundamental reason for Feng's rejection of men or why the Tao (or longevity) cannot be as important a concern for Feng as her exclusive love for Shiyiniang. Both may be equally valid as reasons for her refusal of a man's sexual advances. But there are some questions that we must ask first about the basic precepts that she claims to follow as a Taoist adept. Then perhaps we can better understand the connection between a woman's pursuit of immortality and her exclusive love for another woman.

Taoism as a cult of immortality and longevity has a long history in China, and it is a highly eclectic practice. Consequently, it cannot be claimed that there is a unified Taoist discourse on sex. This granted, the first thing that one notices about Taoist writings on sex is that sexual techniques are old longevity techniques, already existent in the Han (206 B.C.– A.D. 220).[35] The ancient Taoist manuals on "the art of the bedchamber" are invariably directed at a male audience, as Charlotte Furth points out, and this discourse has important implications for female as well as male sexuality.[36] A basic proposition in these manuals is that the yin and the yang should mingle and complement each other in sexual intercourse so that a healthy balance can be struck in both the man and the woman. For this purpose, sexual climax is essential for both sexes. At the same time, it is maintained that, if the man conserves his semen in ejaculation, he can return this essence to repair his brain.[37] Related to this fundamental belief in the importance of semen is the theory of "nurturing the yang by plucking yin essence." Put in grisly terms, this is *sexual vampirism*.[38] It is said that, with the proper technique of semen conservation, a man can enhance his own health by copulating with many young girls. In a similar vein, a legend about nurturing the yin also appears in the ancient bedchamber manuals; the Queen of Western Paradise—a woman—absorbs the yang essence of the young boys with whom she has intercourse to nurture her yin, for her own perpetual beauty and youth.[39] Nowhere is it emphasized in these manuals that the female Taoist adept should refrain from sex for the purpose of longevity. When "Feng Sanniang" is read side by side with the ancient Taoist bedchamber discourse, it seems peculiar that Feng states that her pursuit of longevity and the Tao prohibits sex.

However, it cannot be denied that many sects of Taoism had a very spiritual orientation and placed great emphasis on the purification or refinement of the body in order to achieve the highest form of immortality.[40] Such schools, according to Isabelle Robinet, asserted that "the tendency toward sexual practices was only a feature of 'popular' or vulgar Taoism."[41] For example, Ute Engelhardt observes of the seventh-century Taoist text *Sheyang zhenzhongfang* (The pillow book of the method for nourishing life): "Most interesting . . . is the clear rejection of sexual practices and the warning against any deep involvement in sensual relationships with the other sex. Female adepts should not get pregnant, and male practitioners should not approach pregnant or menstruating women. Both should rather strive for more self-reliance and venerate the goddesses on high but not dream of engaging in sexual intercourse with them. This is contrary to the shamanistic visions frequently found in Tang poetry and also in certain Shangqing documents. Here the goddess descends and has a physical relationship with the adept—then always male."[42]

Obviously, if female adepts are warned against pregnancy, it is impractical or dangerous for them to have sex with men. However, it is unclear whether the book's warning against cross-sex sensuality is identical to an absolute taboo against all sensuality; above all, it is unclear whether sensual acts with the same sex are permitted. The advice that both female and male adepts should "venerate the goddesses . . . but not dream of engaging in sexual intercourse with them" is interesting, for it almost seems that the possibility of sexual intercourse between a female adept and a goddess is implied. At any rate, a text clearly rejecting sexual practices as does *Sheyang zhenzhongfang* would work as a textual authority for Feng Sanniang's rejection of marriage and sex with a man.[43]

Now that it is apparent that there are widely disparate discourses on sex in Taoist writings—some prohibiting and others encouraging sex between man and woman—the absolute prohibition on sex that Feng observes as a Taoist adept must be understood as partly her own choice. Especially when her fox identity is taken into account, her sexual abstinence seems oddly contrary to what is usually imagined about female fox spirits in late Ming and Qing literature, namely, that they are intent on having sexual intercourse with human males in order to obtain the men's yang essence (i.e., the "best" form of human essence), thereby speeding up their own transformation into immortals.[44]

To conclude, Feng Sanniang is not just an unusual woman. She is, in addition, an extraordinary Taoist adept and an atypical female fox spirit. Her strangeness traverses the divisions of worldly humanity (defined by Confucian teachings on human propriety and family/social relations), the Taoist cult, and foxiness. What she exposes is that a binary gender ideology and cross-sex sexuality are the cornerstones not only of the hegemonic definitions of humanity but also of the mythic Taoist discourse on immortality and of the literary imagination about supernatural beings, the fox spirits. Defying the imperatives of femininity and cross-sex sexuality, she is an odd figure in all three realms.

This does not mean, however, that Pu Songling valorizes one woman's love for another. In Feng Sanniang's last speech, addressed to Shiyiniang, Feng refers to "emotion" or "love" negatively as an obstacle in her cultivation of the Tao. By characterizing her passion for Shiyiniang as "emotion" or "love" (*qing*), which is distinguished from "sex" (*se*), she excludes sexual interest from female-female love. Prior to this speech, she has already cried out against sex (i.e., Meng's rape): "If I had not breached the taboo against sex, I could ascend into the primary heaven on my complete realization of the Tao" (5.616). As she speaks against both sex (i.e., intercourse with Meng) and emotion (i.e., her love for Shiyiniang), she can best be categorized as a cultivator of the Tao who has been strongly influenced by Buddhism, which adamantly negates all emotions and desires. Such a philosophical position denigrates not only cross-sex sensuality but also same-sex love. In short, Pu Songling does not allow Feng to affirm her passion for Shiyiniang.

### The Woman-Preferring Woman in Other *Liaozhai* Stories

"Feng Sanniang" can be contextualized by a consideration of several other stories in *Liaozhai* that depict a woman oddly aloof to men but tender to members of her own sex. Such a contextualization will bring the predicaments faced by the committed woman-preferring woman into higher relief. Again, it should be noted that these other stories have not been read as texts that thematize female-female relations. I argue, however, that, in these stories, the virtual woman—whether a parrot fairy or a Taoist immortal—harbors same-sex preference as the kernel of her fundamental difference from "real" women and "normal" human beings. What constitutes her difference in kind is her difference in desire. At odds with normative human society, which is predicated on cross-sex marriage, these women declare celibacy and their indifference to men. They are retained in the human world only by their love for women. However, their same-sex ties make them vulnerable to men's violent and/or sexual attacks. In order to avoid unsavory sexual advances by men, they must leave both the human world and the narrative, severing their emotional ties to women. The threat of compulsory sexual involvement with men makes it impossible for them to choose women and live happily ever after.[45] They must decidedly renounce the world in order to avoid men.

In "Aying" (Aying the parrot woman), the ordinary motif of the fulfillment of a marriage agreement is intertwined with the theme of women's
friendship and eventually yields in importance to the second theme. A
parrot, who was once promised in jest by her owner, Mr. Gan, to Jue, his
younger son, to be his future wife, transforms into Aying, a woman of
unmatched beauty, and marries the boy some years after the father dies.
She wins not only the heart of Jue but also the respect of Jue's elder
brother, Yu, and his wife. In particular, she forges a strong affective bond
with Yu's wife.

However, the Gan family eventually discovers that Aying is not human but an alien creature with magical powers. Fearing that Aying might
endanger Jue's life, Yu bids her to leave. Aying explains that she has married Jue to fulfill Jue's father's promise. Then, in the twinkling of an eye,
she turns back into a parrot and flies away.

Both Jue and Yu's wife miss Aying dearly. Yu's wife, in particular, constantly weeps over Aying's absence. Two years later, while Yu is away
on a protracted trip to another province, his wife and Jue chance to see
Aying when they and other villagers are hiding in a valley to avoid an impending attack by bandits. Aying predicts that the valley will not be a safe
refuge and convinces them to go back to their house in the village. At the
entreaty of her former sister-in-law, Aying stays with her to keep her company. When the bandits show up, killing or kidnapping those hiding in
the valley and ransacking the village, the Gan household emerges mirac-
ulously unscathed because of Aying's protection.

Afterward, Aying frequently returns to visit Yu's wife whenever Yu is
away on a trip. During one of her visits, Jue rapes her. The following morning, she is caught, in parrot shape, by a fierce cat. Her alert former sister-
in-law rescues her and succeeds in reviving her with tender caresses. As
she flies away, still in parrot form, she bids good-bye to Yu's wife: "Sister,
I blame Jue" (7.923)! Bitter over the rape, Aying must leave her beloved female friend in order to avoid further violation.

The story about a bond between a parrot and a woman finds an imitation some decades later in a story called "Qinjiliao" (The bird Qinjiliao)
in Changbai Haogezi's *Yingchuang yicao* (Unusual grass by a firefly window). A maid who has the beauty and caliber of a noble lady is charged
with looking after a talking *qinjiliao* bird. One day, as the maid is taking
a shower, the bird exclaims in anguished longing, "It is a pity I am not a
man; otherwise I would love you even if I die for it!"[46] In a double move,
the bird expresses desire and its own insufficient ability to act on that desire. The transgression of and submission to the human cross-sex sexual

paradigm are simultaneously scripted. Later on, the bird delivers clandestine love letters between the beautiful maid and a man. During one such trip, the bird falls victim to the wanton cruelty of boys who are killing birds with stones for fun. Then the bird appears in the man's dream, in the form of a woman, and explains to him her affection for the maid and her purpose in arranging his marriage with her—she does not want the maid to be married to a nasty man, so she takes it on herself to find the right husband for her. What we see is a structure of triangulation and substitution similar to that in "Feng Sanniang."

In Pu's story "Ji nü" (The weaving girl), a beautiful female immortal appears one night in an old widow's house. She offers to be the old woman's companion because she likes her neatness and pities her loneliness. In bed, seeing the beautiful fairy, and breathing her heavenly fragrance, the old woman cannot but wish that she herself were a man. The fairy reads the old woman's erotic thoughts but merely gently scolds her. Then they live together in joyful harmony and do splendid weaving work. However, the old woman is foolish enough to boast about the fairy's beauty and weaving dexterity. Throngs of women come to their house to see the fairy. Then men come too. The fairy allows women to visit but not men. Eventually, after persistently begging and then bribing the widow, a scholar is granted a glimpse of the fairy. Afterward, he writes a poem in praise of her beauty. On hearing the poem, which includes a description of her bound "lotus feet" loaded with sexual innuendo, the fairy feels herself soiled by the scholar's desire and decides to leave. Prior to her departure, she attributes the whole course of events to her own mistake: she has "fallen into the snares of emotion [*ou duo qingzhang*]" (9.1223). This denunciation of feelings carries an unmistakable echo of Feng Sanniang's condemnation of emotion before leaving Shiyiniang.

What these stories have in common is that the woman-preferring woman—a woman whose love is reserved exclusively for other women and who rejects men's sexual advances—cannot appear as a real human being but must be represented as a different kind. The strategy tactfully symbolizes the odd woman's difference, but it also works to localize defiant female same-sex desire, disfigure it, and eventually exorcise it—the strange—from the human community. The inscrutability and alterity of the other species (such as the fox), which are conventional in the *zhiguai* (lit. "recording the strange") literary tradition, are here reinscribed with a particular significance. They are coextensive with, and almost stand allegorically for, the woman-preferring woman's status as a social anomaly.[47] Moreover, all these stories end in the woman-preferring woman's separation from her companion. Sometimes, that separation is violently imposed, as in "Aying." Other times, the woman-preferring woman is allowed to express her feelings for another woman on the condition that she dispense with the sentiment, renounce it, and negate it. Far from encouraging exclusive female same-sex preference, these representational patterns warn against it.[48] If Pu Songling accepts female-female love, the polygamous arrangement of compulsory cross-sex sexuality sets the limit for it.

### The Woman-Preferring Woman outside Men's Representations

That a fox spirit may transform into a woman, forge an unusual friendship with a human female, and assist the latter to subvert and surmount a woman's destiny is a fantastic idea entertained by Pu Songling but never fully realized in his tales. These elements have reached similarly ambiguous but arguably more subversive expressions in Qing women's literature. To name a striking example, *Bi sheng hua* (Flowers generated from the writing brush) by Qiu Xinru (1805–?)—commonly deemed one of the three masterpieces of Qing women's literary *tanci*—aligns a fox's supernatural powers with female same-sex preference and marriage resistance in a complicated plot.

The heroine of *Bi sheng hua,* Jiang Dehua, is the third daughter of a retired official who has no son. From a very young age she is rigorously educated, and she shows an aptitude for scholarship and poetry as extraordinary as her beauty and virtue. Her parents have already arranged her engagement to her cousin, Wen Shaoxia, when some evil officials, her father's enemies, nominate her to be sent to the palace to be one of the many beauties who render sexual service to the promiscuous Zhengde Emperor. Unless she agrees to go, her father's life is endangered. Therefore, Dehua accepts the imperial order, but en route to the capital she tries to hang herself one night at an inn. She is rescued by Hu Yuexian, a fox spirit who has once warned her about a coming disaster shortly before the imperial order is received by the Jiang family. Having transformed into the exact likeness of Dehua, Hu volunteers to go to the capital to serve the emperor in Dehua's stead. She also gives Dehua a set of scholars' clothes and shoes and urges her to dress up as a man. Subsequently, Dehua calls herself Xiaofeng, gets married to Xie Xuexian, becomes the top candidate in the civil service examination, and also learns the art of war. On the Zhengde Emperor's death, a rebellion breaks out. Xiaofeng quells the rebellion, saves the dynasty, and becomes the prime minister under the new emperor. However, Wen Shaoxia, who is also a top official at the court by this time, recognizes Xiaofeng as his cousin and fiancée despite her disguise. After persistently applying pressure, he succeeds in forcing Xiaofeng to confess to the emperor and the entire court that "he" is in fact a woman. Once her female identity is revealed, Dehua is ordered by the emperor to marry Wen Shaoxia. Moreover, it is suggested by Dehua's father that Xuexian (the wife of Xiaofeng) marry Wen Shaoxia as well.[49] Dehua reluctantly returns to a woman's domestic life. But Xuexian refuses to remarry. Determined to remain chaste and to pursue immortality, she follows the path of her choice with the help of Hu, the fox spirit.

Early in the narrative, the fox spirit Hu transforms into the exact likeness of Dehua and declares to the surprised Dehua:

> Don't you know that I am you, and you are me.
> You must have tender feelings for me, and I for you.
> This is why my humble appearance is as yours.
> You and I share a bond over three lives; it is predestined.[50]

Although the critic Siao-chen Hu has discussed the scene solely in terms of doubling between the women,[51] the last part of the fox's declaration—"You and I share a bond over three lives; it is predestined"—actually uses a formula more commonly employed for expressing either the predestined friendship between members of the same sex or the predestined love bond between a woman and a man. Therefore, Qiu's text embeds friendship and eroticism in the mirroring and identification between women.

As the story unfolds further, something else is eerily homoerotic. The fox spirit plays a crucial role in protecting Dehua from sexual violation by men. Moreover, she assists Xuexian, the woman whom Dehua has married while disguised as a man, to withdraw from the anticipated marriage with Dehua's fiancé. With the fox spirit's help, Xuexian is able to follow her chaste inclination, cultivate her Taoist divinity, and become an immortal.[52] It is striking that, while the author, Qiu, must yield her heroine, Dehua, to marriage with a man and conventional domesticity, she manages to arrange for Dehua's double, the fox spirit, and Dehua's "pseudo"-wife, Xuexian, to form a lasting same-sex bond and to pursue lives independent of men.

In Qiu's text, then, female same-sex preference and resistance to marriage correlate with Taoist divinity and the supernatural powers of an alien, indecipherable fox. The correlation strongly recalls that in Pu Songling's "Feng Sanniang." It is likely that the correlation points to a commonly shared cultural fantasy in Qing China. That women should bond together and pursue self-development in preference to marriage with a man constitutes a social transgression. Whoever so prefers shows an extraordinary desire for self-determination and a refusal to accept the dictated fate of women. In the language of our day, that woman rebels against the shackles of woman's role in society and desires to be an autonomous subject. In the language of the Qing, she is no ordinary, mortal woman. She must be either an immortal or an animal spirit, for acting on such a preference would require supernatural powers. The representational elevation of such a figure to the status of an "immortal" (*xian*) or a "spirit" (*jing*) suggests that a woman's choice of an independent career and female companionship over compulsory marriage entailed a level of agency rarely attained in the real world. Moreover, it was the case that Qing society could better comprehend a woman's resistance to marriage as her desire for divinity and chastity than as her preference for her own sex.

In these late-imperial stories, women who have an uncompromising understanding of their preference for female companionship over marriage must exit the world. They are forced to disappear one way or another—by committing suicide, resorting to a religious life, or simply vanishing—in order to protect themselves from the encroachment of men's possessive desire. Like the morally loose woman in pornography who simulates intercourse with another woman as a prelude to sex with a man, or like the wife in Li Yu's *Women in Love* who is enamored of her husband's prospective second wife, the uncanny, unworldly, and evanescent female spirit who feels tenderly toward her sister-friend but resists sexual violation by men embodies the limits of the discourse on female-female desire in late-imperial China.

## Conclusion

To recapitulate, the tendency of most male-authored creative literature such as fiction and drama during the late-imperial era was not to demonize female-female relations but rather to trivialize them and co-opt them into supporting the institution of marriage, especially the form of marriage most desired by men in theory—polygamy. Rarely did male authors imagine that a woman in a significant relation with another woman could not be brought—by coercion or persuasion—to marriage with a man. It is only in presumably truthful accounts recorded in the *biji* of literati that we gain glimpses of women who had close relationships with other women and committed suicide because they abhorred the thought of marriage. In the light of these general patterns, the tales of odd girls in *Liaozhai* are unique because, in a wildly fantastic genre, the author indulges himself in imagining women who prefer female companionship over marriage, only ultimately to exorcise them by banishing them to an abject realm of evanescence, self-abnegation, and exile.

Throughout this discussion, I have repeatedly run up against the presence of the marriage imperative in late-imperial Chinese sources. This is related to but differs significantly from compulsory heterosexuality. The latter, as Adrienne Rich formulates it, is an "institution" powerfully propagating the conceit of women's "innate orientation" toward or "preference" for heterosexuality; it claims that women need and can be fulfilled only by sexual relationships with men.[53] Despite the coercive nature of this myth, it relies to some extent on the very presupposition of the importance of women's fulfillment to be effective. In contrast, the marriage imperative in the late-imperial Chinese representations that I have analyzed is little concerned with a woman's natural inclination or fulfillment; rather, it sees marriage as simply a woman's duty. Women must marry to fulfill their roles as obedient daughters, wives, and mothers. Such obedience to men throughout one's life defines virtuous womanhood, according to Confucian teachings. Therefore, it may be that *compulsory marriage, compulsory sexual service, compulsory reproduction,* and *compulsory chastity* are more apt than *compulsory heterosexuality* as descriptions of women's fate at the hands of traditional Chinese patriarchy.

The concept of a marriage imperative is especially relevant for our understanding of the literary texts from the eighteenth and early nineteenth centuries. Thanks to historians' efforts, we now have some knowledge about the marriage market during the late-imperial period, especially the high Qing era. In terms of demographics, the male portion of the population outnumbered the female throughout the late-imperial period, which made marriage practically universal for women and very difficult for large numbers of poor men at the lowest levels of society. As Susan Mann synthesizes current research findings by Ted Telford: "No matter how much marriage markets for men improved during the eighteenth century, women were still in such short supply that the population remained locked in a 'marriage crunch' in which 'the vast majority of all women were married and had begun having children as early as human female physiology could possibly have allowed' throughout the late-imperial period." Furthermore, this crunch made it "'extremely unlikely that more than a handful of women could have remained unmarried as Buddhist nuns, maids, prostitutes or "marriage resisters" throughout their adult lives.'"[54] We also now know that the marriage imperative was normalized in part by Qing law. Matthew Sommer points out that formerly sanctioned female prostitution was banned by the Qing state during the legal reforms of the eighteenth century and that the expectations of marriage and chastity were extended to *all* women. The elimination during the Qing of status distinctions in the laws regulating illicit sex meant that the state viewed every woman as a wife and made legitimate marriage the only lawful context for women's sexual activity (at least as far as sex with male partners was concerned).[55]

In short, demographics, economics, and the state ideology all contributed to making marriage imperative for women in late-imperial China, especially during the high Qing era. And this imperative is apparent in the literature by both men and gentry women touching on female-female relations that I have discussed. Female-female desire by itself is of little concern to patriarchy and accorded little significance. What matters from the dominant male point of view is a woman's utilitarian value in marriage and reproduction. To ensure the purity of a patrilineal descent line, a woman's sexual congress with men other than her husband is strictly prohibited—hence the segregation of the sexes and the female chastity cult—but her intimacies with women are inconsequential. What determines a woman's gender conformity or nonconformity is first and foremost her relations with men, not her relations with women. Female-female desire does not render a woman defective or make her a gender outcast as long as it cooperates with the imperative of cross-sex marriage. In sum, female-female desire by itself is not taboo; marriage resistance is.

The plight of the woman-preferring woman in Pu Songling's *Liaozhai* is that of not even possessing the luxury of being the object of a prohibitive law. She is not recognized, and therefore cannot be interdicted, by the law. Her subjectivity is borrowed—she enters symbolic inscription, or the light of day, only through displacement, as someone not quite herself. Rather than her love for women, inexplicable faults—her subhuman condition, her quest for immortality, her vulnerable femininity, and her rejection of aggression perpetrated by men—are enumerated as reasons for her exile. Is it better, then, to accede to this nameless ontological limbo or to become recognized by a high-handed classification system and risk formal condemnation? This is a question that I ask with respect to twentieth-century Chinese discourses on female-female relations, in which the epithet *female homosexuality* became available for marking intense bonding between women as pathology and perversion, having been translated and borrowed from Western discourses on sex.

:: 

The next part of this book will argue that, although the Chinese translation of modern sexual science during the early twentieth century precipitated important changes in urban sexual beliefs and practices, it did not bring about a complete reversal in the understanding of female-female relations, the traditional dismissal, trivialization, and co-optation of those relations by men continuing partly uninterrupted. The shift that occurred was less an abrupt and clean epistemological break with late-imperial beliefs than a matter of reorganization, added complexity, and increased topicality. Instead of being expressed only ambiguously and in a scattered, unconnected fashion (in elite literary inscriptions), personal attitudes toward female-female relations became clearly articulated and were organized around the neologism *nüzi tongxing lian'ai* (female same-sex love). These newly reformulated ideas were disseminated throughout the burgeoning urban public sphere through intellectual publications, both periodicals and books, as well as through popular self-help books on sexual hygiene. Owing to a fascination with science, the public attributed greater authority to medical than to fictional descriptions. Nonetheless, imaginative literature continued to play a significant role. May Fourth fiction taking as its subject matter female-female relations not only represented those relations as they may have existed during that era but also contested the hegemony of medical discourse.

During the 1910s and 1920s, the odd girl who rejected marriage became popularly dubbed *dushen zhuyi nüzi* (a woman believing in remaining single) and, not infrequently, was suspected of practicing homosexuality. However, she could no longer be dismissed offhand by commentators as nonviable and symbolically exorcised from society through a variety of writing strategies since she might very well have the material means with which to support herself and her female lover; that is, she might have a profession.[56] Not unlike the literati who touched on female-female desire in late-imperial times, some male authors of the "new literature" (*xin wenyi*) of the May Fourth era described female-female desire as either a titillating curiosity or a harmless, transitory game that girls would outgrow. Meanwhile, other male intellectuals showed their uneasiness in an occasional short story or social commentary about certain emergent female figures such as the adult female intellectual couple or the masculine woman who could masterfully seduce weak-minded girls.

Among the New Women who experimented with Europeanized forms of fiction and autobiographical narratives during the same era, quite a few wrote about intense love and physical relationships among schoolgirls and female teachers. However, no female writer of the Republican decades was known to have confessed same-sex love as her own preference or chosen lifestyle in adulthood.[57] Uniform silence/absence in this regard suggests that society's disapproval of any woman who preferred female companionship to marriage remained strong throughout the Republican period, showing a significant degree of continuity with the dominant attitude of late-imperial China. Furthermore, while the strength of the women's liberation movement during the May Fourth era may have granted many women a legitimate claim to new lifestyles independent of men, female same-sex love was for the first time conceptualized by the medical community as a perversion, a conceptualization that carried with it an unprecedented stigmatization. New Women were in the main encouraged by liberal, reform-minded male intellectuals to pursue free love with men (but not with other women) as an unquestionable desire and an inalienable right. Heterosexuality, as a naturalized sexual orientation, was thus born for urban middle-class women in modernizing China.

TWO :: **REPUBLICAN CHINA**

# TRANSLATING HOMOSEXUALITY:
# THE DISCOURSE OF *TONGXING AI*
# IN REPUBLICAN CHINA

Whereas emotional and physical intimacy between women, as well as sex between men, was never the concern of physicians in the late-imperial era in China, in the early twentieth century it suddenly appeared in a variety of medical publications, ranging from sex-education manuals to translations of articles on homosexuality appearing in intellectual journals. The medicalization of intimate same-sex relations was, undoubtedly, linked to the importation, often by way of Japan, of Western "sexual science," and it had far-reaching effects on the modern Chinese sexual epistème and culture in general, not to mention literature. However, the exact details of this medicalization have hitherto escaped researchers, including those who woefully lament the presence of a Western homosexual/heterosexual dichotomy and homophobia in late-twentieth-century Chinese societies.[1] For instance, the Hong Kong queer activist Chou Wah-shan, following Frank Dikötter, generalizes about early-twentieth-century Westernizing Chinese elites' view of homosexuality solely on the basis of sex-education manuals, in which homosexuality is tersely cataloged as a male dissipation or an abnormality.[2] Both Chou and Dikötter overlook the intellectual debate over same-sex relations that occurred during the May Fourth era (1915–27).

The medicalization of same-sex relations that began during that period indeed represented a dramatic departure from late-imperial literary depictions of such relations in terms of vocabulary and truth claims. But, more significant, the lively intellectual debate over same-sex relations ignited by the neologism *same-sex love* in the May Fourth public sphere was very different from the narrowness of public opinion and expression in later decades, especially the Maoist period. The formation of a discourse of same-sex love during the May Fourth era and beyond merits scrutiny and is the subject of this chapter. At issue here is an open mind that may protect us from a predetermined agenda to read the Maoist state retrospectively into the Republican past. Also crucial here is vigilance against a Eurocentric dismissal of Third World translated modernity as an inferior copy. More important, May Fourth sources reveal an alternative modern discourse of homosexuality, but we must be patient if we are to allow them to speak, in all their richness, half-uttered sounds, and self-contradictions.

::

In 1931, Magnus Hirschfeld, the founder of the Institute for Sexual Research in Berlin, a key figure in the popularization of the theory of "the third sex," and an activist for homosexual rights, visited China and gave thirty-five lectures (in German with Chinese interpretation) on sexology, including the issue of homosexuality, in the colleges and universities of major Chinese cities. Having fled Germany when his life and work were endangered by the Nazis, Hirschfeld was well respected and heartily welcomed by medical professionals and ordinary audiences around the world, including those in China.[3] The Chinese press "made almost daily announcements and reports of [his] lectures during [his] entire stay."[4]

Although perhaps unique in that he disseminated his ideas personally, Hirschfeld was by no means the only European specialist on same-sex attraction to be introduced to China during the Republican period (1912–49). Among others translated or discussed were Havelock Ellis, Iwan Bloch, Richard von Krafft-Ebing, Sigmund Freud, and Edward Carpenter. Chinese terms were coined for Krafft-Ebing's and Ellis's medical theories of "homosexuality" as sexual "perversion" and "inversion" as well as for Carpenter's view of "homogenic love" as a superior sentiment. A wide spectrum of conceptions of same-sex desire and correlative value judgments could be found in this translated material. Such diversity suggests that Chinese translators were unlikely to take a uniform approach to their

Western source materials, which were themselves diverse. It is precisely in the moment of choice, when the translator has the freedom to cite and appropriate certain materials rather than others, that we witness the possibility of cross-cultural understanding and coalition, rather than bleak, wholesale Western cultural imperialism and imposition in the name of universality. The Chinese translator's agency was, perhaps like all forms of agency, never uncircumscribed, but its existence and function cannot be denied.

This formative Chinese discourse of homoeroticism revolved around the neologism *tongxing ai* (also *tongxing lian'ai* and *tongxing lian*), literally "same-sex love." In defining *tongxing ai,* Chinese writers distinguished it primarily from *nannü zhi lian'ai* (love between man and woman), *yixing zhijian de ai* (love between the opposite sexes), and, simply, *lian'ai* or *aiqing* (love). Attraction between the two sexes was assumed to be the primary or default form of romantic and sexual attraction. Nevertheless, the fact that many Chinese writers took interest in novel Western theories of homosexuality suggests that there was a convergence of local factors necessitating such discussion. Part of the necessity stemmed, actually, from the fact that love between man and woman was being defined, debated, and advocated as young people's right and desire in China during the May Fourth era. Chinese intellectuals' examination of opposite-sex love required an inspection of human affection and attachment in general, for analogy but also for distinction and contrast. The examination extended to, among other things, friendship between man and woman and love and friendship between persons of the same sex. In a sense, to establish love between man and woman as the center of human affection, Chinese intellectuals had to delineate its boundaries and identify relationships that were peripheral to or overlapped with it, including kinship, friendship, and "abnormal" forms of love.

Historical and social circumstances fueled Chinese intellectuals' curiosity about Western "modern science" and their own theoretical reflection on same-sex love. Because of centuries of sex segregation in the past, same-sex bonding was strong and widespread in early Republican China. In fact, close same-sex ties were so common in educational institutions that Western discussions of homosexuality in school inevitably intrigued many Chinese intellectuals. An area of problematization and theorization may indicate discrimination, but it was probably also a privileged form of relationship. Same-sex love in the schools—between students, between student and teacher, and between teachers—was definitely for the Chinese translators as well as for the editors and middle-class readers of urban publications a privileged relationship, more widely recognized and more carefully considered than the same-sex relationships of the uneducated or of adults above a certain age outside an educational setting. Another palpable local circumstance was male intellectuals' anxiety over nontraditional gender roles in the rapidly changing urban society. A concern over blurring gender boundaries prompted them to lend credibility to imported sexology, which conflated same-sex intimacy with unconventional gender behavior and characterized both as *sexual inversion* and an abnormality. In other words, not only did the translated sexual taxonomy introduce foreign ideas about same-sex intimacy, but the appearance of new gender identities such as the New Women in the shifting local socioeconomic order also motivated the urban public to see new meanings in same-sex relations.[5]

Specific in focus, and Western in origin, Republican Chinese translations of texts discussing same-sex love reflect, nonetheless, major tensions in Republican Chinese society. In an important theoretical reflection on translingual practice, Lydia Liu points out that it may be fruitful to consider translation in terms of "invention." She maintains, "Meanings . . . are not so much 'transformed' when concepts pass from the guest language to the host language as invented within the local environment of the latter."[6] If we agree with Liu, then details of Republican Chinese intellectuals' translation of homosexuality are important, for it is precisely through an examination of the way in which notions of *homosexuality* from other languages came to be rendered in Chinese as well as the local significance that these renderings had that we may make major discoveries about Chinese views of sexuality.[7] This chapter is interested, then, in an emergent specialized discourse, but also something more. It is an attempt to shed light on Republican Chinese politics of gender, desire, marriage, class, and subjectivity through an investigation of Chinese *same-sex love* as translingual practice.

### The Significance of the Word Itself

*Tongxing lian'ai, tongxing ai, tongxing lian*—these terms differ slightly in emphasis, but all three are composed of the words for "same," "sex," and "love" and denote "same-sex love." Because one of these coinages—that is, the same string of characters—has been in use in Japanese since the early twentieth century,[8] and because Japanese intellectuals' interest in translating European sexology predated that of Chinese intellectuals,[9] we have reason to believe that *tongxing ai* was a loanword from Japanese and that, on the basis of that loanword, the Chinese invented the variants *tongxing lian'ai* and *tongxing lian*.[10] Not only was *tongxing ai* (or *tongxing lian'ai* or *tongxing lian*) a new coinage, but its individual components were also neologisms or characters used in a fresh sense. *Tong xing* (same, sex) was a new construct, in that, prior to the twentieth century, the character *xing* had not meant "sex" but had been limited to denoting "nature"—the original state, truth, quality, or disposition of something. In Confucianism, *xing* is a specialized philosophical term, meaning "human nature." The canonical discussion of *xing* occurs in *Mengzi* (Mencius), where it is maintained that human nature consists of men's moral capacities and tendencies beyond the desire for food and sex.[11] In other words, the orthodox meaning of the character *xing* has only a tangential, if not reverse, relation to sexuality. The relation to gender is similarly tenuous. A single character denoting "gender" does not exist in classical Chinese. *Xing* was chosen for this purpose out of the need to translate the category *gender* as employed in European languages. This unorthodox usage of *xing* was begun by the Japanese during the Meiji period.[12] By the 1920s, the modern usage of *xing* with the double meaning of "gender" and "sexuality" was well established in Chinese (but not to the exclusion of its old usage as "nature"), making the character similar to the English word *sex*.

Although not quite the neologism that *tongxing* was, the compound *lian'ai*—"romantic love," "love affair," "falling in love," "being in love"— was a novel and exalted concept for Chinese youths during the May Fourth period.[13] Intellectuals advocated *ziyou lian'ai* (free love) between men and women, in protest against Confucian morality and the traditional patterns of arranged first marriages (with the possibility of polygamy), which had dictated the proper segregation of respectable young women from men well before puberty, prohibiting courtship and the free congress of the sexes.[14] In publications, there appeared endless discussions devoted to *lian'ai*—what romantic love is, what its constituents, conditions, and rules are. How should young men and women learn the art of romantic love? Is friendship a prerequisite for love? What differentiates love from friendship? What distinguishes love from mere sexual intercourse such as that which was expected on the wedding night of a traditionally arranged marriage? Some said that romantic love was absolute, while others maintained that it was conditional and changeable. Some believed that romantic love was a special modality of emotion distinguished from other kinds of affection, while others declared that there was no qualitative affectional difference between romantic love and fast friendship. Some put forth the formula that the ideal romantic love equaled the union of two people in both spirit and flesh, while others claimed that "spiritual romantic love" was the most exquisite and highest kind, for it sublimated the animal sex instinct and was sacred. In addition, there were those who doubted that there was any such thing as "romantic love"; they argued that what was usually thought to be romantic love was no more than sex plus the basic feelings that one human being has for another.[15]

It was of tremendous import, therefore, when this exalted, magical discursive construct *lian'ai* was combined with the words for "same-sex" to form the concept "romantic love between people of the same sex." The early Republican intellectuals translated *homosexuality,* not as *tongxing xingyu* (same-sex sexual desire) or *tongxing xingjiao* (same-sex sexual intercourse), but as *tongxing lian'ai* (same-sex *love*).[16] The neologism's difference from traditional Chinese categories of male-male eroticism is apparent, for the latter focused exclusively on the carnal and the sensual. In traditional language, some men could be described as *hao nanse* (fond of having sex with beautiful boys) or *ku ai nanfeng, bu xi nüse* (preferring beautiful boys to women).[17] In a similar vein, some groups of women could be nicknamed a *mo jing dang* (mirror-rubbing gang) based on a slang word for female-female sex.[18] With the category *same-sex love,* however, emotional intensity and sympathy was highlighted. According to the discursive construction of love in the May Fourth period, an erotic component can be taken for granted but is supposed to be only one part of love.

While love between young men and women may have been a difficult process or art that had to be "learned" in the 1910s and 1920s, most educated youths were instructed in single-sex schools (including colleges and universities), where deep sympathy and intimacy—not limited to spiritual intimacy—between best friends often grew. Does this mean that they all had same-sex romantic loves? Was it more natural for them to fall in same-sex than cross-sex love?

The thorny issue surfaced when the distinction between love and friendship was challenged. Although in the 1920s intellectual discussion of romantic love many assumed, as a matter of course, that love is a tangible entity that occurs between a man and a woman, there were radical thinkers who attempted to deconstruct love defined as such. They asked whether love is any different from friendship and whether passionate love cannot just as well take place between same-sex friends.[19] In a 1928 debate between those who questioned or denied the existence of love and their opponents in *Xin nüxing* (New woman), one of the participants, Mao Yibo, objected to the category *love:*

I admit that there exists sexual friendship and that the most intimate rela-
tionship/friendship between a man and a woman is sexual friendship, but
sexual friendship is not something limited to people of the opposite sex.
Even between people of the same sex, haven't there been cases in which, because of the seamless matching of beliefs, personalities, and aspirations, the
most intimate and passionate involvement took place?[20] If this is true, why
should we call some sexual friendships *love* but not others? How do we tell
the difference between a cross-sex friendship and a same-sex friendship?
Should we simply say, like Ellis, that the distinction [between love and
friendship] is blurry? If relationships of the same weight are called *love*
when occurring between people of the opposite sex and *friendship* when
occurring between people of the same sex, I think that such naming is not
only unwise but also superfluous.[21]

Mao Yibo objects to the reification of *love* as a higher category than
*friendship;* he protests against the differential treatment of homo- and
heterosexual bonds in May Fourth discourse. According to him, while
heteroerotic friendship is privileged and crowned with the new title *love,*
homoerotic friendship is not accorded the same status. He believes that,
to be fair, both forms of the most intimate intersubjective bonding should
be named the same. Understandably, while Mao's proposal is that both be
called *sexual friendship,* in the sense of friendship with some degree of
sexual involvement, another strategy that made the same point was to use
the term *tongxing lian'ai* when referring specifically to homosexual love
and *yixing lian'ai* when referring to heterosexual love.

If same-sex love was so common in the 1920s that certain intellectuals
openly protested the construction of male-female free love as the ultimate
love, what would be the result, then, of introducing European sexology—
such as Havelock Ellis's work—theorizing the pathology, neurosis, or abnormality of homosexuality into China at this historical juncture? Would
it promote free association and love between the sexes? Would it threaten
to shift the center of many Chinese youths' emotional lives from a same-
sex to a cross-sex axis? Would it function to intimidate women with newfound economic independence from becoming lifelong lovers with each
other?[22] Would Chinese gay men be affected by the imposition of an unprecedented social stigma?[23]

It appears that the introduction of European sexology did, in fact, bring
about all four effects—not instantly, but gradually; not on a sweeping
scale, but in ever-widening circles—over the course of the first half of the
twentieth century. The medical stigma placed on homosexuality in Republican China was moderate, however, and from it one cannot foretell

that the Chinese Communist Party would, after 1949, harshly denounce homosexuality either as Western capitalist corruption or as a heinous feudalist crime. The ambiguity of the Republican Chinese attitude toward homosexuality will be best illustrated by the partial history of translation reconstructed below.

## Same-Sex Love in Urban Middle-Class Periodicals

When the subject of homosexuality first appeared in Republican China, the phenomenon was not only cataloged in medical sex-education manuals but also represented in translated articles and discussions published in major urban journals on women, gender, education, love, relationships, and sex. The latter kind of representation—journal articles on same-sex love—is especially interesting since the translators could choose among a broader range of Western sources than strictly medical genres and their choice of source material was therefore more likely to reveal their own personal opinions.

Chinese intellectuals chose to translate a fascinating variety of material. Not only did the Krafft-Ebing and Ellis school of sexology, which pathologized homosexuality, receive attention, but so did the contemporaneous Western gay liberation discourse. Iwan Bloch's less judgmental theory of inborn homosexuality is one example of the latter.[24] Another, especially provocative one is the 1920s translations of Edward Carpenter's writings, which often idealize "homogenic love" in the advocacy of gay liberation. These translations reveal a certain degree of open-mindedness about the subject of homosexuality, and their appearance indicates a certain freedom to express dissenting views. Granted, these translations appeared in journals promoting "new knowledge," social reform, and progress; however, the journals were not in any sense underground or marginal. They were, on the contrary, well-known periodicals published by the most successful and prestigious publishing houses, such as the Commercial Press and the Kaiming (Enlightenment) Bookstore in Shanghai. I would hesitate, therefore, to describe the translations as a counterhegemonic discourse. It would be more accurate to say that, in the 1920s, the literate, urban Chinese public had no definite opinion on the nature of same-sex love and that the Chinese intellectuals who had access to theories of homosexuality written in other languages had a great deal of room in which to maneuver.

In June 1911, a few months before the revolution that was to establish the Republic of China, the Shanghai-based *Funü shibao* (Women's times), one of the pioneer women's journals in China, published an article entitled "Funü tongxing zhi aiqing" (Same-sex erotic love between women).[25] Written by one Shan Zai (a pen name) well before the advocacy of the vernacular by the May Fourth intellectuals, the article is in classical Chinese.[26] In it, the author mentions many German and British sexologists by name, and, whenever he includes terminology from European sexology, the words are given in German rather than English, indicating that he may have consulted German rather than English editions of such works as the second volume of Havelock Ellis's *Studies in the Psychology of Sex*.[27] Moreover, Shan Zai shows some familiarity with the prevalence of female same-sex erotic love in Japanese schools, which most likely indicates that he had either lived in Japan or read Japanese publications on the topic.

Shan Zai opens the article thus: "When a woman falls in same-sex love with another woman, it is in fact the same as a man's being fond of having sex with beautiful boys [*Fu nü yu nü tongxing zhi xiang lian'ai shi tongyu nanzi zhi hao nanse*]." The phrase *hao nanse,* or "[a man's] fondness for having sex with beautiful boys" (as opposed to *hao nüse,* "having sex with beautiful women"), is a well-established expression in traditional Chinese, meaning that a man enjoys (certain forms of) homosexual sex, to put it in late twentieth-century parlance. Attempting to put forth and explain the novel idea of "same-sex erotic love between women," Shan Zai uses the well-known male case as an analogy. Shan Zai then goes on to say: "There are different kinds of motives and reasons for same-sex erotic love between women. Modern people study it from a medical perspective, and they have generally claimed that it arises from the inversion of erotic desire [*qingyu zhi diandao Inversion des Sexualtriebs*] and that it is a disease [*jibing*] or abnormality [*bianchang*]. When a woman lacks love for men but feels erotic love for people of her own sex, this is a perversion of erotic desire [*qingyu zhi biantai*]."[28]

In this passage, we encounter almost all the key psychomedical neologisms—*qingyu zhi biantai* (perversion, abnormality, or metamorphosis of sexual desire), *diandao* (inversion), and *jibing* (disease)—that would later recur in modern Chinese medical discourse on homosexuality. Later on in the article, Shan Zai's invocation of names makes the origin of these words and ideas clear—German and British sexology of the late nineteenth century and the early twentieth, particularly the work of Havelock Ellis. Prior to the arrival of European sexology, the Chinese indigenous concept of homosexual liking, *hao nanse,* is basically neutral; it is the balanced opposite of *hao nüse.*[29] The term carries no negative value judgment, no comparison of homosexual taste to either disease or the perversion of an aim-specific, originary "normal" erotic drive. Moreover, it is without dispute a notion dissociating sexual pleasure from procreation. Its limitation resides in the fact that it takes no account of female-female attraction. Modern sexology bestows on female homosexuality a visible status comparable to that of male homosexuality. However, the overall assumption about homosexuality is already negative.

Shan Zai is careful to differentiate between different kinds of female same-sex erotic love. "Those women who have inverted erotic desire," he writes, "would have no romantic feelings even if they see beautiful men. However, not all those trapped in same-sex erotic love have behaved out of inverted erotic desire. Some of them do so because they want to satisfy their erotic desire but have no opportunity to associate with men, and still more indulge in this bad erotic affection out of the curiosity for pleasure. The reasons and motives for the same-sex erotic love prevalent among female students nowadays are difficult to ascertain, but they probably do not go beyond the above reasons."[30] In other words, he dutifully introduces the European sexological idea that some women are determined inverts; they are a special kind of women. Their same-sex erotic love can be distinguished from temporary kinds. Here, the new idea *funü tongxing zhi aiqing* (same-sex erotic love among women) is a category of sexual pleasure and love relationship, containing also a (sub)category of personhood.

After having described same-sex erotic love among women in broad medical terms, Shan Zai comments on the common occurrence of this love in European history and literature as well as in non-European cultures. Among the things that he mentions are Sappho, "Tribadie," and Denis Diderot's *La religieuse* (The nun). Interestingly, in this section, his tone is considerably less judgmental. He says that there are many melancholic, romantic intricacies (*qingjie zhi ai yan*) in women's same-sex love fit for poets and novelists' pens.

Then Shan Zai moves on to Japan's situation and ends the article by discussing the difficulties in "preventing" female same-sex love:

> Recently in the society of female students in Japan, same-sex mutual love is also prevalent. Educators are eager to extinguish it but do not have good methods. . . . To prevent this fashion [*feng*] by abolishing the dorms in women's schools or forbidding close female friends to sleep in the same room is easy to say but difficult to carry out. To instruct female students that, from medical and ethical perspectives, this is an unnatural and unethical behavior is also difficult, for we would have to tell young girls explicitly about the matter. Some educators have said that proper sex education can

sweep away this bad fashion. But it is difficult to explicitly explain such a thing; therefore, nowadays no one is advocating this approach any longer. Indeed, to prevent same-sex romantic love among women, there is no other method besides cultivating women's moral character.[31]

The language here is fascinating. Female homosexuality in the schools is discussed as a "fashion" that might be "extinguished" and "prevented." The trope of "wind"—custom or fashion—presents female homosexuality as a changeable social practice rather than a fixed personal truth. However, this "fashion" behaves like a virulent epidemic. While great anxiety over women's homosexual behavior and relationships is expressed, male homosexuality is conspicuously absent from this discussion of the necessity of and strategies for preventing homosexuality. In other words, although European sexology instills a new awareness of women's homosexuality as a counterpart of men's, that awareness turns immediately to the regulation of female desire but not male. In this case, sexology merely provides the necessary conceptual means for regulating female sexuality. As early women's journals in the late Qing and the Republican period often had a large number of male contributors and readers,[32] Shan Zai's article on female same-sex love in the schools may be a telling example of male anxiety over female sexuality, especially over female sexual pleasure dissociated from men and reproduction, in a modernizing society.

In December 1923, *Jiaoyu zazhi* (Chinese educational review) put out a special issue on the subject of sex education. Among the thirteen articles on such topics as "Introduction to Sex Education," "The Movements of Sex Education in Europe and America," "Life between the Two Sexes and Education," "Analysis of the Male and the Female Sexes," and "Sexual Hygiene and Ethics during Puberty," we find Shen Zemin's "Tongxing ai yu jiaoyu" (Same-sex love and education). This is not an original work; rather, it is a translation of the chapter "Affection in Education" from Edward Carpenter's *The Intermediate Sex* (1908). In his afterword to the translation, Shen indicates why he considers Carpenter's critique of Victorian England relevant:

> Carpenter's essay is targeted at education in England. But isn't the situation he describes common in the schools of China? . . .
>
> China is a place where "the gutter" pointed out by Carpenter is most prevalent. Emotion has been stunted in part by common opinion in society and in part by the traditional institution of marriage. Now schools continue to do such work.

> Shall we advocate the education of emotion or preserve "the gutter"?
> Why don't we gather the courage to recall our own school days! We have all
> gone through life in the schools![33]

Addressing probably adult educators, Shen pleads, via Carpenter, that they show tolerance for and understanding of the same-sex affectional ties, often intense and romantic, that develop between students or between student and teacher in schools. The essay maintains that true comradeship, friendship, and love between students have been unjustly equated with the "wretched" practices and habits that merely provide a sexual outlet. Serious attachments are forced to "exist underground, as it were, at their peril"; they are "half-stifled in an atmosphere which can only be described as that of the gutter."[34] It is imperative that the attachments be openly acknowledged and institutionalized, for affection is an educative force and school the appropriate place for developing it. Carpenter does not explicitly state whether same-sex affection should last beyond the school days, whether serious same-sex comradeship legitimizes same-sex sexual practice, or whether it may be an alternative to marriage. But we can easily gather from his other writings and his own life that he affirms lifelong same-sex unions. The translator, Shen Zemin, cautiously refrains from bringing up such issues in his afterword. However, his evocation of past school days reads like a melancholic lament over some aborted friendship.

Toward the end of "Affection in Education," Carpenter distinguishes women's homogenic attachment from men's:

> The remarks in this paper have chiefly had reference to boys' schools. . . .
> [I]n girls' schools friendships instead of being repressed are rather encouraged by public opinion; only unfortunately they are for the most part friendships of a weak and sentimental turn, and not very healthy either in themselves or in the habits they lead to. . . . [O]n the subject of sex, so infinitely important to women, there needs to be sensible and consistent teaching, both public and private. Possibly the co-education of boys and girls may be of use in making boys less ashamed of their feelings, and girls more healthy in the expression of them.[35]

These are enigmatic remarks. What exactly is "sensible" knowledge about sex for women? Is Carpenter suggesting that girls by themselves cannot figure out what correct sex is? And what are the "not very healthy" habits? Because Carpenter does not go into details, it is difficult to pin down his position. At any rate, one thing is certain: he sees sentimentality as a fault in girls' friendships, and he believes that society is responsible for encouraging women to be unduly sentimental. Coeducation, according to him, can enhance the feelings in boys' friendships, but it reduces the emotionality in girls'. This is a curious corrective proposal, one that implies that boys' friendships will strengthen in spite of the presence, or availability, of girls while girls' mutual love will lessen because boys, supposedly solid in intellect and knowledge, are around.

A comparison at this point of Carpenter on female friendship with Havelock Ellis on female homosexuality can be useful. It is also appropriate since Ellis too was later translated into Chinese.[36] Ellis writes: "Among women, though less easy to detect, homosexuality appears to be scarcely less common than among men . . . ; the pronounced cases are, indeed, perhaps less frequently met with than among men, but less marked and less deeply rooted cases are probably more frequent than among men."[37] Carpenter's and Ellis's ideas are, I would argue, similar in that female same-sex love is considered in many cases a mistaken passion. It is suggested that self-delusional female friendships are possible because society tolerates a greater measure of sentimentality in women than in men and that, when challenged, these friendships may be revealed to be less "deeply rooted" than male homosexual relationships.

In translating Carpenter, Shen Zemin gives no indication of whether the critique of oversentimentality applies to female friendships in China or whether in China in 1923, as in the West during the Victorian period, women's intimate bonds were encouraged and men's discouraged. For such information on the local context, we must turn to another article published in the same year in *Funü zazhi* (The lady's journal), "Nannü de geli yu tongxing ai" (The segregation between the sexes and same-sex love) by Yan Shi (another pen name, gender reference unclear).[38] Yan writes:

> Last semester we received fliers attacking the president of a certain women's normal college. Among other faults, the president was accused of ill management, which led to the popularity of the habit of same-sex love among the students in that college. The question whether the president is responsible put aside, the issue of same-sex love in itself is worth our careful discussion. It is a common phenomenon that same-sex love takes place between student companions in schools—whether in men's or in women's schools. All of us who have had the experience of living in a school can observe it. It is not limited to any one school, although it may be more common in some schools than in others. However, people usually treat such things merely with ridicule, and no one seriously wants to study the matter or to think of some remedy. This is very strange.

We should be aware that same-sex love is a perversion of love. It is harmful to young men and women. Those who experience strong same-sex love are often repelled by the opposite sex, and they refuse to lead a normal married life.[39]

If we can trust Yan Shi, same-sex love was equally common in men's and women's schools in China. The public attitude toward both was, evidently, laissez-faire and not particularly inclined to take the problem seriously. There was ridicule instead of probing interest in causes or corrective measures, although students' same-sex love might sometimes be seized on as a reason for attacking certain school authorities. Yan Shi's own attitude is that same-sex love is a serious social ill caused by sexual segregation and that coeducation must therefore be promoted. Included in the article is a passage from Walter M. Gallichan's *The Psychology of Marriage* (1917) meant to serve as sociological authority. The article concludes with the assertion that only coeducation can prevent same-sex love.

Obviously, there is quite a gap between Shen Zemin's and Yan Shi's attitudes, although both rely on Anglo-American authorities. While Shen Zemin calls for the open affirmation and institutionalization of same-sex attachment among youths, Yan Shi denounces such attachment as an obstacle in the path to normal marriage and a "perversion" (*biantai*), a novel concept in sexology and psychology.[40]

*Funü zazhi,* a major intellectual forum then for Chinese discussions of issues of particular relevance to women (such as women's suffrage, the women's labor movement, women's education, coeducation, male-female socialization, the new gender ethics, love, sex, marriage, motherhood, and divorce), did not always publish negative theories about same-sex affection. In 1925, "Tongxing ai zai nüzi jiaoyu shang de xin yiyi" (The new meaning of same-sex love in women's education), a translation by Wei Sheng (another pen name, gender reference unclear) of an article in Japanese by Furuya Toyoko, appeared.

In this article, Furuya defines *same-sex love* as a form of spiritual love, one that excludes "ugly" sexual intercourse between people of the same sex. Then she theorizes it as an intensified, modern modality of *adoration* or *friendship:*

> Same-sex love in the sense I newly discovered is an emotional rapport between people of the same sex. Traditionally it has been called *adoration* if between the younger and the elder and *friendship* if between equals.
>
> However, because the spirit of mankind has been incessantly progressing upward, feelings have reached amazing fineness and intensity in our

century. If such feelings flourish between people of the same sex, they exert a determining influence on these people, sometimes to the extent of becoming the fundamental affection motivating their lives, dominating the entirety of their spiritual faculties. Therefore, we cannot call it by simple traditional terms such as *adoration* or *friendship*.[41]

Furuya constructs an evolutionary theory of the human emotions and identifies same-sex love as the most recent manifestation of human spiritual progress. In modern women's education, she maintains, same-sex love can work vitally. Love motivates female students to imitate the character, behavior, and intellect of admirable female teachers. Therefore, mechanical, impersonal pedagogy must be forsaken, to be replaced by an education suffused with feelings and the interaction between personalities. Moreover, Furuya points out that love and comradeship between female students cultivate and purify sentimental faculties. Such love is abiding, and it continues even after the women are married and have children, which is proof of the love's purity and spirituality. These positions constitute the so-called New Culturalism as it was applied to education.

Significantly, Furuya mentions Edward Carpenter as one of the first to point out the value of same-sex love in education. Furuya's own contribution, then, is to theorize specifically about the educative power of specifically female same-sex love, instead of subsuming it under male same-sex love as Carpenter did. Furuya is, however, similar to Carpenter in other respects. For example, she elevates the spiritual and eschews the physical in the discussion of homogenic love in schools. She also follows Carpenter in arguing that the prevalence of homogenic love in modern civilization is due to an increase in the intermediate sex—a fact of evolutionary import. According to Furuya, one of the major signs of modernity is that male and female characteristics are converging. As a result, masculine women may attract feminine women, and vice versa. However, in the end, Furuya reminds the reader that the attraction between women of opposite gender types is just one of the many possibilities of female same-sex love. This is an important moment in the text as it frees the imagination of the Chinese reader (who reads Furuya in translation) from the set pattern of masculine-feminine pairing. The reader may observe that the female student's fervent adoration of the female teacher is not so much about opposite-gender role-playing as about identification.

That in the 1920s Chinese intellectuals were particularly fascinated with female homosexuality is apparent in the appearance in a 1927 issue of *Xin wenhua* (New culture) of "Nü xuesheng de tongxing ai" (Same-sex love among female students), a translation by Xie Se (another pen name, gender reference unclear) of "The School-Friendships of Girls," an appendix that Ellis added to the revised and enlarged English third edition of *Sexual Inversion*. That this translation appeared in *Xin wenhua* is particularly significant.

The editor of *Xin wenhua*, "Dr. Sex" Zhang Jingsheng, was a controversial and notorious figure on the intellectual scene in Shanghai and Beijing in the 1920s. He promoted sexual knowledge and the attainment of sexual pleasure and bliss defined solely in terms of male-female intercourse. As Hsiao-yen Peng points out, Zhang appeared as a radical reformer of traditional Chinese sexual mores, deploring Chinese youths' ignorance of sexual techniques and lack of sexual energy. Further, Zhang promoted a female-centered utopia where beauty, art, and love would be the ruling values.[42] We can note, however, that Zhang was criticized by some of his contemporaries, most notably the contributors to the feminist magazine *Xin nüxing*, for being male centered, unscientific, and prone to Taoist superstitions about male and female sexualities. In his writings, Zhang encouraged men to derive pleasure from foreplay alone (*shen jiao, qing wan*) in language that emphasized the conservation of semen in the interest of health, advice that reminded Zhang's opponents of traditional Taoist sexual alchemy. Zhang also advocated female sexual climax by theorizing a temporal or direct cause-and-effect link between female climax, the emission of the ovum, the perfect impregnation, and the generation of healthy, gender-distinct offspring, a theory that his opponents decried as absurd. Finally, Zhang sought to dispel the value conventionally placed on women's virginity by arguing that a sexually experienced woman can give a man more pleasure than a virgin can. The *Xin nüxing* writers found the last—his promotion of women's sexual freedom in a rhetoric that defines women as objects rendering pleasure to men—especially suspect and distasteful.[43]

From my point of view, Zhang's theory about female sexuality is problematic mainly in that it represents an attempt to legitimize female pleasure through reproduction and dichotomous gender ideals. His notion of *xing mei* (sexual beauty) is not just a theory about pleasurable intercourse but also an ideology of gender difference, dictating standards for women's femininity and men's masculinity.[44] One of the effects of Zhang's rigid ideas about gender norms is that he attacked male homosexuality in a vehemently contemptuous language rarely seen in Chinese publications in the 1920s.[45] He deplored the phenomena of the *nan xianggong* (feminine boy actor/prostitute) and the *nü nanzi* (masculine woman) because he believed that they were symptomatic of the Chinese race's lack of sexual desire and consequent degeneration.[46] His reasoning reveals a "masculinity complex" and racial envy that can be attributed to a sense of national marginality, not to mention the possible influence of Krafft-Ebing's early theories attributing homosexuality and gender inversion to heredity (treating them as something like an inherited neuropathology).[47]

The article that Zhang chose to be translated, Ellis's "The School-Friendships of Girls," turns out to be very ambivalent about educated young women's homoerotic activities. I shall discuss the essay's male voyeurism, anxiety over autonomous female sexuality, and phallocentrism in detail in order to argue that it is precisely because the piece offers at once dangerous titillation and phallic assurance that it could be endorsed by Zhang as authoritative as regards women's same-sex intimacy in schools. Moreover, translator as well as journal editor must have implicitly drawn many parallels between women's liaisons in schools in the West and in China since they clearly considered the discussion of the situations in European and American institutions of particular interest.

Ellis recounts several studies of girls' school friendships of a particular kind, called *fiamma* in Italy and *rave* or *spoon* in England. According to the researchers, these friendships are different from usual friendships in that they have many elements characteristic of the sexual love between man and woman, such as madness, passion, exclusivity, and jealousy. In Italy, the word *fiamma* refers both to such a relationship and to the beloved person, who ignites love in another and makes her assume the role of the active, pursuing lover. A flame is most often sparked by the attraction of physical beauty and elegance. It arises between students who do not know each other rather than between familiar, constant companions. In a typical scenario, a boarder chances to see a day pupil or merely hears of her elegance, then falls in love and starts to court and woo her, in which process love letters play a central role.

Ellis writes, "Notwithstanding the Platonic character of the correspondences, . . . there is really a substratum of emotional sexuality beneath it, and it is this which finds its expression in the indecorous conversations already referred to. The 'flame' is a love-fiction, a play of sexual love. This characteristic comes out in the frequently romantic names, of men and women, invented to sign the letters."[48] Although Ellis recognizes a sexual dimension in girls' school friendships, he automatically assigns the status of a play or fiction to them. The unspoken assumption here is that, unlike girls' school friendships, the love between a man and a woman is not a fiction; it is real. Ellis implies that a romance between girls is merely a temporary staging and that their amorous acts and speeches are mimetic rather than serious in intention and consequence.

Besides passing phallocentric judgment, Ellis toils to find unthreatening explanations for girls' school friendships, and he falls into a theoretical impasse. On the cause of the flame friendship, Ellis believes that the "intense desire to love a companion passionately is the result of the college environment," where girls far away from home "feel the need of loving and being loved." He emphasizes that the flame relationship is different from sexual perversion:

> While there is an unquestionable sexual element in the "flame" relationship, this cannot be regarded as an absolute expression of real congenital perversion of the sex-instinct. The frequency of the phenomena, as well as the fact that, on leaving college to enter social life, the girl usually ceases to feel these emotions, are sufficient to show the absence of congenital abnormality. The estimate of the frequency of "flames" in Normal schools . . . [is] about 60 per cent., but there is no reason to suppose that women teachers furnish a larger contingent of perverted individuals than other women. . . . The root is organic, but the manifestations are ideal and Platonic. . . . It may well be that sensual excitations, transformed into ethereal sentiments, serve to increase the intensity of the "flames."[49]

The logic of the passage is tellingly tortuous. Ellis's predicament, briefly, is that, if flames are real expressions of sexuality, then 60 percent is too high a figure for an "abnormality." Therefore, he must maintain that these friendships do not count as sexual relationships and that genuine "perversion" is something else. It does not occur to him that he may solve the theoretical impasse by assuming that sexual feelings between women—whether short-lived or abiding—are normal. Later on, he plainly contradicts his claim that flames do not indicate "congenital" "sex-instinct" when he surmises that "organic" sensual excitations among girls are "transformed into ethereal sentiments." This amounts to his arguing, in spite of himself, that there exists a primal sexual impulse for the same sex that is later suppressed.

What Ellis obstinately regards as the only "normal" "sex-instinct" may in fact be engineered by socioeconomic factors. With a different set of socioeconomic factors operating, alternative manifestations of desire may naturally arise. Apparently, female teachers showed a higher than usual percentage of what Ellis calls *perversion* because they were educated and therefore able to write each other love letters and, more important, to make their own living independent of men or outside conventional middle-class marriage.

In the article, Ellis cites his own informant, an English woman familiar with the "raves" fashionable in English girls' schools. Her independent observations of the duration and causes of raves are enlightening:

> That the "raves" fell and act like a pair of lovers there is no doubt, and the majority put down these romantic friendships for their own sex as due, in a great extent, in the case of girls at schools, to being without the society of the opposite sex. This may be true in some cases, but personally I think the question open to discussion. These friendships are often found among girls who have left school and have every liberty, even among girls who have had numerous flirtations with the opposite sex, who cannot be accused of inversion, and who have all the feminine and domestic characteristics.[50]

Compared with Ellis on flames, the English lady is much more doubtful about the explanatory power of single-sex environments and gender inversion (i.e., lack of femininity).

The translator, Xie Se, is largely faithful to Ellis's essay, departing from the original in only two therefore significant places. First, in rendering the title "Same-Sex Love among Female Students" instead of "The School-Friendships of Girls," he unambiguously locates the subject of the essay within the sexual sphere and particularly within the homosexual spectrum of that sphere, a move that Ellis resists. This shows that Xie Se's conception of homosexuality departs significantly from Ellis's, which pivots around gender inversion and theorizes about the subject's orientation of desire. Xie Se focuses, rather, on the behavior and feelings actually manifested intersubjectively. Ellis's sense that a certain personal essence is the foundation for object choice is absent from Xie Se's creation of the category *same-sex love* out of this essay. Xie's attitude may reflect the traditional Chinese understanding of the self, which is seldom perceived as an autonomous, independent entity, being more often taken to be the site where a set of relations converge. The self takes shape in reference to others and within communities. Therefore, same-sex desire may not be said to properly "belong to" a subject.

Second, Xie Se diverges from Ellis when it comes to the notions of *activity* and *passivity* in sexuality. The English original states that, in a flame, one girl takes on a more active role while the other is passive. In the Chinese translation, these roles (*active* and *passive*) are reinscribed as *juyu fu de diwei* (assuming the role of the husband) and *nairu qizi de roushun* (playing the role of the meek wife). Xie Se derives his notions of *active* and *passive* from conventional matrimony in China, collapsing sexuality into marriage. Compared with Ellis, Xie Se's attitude toward sex strikes one as a fascinating mixture of liberalism and conservatism, indicating the imprint of cultural difference.

In the five journal articles that I have surveyed thus far, *tongxing ai* is primarily signified as a modality of love or an intersubjective rapport rather than as a category of personhood, that is, as an identity. Moreover, all five articles focus on attachments in same-sex schools, recognizing same-sex attachment, especially women's same-sex attachments, as a common occurrence rather than as an uncanny singularity. Two articles (Shan Zai and Yan Shi) denounce homogenic love as perverse; two (Shen Zemin and Wei Sheng) affirm its ennobling capacity or the crucial role that it can play in the refinement of the young. The fifth (Xie Se) is ambivalent, affirming the passionate emotional quality of female students' homoerotic love, yet also preferring to believe that it is merely a temporary phase.

Ironically, it is the denunciatory articles that entertain the idea that there may be same-sex lovers who resist conventional marriage. The affirmative articles, by contrast, focus exclusively on the school phase and eschew the possible conflict between homogenic love and most societies' expectation that adults marry. Carpenter's essay (translated by Shen Zemin) avoids the question altogether, while Furuya's (translated by Wei Sheng) asserts that homogenic love is purely spiritual and can therefore coexist without conflict with the carnal, nuptial union between man and woman.[51] Ellis (translated by Xie Se) strives to remain neutral but succeeds in doing so only by seeing female same-sex love in the schools as a harmless rehearsal for cross-sex love and marriage. We may observe that, in these five articles, homophobia—the attempt to detect improper beginnings and prevent grievous extremes—and a protoawareness of the homosexual identity paradoxically go hand in hand. We may also observe that, to avoid arousing the public's apprehension, writers who champion homoeroticism tend to emphasize that passionate homogenic love is common to humanity, that it is not a peculiarity limited to a minority of people, and that such a universal emotion does not necessarily conflict with marriage.

The most significant of European writings championing homosexuality to appear in China during the 1920s was probably the translation by Qiu Yuan (another pen name, probably Hu Qiuyuan, male) of Carpenter's "The Homogenic Attachment," which appeared in *Xin nüxing* in 1929 under the title "Tongxing lian'ai lun" (On same-sex romantic love). The translator explains in his first note: "Although my translation is bad, I hope it will make people become seriously interested in the issue [of homosexuality]. If people will not simply regard it as 'uncanny' or 'perverse' or as some old thing such as '[a man's] fondness for beautiful boys' [*nanse*] or 'women mirror rubbing' [*mo jing*], I will feel content with my own effort."[52] Qiu Yuan assumes the pose of a humble enlightener facing an ignorant public. He intends to make readers realize that homosexuality is more than a matter of sexual pleasure, as it has been conceptualized in the past. He also hopes that, by providing people with knowledge, he can demystify for the general public the unfamiliar concept of homosexuality. And, most important, and the likely impetus behind his translation efforts, he objects to the sexological notion then gaining currency in China that homosexuality is perverse (*biantai*).

The essay begins with an enumeration of brilliant examples of what Carpenter calls a *homogenic attachment* (homosexual love) in European history, literature, and art. Then the latest relevant scientific discoveries by European doctors are summarized. First, homosexuality is not a morbid, degenerate, or neurotic condition; on the contrary, many of the most outstanding people in history have had strong homosexual temperaments. Second, people with strong homosexual temperaments need not and cannot be "cured." Third, the homogenic attachment can be found in a wide spectrum of people, ranging from those attracted exclusively, to those attracted only occasionally, to members of their own sex (Carpenter, following the German sexologists, calls the former *Urings*). We see, then, that, with the translation of this essay, the Chinese public was introduced, perhaps for the first time, not only to the idea of a healthy social spectrum ranging from mostly homosexual to mostly heterosexual persons, but also to concepts of congenital homosexuality and homosexual identity that carried no implications of pathology or inferiority.

The essay contains other politically and philosophically interesting ideas. Via translation, these ideas too became available to Chinese readers. One such idea is that the desire for physical contact and closeness is an integral part of spiritual comrade love and that the spiritual should not be divorced from the physical. Another is that human sexuality should be freed from the reproductive imperative. This imperative is outmoded and meaningless in the modern age, although in the past a nation's or a community's strength may have depended on population size. Sentiments or attachments have value in themselves, value that should be measured in terms other than whether they end in reproduction. (It should be noted that Carpenter is not privileging pleasure; on the contrary, for him the emphasis should be on sacrifice, courage, and unswerving devotion.) Yet another interesting idea is that there exists within the homogenic attachment the urge to democracy. Because this attachment draws people together even across class lines, it has important implications for the women's liberation movement, allowing women to form alliances and fight their sex's oppression. Carpenter's articulation of the relationship between women's liberation and homosexual love may have struck a sympathetic chord in some feminist readers of *Xin nüxing*.

The translations surveyed above were later overshadowed by Pan Guangdan's 1946 *Xing xinli xue,* a translation of Havelock Ellis's *The Psychology of Sex.* Although Ellis's book is not entirely on homosexuality, it has a long chapter on the subject, and Pan's lengthy annotations containing numerous references to homosexuality in Chinese culture and history (people, institutions, theories, and writings) were especially invaluable. Pan even included an appendix ("Zhongguo wenxian zhong tongxing lian juli [Examples of homosexuality in Chinese documents]") in the volume, in which, besides giving examples of male-male and female-female love, he analyzes indigenous Chinese views of the causes for homosexuality. Not accepting "sexual psychology" wholesale, he raises questions about it. For instance, he doubts the applicability of Ellis's theory of sexual inversion to the adult men who liked boys in Chinese history, for the former showed no effeminacy. He believes that deeper or other causes of homosexuality are yet to be discovered.

While the translators who came before him—Shan Zai, Xie Se, Shen Zemin, Wei Sheng, and Qiu Yuan—have been forgotten, Pan Guangdan is remembered today as a pioneer who introduced European scientific interest in homosexuality to the Chinese public.[53] There are several factors that may have contributed to such a course of events: the earlier translators' imperfect command of English and other foreign languages, the obtuseness of their Chinese prose (which was adversely affected by the foreign syntax), the fact that they themselves did not become prolific scholars or writers, and the ephemeral quality of journal articles compared with books. Another crucial reason is that, unlike Pan, the other writers did not demonstrate a broad knowledge of Chinese homosexual culture and history.

Nonetheless, I will maintain that, like Pan, the earlier translators were serious about East-West parallels and comparisons. Above all, they chose foreign texts that seemed to them the most useful and urgently needed for clarifying, justifying, or criticizing the prevalence of same-sex passionate attachment in Chinese schools (including colleges). On the one hand, there was a serious desire to regulate adolescents' and college students' sexuality. On the other hand, insofar as the problematized erotics in formal education was primarily an upper- and middle-class experience, the regulatory attention that it received also signified social importance and privilege. The early translators' work, not polished in style, and certainly not worth reprinting today, nevertheless represented the moment when Chinese intellectuals first came into contact with modern European theories of homosexuality. These pieces on *tongxing ai* constituted the first modern discourse on homosexuality in China, the site where trite and novel concepts, and foreign and local social phenomena, were first negotiated.

To recapitulate, this discourse on *tongxing ai* was not unified in character. Homosexuality was, as a rule, conceived of as a rapport, which admits contingency, interactive creativity, and the individual value of a specific love object. But the idea of an unchangeable, innate homosexual temperament in the subject of desire (what we now call *orientation*) also appeared in the discourse. Homosexuality was affirmed by some as an ennobling sentiment, a consequence of and a force propelling human evolutionary progress. At the same time, it was decried by others as a danger, as the perversion of desire and gender. Female-female erotic love, especially, gained unprecedented attention. In quite a few articles, great anxiety is expressed over female homosexuality—but not, it should be noted, over male homosexuality. Female homosexuality in the schools is seen as a fascinating modern phenomenon requiring both investigation and regulation.

Two decades later, Pan Guangdan would describe the phenomenon of same-sex love in Chinese schools in the 1920s in relatively trivializing terms:

> Ellis's observation [that "many of us are unable to recall from the memories of school life and early associations any clear evidence of the existence of homosexual attractions, such rare sexual attractions as existed being exclusively towards the opposite sex"][54] might be true of the situation in Europe and America, where social interaction between men and women and coeducation became common at an early date. However, in the schools in China ten or twenty years ago, same-sex love between male students occurred quite a bit. Although it could not be said to form a "tradition" as in some English public schools, even the concrete examples that I can personally identify and remember were numerous. After coeducation became popular in

China, of course, such incidents have become fewer and fewer. Still, even in coed schools, we can find many instances of same-sex love between female schoolmates. Some women even make a mutual agreement not to get married or to marry the same person in the future. Nonetheless, in the final analysis, this is but the temporary expression of emotion. When time and setting change and the women reach maturity, they will separate and follow the paths of heterosexuality and marriage.[55]

These remarks attest retrospectively to the prevalence of same-sex love in Chinese schools in the 1920s. Pan's argument, unlike the debates during the 1920s, fails to indicate the tension between seeing same-sex desire as a product of the environment or an immature phase and regarding it as deeply satisfying, precious, and serious, however fleeting the passion may be. Pan's attitude toward same-sex love in the schools is dismissive compared with Qiu Yuan's or Shen Zemin's, although it is no more heterosexist than Yan Shi's or Xie Se's. One may observe that, in the transition from the 1920s to the 1940s, a liberal discourse that would celebrate homosexual love in and/or out of the school in Edward Carpenter's fashion became less audible in Chinese. The range of Chinese discourses on homosexuality narrowed after the 1920s, in which process Ellis's medical theory of homosexuality, premised on a dichotomy between the normal and the deviant, gained hegemony through repeated citations and translations into Chinese.[56]

### Republican Chinese "Same-Sex Love"— A Discourse of Alternative Modernity

The Republican Chinese discourse on same-sex love departed from previous Chinese views of male-male or female-female attraction in many ways. Besides the fact that its predominant focus was on eroticism in modern-style education, it appended, above all, a supplement of interiority and emotionality to preexisting Chinese terminology for same-sex intercourse and erotic pleasure. Same-sex attraction, thus, became something that could be more than carnal and superficial. It was accorded depth, whether pathological or romantic. Another key aspect of this new discourse's modernity is that women's same-sex love received unprecedented attention as a counterpart of men's. This theoretical inclusion mirrored women's greater participation in social and public life in modern times, but it also signaled the expansion of men's scrutiny into a formerly private realm of female experience. While in previous ages Chinese men were largely content to contain female homoeroticism rather than prohibit it, in the Republican period such containment was no longer possible, and male intellectuals found themselves increasingly having to criticize, regulate, or inhibit women's same-sex attraction.

Remarkably, the Republican Chinese discourse on same-sex love did not make *the homosexual,* an identity akin to a racial minority, the predominant figure standing for same-sex attraction.[57] That is, the idea of there being an extraordinary homosexual nature confined to a small percentage of the population did not become the overruling paradigm for understanding homoerotic desire. This might be viewed as surprising, given the fact that late-nineteenth- and early-twentieth-century European sexology is usually credited, in the West, with discovering, and perhaps also creating, the figure of the quintessential biologically determined homosexual. In contrast, despite their interest in Western sexology, many Chinese intellectuals inclined toward understanding same-sex love as relational and situational.

How this divergence may be interpreted is surely open to debate. It seems to me, however, simplistic to see it as the failure of Chinese intellectuals as readers and translators—that is, as their failure to grasp the West's accurate knowledge about identity—as Frank Dikötter has recently done.[58] Republican Chinese intellectuals' focus on the relational and situational qualities of same-sex attraction may reflect a different but equally valid imagination about human subjectivity—one that sees it as dependent on context rather than as essential and unchanging. In retrospect, and with the hindsight that one of the trends in the contemporary queer movement in the West is precisely to reconceptualize the homosexual identity as a form of "strategic essentialism" or "necessary fiction,"[59] we cannot but wonder whether Republican Chinese intellectuals had some justification all along as they insisted on observing the relational and situational in the homoerotic. In this regard, in criticizing the Republican modernizing elite for failing to master Western sexual science and only selectively appropriating it to "consolidate the widespread distinction between procreative and nonprocreative sexual acts," Frank Dikötter has neither taken into account the full range of Republican Chinese intellectual discussion nor given an adequate representation of early Western sexual science.[60] He seems staunchly oblivious to the fact that nineteenth- and early-twentieth-century European sexology (such as Krafft-Ebing's theories, of which he speaks highly) was an extremely speculative and hybrid genre of writing and had its own cultural historical roots and dire ideological ramifications.[61]

At the heart of the issue is whether one may uncritically embrace *identity,* or fixed orientation, as the only key to a correct and politically useful understanding of sexuality. Even though early sexology provided certain resources for the conceptualization of gay identity, preference, or orientation in certain circles in the West, for many decades the medical discourse on gay "personhood" was a negative and treacherous one. A telling example is that, until 1973, the American Psychiatric Association listed homosexuality as a personality disorder. Medical professionals' horrible treatment of homosexual persons—including subjecting them to aversion therapy, electroshock, castration, vasectomy, lobotomy, psychoanalysis, hormone medication—in twentieth-century America is well documented by Jonathan Ned Katz.[62]

In view of the negative effects of the model of sexual orientation and identity, the historian John D'Emilio, among others, has pointed out that Kinsey's findings in the 1950s of a high incidence of homosexual behavior in the general population was conceptually revolutionary and politically liberating. D'Emilio maintains, "The data [presented by Kinsey] disputed the common assumption that all adults were permanently and exclusively either homosexual or heterosexual and revealed instead a fluidity that belied medical theories about fixed orientations." Moreover, "Kinsey . . . used his statistics to suggest that such a common sexual activity ought not to be punished. Resting on the misinformed view that homosexual behavior was confined to a small number of individuals, society's treatment of homosexuals, he argued, was socially destructive."[63] If it is true that the capacity for homosexuality is not limited to a minority of people, supposedly exceptional in physiological or psychological makeup, but rather to be found throughout the general population, not only will lesbian and gay communities have to be reconceived as having no fast boundaries, but the stigmatizing of homosexual behavior as unnatural, abnormal, or neurotic will also lose its ostensible foundation in rationality. This is not to dispute the point that the establishment of lesbian/gay identities remains a necessary political project, in that people with predominantly homosexual interests ought to have the freedom to define their own orientation as such without being constantly ignored, harassed, restrained, or subjected to attempts to convert, reform, or treat them.

In the light of these tensions, Republican Chinese discussion of same-sex love, with its preponderant attention to the intersubjective and the circumstantial, can be viewed as an alternative modern discourse on homosexuality rather than as a deformed, deficient, and uninformed version of Western sexology. No matter how urgent it may seem to some to recuperate the notion of people's unchanging natures for legitimating erotic difference, we must recognize that there has always been resistance to sexual categories and that the refusal of sexual identity may represent yet another tactic for demanding diversity in a globalizing world.[64]

On closer inspection, furthermore, it might be argued that alternative modern discourses on homosexuality have existed all along even in Western contexts. Despite the claims of many Foucault-influenced studies of sexuality to the contrary,[65] the Greek-Latin bastard word *homosexuality* has not been exempt from indeterminacy and controversy since its coinage. Does *homosexuality* designate behavior, relationship, identity, or fantasy? If it designates identity, is sexual identity a matter of physiology, psychology, orientation, preference, performative repetition, or choice? By no means has there been consensus over the signification of the modern paradigmatic term *homosexuality*. As Eve Sedgwick maintains, competing conceptual models for sexuality coexist, and new models do not simply supplant old ones.[66] It is no wonder, then, that, instead of a radical, total epistemic change, the discursive shift in Republican China from traditional categories of male and female relationships to *tongxing ai* was gradual.

Nonetheless, it cannot be overemphasized that the inclusion of female-female relations within the discourse on same-sex love was a telltale sign of modernity, late-imperial representations of male and female same-sex relationships having been characterized by gender asymmetry—depictions of sex between men constituting a significant erotic mode and those of sex between women appearing primarily only as inauthentic practice. That inclusion was not a sheer positive sign, however, for it meant that, just as some May Fourth intellectuals adopted European sexology's abnormalization of male homosexuality, so too did they abnormalize female homosexuality. At the same time, the institution of concubinage was attacked as vicious, monogamy within marriage advocated, the nuclear family idealized,[67] and love matches privileged over arranged marriages—resulting in the normalization of female desire for the opposite sex. Ultimately, the debate over the meaning of female same-sex love was driven underground—at least in mainland China—to reemerge only with the resurgence of liberal feminism in the late 1980s and the 1990s.

::

In summary, my examination of Republican Chinese discursive formations in this chapter pursued two lines of inquiry. I investigated the translator's agency during the 1910s and 1920s, and I examined the diverse significations of the new taxonomy *same-sex love* in the popular dis-course represented by the urban print media. In both analyses, I showed that it was above all the incorporation of female same-sex relations that distinguished the new discursive domain from the late-imperial discur-sive domain, marking it as modern. My hope is that the insight thus gained into the process of translational appropriation and localization in the early twentieth century can help us better understand the globaliza-tion of Western sexual identities in the Chinese-speaking parts of Asia at the turn of the twenty-first.

The next chapter will continue these lines of inquiry by examining the competing and mutually determining relations between sexological taxonomy and fictional narratives during the May Fourth era.[68] When cre-ative writers wrote about intimate relations among the New Women and called it *female same-sex love,* they did not simply subscribe to the clin-ical explanatory power of the neologism. Rather, their narratives both en-riched and contested its medicalized meaning. It is through fictional rep-resentations that we may gain a fuller understanding of the gender issues that helped motivate the translation of sexology in the first place: the same-sex bonds that occurred among the New Women of the May Fourth generation. How the discourse on same-sex love is intermeshed with other discourses such as feminism and nationalism, and is refracted by the gen-der difference in writing, is most intriguing.

# FEMALE SAME-SEX LOVE
# IN MAY FOURTH FICTION

## Women's Homoerotic School Romance: From Science to Fiction

As discussed in the preceding chapter, intimate female relationships gained unprecedented topicality in China during the 1920s and were debated in terms of the neologism *same-sex love* in the major intellectual journals on the woman question, gender, sexuality, and education.[1] As Western-oriented Chinese intellectuals tried to enlighten themselves and others about love and sex, they stumbled on sexological definitions of sexual normality and perversion and appropriated them to interpret and regulate local practices, including women's relationships. During the same period, May Fourth writers experimenting with Europeanized narrative forms by no means neglected female-female relations. *Xin wenyi* (new literature) thus competed with a discourse on sexual enlightenment based on sexual science for symbolic authority over the meaning of same-sex love.[2]

Not uncommonly, writers of modern vernacular fiction applied the novel taxonomic term *same-sex love* in their descriptions of women's relationships and, therefore, participated directly in defining the unfamiliar category for urban readers. On occasion, it was the literary critic who brought fictional narratives into competition with sexual science to define *female same-sex love*. For instance, in a lecture on literature in 1927, Zhao Jingshen made a brief attempt to analyze modern vernacular short stories in the light of Ellis's and Freud's theories of abnormal sexual psychology. He identified Lu Yin's "Lishi de riji" (Lishi's diary; 1923), Ye Shaojun's "Bei wangque de" (The forgotten; 1922), Zhang Yiping's *Qingshu yishu* (Love letters; 1926), and Zhang Ziping's *Fei xu* (Flying catkin; 1926) as fictional representations of female homosexuality and Ye Dingluo's "Nan you" (Boyfriend) and Huang Shenzhi's "Ta" (He) as stories about male homosexuality. And, in the 1930 expanded version of the 1927 lecture, he also identified Ling Shuhua's "Shuo you zhemo yihui shi" (Rumor has it that something like this happened; 1926) as a story about female same-sex love by a female writer.[3] While on the surface such classifying and cataloging seemed simply to explain modern Chinese fiction in terms of sexual science, in fact it instructed the urban Chinese public about same-sex love in the fiction writer's or critic's own terms. Furthermore, the literary critic could exercise authority over the meaning of same-sex love by discussing non-Chinese as well as Chinese literature.

Zhao Jingshen's interest in fictional representations of female same-sex love certainly extended to non-Chinese literature. In 1929, writing in *Xiaoshuo yuebao* (Short story monthly) about the banning of *The Well of Loneliness* in Britain, he summarized the plot of Hall's novel in a humorous tone, implying that what agitated the English was simply an ordinary love affair between two women.[4] In 1925, Zhou Zuoren, another renowned critic, translated a celebrated poetic fragment by Sappho—"To a Beloved Woman"—into Chinese for the literary journal *Yu si* (Threads of talk). Following Longinus's remarks in *On the Sublime*, Zhou praises Sappho's poem as an excellent portrayal of the love frenzy. He points out that "women's same-sex love" is sometimes called "sapphism" since Sappho's relationships with women were reputedly romantic. He then protests that appropriating Sappho's name in such a way is unfair to the poet because her friendships with women were not necessarily as "perverse [*biantai*]" as those properly classified as "same-sex love [*tongxing lian'ai*]."[5] As a literary critic, then, Zhou plays a double, if not self-contradictory, role in defining *female same-sex love:* on the one hand, he commends the poet for her outburst of passion for another woman and maddening jealousy because of her lover's slight; on the other hand, he advises his readers that same-sex love is perverse.

Although fiction writers rarely so worshiped science as to conceive of their own stories as studies of female same-sex love, their depictions of intense female-female relations nonetheless worked out the same social concerns and anxieties that motivated other intellectuals to translate and appropriate Western science (in all its permutations as medicine, psychology, and sociology). May Fourth fiction and translated science addressed the same audience—the urban educated middle classes—about the same local issues. Above all, fiction writers' attention to the boarding school as the predominant location of female-female romantic love rivaled translators' interest in applying Western theories of homosexuality to the situations in Chinese girls' and women's schools. And that combined attention created a discursive phenomenon that might be called *the female homoerotic school romance.*

Most of the fictional narratives about female-female relations, moreover, appeared first in the same public space—the periodical press—as did the translations of sexological treatises on homosexuality and translators' remarks on local same-sex practices. Fiction writers thus participated directly in the social debate about and negotiation of women's same-sex romantic relations in the burgeoning public sphere of the May Fourth era.[6] This public sphere, in which the periodical press played a vital role, was where the educated class could share opinions in an extrafamilial realm independently of the state. Since the late Qing, and through much of the Republican era, newspapers and journals proliferated, carrying works of fiction (*xiaoshuo*) as well as journalism and criticism. Often, it was in fiction that the reformist and revolutionary elites articulated their hopes for the modern nation and rehearsed enlightenment ideals for a sizable urban readership.[7] This public sphere facilitated by the periodical press was centered in Shanghai and Beijing but by no means restricted to these two cosmopolitan metropolises. Many periodicals of the time circulated nationally and even internationally. For instance, the feminist journal *Xin nüxing* (New woman), which was based in Shanghai and boasted a circulation of ten thousand in 1926, was distributed by the postal system to subscribers in addition to being sold in twenty-nine cities all over China and in three overseas locations (Tokyo, Taiwan, Singapore). The national/transnational reach of the magazine was evident, moreover, in its regular publication of Chinese intellectuals' writings submitted from many Chinese cities distant from Shanghai and from Europe, the United States, and Southeast Asia.[8]

May Fourth translations of sexual science provided the basis for a discourse promoting sexual enlightenment, but that discourse was not without its ideological limitation. As discussed earlier, when translators of sexology attempted to make sense of the prevalence of same-sex relationships in the 1920s, many could not hide their anxiety over intimate female relationships in particular. Anxiety was strongest about the fact that some women might decide not to marry. Other intellectuals also openly voiced their concern over long-term relationships between women. Chen Dongyuan, known for his pioneering research into the lives of women in China's lengthy history, apparently associated the menace of female homosexuality with independent career women of the modern type. In 1926 he observed: "Marriage is often a difficult problem for modern women of the intellectual class [*xiandai zhishi jieji de funü*]. As a result, things like 'intimate female friends swearing a bond' [*bai xiangzhi*] are hard to avoid. There is a group of female teachers in our province—Anhui—who often make their male and female acquaintances suspect that they have organized a secret 'Refuse-to-Marry Party' [*bu jia dang*]. I wonder if there are similar phenomena elsewhere."[9] In his seminal work, *Zhongguo funü shenghuo shi* (The history of the lives of Chinese women), after describing women's same-sex unions in Canton, Chen complains: "It is against nature if women refuse to marry because of same-sex love [*tongxing lian*]. It is harmful to women's health. Ever since [women's] means of livelihood changed in modern times, more and more women past the marriageable age indulge in same-sex love. It is a serious problem."[10]

It is startling that someone who seemed to care about women's oppression in traditional China and who praised women's achievements highly would nonetheless view women's independence and same-sex partnerships so negatively. It is possible that, precisely because Chen took women's demand for emancipation seriously, he could not but feel threatened by their same-sex relations. Paradoxically, in these passages, Chen conceptually trivializes female same-sex relations in order to justify his own regulating impulses. He presumes that women can be fulfilled only by marriage and that same-sex love is merely an inferior substitute for those "past the marriageable age." It seems that, while the women of his day could not necessarily be forced to marry (since some of them were economically independent and able to make their own choices), the newly translated discourse on sexual health and women's natural biological needs furnished a new armory of rationalizing tools with which the male intellectual could regulate women's sexuality and constrain their life choices.

Another striking limitation of the sexual-enlightenment discourse was that it severed female-female spiritual love from female-female carnal desire on a scale of respectability. Some translators chose their material specifically in order to reassure their audience that women's same-sex love was purely spiritual and therefore fully compatible with cross-sex love and marriage. Others, by contrast, defined women's same-sex love simply as an unhealthy sexual practice. The work of both exuded a discomfort with physical, and especially sexual, intimacy between women. Borrowing their authority from European male doctors, they denigrated erotic interchange between women as immature, immoral, unsatisfying, unhealthy, and abnormal—either physiologically or psychologically. Female-female lust, like long-term female-female partnership, was thus highly contentious in May Fourth intellectuals' discussions of sexuality and gender. The legitimacy of lust between women was called into question and bluntly denied.

The enlightenment intellectuals' disapproving attitude toward female-female lust formed a stark contrast with their discourse on women's sexuality elsewhere. Women's sexuality was a focal point in the reform of heterosexual mores during the 1920s. May Fourth male intellectuals' attack on the traditional cult of female chastity (*zhencao*) and their advocacy of "freedom of love" (*ziyou lian'ai*) (i.e., a youth's freedom to associate with the opposite sex and thereby experience love), monogamous marriage (*yifu yiqi zhi*), and the right to choose one's own marriage partner all entailed the presumption of an autonomous sex drive in women. Unless the notion of autonomous female desire was mobilized, Chinese men could neither convincingly advocate egalitarian love relations between men and women nor promote a notion of marriage that was based on physical as well as spiritual love.

It was during this period that the writings on love and marriage between the sexes by Edward Carpenter and Marie Stopes were introduced. Their popularity in 1920s China showed that, to a considerable extent, the May Fourth campaign promoting male-female romantic love and the liberation of women's sexuality paralleled the British attempt to reform Victorian heterosexual mores and to cast off normative beliefs about good women's asexuality. During the 1920s, Chinese New Women of respectable economic or social backgrounds gained—in the discussions in intellectual magazines at least—the right to sensuality and orgasm in marriage and possibly also in the courtship leading up to it. A woman's taking pleasure in sex with her male lover/husband became accepted by some as a right rather than as a vice, as excess and lasciviousness (*yin*).

However, this sexual-enlightenment discourse, which revolved around such key words as *sex, free love,* and *marriage,* did not grant women the right to homosexual orgasm. That idea appeared only when the practice was abhorred as an unspeakable depravity or intimated to be a health risk. It did not occur to most male intellectuals that women's autonomous sex drive should include the capacity or desire for an orgasm so defined. They conceived of a woman's autonomous sex drive as aim specific, as directed at men as objects. Some also conceived of female orgasm, not as an end in itself (i.e., as something desirable because pleasurable), but as a means to some other end. Zhang Jingsheng, for example, linked female orgasm closely with ovulation and propitious impregnation. Other intellectuals promoting sex education disagreed and severely ridiculed his work as unscientific and male centered.[11] Yet, tellingly, in this debate among male intellectuals on female orgasm, all the participants focused on a woman's reaching climax during male-female intercourse. No one brought up the possibility of female orgasm in autoerotic or same-sex situations as the best argument against Zhang Jingsheng's justification of it for the sake of reproduction. Were they simply supremely confident that women could not find sexual pleasure without men? Or could they not bear to think that men were dispensable?

The May Fourth sexual-enlightenment discourse acknowledged spiritual love between women as love. It frowned on caresses and kisses between young girls. And it flatly rejected orgasmic sex between women. Against this backdrop, what role did creative literature play? To what extent did fictional narratives assist in, or resist, the physiological, psychological, and moral inspection and evaluation of female-female relations? Insofar as fiction can be distinguished from the arguments of the sex educators, it should not be dominated by terminological definition, schematic classification, moral or scientific pronouncement, or explicit evaluation. Is fiction, therefore, freer to fantasize or more in touch with experience, and can it therefore explore female-female lust in depth?

As I will demonstrate below, female-female carnal desire is trapped between insignificance and ignominy in May Fourth fiction, the narratives of which constantly erase the possibility of a positive, nontrivial meaning of female-female lust. My strategies for reading these narratives therefore differ, depending on whether the author is male or female. Of men's graphic depictions of female-female sex, I insist on asking, What strategies does the author employ, not only to conjure up the spectacle of female-female sex voyeuristically, but also to suppress its threat so that a vertiginous masculine pleasure does not turn into a truly subversive feminine power?[12] Of women's depictions of female-female sex, which tend to treat female-female eroticism more decorously, I ask, How can female-female sex be culturally significant—recognized as physically gratifying and ecstatic without, at the same time, being demonized or deemed degenerate? What does a positive female-female sex scene look like? Many fervent gazes, embraces, and nighttime chats between women have been taken at face value by readers and granted no cultural significance beyond straightforward depictions of friendship and sentimentality. Meanwhile, the few explicit depictions of female-female physical desire cover themselves with disclaimers. I mean to read more into these texts, as portrayals of positive female-female lust, but also to question them, as expressions of fear. This is not an accusatory project, for the task of creating a positive portrayal of female-female lust is not easy. Perhaps it can be accomplished only in metaphors and dreams.[13] Perhaps it can be written, not through exhibitionism, but only through total immersion, becoming intuitive and fluid and no longer concerned with rules and clarity. Perhaps it can be accomplished if a woman writes, not for everyone, but only for her intimate doubles.

## Lu Yin: In Excess of Lesbian Spirituality

Among May Fourth fiction writers, Lu Yin (1899–1934) dwells most persistently on female same-sex attachment, primarily as a spiritual, ideal, and liberating love, surpassing cross-sex love and marriage. In numerous short stories, she expresses anxiety with respect to, or dissatisfaction with, the institution of marriage. As Wendy Larson observes, she repeatedly critiques "heterosexual marriage as damaging for both women and men but more so for women."[14] And several critics have noticed recently that the sensibilities in Lu's often autobiographical fiction verge on the lesbian. Hsiao-yen Peng, for example, argues that the novella *Haibin guren* (Old acquaintances by the seaside; 1923) explores the extreme difficulty that girls have "shift[ing] from adolescent love for the same sex, which is not necessarily lesbianism, to the adult love for the opposite sex." Peng maintains that characters in the story consider same-sex love superior to heterosexuality because it does not cause anxiety about sexuality. She admits, however, that "Lishi de riji" (Lishi's diary; 1923), another story also seemingly asexual, thematizes "lesbian love, considered . . . taboo by society."[15] In a similar vein, David Der-wei Wang maintains that Lu Yin "tentatively probes [*tanchu*]" the subject of lesbianism in some of her works. He argues that, although "these same-sex relationships seldom contain expressions of physical desire, in tenderness of feelings they fully rival the romance between man and woman. Both 'Lishi's Diary' and *Old Acquaintances by the Seaside* bring the matter into play." [16] Both critics, moreover, point out that Lu's stories of female bonding contain many traces of her attachment to Shi Pingmei and other female friends from Beijing Women's Normal College. Wendy Larson further notes important cross-class similarities between the all-female literarily inclined group in *Old Acquaintances* and the real-life all-female societies formed among silk factory workers in early twentieth-century Canton. Both "marked heterosexual relations as the source of women's downfall. Once a woman began a relationship with a man, whether inside or outside marriage, she placed herself within a circle of practices determined by social custom. And the social custom in question, of course, sprang from concepts of moral virtue." [17]

While Peng and Wang consider the female bonding in Lu Yin's writing lesbian or quasi-lesbian, Meng Yue and Dai Jinhua attempted in their early collaborative work to distance it from "homosexuality": "In the world [of Lu Yin's works], the only love that can be in harmony with reason is love for the same sex. But, apparently, this is different from homosexuality in the sense of gender inversion [*xingdaocuo yiyi shang de tongxinglian*]; it is, rather, a utopia existing in the minds of girls, a women's nation that expels men and the desires for men (sexual threat and sexual anxiety). . . . Lu Yin seems to want to oppose the unfeeling, irrational feudal laws of social decorum with this innocent nation of sisters where feeling [*qing*] exists in harmony with reason [*zhi*]." [18] Although, as observant critics, Meng and Dai do consider women's friendships in Lu Yin's works, particularly in "Lishi's Diary" and *Old Acquaintances,* intense and romantic, they have reservations about classifying these friendships as homosexual. This would be logical if the carnal sex act is indispensable to their definition of *sexuality*. Female-female love in Lu Yin's fiction falls short of this particular criterion because the close friends do not—at least on the textual surface—indulge in erotic fantasies about, much less engage in sex acts with, each other. Most of the female friends in Lu Yin's fiction are courted by, become romantically involved with, and eventually marry men. However, what motivates Meng and Dai's commentary here is not the absence of lust. Rather, these passionate female friends do not fit the model of "gender inversion." As the early-twentieth-century sexological theory of homosexuality as "sexual inversion"—confusing sexual relations with gender identity—is in fact an inadequate definition of homosexuality, it is problematic that Meng and Dai perpetuate such a model in their writing. Their inherent assumption about what constitutes homosexuality or lesbianism is limiting, and therefore counterproductive, where it should instead allow for difference and the possibility of its being a utopian lifestyle choice.[19]

A more fruitful way to examine the issue, I propose, is to return Lu Yin's autobiographical fiction to the context of the discussion of women's same-sex love in her era, so as to understand how her work signified female *same-sex love* (*tongxing lian'ai*) then and bestows meaning on *lesbianism* now.

The female friends in Lu Yin's fiction do not subscribe to a biological, essentializing, and particularizing model of same-sex love; rather, they consider female same-sex love to be a life option superior to a constrained domestic life. As Meng and Dai point out, the educated middle-class woman in Lu Yin's fiction typically considers a man's love dangerous because it threatens to engulf her, at a moment when she is only newly awakened to feminist consciousness and has only recently liberated herself from her father's household, in marriage and thus another man's prisonhouse.[20] Love between one woman and another, on the contrary, is at once emotionally satisfying and supportive of the pursuit of artistic and professional self-fulfillment. While previous critics have not made the connection, the idealized female bonding portrayed by Lu, in fact, closely parallels the phenomenon of nineteenth-century "romantic friendships" among middle-class intellectual women, the first generation of "New Women," in Western Europe and America. For them, in Esther Newton's words, "the battle to be autonomous was the battle to stay single and to separate from the family sphere. Ironically, they turned to romantic friendships as the alternative, replicating the female world of love and commitment [that of the Victorian domestic sphere] in the new institutional settings of colleges and settlement houses."[21]

Lu Yin's and many other May Fourth writers' works reflected a similar situation in China. School friendship occupied a special place in the lives of intellectual New Women, a phenomenon that can be attributed partly to the fact that formal higher education for women was in a nascent stage in this period.[22] Western-style elementary schools for girls were established in China by Western missionaries only in the second half of the nineteenth century. At first, their only students were foundlings and girls of the poorest families, attracted by the free room and board and the allowances. Gradually, as such an education proved its utility, similar schools catering to the gentry began to appear. Around the turn of the century, formal education for women had become so prestigious that schools instituted entrance exams and, instead of paying women to be educated, charged high tuitions. During the Republican period, the number of women receiving formal education grew, but essentially only relatively wealthy families could afford to have their daughters educated beyond the elementary level. Thus, women pursuing higher education during the May Fourth period constituted an extremely select group and brought with them to the experience of same-sex love the emotional and cultural baggage of the isolated intelligentsia—innocence, alienation, melancholia, romanticism, idealism, and ambition.[23] Female same-sex bonding in school was not simply a matter of physical pleasure; more often than not, it was about camaraderie and a creative search for the self.

In *Old Acquaintances,* the protagonist, Lusha, and her female classmates give one another intimate emotional and intellectual support. As Lusha falls in love with a man, classmates comment: "In recent years she has had great opportunities for gaining importance in society. Marriage would make a waste of her talents."[24] Like the early feminists in Europe and the United States, an intellectual Chinese woman in the May Fourth era had better stay away from marriage and childbearing if she desired to remain independent and to make a (nondomestic) contribution to society. For camaraderie and morale, she relied on female classmates, relatives, or colleagues who, like herself, might be trying to break away from traditional women's roles as wives and mothers in order to become educators, writers, doctors, or social reformers. In society, these women were defined by their resistance to marriage, labeled *dushen zhuyi nüzi* (women who believe in remaining single) when they were taken seriously, *bu jia dang* (the party of women who will not marry) when they were not.[25]

In North American scholarship, there has been charged controversy over whether nineteenth-century women's romantic friendships such as "Boston marriages" are comparable to the "lesbianism" of the twentieth century. Some critics argue that the linkage that psychologists/sexologists such as Freud and Ellis made between bourgeois women's romantic friendships and working-class women's "homosexuality" and cross-dressing at the turn of the century was "devastating" to many middle-class romantic friends. Esther Newton believes that the association with sex defiled the value placed on spirituality by romantic friends, and Lillian Faderman argues that the sexological labels *pathology* and *perversion* "morbidified" women's romantic friendships.[26] In this regard, it should be pointed out that, during the interwar period in China, the politics of naming was considerably different from that in late-nineteenth-century Europe or America. May Fourth educated women self-consciously associated their romantic friendships with the neologism *same-sex love.* Judging from contemporary discussions and representations, many of them embraced the term in spite of its connotation of physical eroticism. *Female same-sex love* was considered a common romantic devotion and physical attraction by both women themselves and male intellectuals. Nevertheless, society in general disapproved of the practice, regarded it with suspicion, and sought to delimit it. I have already dealt to some extent with the ideological tension (see chap. 4). To continue that investigation, it is necessary to turn to Lu Yin's inscription of the line between cultural legitimacy and illegitimacy, purity and impurity, in a good middle-class New Woman's same-sex love. In the life that Lu turns into textual performance, lesbian lust is an (im)possibility.

*Old Acquaintances* is the exemplary story of spiritual female-female love in Lu Yin's literary corpus. It is unique in May Fourth literature on female same-sex attachment in that it depicts the intersubjective dynamics, not only within the relationship between a female romantic couple, but also within a closely knit community of female romantic friends. The fact that so many female characters populate the text, and that their stories intertwine with one another, has been faulted as an inability to control the narrative, a symptom of the author's perturbation about life and the future.[27] But such criticism misses the story's chief merit. It is precisely because the story presents us with a maze of relationships, some passionate and some polite and intellectual, that it is a successful depiction of a women's community.

This beautiful women's community scatters as the women graduate from college, get married one after another, and give up the career ambitions that they had while in college. Ending with the despondent longing of the protagonist, Lusha, for the camaraderie of her school days as a paradise lost, the story nevertheless articulates the ideal of lifelong female same-sex commitment. Lusha and her friends wish to build a house by the sea where they can live and pursue intellectually rewarding work. Some of them would write their great literary works sitting by a window overlooking the ocean; others would teach innocent children in a seaside village and come home in the evening to join the rest for storytelling. It would be a blessed world.

One thing, however, is absent from this portrayal of a women's utopia—physical sex. The absence prompts Meng Yue and Dai Jinhua to conclude their study of Lu Yin thus: "The ideal women's nation . . . can at most pose a shadowy threat to the feudal social order. It cannot be a truly subversive or destructive power. . . . Women's sexual desire—the restless whispers of the 'slumbering body' repressed in the text—eventually will disintegrate the women's nation from within."[28] Such an assertion is possible only if it is assumed that women's libidinal desire, repressed in the text, can be directed only at men. But why can it not be directed at women? Meng and Dai unduly neglect Lusha's lament before describing the women's utopia: "The human world can be compared to a water vat for lotuses and people the little insects in the vat. No matter how intelligent, we will never be able to break out of earthly confines" (2:148).

If the house by the seaside inhabited by female friends "can only be an ideal impossible to realize" (2:148), as Lusha laments, might the reason not be precisely that Lu Yin/Lusha senses that such a house is inherently too dangerous and nonconformist for society to tolerate and that, for this reason, it cannot be allowed by society to exist? Instead of arguing that sexual hunger will eat away at the women's house from within, I see the issue to be social constraint imposed from the outside. Society would discountenance a sexually self-sufficient women's community. Lesbian spirituality and lesbian sex, two seeming antitheses, are in fact related in declaring independence from male sexuality. Although lesbian sex is buried in the text's silence, yet, like lesbian spirituality, it is the cause of Lusha's (and Lu Yin's) personal anxieties and self-disavowals because social prohibition is anticipated.

Critics generally perceive the female-female romantic love in Lu Yin's writings as asexual or "pure." Taking that observation as a point of departure, I wish to bring out the lesbian physical desire that subtends lesbian spirituality in Lu Yin's work. How can we talk about lesbian spirituality? Is repression operative? Yet repression is always already a matter of construction. With society's molding of Lu Yin and her female peers in one of the first women's colleges as unconventional but respectable women,[29] their desire for physical intimacy with other women cannot but be fashioned according to a romantic rhetoric that is more sentimental and aesthetic than lustful. Still, the idyllic in her work is also sensual and ecstatic. Sensuous pleasures take her characters unawares. Lesbian enjoyment emerges in displaced forms, such as dream symbolism and her own travel to another country—Japan. It is as if, in moments when ordinary social and cultural regulation of the good New Woman's body relaxed, her physical lesbian desire faced twilight.

This interpretation is particularly plausible when we shift our attention from *Old Acquaintances* to a shorter work, "Lishi's Diary." While the two texts were written in the same year, 1923, and share many themes, such as the encroachment of heterosexual courtship and marriage on female friendships and fantasies about a women's utopia, "Lishi's Diary" is a much more impassioned and self-conscious declaration of lesbian love in protest against compulsory heterosexual love and marriage than *Old Acquaintances* is. Not only is the neologism *tongxing de ailian* (same-sex romantic love) used in the story to indicate that Lishi is aware of current discussions of homosexuality and her own conscious choice.[30] But physical lesbian desire, which surfaced as a concern in May Fourth discussions of women's same-sex love, also gains a highly symbolic visibility. Even though in *Old Acquaintances* Lu Yin claims—through Lusha—that she "advocates a spiritual life [*zhuzhang jingshen shenghuo*]" (2:150), she has nonetheless written, either consciously or inadvertently, of the secret and ecstatic commerce between female bodies.

The plot of "Lishi's Diary" may be summarized as follows. An anonymous narrator publishes the diary kept by her close friend, Lishi, who died of melancholia. In the diary, we find that Lishi, a female student, corresponds with two friends, one a young man named Guisheng and the other a young woman named Yuanqing. Guisheng lives in another city, while Yuanqing is actually Lishi's schoolmate. One day, a former schoolmate, Wenwei, visits Lishi, and Lishi discovers the truth about marriage from her. Wenwei has been married for three years. By all appearances her marriage is happy, but she complains that her energy is completely taken up by household management and her daughter and that marriage is boredom and bondage. Lishi feels depressed after the conversation. She confesses to Yuanqing that for Guisheng she feels merely friendship. She has never been inclined to go to men for comfort because she feels fettered when she interacts with them. Yuanqing sympathizes with Lishi. Consequently, the tenor of their relationship changes: "It was ordinary friendship; now it is same-sex romantic love [*tongxing de ailian*]" (1:188). They make long-term plans and talk about the pleasure and comfort of living together in the future. Lishi dreams that night that they row a boat in a lovely stream in an idyllic moonlit landscape.

Yuanqing is forced by her mother to move to another city and to date her cousin as a prelude to their marriage. As a result, Yuanqing writes Lishi before departure: "Our ideal life is not allowed by them! . . . Ah, Lishi! why didn't you plan ahead! Why didn't you dress up in men's clothes, put on a man's hat, act like a man, and visit my parents to ask for my hand? Now they know you're a woman, and they would not let you marry me. They have found a 'capable youth' for me!" A few weeks later, however, Yuanqing writes Lishi again, in a completely different tone: "Lishi, our opinion of life was childish. Love between people of the same sex [tongxing de ailian] will never be allowed by society in the long run. Listen to my advice. Wake up!" (1:191, 192). Betrayed, Lishi loses her will to live. Not only does Yuanqing forsake her, but she also sends Liwen, a young man full of machismo, to court her. Such insensitivity breaks Lishi's heart. She bitterly resents God for dividing mankind into males and females. Soon she dies of melancholia.

In the story, letters figure importantly, forwarding the amorous relationship. Lesbian love encourages literary production, and writing produces the distant, longed-for aura of the love object despite the fact that Lishi and Yuanqing go to the same school. Lishi's love for Yuanqing culminates in the dream that she transcribes after she and Yuanqing first confessed their mutual affection. As Lishi says, "What appeared in my dream is what we daily long for" (1:189); the dream is the most elaborate textual description in the story of how the women envision a common life.

The dream is set in a rural and natural landscape, far removed from city life. It suggests a wish to tear away from social conventions and institutions. Lesbian union may thrive in a hermitage, but it will not survive in the present civilization. A seeming innocence suffuses the dream:

> I dreamed of a clean, neat hut by a stream. In front of the hut grew two willow trees, and willow branches kissed the roof. A small boat was tied to the willow trunk. It was sunset, and clouds covered the sky. Yuanqing and I sat in the boat. We rowed it in the clear ripples deep into bushes of reeds. Then, suddenly, a light rain fell. We buried ourselves in the bushes, so we could not see the rain but could only hear the raindrops. A long time passed, and it became night. We rowed the boat homeward. At this moment, moonlight shone through the thin clouds and turned the water into blocks of jade. Yuanqing asked me to visit the Crystal Palace in the stream, so I dived into the water. Then, suddenly, I woke up with a start. (1:188–89)

Unlike the ideal life projected by Lusha in *Old Acquaintances,* that propounded in the dream consists, not of a joint intellectual adventure, but of a collaborative experience entirely sensuous, bodily, soothing, at one with nature. Certainly, no explicit erotic thoughts appear in the dream. But its imagery—rowing a boat in water, entering a bush of reeds, and looking for the legendary Crystal Palace in the water—is all peculiarly reminiscent of female sexual arousal and the exploration of female erogenous zones—wet vagina, pubic hair, clitoris, and cervix. That Lu Yin was interested in the prophetic, symbolic, and even sexual qualities of dreams is made clear in "Fuqin" (Father; 1925), in which a tormented young man dreams of his stepmother holding and kissing a bouquet of red roses. It is as though censorship lapsed while he was asleep and he fulfilled his wish of declaring his incestuous love and was accepted by the stepmother.

As Zhang Jingyuan has pointed out, Freud's theory of the interpretation of dreams had been introduced in China by 1920.[31] Many May Fourth male writers, such as Guo Moruo and Lu Xun, were interested in experimenting with dream symbolism as the disguised, condensed, or displaced expression of a character's unfulfilled wishes, especially sexual wishes, thereby adding psychological depth to their fiction.[32] It should not be surprising if Lu Yin, as a female writer, similarly had the Freudian theory of dreams as a usable system of erotic symbolization in mind when she created the highly sensuous dream scene in "Lishi's Diary." That Lu Yin may have arranged—be it deliberately, intuitively, or unconsciously—to have her self-declared lesbian character reveal in the displacement and condensation of a dream her desire for genital consummation of her relationship with her girlfriend has hitherto not occurred to critics. And my reading of the idyllic scene as an exploitation of Freudian ideas or allusions to female-female genital sex may be automatically rejected by most critics as perverse. But "perversity" as a reading strategy is precisely what is necessary. To understand how a society in which heterosexuality reigned supreme may have limited Lishi's/Lu Yin's expression of physical desire for another woman as well as readers' reading strategies, one must resist the apparent interpretation and move beyond the "natural" and reasonable (in this case, the idyllic or the pure). What appears natural is in fact culturally produced and enforced.

Physical lesbian desire enters Lu Yin's autobiographical writing through yet another form of displacement: travel and temporary cultural dislocation. With her second husband, Li Weijian, Lu Yin made a trip to Japan in 1930. In *Dongjing xiaopin* (Notes from Tokyo; 1930–31), a series of short personal essays that she sent from Japan to *Funü zazhi* (The lady's journal) in Shanghai for publication, Lu Yin subjects Japanese women to scrutiny, including a voracious, desiring gaze. These essays on her negotiation between Chinese and Japanese cultures, which have received scant comment from critics, are in my assessment the key to unveiling Lu Yin's carnal desire for women and its predicament.

According to her biographers, Lu Yin suffered from depression after her first husband's premature death in 1927. She did not regain her enthusiasm for life until she fell in love with the young poet Li Weijian in

1929. It is not surprising that her newfound love for life included a fascination with sexuality, as can be seen in her writings from the period. What
is remarkable is that it is immediately after her happy remarriage in 1930
that her interest in the erotic dimension of other women's existence
peaked. Although her desire to know other women sexually is arguably
routed through men and articulated from a masculinized position, Lu Yin
never loses sight of her identity as a woman. Her masculine identification
in the expression of same-sex carnal desire is worth probing as historically conditioned.[33]

There are three levels on which Lu Yin's observations of Japanese
women may be understood. On the first level, they are marshaled in the
form of a travelogue, or amateur ethnography, intended for a Chinese audience. On the second level, Lu Yin shows a particular interest in Japanese women among all aspects of Japanese society because of her feminism. She places herself in a sociopolitical alliance with Japanese women
at the same time as she expresses a personal sympathy and concern for
them. On the third level, which is also the most intriguing, Lu Yin admires Japanese women aesthetically and erotically. This erotic objectifica-
tion is not necessarily the desire for the exotic or the foreign. To a large
extent, it plays itself out as misrecognition—the fulfillment of her fantasies about Chinese women after deferral. When Lu Yin encounters Japanese women—most notably when she plays the voyeur in a public bathhouse and the red-light district—she makes an incursion into their erotic
aura, something that social decorum has kept her from doing in China. In
other words, her recognition of Japanese women as sexually desirable and
pleasurable objects is a compensation for previously thwarted curiosity
about and desire for Chinese women as much as a discovery of the desirability of Japanese women.

Japanese women play a determining role in Lu Yin's negotiation of
Chinese and Japanese cultural differences. Their friendliness, loyalty, and
beauty seduce her, and, as a result, she becomes receptive to Japanese culture as a whole. In the essay "Linju" (Neighbor), she confesses her prejudice against the Japanese people and how it changes on visiting Japan. In
China, she has hated the Japanese and imagined them to be no better than
"malicious tigers and wolves." Even on the ship to Tokyo, she gets stereo-
typed impressions of the Japanese passengers. She resents the Japanese
men on board for being conceited and arrogant and treating the Chinese
passengers badly. And of the Japanese women—who behave with "lamb-
like docility toward men"—she laments: "Although their gentleness did
not arouse our indignation, it made us sad. 'The most pliable women in

the world! Why do you willingly be men's slaves and puppets!' I could not help yelling. It is a pity that they could not understand my words. They probably took me for a lunatic" (2:46). Undoubtedly, a sense of national superiority hides in this criticism of Japanese women's meekness. Fueled by nationalist anger and pride, Lu Yin assumes that Chinese women have stronger characters and experience greater personal freedom. Nevertheless, she identifies with Japanese women as women, which is why she cares about them as a group. Her concern for their social status as women takes precedence over sentiments of national antagonism.

On her arrival in Tokyo, Lu Yin discovers that many Japanese people behave courteously and helpfully toward foreigners. She regrets her past narrow-mindedness. The key to her transformed attitude is her neighbor, a plump middle-aged woman who volunteers to bring Lu Yin water daily from the well and, moreover, shares homemade pickles, chili powder, and an extra apron with Lu Yin. As their relationship takes shape, gender supersedes nationality. Although Lu Yin identifies herself primarily as a Chinese writer and intellectual, sympathy and friendship grow out of a shared social role—a woman in charge of a kitchen. Clumsy, and in need of help with domestic management, Lu Yin discovers that, far from being deficiencies, her elderly neighbor's loyalty and generosity and deference to others are her strengths.[34]

Meanwhile, Lu Yin's attitude toward younger Japanese women also changes, for a different reason. While previously she was eager to raise their consciousness and urge them to revolt against men's domination, she now sees in them incarnations of classical feminine beauty. One day, she observes a pretty waitress stationed outside the café next door dressed and made up in traditional Japanese style in order to draw male customers in. She praises the young woman's winsome looks and smiles by citing classical Chinese poetry. Then, on witnessing the waitress's success, Lu Yin teases herself: "Those who want money have gotten hold of money. Those who want to have fun get fun. Cause and effect have worked out perfectly. . . . Why should you be hypersensitive and full of bitter grievances!" (2:40). In Lu Yin's transformation from a critic of women's slavery to an admirer of the erotic appeal of commodified female sexuality, we find lesbian desire colliding with radical feminism.

Lesbian desire occupies an awkward yet challenging position in a world structured by the sexual supremacy and economic dominance enjoyed by men. At times, lesbian desire flows conveniently alongside men's desire for the female body, but, at others, it clashes with men's gratification and finds the commodification of women for men deplorable and degrading.[35] In Japan, Lu Yin soon discovers the seamy side of female prostitution, and she is forced to reconsider her romanticized view of it. In "Liudao zhi yipie" (A glimpse of Yanagi Shima), she recounts her naïveté about and subsequent disillusionment with prostitution.

She begins the article by confessing that she is attracted to "secret lifestyles." Above all, she finds the life of the prostitute mysterious and wishes to find out more about it. Lu Yin reasons, "Naturally, this is because I lack the qualification for visiting prostitutes. For rich men who are used to carousing in the brothels, it is of course no big deal" (2:56).

Besides measuring herself against men, Lu Yin reveals her desire to cross-dress: "When I was still in China, I had often daydreamed about masquerading as a man so that I could visit a brothel to have a look at prostitutes' flirtatious smiles and luxurious, dissipated lives. Perhaps I could discover some new life there. But I have too short a stature to pass as a man. Moreover, Chinese society is so obdurate that I never dared to try, for, if unfortunately I were found out, people might have dreadful suspicions about me" (2:56). Whatever these "dreadful suspicions" might be, Lu Yin finds her stay in Japan an excellent opportunity to act out her fantasies away from home.[36] In the new cultural environs, she is practically anonymous and therefore harbors no fear of scandal. Consequently, one day she suggests to her local guide that he take her and her husband to observe Japanese prostitutes. Because a woman cannot easily gain access to high-class courtesans, they agree instead to take a stroll in Yanagi Shima, a district where lower-class sex workers congregate.

For this expedition Lu Yin dresses in drag. Not that she disguises herself as a man. Rather, she takes off her Chinese garments and puts on a Western skirt, shirt, and blazer in order to masquerade as "a Japanese New Woman." No doubt, to some extent Lu Yin honestly identifies with the New Women of her host country. But the gesture bespeaks even more her discomfort with remaining in her customary cultural identity while embarking on a journey considered transgressive and forbidden by her usual self. At any rate, she is excited as they set out. But, as night falls and they approach the brothels, she becomes timid and follows her male companions in trepidation. Entering a dark alleyway, she sees women's faces like white masks through small windows on the doors of the houses. The sight quickly turns surrealistic:

> In the dim light, when I suddenly spotted their faces with simulated coquetry and lasciviousness, a chill ran down my spine. I did not believe it was the human world. I felt as if in a nightmare: I had been taken by two

ghost soldiers to hell. In a yard filled with puss, blood, and stench, numerous brightly colored flowers were displayed. Behind each flower hid a woman with a gaping nose, festering eyes, and rotten ulcers all over her body. They watched me in tears as if they wanted to tell me something, but I shut my eyes and was too scared to lift my head. All of a sudden, those ghost soldiers took me out of the yard again! (2:59)

"Come, let's have fun, brother!" The phrase resounding in the alley does not entice Lu Yin but rings like a cry of humiliation and misery in her ear. She realizes that she is repulsed because she is, after all, a woman, not a man. Eventually, an old prostitute trying to grab hold of a customer notices that Lu Yin is a woman. Humiliated and angry, she rebukes Lu Yin for setting foot in that part of town. She calls her "a modern woman disobeying the chaste rules of women" (2:60) and dares her to go inside a whorehouse. The rebuke effectively spotlights Lu Yin's predicament for us. Caught between man and whore, Lu Yin the New Woman is awkward and out of place. She has imagined that she can flirt like a man with a prostitute—the most eroticized and sexually available woman in Japanese society as well as Chinese—but her same-sex desire finds no hospitable place in the existent structure of sexual traffic. Unless she willingly and boldly takes on a markedly deviant status, she will never be able to walk into a brothel and demand her share of its pleasures. Furthermore, fundamentally, her desires and the sex trade have limited overlap. As a New Woman who prizes the intellect and mental labor, she abhors women who soullessly sell their bodies in order to earn a living. She and the sex workers may be of the same gender, but they are from such different social strata and their outlooks on life are so different that finding an egalitarian lesbian erotics to unite them is out of the question. Furthermore, Lu Yin is in danger of being taken for a prostitute herself by the men cruising among them.

Essentially, Lu Yin, as a New Woman of the upright, proper kind, one who remains enthralled by mainstream conceptions of decency and progressiveness, has very few choices when it comes to obtaining homoerotic satisfaction.[37] From a traditional Chinese point of view, she is deemed bold because she actively pursues free love with men as well as remarriage; however, situated in the context of the intellectual campaign for free heterosexual love and marriage, she is in the vanguard and not at all deviant or marginal. Being the exemplary, appropriate New Woman, however, she always stops short of acting on, or even acknowledging, her carnal lesbian desire.[38] She respects her refined upper- and middle-class female romantic friends too much to pursue sexual relationships with them, knowing that society already considers love between women to be a perversion. And to pursue lower-class women would be to embrace decadence and to replicate the patriarchal commodification of them as sex objects—and therefore unthinkable. Consequently, Lu Yin's carnal lesbian longing must be smuggled into action through a seemingly asexual practice legitimated by Japanese culture. She finds tremendous excitement in bathing with other women in the bathhouse. Typical of sublimation, she rationalizes her rapture in terms of aesthetics.

Lu Yin describes her visit to the bathhouse in "Muyu" (Taking baths). Freshly arrived from China, she discovers that traditional Japanese bathing facilities are designed, not for private baths, but rather for communal bathing.[39] In general, she finds that, unlike the Chinese, the Japanese are not overly modest. Men and women can look at each other's uncovered bodies freely: "One finds men wearing flimsy shirts and shorts in the street. . . . And sometimes naked women can be seen through windowpanes, watching passersby unruffled." On entering a women's bath for the first time, Lu Yin marvels that the dozen women inside are stark naked. Reluctantly, she bares her own body, then rushes into the pool and hides in the water. It is not until she finishes bathing and gets dressed again that she relaxes and dares to look around:

> The other women were lovely and languorous after their bath. And how natural they looked! Facing the glossy mirror, they combed their hair and applied powder and rouge to their faces, all the while without a stitch of clothing on. They stood up, sat down, and knelt on one knee, adept in all varieties of postures. I feasted on the sight. I wanted then to sing the praises of the beauty of the human body—the smooth skin, the voluptuous curves, and the round, fat toes—everything displayed the art of nature. . . .
>
> I admired their bodies as I put on my socks. When done, I felt embarrassed to be sitting there staring at them. So, picking up my towel and dirty clothes, I left the place where the flesh [se xiang] of women was displayed.

On her way home, Lu Yin senses that her "nerves were excited." She wonders whether the Japanese are exceptionally fortunate to be able to cast off "hypocrisy and bondage" (2:48, 49).

In the sundry essays written in 1930 and 1931 in which Lu Yin compares Japan and China, nowhere does she lean so decidedly toward Japanese culture as in the essay on bathing. As if to deny the libidinal significance of her pleasure, she frames the whole liberating experience with a discussion about the aesthetics of the human body and the superiority of nature over artifice. From the moment she opens the essay, she tries to strip nudity of erotic connotations and to imply that it is a banal, original state by recognizing that humankind is simply a species of animal: "Homo sapiens [*renlei*] are mysterious animals indeed. We like hiding and concealing. This is especially true of women, who are always wearing masks. . . . Therefore, it is rare that one can behold the beauty of the human body" (2:47). Peculiarly, what Lu Yin means by "the beauty of the human body" here and throughout the essay is exclusively the beauty of the female body. Her attention to humans as a species is lopsided indeed. She does not touch on male beauty at all but praises the feminine physique profusely.[40]

This preoccupation persists when Lu Yin investigates cultural differences in attitudes toward the female body. First, she mentions female models in modern art circles and Western dancing girls as performers of nudity, expressing discontentment with the contrivance of the former and the artificial embellishments of the latter. Then she criticizes China for its treatment of women's bodies. According to her, China is especially against the voluptuous body, even clothed, not to mention nude: "The teachings of decorum are strict in China. It suppresses the rich curves of the female body with chest bands and waist girdles, turning a human into a wooden idol." For Lu Yin, this cultural practice of eliminating women's sexual difference from the sphere of vision stems from the "extreme care that ancient Chinese sages took to prevent erotic attraction between men and women" (2:48, 49). She glosses over the fact, however, that essentially it is her own visual deprivation, as a woman regarding women, that compels her to protest. What dissatisfies her is, not exactly Chinese sages' obsession with keeping women hidden from men's gaze, but more specifically their ready association of the female body with obscenity, which somehow disallows the enjoyment of nakedness among women themselves.

Even in the Japanese bath, Lu Yin is not free from her habitual cultural mind-set. She shies away from showing her body to other women, as if ashamed, but watches other women with relish. Although nudity may be nothing for Japanese women, it is obviously an unusual stimulation for Lu Yin. Her excitement can hardly be read as what she claims it to be, a simple release from artifice. Women's nakedness is for her, after all, an arousing, if not obscene, "sight of the flesh [*se xiang*]" (2:49).

Compared with the objects of her gaze, Lu Yin's body appears always asexual and far from voluptuous. She objectifies other women, but never herself. There is a gap in the text, an uncertainty about the femininity of her own physicality. Can it be that a debilitating masculine mask arrests her action? The women's bathhouse is not merely a place in which to admire women but also one in which to compete with them. Lu Yin's response to the situation is to hide herself, to immerse herself in the bath, gazing at women like a man whose body is not gazed at in return. While masculinization—the adoption of a cerebral masculine persona—safely facilitates her chivalrous appraisal of other women's sex appeal, it also prevents an unreserved lesbian encounter from taking place. Lu Yin cannot melt with a desirable woman unless she strips herself of phallic protection and impenetrability. If as a spectator she cannot go all the way, that is, if she cannot act like a masculine manipulator of women's bodies, she must learn to proffer her own body to other women so that an interactive, egalitarian erotic dynamics can come into being. In the bath, Lu Yin's lesbian lust cannot truly take flight, for she has not yet liberated the sex appeal and sexual energy of her own female body.

### Female-Female Eros as Represented by Other Writers

Other May Fourth writers wrote more explicitly about female-female physical behavior than Lu Yin did. Ling Shuhua, for example, provides carefully chosen details hinting at girls' kissing and fondling. And Ding Ling goes even further, stating bluntly, for example, that some female teachers have had sex with other female teachers. Even these authors seem to need to distance themselves from female-female eros, however, the former disclaiming her own inspiration, the latter throwing an unsympathetic light on intellectual women's same-sex relations. (Among male writers, Yu Dafu and Zhang Yiping construct graphic scenarios of female-female sexual aggression, but these are clearly thinly disguised male fantasies that are more about expressing men's concerns than about seriously tackling the issue of female-female eroticism.) Intensity of eroticism is, of course, never determined simply by explicitness. Whether certain activities appear in a text hardly speaks to its erotic value. Lu Yin's stories about her enchantment with other women are compelling and endearing mainly because of her struggle with cultural confines. Moreover, the erotic value of her appreciation for other women's sensuous bodies is enhanced by her lifelong concern for other women's welfare.

"Shuo you zhemo yihui shi" (Rumor has it that something like this happened; 1926), by Ling Shuhua, an important female member of the Wenxue yanjiuhui (Literary Association), makes a good starting point for a discussion of more explicit female-female eroticism. The story is a rewriting—at the author's request—of "Ta weishenmo huran fafeng le" (Why did she suddenly go crazy; 1926), by Yang Zhansheng, a male member of the Wenxue yanjiuhui.[41] And it follows the basic plot of the earlier work.

In Ling's story, two female students, Yingman and Yunluo, fall in love with each other after they are cast as Romeo and Juliet in their school's production of Shakespeare's play. Outside rehearsal, they engage in tender embraces and kisses and even share a bed in the dorm. One day Yunluo (Juliet), in tears, tells Yingman (Romeo) that her mother wants her home to meet a marriage prospect. Yingman asks her not to go and to think of herself as being married to her. They will live together all their lives, as two female teachers in their school do. Feeling that she must obey her mother, Yunluo cannot bring herself to commit to Yingman, but neither can she bring herself to reject her outright. When what is originally meant to be a brief visit drags on, Yingman blames it on a military conflict in the Jiang-Zhe region. But, eventually, she overhears classmates discussing Yunluo's situation and, learning the truth, that Yunluo has married, faints dead away. In her delirium, she seems to see Yunluo but cannot quite tell whether she is crying out for help or smiling.

If we compare Ling Shuhua's text with Yang Zhensheng's earlier version, we find that Yang's is barren but that a lively imagination animates Ling's. She tells the story through rich, sensitive, and suggestive details about girls' school and dorm life, and she builds up to the physical and psychological intimacy between the two protagonists gradually. Yang, by contrast, speedily attributes the love affair to the lack of a proper emotional outlet: "They [Gu Yingman and Deng Yunluo, Yang's protagonists] had been good friends. After they acted together onstage as Romeo and Juliet, they grew even more intimate. Gu Yingman had a forthright, somewhat manly character. Deng Yunluo was about eighteen, at an age when her need for love was just budding. They happened to be born in a nation governed by decorum. They could not obtain the proper association with men. Therefore, they fell in love with the same sex [*tongxing jian zhongqing qilai le*]."[42] Such an explanation of same-sex love—attributing it to contrary gender role-playing, the inherent masculine temperament of one girl in the pair, and the improperly restrictive same-sex environment—corresponds to notions popularized by imported sexual psychology.

In Ling's rewriting, by contrast, it is suggested, not only that Yingman and Yunluo are in love with each other, but also that many other of their classmates have formed intimate partnerships. Speaking firmly as a woman, Yingman points out to Yunluo that same-sex love surpasses the love of men: "Teacher Chen Wanzhen and Miss Chu have been living together for five years. Why can't we follow their example? Don't think about the difficulties only. I believe my love for you is much deeper and will last longer than any man's love for you. You understand, don't you? Can't you think of yourself as being married to me?"[43] The fact that Romeo can give an example of lesbian union is especially provocative. It seems common knowledge in the school that two female teachers have been living together as long-term companions. No public censure is indicated. The pressure that tears the young female lovers apart comes solely from Yunluo's family.

In her time, Ling Shuhua was called a writer of the Xin guixiu pai (the New Boudoir School), meaning that she was rather conservative in her choice of subject matter and less than defiant in her criticism of tradition. Yet this story argues to the contrary. Although the title reads like a disclaimer—distancing the author from the narrative and any opinions expressed therein, implicitly or explicitly—the text itself shows genuine sympathy and understanding for female lovers. Its insight is unique and unchained by Yang's earlier version. Ling is especially daring in asserting that the relationship between the two teachers is essentially the same as that between Yingman and Yunluo, that same-sex love can be the chosen lifestyle of adult women as well as a maddening passion between adolescents.

Another May Fourth story to tackle the subject of cohabiting female teachers is "Shujia zhong" (Summer break; 1928) by Ding Ling, who gained literary fame in the late 1920s for her bold representation of female desire. In "Shujia zhong," a number of young women teach at an elementary school, Zili nüxue (The Self-Reliance Girls' School), in a hot, humid provincial town. These women have sworn to stay single so that they can devote themselves to teaching. However, they pursue this path, instead of marrying and becoming housewives, mainly because they have been enchanted with the notion of women's emancipation as disseminated by elite intellectuals in the trend-setting cities. They lack, in fact, a passion for teaching and the moral and intellectual integrity to fuel the self-development that will lead to productive lives. As they grow older (into their mid- and late twenties), they secretly regret not having taken advantage of opportunities to become romantically involved with men or enter marriages arranged by their families. They come to long to find suitable men so that they can marry and leave off teaching. But, before they find men, they pair off as lovers or special "friends," and "they do with each other whatever newlyweds do."[44] Yet rarely does a day pass among them without jealous bickering. Their self-doubt and boredom are aggravated during the summer months as, then, they do not have even the daily classroom routine to preoccupy them. At the end of the summer vacation, another semester starts. Life falls back into its depressing, repetitive cycle even as it seems to be filled with activity again.

The pessimism and sarcasm that pervade the story expose a serious social problem. Are these women to blame for their own misery because they are not ambitious enough? Given the limited choice of professions then available to women, most of the characters have turned to teaching, not because it suits their abilities and interests, but because it is their only option. It is, therefore, not surprising to find that they do not bond as enthusiastic partners in a common enterprise. A future of female cohabitation lacks excitement and luster. Marriage with prosperous men can at least provide economic comfort, even vicarious career success.

Nonetheless, the contempt for female homosexuality revealed in the text is chilling. Through a critical speech delivered by the character Zhiqing, who is unpopular among the other women and, therefore, bitter, Ding Ling attributes the women's lack of enthusiasm for their profession to their sexual experimentation in school; instead of focusing their energy on their studies, they looked for girlfriends among their schoolmates and learned to kiss, embrace, write love letters, and conduct oratorical lovers' duels. Same-sex love affairs among female teachers are a continuation of a "ridiculous" and detrimental practice among adolescents.[45]

Ding Ling unflinchingly discloses the sexual nature of certain relationships between women teachers, but the plot degrades lesbian eroticism to the level of a second-rate sexual outlet and a form of self-deception. The denigration of female homoeroticism is apparent, for example, in the way in which the relationships between two pairs of lovers—Jiaying and Chengshu, Dezhen and Chunzhi—are presented. It is repeatedly suggested, for example, that the homely and emotionally dependent Chengshu unjustly deters the prettier and younger Jiaying from having relationships with men and, ultimately, a wholesome family life. Jiaying therefore resents the possessive Chengshu, and her dissatisfaction and ennui pervade the text.

The relationship between Dezhen and Chunzhi is similarly fraught with dissatisfaction and ambivalence. Dezhen has just become engaged and has been preparing her trousseau zealously. And, as can be imagined, the engagement causes constant friction between her and Chunzhi. After a fight between Chengshu and Jiaying has ended, the narrator remarks:

> Their love survived, and life went on without change, since no one worthier of love was likely suddenly to appear, and since neither wanted to realize that the sentimental relationship in which they sought comfort could not satisfy their real needs and desires. Similarly, Dezhen and Chunzhi continued to be lovers amid intermittent fights until Dezhen's wedding day. Despite the fact that they would hurl invectives and even threaten bloodshed during their arguments, it all seemed to be no more than unconscious angry words. Afterward, Dezhen would make peace with Chunzhi by reiterating her love and at the same time prepare the dowry for her own wedding in high spirits. Chunzhi sneered at Dezhen and pointed out to others how ridiculous Dezhen was to look forward to marriage with such eagerness. Nevertheless, she spent entire days helping Dezhen embroider flowers on handkerchiefs and shoes. Couldn't she tell that the handkerchiefs and shoes were all prepared for a man's enjoyment?[46]

Both Dezhen and Chunzhi regard marriage as more legitimate than a same-sex relationship. Even the jealous Chunzhi's criticism of men and conventional marriage is halfhearted. Thanks to the lack of faith that exists between them, the two women's relationship is reduced to little more than an old, dull habit or a second-best alternative.

The pessimism about female-female love expressed in "Shujia zhong" enters an interesting dialogue with the attitude toward female-female relationships to be found in Ding Ling's renowned "Shafei nüshi de riji" (Miss Sophia's diary), published three months before "Shujia zhong." In an eloquent reading of this celebrated text, Lydia Liu has shown Sophia's disenchantment with men's romantic love and her overall ennui, an ennui exacerbated by the loss of her female soul mate, Yun, who has languished and died in a disappointing marriage.[47] Sophia's only consolation is keeping a diary that is addressed to Yun and expresses her love for her.

In these two stories, a fulfilling female-female love relationship is either lost (owing to the intrusion of men) or realized only with difficulty. It is clear, not only that Ding Ling doubts that a romantic understanding can be reached between man and woman, but also that she finds it unlikely that happy, satisfying female-female unions can be maintained in a world dominated by men. In a society characterized by gender inequality, few women can resist the material and symbolic benefits that marriage provides. Few women are able to value other women as people deserving of trust, devotion, and commitment. Therefore, betrayal, dishonesty, and resentment almost of necessity plague female homoerotic relationships.

Ding Ling's criticism of these relationships does not, however, end in a simplistic assertion of the superiority of heterosexuality to female homosexuality. She debunks the contemporary myth of a liberating, fulfilling heterosexual love with equally trenchant sarcasm. She searches restlessly for something greater than romantic love to believe in. It is perhaps for this reason that she later took a clear turn toward socialism, hoping to achieve some sort of overall economic and social restructuring.

The stories by women writers analyzed thus far in this chapter all carry with them a certain authenticity—the minutiae of women's relationships presented in the texts seem almost to have grown out of the writers' own experiences and observations. By contrast, in the male writers' works to which I now turn, female-female physical relations are trite, thinly disguised fantasies introduced to serve men's nationalist or erotic interests. Yu Dafu's *Ta shi yige ruo nüzi* (She is a weak woman; 1932) stereotypes female homosexuality according to the medical theories of the third sex and gender inversion to create a homology between personal and national pathologies. In this novella, a tall, strong female student, Li Wenqing, who has a low voice and coarse skin and who stinks, seduces the pretty young girls in the school dorm. She sleeps with and abandons one girl after another, including the protagonist, Deng Xiuyue, an angellike beauty who loses her virginity to this monstrous masculine woman. Deng subsequently embarks on a tempestuous erotic life with male teachers. After a few years, she gets married to a poor writer. When her husband is unable to support her, she hits on the idea of dating and getting money from one of her former lovers, but she is raped and beaten by him. At the end of the novella, she is gang-raped, killed, and mutilated—her breasts cut off—by soldiers during the Japanese invasion of Shanghai in 1932.

What corrupts Deng, then, is the monstrous third-sexed woman. Had Deng not been prematurely introduced to sexual relations, she might instead have developed her intellect—becoming reliant on her mind instead of on her body—and worked for the great socialist cause, as one of her classmates, Feng Shifen, does. Female-female sex in the school is represented as detrimental, divorced from spiritual communion, sympathy, and self-improvement for the national good. Moreover, the image of the coarse, masculine woman, Li Wenqing, is juxtaposed with that of an effeminate, effete man with whom Li has a sexual relationship at one point. Yu Dafu was apparently mindful of the sexological descriptions of both male and female sexual inversion and keen on exploiting these concepts of gender abnormality to symbolize social disintegration and chaos, not to mention the impotence and loss of virility that he saw as characterizing the Chinese nation. His portrayal of female-female sexual relations was nothing but a way in which to articulate impending national doom.[48]

In "Songluo shan xia" (Under the pine hill) by Zhang Yiping (1902– 46), a lesser-known male writer, we find an example of female-female eroticism exploited for men's voyeuristic pleasure.[49] Zhang's *Qingshu yishu* (Love letters; 1924), the collection of stories in which "Under the Pine Hill" first appeared, is characterized by an overt eroticism combined with soulful yearning across both time and space. And the frontispiece to the volume, a reproduction of William Blake's illustration *The Reunion of the Soul and the Body*, sets the tone for the collection in general and for "Under the Pine Hill" in particular, which is positioned first in the volume.[50]

Blake's illustration—one of a series created for Robert Blair's poem "The Grave"—is intensely erotic.[51] Following Blair's lead, Blake shows the soul and the body as partners rushing into each other's arms, never again to be sundered.[52] The body, represented as male, has just sprung from the open grave and still has a shroud about his loins. Naked, muscular, and kneeling in a strained posture with arms extended toward the sky, he craves to receive. The soul, represented as female, is descending from the open clouds. Draped, lithe, with head downward, she imprints a kiss on the male figure's lips as if to infuse him with life in preparation for life everlasting.[53] The image can, therefore, also be interpreted as a lovers' embrace, a literal reading entirely in tandem with the religious meaning of the image.[54]

*The Reunion of the Soul and the Body* may celebrate synthesis and not division, yet the symbolism employed in it is deeply entrenched in a dichotomous, binaristic logic that borrows from cross-sex sexuality, normativizing heteroeroticism and erasing homoeroticism. Binarism casts the soul and the body as opposites rather than as symmetrical echoes or reflections of each other, conceiving of the reunion of body and soul as opposite rather than same gender. Had Blake chosen to depict two male figures—one muscular and solid (the body), the other lighter and evanescent (the soul)—the image would still have worked.[55] However, he implicitly rules out such a homoerotic image as inappropriate. Furthermore, by instituting the body-soul theological opposition and then celebrating the pair as inseparable, Blake naturalizes and glorifies opposite-sex sexuality in the death-defying merging of body and soul.

In choosing this image to serve as the frontispiece of a collection of love stories, Zhang Yiping pays explicit tribute to Blake's heteroerotic Romanticism. Apparently, Zhang aims at embodying the imported Western paradigm of love—(heterosexual) unions at once spiritual and physical—in his creative writing. Nevertheless, as noted earlier, the volume begins with "Under the Pine Hill," which is structured as a love letter from a young woman to her boyfriend, telling him about her same-sex lover (*tongxing lianren*) and lamenting her death—in response to his own admission of having had a same-sex experience. Can the story be the product of either unconscious desire or a traditional/indigenous Chinese homoerotic ambience that escapes Zhang's manifest intention to promote Western-style heterosexuality? How subversive of the modern hetero-romantic paradigm can the story be?

In the end, female sexuality in "Under the Pine Hill" turns out to be powerless to exit the circuit of male desire. It is male homoerotic love, mentioned but never shown in the story, that invites and authorizes confession, reminiscence, and commemoration of female homoerotic love. Does the positioning of this story at the front of the volume then imply that same-sex love is a preparatory, preliminary, initiatory, or immature stage of a young person's sexuality? It is as if the book argues that its seven stories of heterosexual love are predicated on the loss and demise of homosexual love. The narrator of "Under the Pine Hill" mourns her same-sex lover and thus kills her yet again because mourning is double-edged. Ostensibly, mourning reactivates memory, denies amnesia, and keeps the loved one alive. However, it also finalizes death and is, therefore, conducive to psychological acceptance. Writing thus performs a double ideological function: it both creates a monument and buries the dead. At the end of the story, the bond between the female narrator and her male lover is intensified rather than shattered by the sharing of memories of past homoerotic love affairs. And the narrator's daring description of female-female sexual experimentation serves only vicariously to excite her male lover/male readers. It is in such a structure engineered by a male writer that we experience most fully the ideological limits of May Fourth intellectual discourse on female-female desire.

### Literary Inscriptions beyond the May Fourth Era

As demonstrated above, throughout the 1920s, although representations exploring female same-sex love are few in number, they can easily be found in the works of major fiction writers. Among female writers, Lu Yin was most critical of the destructive effects that heterosexual marriage had on women and most self-conscious in idealizing female-female lifestyles as a utopian alternative. Ling Shuhua daringly suggested that same-sex romantic companionship among female students and teachers was common. Both Lu and Ling allowed their same-sex-inclined female protagonists to argue that female-female love was superior to heterosexual love and marriage. Ding Ling, by contrast, offered bitter portrayals of same-sex relations among New Women as little more than a temporary sexual outlet. Among male writers, Zhang Yiping carved out the role of a male voyeur. And, in the early 1930s, Yu Dafu deployed sexological characterizations of sexual inversion to metaphorically represent social disorder and national weakness.

Yu's demonization of female-female sexual practice and inverted gender traits invites the reflection that, as Japanese military aggression escalated in China during the 1930s, growing Chinese nationalism and the leftists' zealous call for socially engaged literature may have cast an unflattering light on female-female romantic love (as well as heterosexual love), making it seem self-indulgent and irrelevant to the crisis at hand and, hence, an unfitting subject for a writer, unless it was being condemned.[56] Indeed, to a certain extent such speculation is justified, for, after the early 1930s, fiction writers' references to same-sex love became relatively rare compared with the May Fourth era. What also seems likely is that, as the discriminatory sexology of the Krafft-Ebing and Ellis variety steadily accumulated authority through repeated translation and citation in popular manuals on sexual hygiene and psychology through the 1930s, few fiction writers were disposed to regarding same-sex love as a positive personal matter, regardless of the national crisis looming large on the horizon.

Yet, ultimately, the situation prevailing throughout the 1930s and 1940s was more complex than might be suggested by the work of Yu Dafu. Same-sex love had not yet become taboo, and there were scattered, if admittedly infrequent, references to the sexological concept in writers' representations of female-female relations. Xie Bingying's *Yige nübing de zizhuan* (The autobiography of a woman soldier; 1936) is an especially instructive example because the candid confession in the autobiographical mode of having in the past engaged in same-sex relations suggests that same-sex love was not perceived as an unspeakable evil by either the patriotic author or her intended audience.

In one of the subdivisions of her fascinating narrative, Xie relates the "troubles of same-sex love [*tongxing ai de jiufen*]" that had occurred during her school days.[57] After finishing the advanced elementary school (*gaoxiao*), she was admitted to Changsha shengli diyi nüshi (Changsha's

Provincial First Women's Normal College) in the early 1920s.[58] Because she was "born with a male personality [*shenglai jiu you nanxing de xingge*]," quite a few romantically inclined female college classmates were drawn to her and fell in love with her. Interestingly, the patriot Xie did not criticize same-sex love as fundamentally at odds with the interests of the nation but rather reminisced of it fondly and with good humor. Her main objection to it was that the five female classmates attracted to her had all madly wanted to monopolize her attention and that each of them had been irrationally jealous of perceived rivals. Instead of being possessive of, and being possessed by, a particular friend, Xie wished that love could be "shared among all [*dajia xiang'ai*]."[59] In this sense, Xie presented herself more as a philanthropist than as someone immune to the love of the same sex.

As Xie's narrative progresses, youthful female same-sex love ceded importance to her budding longing for romance with the opposite sex (*lian'ai*), to the Nationalists' Northern Expedition to unify China, to her joining the army, and, finally, to her repeated struggles to escape from an arranged marriage and imprisonment by the feudal family. Her joining the army in 1926, in particular, was a decisive turning point in her life. Her enchantment with romantic love with men was superseded by her dedication to overthrowing the old social order in China and her resolve to liberate the oppressed masses from poverty and hardship. In the section "Dapo lian'ai meng" (Break the dream of romantic love), she reported a song that she and other women soldiers had learned to sing:

> Make haste to study! Make haste to practice! Work hard to be the vanguard
>     of the people!
> Overthrow feudalism! Break the dream of romantic love!
> Accomplish social revolution, great courageous women!

These youths' former notions of romantic love were promptly replaced by a new conviction that the only (opposite-sex) love worth pursuing was the "comrade love between like-minded revolutionaries [*geminghua de tongzhi ai*]."[60] The priority was clear: personal love had to serve the cause of emancipating the masses.

Despite the fact that Xie learned to subsume her emotions and desires and redirect her energy to the cause of nationalism, she nonetheless recounted the popular practice of same-sex love in her college and the episode of same-sex love in her own past instead of erasing them from her life story altogether. Her openness in this regard suggests that female same-sex love was far from being singled out as especially decadent, degenerate, and unforgivable by nationalistic youths like herself on the eve of the Sino-Japanese War.[61]

Although Xie's confession of same-sex entanglements is unique among the works of women writers, it had a precursor in the autobiography of the left-wing male writer Guo Moruo, *Wode younian* (My youth; 1932), in which Guo depicted the prevalence of male-male love and sex in school and his own relations with male lovers. Guo reminisced about his life in an advanced elementary school (*gaodeng xiaoxue*) in Jiading, Sichuan, right after the traditional civil service exam was abolished in 1905. He enrolled in the school when he was not yet thirteen. During his first semester there, he became close friends with Wu Shangzhi, a boy whose personality, face, and demeanor were of a "meek and tranquil beauty [*xunjing mei*]." Guo wrote, "His character was quite the opposite of mine. But we became very intimate; our intimacy surpassed the feelings between brothers and the closest kin [*bi xiongdi gurou jian de qinggan haiyao qinmi*]." Commenting on how often he and Wu broke up and then renewed their friendship, Guo wrote, "The situation was as if we had been in same-sex love. In fact, our affection for each other was more serious than love."[62] After Guo went to middle school in 1907, he fell in love with another flower-like boy. Describing the second love affair, Guo dwelled unabashedly on the sexual aspect of their relationship—kisses, passionate embraces amid cries of "I love you," and sleeping over in a hotel. Such frankness indicates that, although nation building was the foremost concern of revolutionary youths and intellectuals in the 1930s, same-sex relations were not automatically associated with national weakness, nor were they necessarily feared and condemned as the symptoms of dissolution and mental illness.

### Looking Beyond Republican China

Diverse as they may seem, the fictional representations of and translations of sexological discourse about female same-sex love that appeared during the May Fourth era are inherently ideologically limited in that they do not explicitly affirm long-term female-female partnerships and female-female lust. The defiant celebration of sex between women and of a combative will to legitimate long-term female-female partnerships beyond those formed in adolescence will not be seen until the last decade of the twentieth century. By making such a statement, I am merely observing the pronounced difference between eras. In no way am I prescribing a teleology or destination for literary evolution. Nevertheless, the opening up—in literature at least—of alternatives for female sexuality and women's life choices should be acknowledged as a positive plurality, regardless of whether these alternatives are considered by the writers proposing them to be representations of lesbian sexuality and identity. These insurgent articulations by women of female same-sex practices at the turn of the millennium constitute the subject of the second half of this book. Because of the sheer volume of such works produced—for both elite and popular audiences—my approach will of necessity be selective and illustrative rather than comprehensive, highlighting certain unprecedented dimensions of recent discursive formations, especially those found in serious literature.

My analyses of the literature of post-Mao China focus on two novelists whose inscriptions of female homoeroticism stand out as the most innovative in that context—Lin Bai (b. 1958) and Chen Ran (b. 1962). Meanwhile, across the Taiwan Strait, the growing lesbian identity movement, one of the more prominent new social movements in Taiwan after the lifting of martial law, has been especially robust compared with the development of similar movements in other Chinese-speaking societies.[63] The radicalism of this burgeoning sexual politics in Taiwan is worth studying, and I highlight its militancy by analyzing two clusters of formations. Both occur in the context of a highly mediated public sphere. One is a series of debates among feminists and lesbian activists over the significance of lesbianism for the overall women's movement; the tension erupted in Taiwan during the mid-1990s, and the reverberations continue. The other is the emergence of lesbian autobiographical writing. Although other queer-identified novelists such as Chen Xue and Hong Ling have also published significant work and won acclaim from local critics, here my primary example is Qiu Miaojin (1969–95), a lesbian-identified writer who single-handedly created two local terms for referring to lesbians that have garnered huge followings among lesbians in Taiwan—*eyu* (crocodile) and *lazi* (lez). Indeed, Qiu is nothing less than a cult figure.

All four key nodes of discursive formations—the writings of Lin Bai, Chen Ran, and Qiu Miaojin and the contentious debate among Taiwanese feminists and lesbian activists—are chosen for analysis here because of their potential to illuminate the high gender stakes involved in the politics of lesbian sexuality and identity and because they demonstrate the unique ways in which female homoerotic literatures and lesbian feminisms complicate/enrich what Mayfair Yang calls *the transnational Chinese women's public sphere(s)*.[64] The concept of the public sphere is (as we have seen) useful for understanding the May Fourth era, during which, because of the weakness of the state and the protection provided by foreign concessions (in Shanghai, e.g.), Chinese intellectuals could openly debate a broad variety of cultural issues, including gender and sexuality. Yang's call for an examination of women's unique contributions to the public sphere is especially compelling in the context of turn-of-the-millennium transnational China, where apparently governments can no longer dominate all social activity and public discussion. Women's movements and feminist discourses have been striking developments in Chinese societies since the 1980s, and the public debate and contestation surrounding female same-sex eroticism and lesbian subjectivity are part and parcel of these developments.

THREE :: CHINA AFTER MAO

# THE BRAVE NEW WORLD OF
# POST-MAO CHINA: AN OVERVIEW

### Reading the Silences of Maoist China

The year 1949 saw the founding of the People's Republic of China (PRC). Soon thereafter, or so it seems, complete effacement of female same-sex love as a topic for public debate and artistic representation came about with the onset of Maoist totalitarian control. In Mao's China, the category *same-sex love* was largely erased from the public arena, and it disappeared from the print media as well. Harriet Evans's research reveals that, in the 1950s, 1960s, and 1970s, the official discourse on sex in the journals of the women's and youths' organizations contained no mention of homosexuality; and, according to a 1990 source that she cites, in the early years of the PRC homosexuality was declared not to exist in liberated China.[1] In my own research on the Maoist period, I have found only one post-1949 publication that discussed homosexuality and other sexual variations openly—but only as perversions. Not surprisingly, the book, by Zhang Minyun, is a study of the development of modern sexual science in the West and Japan since the late nineteenth century, and it was published in Shanghai in 1950, a year in which the Chinese Communist Party

(CCP) had not yet firmly established its control over most aspects of social life and thoroughly nationalized public culture.[2] Once the CCP tightened its grip, however, the mere mention of homosexuality became taboo in all material destined for public circulation.

That, under the Communists, the term *same-sex love* became unmentionable, an abomination, and disappeared altogether from circulated print should not, however, lead one naively to presume the absence of either homosexual desire or same-sex sexual behavior in Maoist China. Moreover, the not unusual display of beautiful, heroic bodies (female as well as male) and same-sex physical contact in the visual arts (films, posters, and revolutionary model operas) could, since never explicitly sexualized, very well have appeared ambiguous to the individual viewer and been interpreted in a wide variety of ways, including but not limited to erotic fantasy.[3] *Wutai Jiemei* (Stage sisters; 1965), one of the director Xie Jin's best-known films, foregrounds the intense bond between two regional opera actresses, a relationship that may have struck some viewers as little different from love. In a fascinating memoir, Xiaomei Chen reflects on how keenly she, as a youngster, felt the allure of the voluptuous bodies of heroines in revolutionary visual art.[4] More explicitly, in her controversial novel *Yige ren de zhanzheng* (One person's war; 1994), the female writer Lin Bai describes her protagonist Lin Duomi's precocious erotic feelings as a child growing up during the Maoist period. One of the decisive moments in Duomi's sexual awakening was when she waited on a lead dancer in the revolutionary model ballet *Baimaonü* (The white-haired girl) as she changed clothes backstage. There, standing next to the adult woman's full, naked body, young Duomi was overwhelmed by a surge of vertiginous pleasure as well as unnamed anxiety, all the while oblivious to the austere message of class oppression conveyed by the ballet.[5]

In everyday life in Maoist China, emotional intimacy and constant physical proximity between those of the same sex may have been common; in fact, same-sex relations may have been less inhibited than premarital male-female intimate relations were. The 1985 film *Nüer lou* (Army nurse), directed by the female director Hu Mei, offers an interesting interpretation of the norms of friendship and intimacy during the Cultural Revolution (1966–76). The main female characters in the film—teenage girls who are Red Guards in a city at the start of the Cultural Revolution—are sent by the state to a hospital in the northern mountains to work as nurses. There, the young women become emotionally attached to one another and take physical closeness for granted—little wonder, given that they share a bedroom and thus have little privacy. By contrast, emotional

bonding between men and women prior to marriage is taboo, as is physical contact between the opposite sexes, other than that required/justified
by work (here, the contact required in a clinical setting).[6] A strong contrast between the possibilities of same-sex intimacy and a stringent taboo
on premarital male-female contact during the Cultural Revolution is also
at the center of the drama in Anchee Min's allegedly autobiographical
novel *The Red Azalea* (1994).

As Min's sexy account of her life as an urban educated youth (*zhiqing*)
sent to toil on a farm became a best-seller in the United States, many other
memoirs of sexual awakening and other experiences during the Cultural
Revolution saw print (in Chinese) in China in the late 1990s. These eroticized first-person narratives recount many male-female sexual liaisons—
despite the revolutionary taboo on bourgeois, individualistic romantic
love and extramarital and premarital sex. Not surprisingly, same-sex sexual relationships also appear in such memoirs. An example is "Gebi e lian"
(A nightmarish affair in the Gobi), by one Long Sheng, which appeared in
a three-volume collection of memoirs entitled *Zhongguo zhiqing qinglian
baogao* (Educated youths report on their love and romance; 1998). The
author (one of the more than one hundred people who submitted "authentic stories") relates the political persecution of a young effeminate gay
man. The "story" centers on two young men, the narrator, Liu Ying, and
one Jiang Xiaobo, both members of the Xinjiang Production and Construction Brigade. One night, on awakening from a dream in which he had
been rejected sexually by a young woman whom he admired, Liu discovers that Jiang, already known as a *tuzi* (rabbit, i.e., one who takes the passive role during male-male anal sex) and to be *nanren nütai* (of woman-
like deportment, voice, and appearance), has performed oral sex on him
while he was asleep. Feeling violated, Liu causes a scene, which leads to
the brigade's investigation of Jiang. During the investigation, it is revealed
that Jiang, having offered himself for penetration, has had anal sex (*jijian*)
with eighteen other members of the brigade. Jiang was henceforth labeled
*huai fenzi* (a bad element) and, whenever there was a political point to be
made about anything, put on public trial. Liu was indignant that, because
of his effeminacy, Jiang was scapegoated and that none of the other young
men who had willingly engaged in anal sex with him were punished. But
there was little that Liu could do to help him.[7]

Moving beyond the politically suspect and clandestine sexual activity
of the educated, Neil Diamant's research in newly opened archives containing information collected about the residents of Shanghai and Beijing
between 1949 and 1968 suggests that sex among working-class men and

women outside monogamous marriage occurred frequently, resulting in many out-of-wedlock and other illegitimate pregnancies. The ravenous appetite for and casual attitude toward sex on the part of both men and women defied official attempts to regulate sexual activity and make people toe the official Party line. Hence Neil Diamant writes, "Contrary to expectations of China scholarship . . . [my] sources show that factory workers, tailors, peddlers, seamstresses, and clerks often entered into friendship, marriage, and sexual relations driven by status and economic concerns, urban or rural residence, sexual desire, and the pursuit of fun and leisure more so than by politics or political class." While most instances of intractable engagement in sexual activity that Diamant found in the records were cross-sex in nature, he did encounter one same-sex instance, where a female worker (who happened also to be a Party member) fashioned a rubber dildo to have sex with a married woman and, furthermore, urged her lover to divorce her husband. No dire political consequences seem to have ensued as a result of the sexual relationship itself even though it was common knowledge among the women's coworkers.[8]

In sum, we are now acquiring through a variety of sources complex and at times contradictory perspectives on sexual activity and other romantic behavior, both same sex and cross-sex, previously hidden beneath the official discourse on love, sex, and marriage between the 1950s and the 1970s. And the recently engendered, post-Mao debate over sexuality in general and same-sex relations in particular, a debate as open as that of the May Fourth era, has spurred a reevaluation of the Maoist past. Post-Mao China's economic reform and reintegration into the global capitalist system, manifested in part in the rapid development of all varieties of print and electronic media and a flourishing publishing industry, furnished the necessary social, economic, and technological infrastructure for new cultural formations. Among other developments are the resumption of transnational flows of sexual epistemology, images, and practices into and out of China, a phenomenal new spate of public discussions of love and sexuality, and the rise of the second wave of liberal feminism, May Fourth feminism being the first.[9]

### From Silence to Contending Discourses

In the 1980s, when homosexuality first emerged in the PRC as an ambiguous medical and legal issue, it was as if a long-standing silence had been broken. The perspective of Wan Yanhai, a medical school graduate and public-health advocate who initiated the AIDS hotline and the "men's world" salon in Beijing in 1992 and started the newsletter *Aizhi jianbao* (Newsletter of love and knowledge) in 1994, is representative: "For a very long time, China's law, mass media, and scientific reports never mentioned homosexuality. The Chinese had access to few foreign or classical Chinese materials concerning homosexuality. Public discussions of homosexuality in the mass media did not begin until the 1980s." Writing in the mid-1990s, Wan commented, moreover: "In mainland China, the status of homosexuals in society is like that of the bad elements [*huai fenzi*] during the Cultural Revolution. Although there is no law explicitly defining homosexuality as illegal, there have been nonstop criminal and administrative punishments."[10] On the basis of interviews conducted in 1994 with more than two hundred gay men in fifteen mainland Chinese cities, An Keqiang, a Taiwanese journalist, finds the fact that, in the PRC, homosexuality per se is not criminalized to be no sign of an enlightened attitude on the part of the government: "In the early years of the People's Republic, those who were discovered to have engaged in homosexual behavior were made to wear a big sign and paraded through the streets. The character written on the sign, composed of the upper half of the character *nan* [male] on the top and the character *nü* [female] on the bottom, meant 'neither male nor female.' Later, during the Cultural Revolution, homosexual behavior was called *jijian zui* [the crime of male-male anal intercourse], and one could be sentenced to the labor camp because of it. Since the economic reform and open-door policy began, the regulation concerning 'hooliganism' [*liumang xingwei*] has been subjectively applied by the police to those found to engage in homosexual acts, even though there is in fact no specific law criminalizing homosexuality."[11]

Taken together, Wan's and An's remarks point to the fact that, between the founding of the PRC in 1949 and the 1970s, public mention of homosexuality was extremely rare in mainland China. In terms of punitive practice, male-male sex acts might, if discovered, incur punishment. However, such acts were understood as gender transgression or sodomy, not homosexuality. Moreover, punishment was not stipulated by law but meted out haphazardly—by participants in mass, Party-mobilized campaigns, by the police, or by the relevant work unit. As late as the criminal code put into effect in 1980, no mention was made of homosexuality. What can be found instead was a law (no. 160) criminalizing activity that fell under the indistinct, catchall category *hooliganism* (*liumang zui*), in which man-boy rape and male-male sodomy by force or threat fell.[12] The PRC's official dictionary of the modern Chinese language (the writing and compilation of which were finished in 1965 but the publication of which did not occur until 1973, after the most destructive phase of the Cultural Revolution had passed) included *tongxing lian'ai,* the Republican neologism for *homosexuality.* The entry is tersely worded, defining *homosexuality* as "the love relationship that takes place between men or between women, a form of psychological perversion."[13] However, the specifics of early-twentieth-century medical theories of homosexuality as gender inversion and psychic pathology did not resurface in the urban popular consciousness until a multitude of publications about sex appeared in the 1980s and 1990s, with the redevelopment of a market economy and the reintroduction of Western culture.

The reemergence of the taxonomy of homosexuality into public discussions in the PRC is part and parcel of the "sexing" of Chinese society and culture after Maoism. Sex has become one of the most prominent discursive formations and commercial enterprises in the PRC since the 1980s.[14] Much of the early phase of this sexing process took place in the arena of popular science. A multitude of books on sexual psychology, sexual culture, sexual history, sex education, and sexual behavior were published between the mid-1980s and the early 1990s, many of which included sections that dealt with homosexuality. For instance, Liu Dalin's pioneering survey of sexual behavior in China differentiates between homosexual behavior and homosexual identity and explores the incidence of various forms of homosexual behavior in China.[15] However, most texts claiming to offer scientific knowledge of sexuality simply rehashed Western sexological theories of homosexuality as gender reversal and psychological abnormality. Many were, in fact, simply reprints of Republican-era books, such as Pan Guangdan's 1946 translation of Havelock Ellis's *The Psychology of Sex* and Zhang Minyun's 1950 *Xing kexue.* The stereotypes about homosexuality rampant in the medical literature led the Hong Kong sociologist Chou Wah-shan to comment in 1996 that the medical profession in the PRC commonly held homosexuality to be a form of mental illness, a view that was especially outmoded as it saw the problem as being one of inverted gender identity.[16]

Meanwhile, some Chinese physicians and specialists have begun to adopt current Western medical thinking, and they have begun to speak out for the right of homosexuals not to be subjected to treatment and also to introduce the concept of sexual orientation both to the medical establishment and to the general public. In 1994, a breakthrough occurred. The disease model of homosexuality was debunked in a joint statement made by more than fifty experts in sexual science, psychiatry, public health, law, and ethics at the end of a groundbreaking conference, "Aizibing jiaoyu yu teshu xing wenti yantaohui" (Meeting on AIDS education and special sex problems).[17] More significant, in April 2001, Zhonghua jing-shen kexue hui (the Chinese Psychiatric Association) finally decided to de-lete homosexuality from the latest edition of *Zhongguo jingshen zhang'ai fenlei yu zhenduan biaozhun* (The Chinese classification of mental disor-ders), published by the association.[18]

The depathologization of homosexuality by the Chinese Psychiatric Association, together with the state's 1997 excision from the new crimi-nal code of the nebulous category *hooliganism,* has been hailed by many mainland Chinese homosexual persons as progress.[19] In the two decades since the start of economic reform, then, the mainland Chinese public has undergone a period of frequent exposure to the question of homosexual-ity, during which homosexuality has been constructed in radically varying ways in a multiplicity of discourses. Initially, pathologizing, sensational-ist, debasing, and criminalizing representations of homosexuality prolif-erated with the development of a new commercial market of print and mass media between the 1980s and the mid-1990s. However, two major social institutions—the judicial system and the psychiatric establishment—have at the turn of the millennium officially relinquished, at least in the-ory, their regulatory power over homosexuality.

### The Relative Invisibility of Lesbians

Amid these complex developments, a significant number of works de-scribing homosexual existence in contemporary mainland China have been produced by local and transnational Chinese journalists, sociolo-gists, and activists and, more recently, by international activists and an-thropologists. The quality of these reports has varied, but the subject in focus is the same—gay men. Representative of PRC journalism in this re-gard are two books by Fang Gang: *Tongxinglian zai Zhongguo* (Homosex-uals in China; 1995) and *Zhongguo bianxingren xianxiang* (The phenom-enon of Chinese transsexuals; 1996). At the height of the Taiwanese media fever for lesbian and gay coverage, the journalist An Keqiang wrote a re-port about gay men in the PRC, which came out in Taiwan as *Hong taiyang xia de hei linghun* (Black souls under the red sun; 1995). The Beijing soci-ologist Li Yinhe and her collaborator, Wang Xiaobo, conducted interviews and questionnaire surveys with some forty gay men (mainly in Beijing) and published the results as *Tamende shijie: Zhongguo nan tongxinglian qunluo toushi* (Their world: A penetrating look into the Chinese gay male community; 1992).[20] Chou Wah-shan collected the life stories of (predominantly male) homosexuals in Beijing, publishing them as *Beijing tongzhi gushi* in 1996. On the American anthropological front, Lisa Rofel researched gay life in Beijing in the late 1990s, a project that resulted in "Qualities of Desire," a nuanced theoretical reflection on the desire for cultural belonging among cosmopolitan gay men in the PRC. In addition, Ruan Fangfu, Wan Yanhai, and Gary Wu have been contributing to Chinese gay activist work in China and the United States (either by traveling back and forth between the two countries or by means of the Internet) since the late 1980s and early 1990s. Almost without exception in such works and projects, the gay man—and, more specifically, the gay man in metropolitan Beijing—takes center stage.

By contrast, only a small amount of journalistic and sociological literature on homosexuality produced in the PRC has touched on the issue of lesbianism.[21] Tamara Chin suggests that this is because no lesbian subculture has yet appeared—at least one recognizable by Western standards. Chin argues that gay men in the PRC are visible—and their subculture therefore recognizable—because their behavior (e.g., cruising public parks and toilets) mirrors that of gay men in the West and the spaces that they occupy are clearly marked as gay. By contrast, it is difficult to find in China any public space specifically marked as lesbian.[22] A more provocative hypothesis, one suggested to me by women from the PRC on several occasions (and one with which Chin does not necessarily disagree), is that close relationships are so common among Chinese women that intimate behavior is simply taken for granted—by women themselves and by society. No one knows whether it counts as homosexuality; hence, there is no special need to talk about it. In other words, that the lesbian subject is largely (but not always) absent from popular journalistic and sociological accounts in the PRC is certain, but the cause of that absence is disputable.

That gay men have such a high profile in the PRC is not entirely an advantage. The majority of media coverage accorded them is distastefully fanciful and biased, based on fabricated reports and uninformed opinion. It tends to attribute homosexuality to mistaken gender identity and, worse still, portray gay men as promiscuous, doomed by AIDS, and a menace to society. Even those few writers who have made an effort to collect accurate data directly from gay men would be hard-pressed to deny that their reports can be unethical (in that they amount to little more than outing) and voyeuristic. For example, Fang Gang, usually regarded as a conscientious reporter, one who collects his stories rather than inventing them, was sued in 1999 for outing the manager of a Beijing gay disco, who was as a result of Fang's story ostracized by family and friends and unable to find work.[23] Perhaps the relative invisibility of the lesbian subject in the media is, then, just a mixed blessing and not an absolute curse. Women who desire primarily other women have largely been spared being subjected to objectifying scrutiny and being misunderstood and misrepresented, the negative aspect of invisibility being that the fact that theirs is a distinctive lifestyle and identity is not commonly recognized.

### Young Cosmopolitan Lesbian Subjects

That being said, it must be pointed out that globalization is moving at such a fast pace in the PRC that the cosmopolitan lesbian subject that was invisible when I visited Beijing in 1995 had become visible a short three years later. When I returned to Beijing in late 1998, what I found were spirited, confident lesbian-identified women in their early twenties who called themselves *tongzhi,* a term that meant "comrade" in its Communist origin but had been appropriated by the lesbian and gay movements in Hong Kong and Taiwan in the early 1990s as an umbrella term for those who identify as lesbigay, transgender, or queer.[24] Accompanied by local friends, I had the chance to meet and chat with a group of these women in a pub. Some of them had just attended, along with some other thirty lesbians, the first mainland Chinese "Nü tongzhi huiyi" (Convention of lesbians) held in Beijing on 2–3 October 1998,[25] and all of them were very excited about starting a community newsletter, *Tiankong* (Sky), the first issue of which appeared in March 1999. What will come next? I asked. Is it identity politics (*shenfen zhengzhi*) that you want? Not knowing whether they understood the term the same way as I did, I heard one of them answer, "We want life, not politics." Another elaborated, "It's a matter of strategy. Talking about politics right now will get us nowhere. The initial aim of our newsletter is to provide useful information and an avenue of exchange for people within the circle [*quanzili de ren*]. We must wait before moving on to another stage."[26]

In addition to *Tiankong*—which, according to Shi Tou, a painter who serves as the newsletter's editor, does not circulate publicly because she and her friends have never applied for a government permit, an application that they do not expect would be granted—the Internet has been a valuable communication resource. One of the women told me that she had been dating other Beijing women whom she met through the Internet as well as chatting with people overseas. Thus, the voices of the new cosmopolitan lesbian subjects, as they currently exist in mainland China, are audible globally, in cyberspace, in addition to being grounded in local women's social circles and discussion groups.[27] Despite having made such progress, however, mainland Chinese lesbians still held back from following the lead of Taiwanese lesbians, who ten years earlier had declared their collective existence publicly, through the mainstream media. Given the tight control of the media exercised by the mainland government at the time, activists felt that it was impossible to engage in similar tactics. However, the atmosphere seems recently to have relaxed somewhat— enough, anyway, that, on 20 December 2000, Shi Tou and Cui Zien, a male writer and film researcher at Beijing Film College, came out publicly on the HNST (Hunan weishi or China Hunan Satellite Television) program "You hua hao shuo" (Talk it easy)—a first in mainland China. Along with the sociologist Li Yinhe, Shi and Cui discussed same-sex love with members of the studio audience. The conversation was very positive and lasted forty-five minutes. HNST has 300 million regular viewers in China, so it is likely that some tens of millions watched the show.[28]

Even more recently, in January 2002, the glossy magazine *Xiandai wenming huabao* (Modern civilization pictorial), whose registered publisher is Zhongguo shehui kexue yuan, the Chinese Academy of Social Sciences, put out a special issue on homosexuals in contemporary China entitled "Tongxinglian yu women tong zai" (Gays and lesbians are with us). While the special issue was dominated by stories about gay men and recent gay-themed fiction, film, and avant-garde theater from Hong Kong and the mainland, a few articles about lesbians did appear.

The first, Shi Tou's "Shi Tou yishu zuopin xuan," consists of reproductions of selected paintings (mostly oils) of Shi Tou, accompanied by a brief manifesto written by the artist. Some of her paintings—the *Wugi* (Weapons) series—depict strong, statuesque nude women whose body parts (hands, heads) have metamorphosed into knives, guns, and other mechanical weapons. As Shi explains, these weapons represent an "incisive, critical look directed at our world, courageous and fearless [*yong pipan de yanguang duizhun women de shijie ba, bufa yingyong yu wuwei*]." Other paintings—the series *Yuanyang hudie* (Mandarin ducks and butterflies)—portray young female couples swimming and hugging happily in multicolored pools. The liquid dreamscapes seem to suggest that the artist's visions of blissful, carefree female-female intimacy are somewhat fantastic and utopian in character.

The special issue of *Xiandai wenming huabao* also contained two articles about the love experiences of three anonymous lesbian-identified women aged between nineteen and twenty-five who were interviewed in

Beijing bars.[29] It remains to be seen to what extent and in what manner young cosmopolitan lesbians can further occupy representational space in the commercial media.

## Fictionalized Lesbian Voices

Mainland Chinese lesbians may not have the same kind of public media presence that gay men have, but they do have a public presence in a wealth of *fictionalized* voices of female homoerotic desire. These fictionalized female voices have been subjected to conservative academic and other forms of unofficial moralist criticism as well as the vagaries of state censorship. They have also been appropriated by profit-oriented publishers and voyeuristic readers. Still, they are opening more lines of communication than their critics can shut down. The voices' polysemy and the emergent interpretive and critical strategies that help bring out that polysemy constitute what I call *the third space* of female homoerotic fiction in post-Mao China. This space, I contend, is carved out by certain novelists and readers who probe female-female desire from socially marginal perspectives and/or with a strong diasporic sensibility. The immediate forebears of those presently enriching and extending the third space are female writers such as Zhang Jie, Liu Suola, and Wang Anyi, who in the mid- to late 1980s pioneered fictional representations of poignant female friendships and tested the constraints imposed on female bonding by heterosexual relationships and marriage.[30] These earlier writers, however, rarely explored physical desire between women and generally shunned the notion *homosexuality*.[31] Their limitations are the ground on which such remarkably persistent and daring writers as Lin Bai and Chen Ran have been building since the 1990s. The sophisticated cultural work that Lin's and Chen's female homoerotic fiction performed for over a decade is especially significant in that it predates the public presence generated by Shi Tou and her fellow activists.

In the two main chapters of part 3, then, I read Lin Bai and Chen Ran in detail. These two writers broke onto the literary scene and ascended to prominence within essentially the same time frame—from around 1986 to the late 1990s. Therefore, my choice to discuss them separately represents, not a chronological, but a thematic ordering. Turning first to Lin Bai, I examine censorship, the hypothesis of sexual liberation, and the representability of female sexuality, compelled by the moralistic reaction against her work. At the same time, I am both intrigued by and dissatisfied with certain liberal PRC critics' justification of Lin's depiction of female-

female eroticism in terms of "female consciousness" and "feminine writing," a justification that repeatedly characterizes the same-sex eroticism depicted by Lin as consistent with an essential, if mysterious, femininity. Such readings must be contested, for Lin's narratives of female same-sex desire are, in fact, beset with recurring tropes of marginality, fear, irreconcilable difference, and exile. What she inscribes, in other words, is a particular female identity that has a specificity of marginality—arguably a female homosexual identity in denial. My disagreement with the mainstream—moralistic or liberal—critics in China, finally, leads me to reflect on the global circulation of texts and the politics of diasporic/transnational reading. When I move on to the work of Chen Ran, I am motivated to reflect on another set of issues. In post-Mao China, both a new wave of unofficial, liberal feminism and the new consumer culture have validated gender difference as a rediscovered truth. As essentialist beliefs about gender, with implicit gender hierarchies, are constructed and propagated by elite as well as popular discourses, Chen's advocacy of a "gender-transcendent consciousness" is unique. Her essays and fictional works challenge the facile hypothesis that there has been a liberation of gender and sexuality in China after Maoism.

# LIN BAI'S NARRATIVES OF FEMALE HOMOEROTIC DESIRE

## At the Juncture of Censure and Mass Voyeurism

Since Mao Zedong's death, fiction writers in the People's Republic of China (PRC) have unremittingly pushed the limits of sexual representation. The liberation of desire was considered a project integral to the restoration of subjectivity to individuals, a topic that dominated Chinese intellectual discussions in the mid-1980s.[1] In this cultural milieu, many works rescuing human desire from sexual puritanism, state repression, the institution of marriage, and the pragmatism of procreation appeared, for example, Zhang Xianliang's *Nanren de yiban shi nüren* (The other half of man is woman; 1985) and Wang Anyi's three novellas about illicit love (*san lian*), *Huangshan zhi lian* (Love on a barren mountain; 1986), *Xiaocheng zhi lian* (Love in a small town; 1986), and *Jinxiugu zhi lian* (Love in a brocade valley; 1987). The trend for literary explorations of sexuality continued into the 1990s and the new century, a period characterized by a vastly different cultural economy, in that elite ideologies such as aesthetic humanism have lost their luster and cultural production is now complicated by the market competition for audience and profit.[2] The most scandalous and best-selling erotic publication in China in the early 1990s was probably *Fei du* (The abandoned capital) by Jia Pingwa, in which the combination of a traditional vernacular style and numerous sex scenes—even though often only insinuated[3]—made critics liken the book to the Ming-dynasty erotic masterpiece *Jin ping mei* (The golden lotus).[4]

Then, in 1996, something peculiar happened. The editor responsible for the publication of *The Abandoned Capital* advised a female writer that, if she wanted to find a publisher willing to put out a work that she had finished some time earlier, she would have to delete its entire first chapter, and make significant changes throughout the rest of the novel, because of inappropriate sexual material. Who was this author? And what was this novel? How can it be judged obscene compared with *The Abandoned Capital,* the modern *Golden Lotus*?

The writer was Lin Bai, and the novel was *Yige ren de zhanzheng* (One person's war). On its completion in 1993, the work was rejected by several serious literary magazines before being accepted by the avant-garde journal *Huacheng* (Flower city), based in Guangzhou. Fortunately, this first publication, in early 1994, was uneventful and not controversial. However, things did not go so smoothly when, on reissuing the novel in July 1994 as a self-contained work, another publisher, Gansu People's Publishing House (Gansu renmin chubanshe), used a photograph of a nude woman on the front cover. In no time, the book was denounced as pornography (*chungong*) and as obscene (*huangse*) in the pages of *Zhonghua dushu bao* (The Chinese book review), published by Xinwen chuban shu (the Bureau of Press and Publications), the central government office in charge of censorship.[5] Several writers and critics defended Lin's work in the pages of the review, but by then *One Person's War* was notorious.[6]

Attempting to remedy the situation, Lin retrieved the copyright and began looking for a new publisher, one who would not package her work in a way suggesting that it was sexually stimulating. But, even after contacting seven different publishers, Lin's agent could find no one willing to touch the project. Even the editor responsible for the publication of *The Abandoned Capital*—whom the agent contacted for advice—urged that *One Person's War* be revised.[7] Indeed, it was not until 1996, after Lin broke down and prepared a censored version of the novel, that her agent was able to sell it to a publisher—and even then only a publisher in Inner Mongolia. So what was wrong with the novel? How could *The Abandoned Capital,* which has graphic sex scenes on almost every page, so readily find a reputable publisher and *One Person's War,* which in fact contains very little explicit sex, face so much opposition?

When I interviewed Lin in 1998 and heard her describe the puzzlement, anger, and despair that she felt in 1996 in reaction to the public reception of *One Person's War,* it occurred to me that what was at issue was, not the amount of sex, but the implicit hierarchy of sex that existed in society.[8] What made the difference for the censors—whether they were aware of it or not—between *One Person's War* and *The Abandoned Capital* was the nature of the sex acts described, the method of narration, and the gender of the author.[9] Only pleasurable heterosexual sex is described in *The Abandoned Capital,* the novel is cast as a third-person narrative, and the author is a man. By contrast, the only heterosexual sex in *One Person's War* is absurd or painful, the novel contains vivid descriptions of female autoerotic activity and homoerotic relationships, it is cast as a first-person narrative, and the author is a woman. To make matters even worse, all indications were that the novel was meant to be autobiographical.

Reactions to *One Person's War* were extreme. Some, such as a review by one Ding Laixian (about whom little is known, not even his or her gender), took a hypermoralistic stance and attacked the novel's feminist position. With tortuously circuitous logic, Ding asserted, for instance, "Ignore the so-called feminism. . . . Here I do not want to quote the Bible on the principle with which God created man and woman, nor do I want to analyze in detail the deep meanings of male and female anatomical structures. All I want to say is that a woman, being a woman, knows that a woman's real happiness (including sexual pleasure in a real sense) cannot derive from her ineffectual and self-tormenting efforts all by herself. . . . Rather, her happiness can result only from hand-in-hand cooperation with man. . . . That a woman (or female protagonist) pursues strange stimulation when she is lonesome sounds just as scary as a drug addict's compulsive use of poison." Ding went on to take a dim view of women writers' depiction of unsavory sexual subject matter: "The present situation in the artistic world of China is very worrisome, and the pursuit of novelty must not go on. If it continues, it may obliterate the little success that women's literature has achieved so far and lead to a flood of virtually pornographic novels like *One Person's War.* In view of this, many people have already raised their voice in sincere cries: Certain self-styled women writers should have some basic sense of responsibility and love [for society]."[10]

The invocation of religious authority, the glaring biological essentialism, the extreme self-righteousness, the attempt to silence women writers—all these things are astounding yet sadly familiar. As the female critic Xu Kun incisively points out, regardless of Ding's gender, his or

her position is male centered in that it "merely rehash[es] the require-
ments of women that men have made for hundreds or even thousands of
years."[11] The moral-minded Ding was irked, above all, by autonomous female sexuality and found it distressing that a woman would flaunt such
sexual practices publicly instead of being "a nurturing force . . . docile and
tranquil . . . modest and humble."[12]

Meanwhile, another kind of reader delighted in learning a woman's
well-kept sex secrets. This was made abundantly clear by the fact that,
during the months that the Gansu edition of *One Person's War* was available, the novel sold well, in the tens of thousands.[13] The private content
of the novel fed right into mass voyeurism. The more shocking the material, the better. By using the word *voyeurism,* I mean to call attention, not
so much to actual secretive looking, as to the publishers' creation for readers a *fantasy* of voyeurism. Although the fact of the matter is that Lin took
the initiative in choosing what is essentially an autobiographical narrative form and in challenging the dominant fiction of female passivity
and gentility with her powerful descriptions of female desire, the profit-
oriented publisher nonetheless encouraged potential readers to position
themselves as voyeurs—occupying a position of mastery, detachment,
security—and to position the author as the mere object of their gaze. In
other words, the marketing machine inculcated the illusion of voyeuristic
control in the masses so that they could consume Lin's novel as exciting,
and yet distant and nonthreatening, entertainment. In fact, the need to
tame women's unruly writing with seductive and reassuring framing has
led to publishers' pervasive use of corrupt/vulgarized versions of the
French feminist slogan "écriture feminine" in promoting women's writing, ambiguously emphasizing the intimate link between women's writing
and the body.[14] As Dai Jinhua, the prominent Beijing-based feminist
critic, has pointed out, catchphrases such as "My body, my self, and my
monster" embellish the covers of many of the works of PRC women writers. Dai remarks, "By means of repackaging, male publishers and critics
transform women's self-narrative and self-questioning into the [object of
the] lustful gaze of the male voyeur."[15]

Since Dai does not spell out the general implications of her observation, I think that Kaja Silverman's theoretical reexamination of voyeurism
is extremely pertinent here. The classic definition of *voyeurism*—as, for
example, in the work of the psychoanalytic semiotician Christian Metz—
considers it as equivalent to scopophilia or the desire to see, as "*concretely represent[ing] the absence of its object* in the distance at which it
maintains it and which is part of its very definition: distance of the look,

distance of listening."[16] Within this definition (which can be applied to the "cinema spectator" [Metz's term] as the prime example), the distance between voyeur and object enables mastery and sadism.[17] Silverman, on the other hand, identifies in the Freudian concept of the primal scene an even more originary form of voyeurism, where distance is conducive to passivity and masochism. She maintains with regard to the primal scene: "Far from controlling the sounds and images of parental sexuality, the child held captive within the crib is controlled—indeed, overwhelmed—by them. . . . The mastering, sadistic variety of voyeurism discussed by Metz can perhaps be understood as a psychic formation calculated to reverse the power relations of the primal scene—as a compensatory drama whereby passivity yields to activity through an instinctual 'turning around' and reversal."[18] I argue that such an instinctual turning around is precisely what is at work in fantasies of voyeuristic reading. In the profit-minded packaging of *One Person's War* and other first-person narratives by women writers for the consumer market, the myth of an active and mastering voyeur is subtly fabricated and imparted. Since such narratives are, regardless of their authors' actual intent, routinely labeled *nüxing si xiaoshuo* (novels of women's privacy) and *nüxing zixuzhuan* (women's autobiographies),[19] which supposedly spring without mediation from the authentic experience of the female body, what is at stake is precisely a reversal of power relations, whereby any assault on traditional morality, conventional aesthetics, and male literary domination that women's verbal-artistic constructs launch is canceled out, and whereby women writers' defiant candor is reimagined as secrets waiting to be pried open by the male reader/voyeur.

It is difficult to imagine that Lin, a dedicated writer, had wanted to provoke either moral censure or mass voyeurism with *One Person's War*. Her novel—motivated in the first place by an urge for self-expression—was unwittingly caught in a struggle between two unsympathetic factions: one part of society wanted to ban it, to silence it forever, while the other commodified it, appropriated it for popular consumption. Eventually, as already noted, Lin agreed to prepare a revised version herself—a move that signaled her compromise with the contending forces—paving the way for the novel's 1996 reissue by an acceptable publisher.

The history of *One Person's War* shows that, the moment sex is liberated from silence, repression, and prohibition, a new set of social players is likely to appear on the scene, those who profit by the articulation of sex until a new equilibrium of power is reached. Sex is not so much set free as incorporated into a new social regime, where power, now distributed widely, is obscured because it is much more diffuse and mobile than before.

The hypothesis of liberation, like that of repression problematized by Foucault, cannot, in other words, be taken at face value.[20] Inherent hierarchies of gender and pleasure are constructed through the very proliferation of sex. Harriet Evans maintains that, although there has been an explosion of sexually explicit material in popular discourse in China since the early 1980s, "all sexual activities not bound by the parameters of legally recognized marriage have consistently been represented as immoral and harmful, in social, psychological and sometimes physical terms. . . . Autonomous female sexuality, mediated neither by patriarchal control associated with marriage nor by the demands of reproduction, constitutes a threat to the model of sexual and marital harmony upheld by the dominant discourse."[21] Mayfair Yang, focusing not on the pattern of moral condemnation but on the actual gender and sexual subject positions that are positively produced and signified, proclaims:

> It is clear that the new consumer culture is based on a fundamental gender bifurcation, and the exaggeration and celebration of gender difference and sexuality. However, this gender construction is also an asymmetrical construction, so that there is the knowing and controlling male gaze and the female object of contemplation and desire. As Laura Mulvey shows, in this new patriarchal structure "woman . . . stands . . . as signifier for the male other." That is to say, . . . in this sexual economy, women are (literally and economically) invested with the quality of "to-be-looked-at-ness," and their function is to provide a contrastic background against which male subjectivity is foregrounded and brought into sharper relief.[22]

Small wonder, then, that, when a woman writer's unveiling of her sexual body through inscription does not provide a smooth mirror in which the heterosexual male subject can see his own image, reaffirming his desirability and potency, a crisis of masculinity occurs.[23] And the crisis cannot be resolved without a flurry of efforts to tame the unruly female figure through discourse. Slapping a sexually charged photograph on a book's cover and marketing it as *nüxing si xiaoshuo* (i.e., a work about women's privacy) represent but one manifestation of the taming discourse, which operates opposite moralist outcries in a complicitous relationship. More intriguing, even those seemingly sophisticated attacks on *One Person's War* that move beyond simply vehemently accusing the novel of depravity denounce it as an instance of "female narcissism" (*nüxing de zilian*), because the female image presented for inspection does not function simply as a signifier for the male other.[24] Instead of reflecting the heterosexual male gaze back on itself, the woman as mirror has had the gall to see and desire herself and other women. The heterosexual male critic finds it soothing to affix the psychoanalytic label *female narcissism* to the female circuit of desire that excludes him, because its threat is momentarily contained by the connotation of immaturity and infantilism that inheres in his "diagnosis."[25] In this manner, he takes refuge in the illusion of analytic impartiality and modernity and continues to look without ever being forced to recognize the true nature of the image on display. In Luce Irigaray's words, "In this economy any interplay of desire among women's bodies, women's organs, women's language is inconceivable. And yet female homosexuality does exist. But it is recognized only to the extent that it is *prostituted to man's fantasies.*"[26]

### The Third Space and Transnational Reading

Taking it, then, as given that diverse social forces have articulated themselves through the censure and commodification of *One Person's War*, what more can we say about the novel? Does the fact that Lin Bai was able to include a definitive, complete version of the notorious text in her collected works, published by a prestigious press in 1997, mean that there has emerged a "third space" where the novel faces neither censure nor mass voyeurism? How will a reading of her text appear in this third space?[27]

The third term has enjoyed a certain prestige in contemporary theory in that to it is symbolically attributed the capacity to unsettle or move beyond a dualistic bind. Thus, we have Gilbert Herdt writing on the multiplicity of "third sex, third gender" to deconstruct sexual dimorphism, Marjorie Garber explicating cross-dressing and bisexuality as the third terms in gender and sexuality, Gloria Anzaldúa refiguring the hybrid borderland as the third country, and Homi Bhabha defining the third space of enunciation as a contradictory and ambivalent space in the structures of meaning and reference that makes all cultural statements and systems always already impure.[28]

The sense in which I am using the third term is to be distinguished from these previous formulations, even as it resonates with them. What I mean by *the third space* is specifically a social space where the reception of, for example, *One Person's War* is not confined by the dichotomous, or, rather, complementary, relation between censure and voyeuristic economy. The third space, I contend, is not a discrete arena isolated from moralism and commercialism. Nor should it be idealized as the interstices between colonizing forces in which the subaltern (in this case, Lin Bai) manages to speak.[29] Commenting on the marginalization and appropriation of women writers' (semi)autobiographies by "the cacophony of the market and the loud patriarchal voices" in 1990s China, Dai Jinhua has located the resistance to new and old forms of male domination in the literary female voice itself—in its forcefulness, clarity, introspection, and full consciousness of "the present state of women's gendered existence."[30] In a similar vein, Mayfair Yang argues that post-Mao women writers' exploration of taboo subjects—gender and sexuality—has carved out a "women's public sphere in print."[31] As these critics ascribe agency to women writers' voices, however, the equally important agency of interpretation has been effaced. I contend that, while *One Person's War,* for example, may justly be intended as an act of social intervention, its challenge to the status quo can be recognized and, thus, magnified only if the overall social space in which it finds itself is no longer monopolized by a monolithic or even a dualistic system of meaning. Therefore, by devising the concept of the third space, I wish to introduce a complex, layered landscape where, in addition to censors, profit-seeking publishers, and voyeuristic consumers, other, less obvious social players are involved in appropriating Lin's work and may be used by it. In fact, players may be acting in plural capacities simultaneously. Lin's narrative is, thus, full of double entendres as it negotiates with overlapping forces and discourses, marginal as well as mainstream. What surfaces in the third space is, simply put, the possibility of multiple reading practices that bring out the polysemy of the novel and constitute it differently for different purposes.[32]

One gets a glimpse of the broadening out, if not the initial opening up, of such a pluralistic space in the republication of *One Person's War.* The fact that the Jiangsu Literary Publishing House took a serious interest in Lin's work has reframed the controversial novel as high art. Not only does the elite publication venue cast Lin's stylistic experiments in a positive light, but the novel also comes to assume the tactical position of a sophisticated text that invites attention and innovative interpretation from professional readers. Several years after the initial controversy caused by the novel, Xu Kun noted the proliferation of academic critics' interpretations of *One Person's War* in particular and women's individualized writing in general in terms of a broad variety of theoretical frameworks, including "postmodernism," "the narratology of the body," "female poetics," "realism," "writing at the margins," and, last but not least, "feminism."[33] These new academic interpretations and the novel's reappearance as part of the author's collected works are, one might argue, all part of the same positive trend and mutually reinforcing. Although its new guise does not deter the prurient and the commercially minded, the novel now readily lends itself to feminist criticism in mainland China and is commonly hailed as a radical example of women's writing or, simply, Chinese feminism.

I would argue, however, that, so far, professional critics operating in the third space within China have glossed over the lesbian content of the novel by treating it as an expression of feminine sensibility and feminist principles.[34] By contrast, it is private readers who have taken bold strides in other directions. Lin professed during her 1998 interview with me that she frequently received letters of admiration from "female homosexuals" (nü tongxinglianzhe) who claimed to see their own reflections in the psychological experiences that she fictionalizes. Taking these marginal readers' agency as an example, I argue that, if approached from a queer angle, One Person's War is unusual in having problematized homophobia instead of homosexuality. The novel refuses to naturalize heterosexual monogamy, which, as Harriet Evans documents, is "the single uniform sexuality" that the official discourse on sex of the Maoist era tried to produce and the hegemony of which has not been seriously disturbed even after the death of Mao.[35]

I demonstrate, moreover, that the third space is ineluctably complicated by transnational circulation; that is, the authorization of overseas editions and the extent of the Chinese diaspora have made it practically impossible to draw the geographic boundaries of the readership of a particular literary work in Chinese.[36] Highlighting as it does only one of the signifying possibilities of a text that circulates transnationally, my particular reading is diasporic in that I choose to hark back to the mainland Chinese context out of a sense of cultural affiliation.[37] But, at the same time, my reading strategy is precisely that which cannot happen at the level of public discourse in China. My interpretation carries with it an awareness of the predominant responses to the novel in China even as it tries to resist their domination and, ranging as far afield as possible, tap into and negotiate with Western terms of analysis. Such a diasporic reading draws its particular strength, obviously, not from the mainstream Chinese uses of One Person's War, but from the transnational exchange aligning certain marginal elements in the Chinese field of force relations with global theory.

Fundamentally, the liberty to explore Lin's narratives of female-female relations with a specific eye to queerness is by no means the monopoly of the Chinese diaspora, for even readers who live in China can find such a strong sense of alterity in themselves that they contest mainstream readings. The borders of the diaspora, like those of the homeland, are, thus, shifting and difficult to draw in terms of physical location alone. Rey Chow argues, "If, as William Safran writes, 'diasporic consciousness is an intellectualization of [the] existential condition' of dispersal from the homeland, then 'diasporic consciousness' is perhaps not so much a historical accident as it is an intellectual reality—the reality of being intellectual."[38] Indeed, a diasporic subject at home is Lin Bai herself—her depiction of dissident sexuality imparts such a powerful sense of alienation and alterity that it almost seems as though, by thinking critically, she had already sent herself into exile in her own country, at least in terms of her imaginary life.

### The Fictional Production of Memory

Prior to the initial publication of *One Person's War,* a certain critical momentum had already been building around other works by Lin Bai. However, it is only in hindsight, when her earlier short stories can be placed alongside her autobiographical novel, that we suddenly realize that she has been working on the same motifs over and over again: irreducible individual difference, unspeakable yearnings, the attempt to break out of isolation, fear, and despair. She draws homologous pictures of lesbian marginality that invite, first of all, an overview of her oeuvre.

Born in a small town in Guangxi Province of southwest China in 1958, Lin Bai attended college from 1978 to 1982. Primarily a poet when she was young, she dabbled in fiction on the side. The breakthrough in her literary development took place around 1987, when her short stories were first accepted by prestigious journals outside Guangxi such as *Renmin wenxue* (People's literature) and *Shanghai wenxue* (Shanghai literature). From then on she devoted her creative energy to fiction rather than poetry. In 1989, she won acclaim from innovative writers and critics such as Ye Zhaoyen and Zhu Wei for the story "Tong xin'aizhe buneng fenshou" (Unable to be separated from the beloved), in which the female protagonist forms an erotic bond with her dog. In 1990, Lin moved from Guangxi to Beijing, the capital of Chinese cultural production. After a two-year fallow period, she experienced a burst of creativity and, in 1993, produced in quick succession several major works that would establish her as one of the most important contemporary women writers in China: "Pingzhong zhi shui" (Water in a bottle) and "Huilang zhi yi" (The bench on the interior balcony) as well as *One Person's War.*

The publication of "Water in a Bottle" and "The Bench on the Interior Balcony" in the literary bimonthly *Zhongshan* (Bell mountain) in 1993 earned Lin a reputation as a woman daring to touch on female homoeroticism. The stories were accompanied by an essay by Chen Xiaoming, the well-known critic of Chinese avant-garde literature and postmodernism. Chen begins the essay by admiring the exoticism of Lin's personal aura and her audacity in probing forbidden subject matter. Slipping effortlessly from the issue of geographic marginality to women's marginality, he characterizes female desire as mysterious and peripheral and attributes Lin's mastery at representing that desire to her upbringing in the remote southwest. Particularly intriguing for Chen—in the same way in which a remote, forbidden country is intriguing—is desire between women. He uses the word *nüxing tongxinglian,* or "female homosexuality," when characterizing the essence of the female relationships in Lin's stories. His essay therefore constitutes one of the earliest instances in China of a critic announcing the presence of female homosexuality in contemporary women's literary writing.

For Chen, Lin's narratives reveal the private world of essential femininity, which resists socialization. A woman's desire as constructed by Lin is an enclosed world; it is narcissistic (*zilian*) and selectively accepting of other women but decidedly rejecting of men. Chen claims, "In some sense, homosexuality is nothing but narcissism extended and magnified." Specifically, in "The Bench on the Interior Balcony," Chen finds Lin mixing two incongruous narrative strands: a masculine discourse about revolution, conspiracy, and violent politics runs parallel to a sentimental, nostalgic tale about two women's love. Between the two there is little interaction: "The male story cannot penetrate the female one. . . . The nostalgia and refined elegance of the tale about women float like an enigma above the tale about men." [39] For Chen, Lin turns the writing of female desire into self-referential solipsism, a distancing from present reality that is both geographic and temporal. He complains that the story's challenge to male authority and sexual politics is limited because it confines itself to the margin and does not confront patriarchy.

Since Chen's essay appeared, Lin's name has become essentially synonymous with female homoerotic literature. Literary critics in China are bound to mention Lin (as well as Chen Ran, another female writer) when they identify examples of female homosexuality in contemporary Chinese fiction.[40] Similarly, the issue of desire between women is hardly ever absent from any discussion of Lin's works. In general, however, critical considerations of Lin rarely depart from the framework and tone set by Chen Xiaoming.

There is to date no systematic attempt in the mainstream critical establishment of China either to evaluate the sociological significance of contemporary writings of female homoerotic desire or to understand the unique historical, cultural, and stylistic issues that these writings raise. This neglect has stemmed in part from the virtual invisibility of lesbian subjects in the PRC, for, even in the recent sociological studies and popular journalistic accounts specifically investigating the existence of homosexuals in China, gay men take center stage.[41] Also contributing to the neglect is the disdain with which homosexuality is viewed in general. Most literary critics are reluctant to soil their reputations (and the reputations of the creative writers whom they study) by focusing on such a socially marginalized topic. Considered trivial, homosexuality affords little symbolic capital, and a critic's expending any sustained effort on the topic is likely only to diminish his or her status. This, in fact, is the interpretation of the novelist Chen Ran, with whom I discussed PRC literary critics' lack of sustained interest in female and male homoerotic literature.[42] The absence of queer theory in the otherwise globalizing field of literary theory in the PRC is singular and forms a stark contrast to the proliferation of queer theory and antihomophobic cultural studies in Taiwan.

To read the lesbian desire in Lin's works seriously, then, is to read against local hegemony. An analysis that seeks to show the nontriviality of lesbian matters automatically declares itself to be translocal and transnational practice. The exploration of queer sexualities is where transnational and diasporic interpretive tactics may critically supplement the broadening third space in China.

For readers accustomed to lesbigay and transgender identity politics in the West or even in Taiwan, the half-dozen female homoerotic works that Lin has produced thus far seem tame because they afford nothing as confrontational as lesbian defiance and empowerment. Even though some of her stories are shockingly violent, portraying women revenging girlfriends who have been sexually abused by men, such characters' actions usually have the attendant effect of being self-destructive.[43] Lin's unique contribution to the female homoerotic imaginary lies, I contend, elsewhere. The most interesting of her narratives are fables of origin that subtly denaturalize contemporary discrimination against homosexual women in the PRC by revealing that discrimination to be either a relatively recent phenomenon or a product of socialization. Her nostalgia for the past is shrouded in fantasy and marked by the melancholia of an irrecoverable loss, a melancholia that is particularly poignant as it reflects a genuine dilemma that traps anyone trying to fend off collective amnesia. That is, despite concerted attempts to remember, one will likely never know with certainty exactly how lesbian desire became a mode of abject sexuality in modern China. Did the stigma always exist in history? If so, what has changed between past and present to give it such force, and why?

Lin's best works evoke these questions about a gap in the collective memory of society. Similarly, they problematize personal history as well. In *One Person's War,* the desire of the narrator and protagonist, Lin Duomi, for others of her sex is spontaneous in youth but is gradually repressed as adulthood approaches. Duomi's recollections of her childhood experiences reveal that her fear of same-sex intimacy is the result of socialization (wherein lies the inherent critique of conformity with the prevailing sexual mores). Complicating things, however, are the fickleness of memory and the temptations of fictionalization. The act of remembering is, for Lin, embedded in the act of fictionalization. Separating the two proves to be impossible, and the uncertainty of historical truth only spurs her desire to discover the past by telling stories.

Representative of Lin's nostalgic return to an imaginary place in time prior to homophobia is her "The Bench on the Interior Balcony."[44] The story, narrated in the first person and in a fragmented manner, is about a mysterious incident in which a young woman was involved during her travels in southwest China a decade earlier. In 1982, right after the narrator graduates from college, she embarks alone on a sightseeing trip across the mountainous southwest and, one day during the rainy season, finds herself in the small town of Shuimo. As she wanders around in a cold, misty rain exploring the old houses and narrow streets at the heart of the town, she chances on a rundown, deserted mansion and an old woman who lives on the top floor, guarding it. On first encountering the narrator, the old woman praises her beautiful eyes and asks where she has come from. Inviting her into her room to sit down, the old woman—whose name is Qiye—tells the narrator that she once served the third mistress (i.e., the third wife in a polygamous household) of the house some forty years earlier. The narrator learns that the mansion used to belong to the wealthy Zhang family, that the master, Zhang Mengda, was targeted as an antirevolutionary element and executed by the Communists after the area was liberated, and that the third mistress, Zhu Liang, disappeared soon afterward. A picture of the beautiful Zhu Liang stands right next to Qiye's pillow, which makes the narrator think that an unusual relationship existed between mistress and maid. Qiye tells the narrator that her eyes remind her of Zhu Liang's, insisting that the two must be somehow connected. Her remarks make the narrator sense the approach, as if from afar, of something enigmatic and important, yet they also bewilder her and make her suspect some sort of trap. Feeling faint, the narrator accepts Qiye's invitation to lie down while the old woman burns dried herbs to ease the headache that has come on her. As the two women continue to talk, Qiye tells the narrator that no one knows what happened to Zhu Liang. However, the narrator intuits that Qiye, who was in her teens at the time, does in fact know. Eventually realizing that she has been stricken with a bad case of the flu, the narrator leaves the mansion and takes a room in a small hostel across the street. While she nurses her illness, her mind is occupied by the story of Qiye and Zhu Liang. In a fever-induced delirium, she is vaguely aware that Qiye drops in once to check on her. She dreams that night in her fevered sleep of finding the mummified body of a woman in a secret chamber in the mansion. Awakening terrified, she hitches a ride and flees the town first thing the next morning.

In a recent essay, Chen Sihe discusses Lin's stylized treatment of homo-eroticism in "The Bench on the Interior Balcony." He argues that Lin's subject matter is admittedly "profane" (*weixie*) and "puzzling" (*kunhuo*). However, it is "purified" (*jinghua*) and redeemed by the beauty of her language and also by the radical awakening of "female consciousness" (*nüxing yishi*) represented in the text. He cites a crucial passage describing how Zhu Liang makes the teenage Qiye massage her all over while giving her a steamy bath every evening, observing,

> This decadent [*tuifei*] description embodies the aesthetics of the "beauteous poison" [*meili de duyao*]. The setting sun, the naked woman, and the undeveloped young girl constitute a picture impregnated with meaning. The sun shines on the body of the naked woman as if the last rays of masculine power were hovering over it. However, the sun is setting, and its light gradually dims on the naked woman. Meanwhile, darkness approaches. The darker it gets, the more delighted the two women become, for darkness is their home. In the dark, they grope for their own ways of pleasuring each other's skin and flesh. The two women satisfy each other's feminine urges for sex and life. The story sets up the old mansion as the border separating outside/inside, that is, two opposite worlds. The former is masculine, political, and teeming with conflict and murder, while the latter is feminine, sensual, and pregnant with the essence of solitude and beauty.[45]

Despite Chen's professed intention of affirming the beauty and feminist self-assurance in Lin's depiction of female homoeroticism, he reinscribes a gendered hierarchy with the tropes of light and dark and employs a heteronormative vocabulary that repeatedly presupposes homoeroticism to be an illegitimate other—profane, filthy, poisonous, and decadent. In his analysis, the secret world of female-female desire is the last haven in the face of the turmoil of revolution. This opinion reaffirms Chen Xiaoming's judgment that Lin depicts the desire between women as a self-contained and self-isolating women's community.[46] But what does it mean? Are women in Lin's story indeed free to disidentify with the nation and to absent themselves from politics? Can women create bonds strong enough to resist the encroachment of male authority and state power?

In fact, in Lin's text, the attraction between women is strong, and they show each other great tenderness, but the bonds between them are subject to devastation by outside forces. The gorgeous mansion that Zhu Liang and her maid inhabited proves no safe haven after all. It is invaded, Zhu Liang's husband seized and executed, and his possessions plundered and divided among the mob, she herself barely escaping the degradation of rape, and Qiye left with nothing to remember her by but a photograph and some bedding that she once used. Years later, it is with the ephemeral power of personal memory that, in guarding the deserted mansion (which had once been used as government office space), Qiye is keeping her mistress alive. When the narrator stumbles on her and discovers the hidden love affair lost to the passage of time, she is stunned. She senses the summoning power (*zhaohuan*) of Zhu Liang and Qiye, yet she resists their call as witchcraft (*gu*).

Neither Chen Xiaoming nor Chen Sihe is willing to acknowledge the gravity of society's interference in women's relationships or to confront the presence of homophobia, despite the fact that one of the most striking features about Lin's text is that it interlocks homoerotic desire with social regulation and internalized fear. The story is not so much about the love between Zhu Liang and Qiye forty years earlier as it is about the female narrator's reaction to it. Consider, for example, how Lin's text lingers over the motif of a lonely, wandering traveler. The narrator comes on an empty mansion. She is filled with anxiety and fear, but, propelled by a mysterious curiosity, she persists in exploring the structure until she is terrified to find an empty tea cup on a bench on the interior balcony and a room with the door standing open. In the dark, lonely room, she finds an old woman and the photograph of a beautiful young woman.

Highlighted in this process is the unexpected yet fated encounter between three—not two—women: the narrator, Qiye, and Zhu Liang. Same-sex attraction is prominently foregrounded as Lin disregards the chronological order in the diegetic world and has the narrator start her narration with the following encounter:

> I once saw a photograph of Zhu Liang in her youth. It was a black and white picture of a woman sitting, showing her whole figure. The contrast between light and dark and the depth of perspective were great. The woman wore a *qipao* dress with high slits that reached her thighs, which was popular in Shanghai in the 1940s. Her waist was tiny and her face gloriously beautiful. Her beauty beamed like an eternal light, which enveloped her youthful form from head to heel. She sat in her photograph and gazed at me through half a century. Her looks dazzled me.[47]

After establishing that her gaze met that of Zhu Liang, the narrator returns to her earlier encounter with Qiye, Zhu Liang's personal maid, and routes her own desire through an observation of Qiye: "When Qiye told me that Zhu Liang had ceased to be a long time ago, her voice was full of nostalgia and affection. She sounded like an old man reminiscing about a love deeply inscribed in his heart, which was so beautiful and yet so tragic, unforgettable even after death" (199).

At the same time as the narrator perceives Qiye's abiding love for Zhu Liang, she complains of becoming confused and dizzy, as if hit by a heavy object. Later on, she maintains, "If Qiye had been a dirty old man, seeing a woman's picture next to his pillow would certainly not have terrified me. For any man, regardless of his age, identity, and status, to miss any woman, regardless of her age, identity, and status—their relationship can always be grasped in terms of a beautiful love affair" (215). Zhu Liang and Qiye might have been free to love each other before the Revolution, but the narrator, a daughter of the Revolution, finds their relationship shocking and slightly repulsive. A nameless fear of same-sex intimacy controls her. In college, she was shy about revealing her body to other women in her dormitory's public showers. She is now struck by the contrast between her own timidity and Zhu Liang's boldness in baring herself in front of Qiye. She cannot but fantasize that part of Zhu Liang's enjoyment as Qiye massages her moist, naked body came from the excitement of overcoming a similar fear.

Although the narrator constantly compares herself to and distinguishes herself from these two women of an older generation, there is no indication in the text that the narrator is, in fact, reliable.[48] It is perfectly possible that the stories buried in the deserted mansion are nothing but the narrator's fantasies. The vision of Qiye massaging her mistress in her bath exhilarates the narrator, but it also terrifies her and makes her ill. The narrator's journey is an inward one, and her unexpected discoveries are of her inner desires and fears.

Seen in this light, details in the narrative that reveal an uncanny resemblance between the narrator and Zhu Liang take on special significance. Indeed, Zhu Liang is the narrator's mental projection and mirror image. Their eyes look alike, and they both come, we eventually learn, from Bobai County. The narrator also describes how, during one of her conversations with Qiye, she is suddenly seized with the fear that Qiye will urge her to take off her drenched clothes and put on something of Zhu Liang's. Despite her fear of being identified with Zhu Liang, the narrator accepts when Qiye offers her bed to her and lies down. Qiye burns incense to relieve the narrator's headache, just as she would perfume the room for Zhu Liang. As the narrator's nerves are calmed, her mind begins to roam about the mansion as if it were a familiar haunt to her, as if she, the narrator, were none other that Zhu Liang. She begins to travel, if you will, through both space and time, visualizing events from the past as if witnessing them. The extreme familiarity and felicity with which the narrator reconstructs scenes of Zhu Liang's life on this occasion blur all distinctions between three temporalities: the last days of Zhu Liang; the narrator's visit to Shuimo in 1982; and the moment when the narration is supposedly taking place, some ten years later. The merging of temporalities reinforces the suggestion that Zhu Liang is a figment of the narrator's imagination—her hidden self—even as the narrator ostensibly resists this possibility.

Under the sway of her vision of Zhu Liang's love affair and her mysterious end, the narrator eventually meets Zhu Liang herself. In her fever, the narrator wanders into the back garden of the Zhang mansion, looking in vain for Qiye. Pushing open a door hidden behind a huge water vat, she finds herself in a narrow, secret passage. Wafting from the depths of the passage is the smell of Qiye's incense. She gropes forward. Her muscles tense up, and her palms start to sweat. She is about to see something. She recounts,

> I seemed to see a woman sitting ahead of me. I cried out Qiye's name, but nobody responded. The woman did not move, as if she had not heard me. I forced myself to walk up to her. The woman's head was lowered, so I couldn't see her face. All I could see was that she was wearing an

old-fashioned *qipao* dress, which reminded me of the picture next to Qiye's pillow. I thought to myself, This must be Zhu Liang. I called to her softly, but still she did not pick up her head. I reached out my hand and forced myself to touch her. An icy cold and hard sensation pierced my fingertip. I turned around and ran in fright. In my haste, I stumbled into a switch; thereupon the mummy (or mannequin?) straightened its stiff neck and emitted a sound resembling a woman's sigh. (233)

Frightened out of her wits, the narrator wakes up in her hostel to find that it was just a nightmare. She feels fortunate, but she decides to leave immediately the next morning. She reasons, "I felt that, if I stayed any longer, I would definitely become controlled by some witchcraft [*zhong gu*]. The wrinkled face of Qiye, the mummy of Zhu Liang in my dream, and the beautiful figure in the black and white photograph—all these things were bending toward me like cool leaves in the air, carrying the odor and filaments of deceased time, and weaving a space that I could tell neither true nor false. The space was becoming more and more real, making it difficult for me to escape" (233).

Phantasm or not, the beautiful Zhu Liang and everything that she represents beckon to the narrator, who finds the solicitation overpowering. She is attracted, yet that attraction only makes her want to flee. Although she successfully conveys that she has experienced great fear, she is never able to articulate what it is she fears and why it is that she must escape the very thing that she finds so compelling. The narrative hints only that the 1949 Revolution is an important marker of change. Zhu Liang's world exists no longer.

At this point, it would be reasonable for us to wonder about the validity of Lin's imaginative speculations. Would such intimacy between women have developed unhindered in a traditional Chinese household? Would it perhaps even have been expected? Can it be that, as the story implies, such intimacy was the result of the limited social opportunities available to women in "feudal society," their lack of political power, and their general isolation from men? And can it be that the new society ushered in by the Communists was meant to do away with this aspect of women's lives?

Here, two reading strategies suggest themselves. The first is to dismiss Lin's choice of the presocialist setting as a random and gratuitous one—it means nothing more than the allegorization of another era in order to represent something that cannot be represented explicitly in a present-day context and can be exchanged with any other remote setting. The second is to give some careful thought to the *specificity* of the choice of the

presocialist era. I argue that Lin's evocation of same-sex intimacy in pre-
revolutionary times and the shattering of that intimacy around 1949 appears, on examination, to be more than a matter of whimsical projection.
Early in the twentieth century, the sociologist Pan Guangdan conjectured
that Chinese women in traditional households commonly had bosom
friends in the females' quarters, which were secluded from the outside
world, and that the relationships were in essence similar to homosexual
love as described by modern Western sexologists such as Havelock Ellis.[49]
Lin is making a similar speculation. The paradoxical combination of wom-
en's confinement and a private emotional world shared only by women is
packed into a relationship between mistress and maid in an old-fashioned
polygamous household in the presocialist era. What appeals to Lin, in
particular, is the class privilege traditionally enjoyed by certain women.

As Lin would have it, elite socioeconomic status licenses and facilitates a woman's pursuit of same-sex pleasures—Zhu Liang has the un-
encumbered and wondrous freedom to procure a maid suiting her fancy,
demand that that maid render erotic services, and in general explore
same-sex desire at her leisure. Although before the Communist takeover
many coastal Chinese cities had been experiencing Westernization for
almost a century, resulting in a modernity that some deem colonial, the
modernizing process was in essence an uneven geographic development.
It is not surprising, therefore, that Lin appropriates orthodox Communist
historiography and casts a provincial town in the Republican hinterland
(the fictionalized Shuimo) as more feudal than modern. While readers
may find the "liberty" accorded the women in this fictionalized feudal
world questionable and hardly to be envied, Lin's imagining of the Revolution is nonetheless critical of the violent disruption of private female-
female bonds. With the decree of the new Marriage Law of 1950, the Chinese Communist Party upheld "free-choice monogamy" as the key to
destroying feudal patriarchy.[50] Heterosexual monogamy thus became the
only legitimate context for sexual activity, and all other forms of sexually
intimate relations (such as premarital, extramarital, or same-sex sexual activities) were relegated to an unspeakable illicit netherworld and erased
from the public imaginary. Lin's artistic reconstruction of the past expresses an inexplicable longing for a time when the circulation of desire
in a household could be much more polymorphous than rigidly codified
heterosexual monogamy.

Class hierarchy notwithstanding, the maid, Qiye, is much more than
a passive object. She reciprocates her mistress's desire and continues to
yearn for her many years after her death. Mutual attraction is possible

even in a relationship structured by unequal power. Or so Lin Bai would like us to believe. What she actually succeeds in demonstrating, however, is that present-day prejudice unavoidably colors one's perception of the past—her narrator cannot help but project her own fear of same-sex intimacy onto Zhu Liang even as she fetishizes her dazzling and nonchalant gaze as the emblem of one woman's courage to demand and enjoy the caress of another.

### One Person's War

Besides envisioning an originary moment at which the private world of female-female bonds was intruded on and shattered by the power of the Communist state over citizens' bodies, Lin explores the devastation of an individual's natural ability to enjoy same-sex intimacy. An escape from the beautiful and seductive figures prominently in "The Bench on the Interior Balcony." It is further elaborated in *One Person's War,* finished a few months later. In both works, Lin represents the fear of same-sex intimacy in the form of abjection—the forced "expulsion" of elements from the self in order to establish the boundaries of the body.[51] Lin traces the process whereby socialization fetters a woman's desire for other women and turns a spontaneous chemistry into the unclean. This is where her text upsets moralistic expectations, which take the obscenity of homoerotic desire as a given. Even though Chinese critics have so far either overlooked this issue or avoided calling homophobia into question, Lin's insight into the internal contradictions of lesbian self-hatred is ambiguous enough to allow for a serious discussion of same-sex attraction and discrimination against those so oriented. In fact, Lin's essentialist claims about her protagonist's homosexual nature may even be considered an example of the "reverse discourse" described by Foucault, in which "homosexuality [begins] to speak in its own behalf, to demand that its legitimacy and 'naturality' be acknowledged, often in the same vocabulary, using the same categories by which it was medically disqualified."[52]

*One Person's War,* the story of the life of Lin Duomi, is told as a first-person memoir.[53] It opens with a little girl gazing at and pleasuring herself in front of a mirror. The image is echoed at the end of the novel, this time with a grown woman watching and penetrating herself. The little girl has matured and experienced adventure, love, and marriage. However, unable to find affection and trust in her male lovers, and equally unable to find a passage leading her back to the primordial women's paradise of her fantasies, she becomes her own lover once more.

It is not difficult to see why this novel caused a scandal in 1995. Praised by Dai Jinhua as representative of the awakening of female consciousness in China in the 1990s,[54] it provoked a certain amount of anxiety on the part of men about women's revolt and autonomous sexuality and the blockage of men's sexual access to women. As discussed earlier, during the debate that broke out in *Zhonghua dushu bao,* attacks were launched by an amateur writer, Ding Laixian, who was offended by Lin's depiction of female autoeroticism. Equating a woman's personal and social struggles with hostility toward men, Ding urged women to obey "the complementary law of the gentle, subservient yin and the active, dominant yang." Ding warned that women writers and critics had better stop advocating women's "pursuit of weird sensations by themselves" and claimed that *female consciousness* ought to mean women's realization of the importance of their predestined roles as the loving mothers of mankind.[55]

Such a grievous misreading throws into sharp relief what is most threatening about Lin's work from a conservative, patriarchal point of view—a woman's autonomous sexuality, which is interpreted as a direct attack on men. The voice of patriarchy blames Duomi for withdrawing from men, completely overlooking the fact that she has been hurt many times by them—and by one man in particular, a cold man, one incapable of reciprocating her passionate and abject love. The origin of autoeroticism in Duomi's life is, thus, twofold. The act of masturbation, discovered instinctually as a child, is first and foremost autonomous and spontaneous. By the end of the novel, however, it is also socially reinforced, a response to disillusionment.

Far from the crude assumption that the *one person's war* of the title is simply Duomi's declaration of war against men, her personal declaration of independence, as it were, the words allude to many different battles, including one against the self. As the epigraph to the novel, Lin quotes her 1989 short story "Tong xin'aizhe buneng fenshou" (Unable to be separated from the beloved): "The war of one person means that one slaps oneself with the hand. One blocks oneself like a wall. One destroys oneself like a flower. In the war of one person, a woman marries herself."[56] The war is waged by Duomi, not only against a society dominated by men, but also against herself. Duomi confesses that she has had a strange impulse to subordinate herself to men and to let them objectify her, all because she has known nothing but complete freedom since having lost her father at age three. But hidden deep in her unconscious is a fear of such freedom, a need of boundaries, a need to obey—and a longing to be protected by a man. Only after she has experienced humiliation and debasement at the hands of a series of selfish and unloving men does she realize the worth to a woman of freedom and self-reliance.

The originality of the statement that Lin makes in *One Person's War* is twofold. First, Duomi's insight into her own weakness exposes the issue of gender subordination as much more complicated than it seems to be at first glance. In order to love herself fully, Duomi must overcome her own masochism. Second, the image of *one person's war* perfectly describes Duomi's self-defeating relationships with women. Throughout her memoir, Duomi's wholehearted, passionate admiration for beautiful women far outweighs her attraction to men. However, she blocks her own approach to women like a wall and crushes her own same-sex desire like a flower. As a result, she finds herself in the end alone.

Early in the memoir, Duomi asks herself whether women, instead of men, are her real love interest. She tries to recall exactly what she feels when confronted with the bodies of beautiful women. She reminisces that, as a little girl, she worshiped a dancer named Yao Qiong, who specialized in the model ballet role of the White-Haired Girl in *Baimaonü* (The white-haired girl). Once, when Duomi followed her backstage, the dancer let her hold her clothes while she changed. Duomi describes the moment of physical proximity as one of utmost excitement and fright: "A girl who had no inner strength stood in front of the naked body of Yao Qiong, her eyes averted, avoiding temptation. She always evaded. Evasion was the miraculous exit whenever she faced temptations" (36). Not even the austere revolutionary content of *The White-Haired Girl* can deter the precocious Duomi from sensing the erotic pull of the dancer. Meng Yue has pointed out that, when the feature film *The White-Haired Girl* was adapted for presentation as a model ballet during the Cultural Revolution, the title character was stripped of the few feminine, sexual attributes that she possessed, becoming the ultimate symbol of class oppression.[57] Here, in Duomi's reminiscence, the process is reversed; the ideological trappings are stripped away and the erotic female body revealed. And, here, too, Duomi's professed timidity is undermined. At least, she is not afraid to face desire experienced in the past, a time characterized by the suppression of sexual expression by the state.

Elsewhere, Duomi recalls a young woman named Nandan who fell in love with her when she, Duomi, was twenty-seven. Although in the end she rejected Nandan, Duomi is perfectly aware that the incident revealed something important to her. She comments, "Nandan returned me to my original state. This was what she meant to me. She cleared a path and led me back to the past. She soaked me in an absolving bath" (48). One memory that Nandan revived—as if clearing away accumulated dirt—was a game that Duomi had played at age six with another little girl in the neighborhood—pretending to deliver babies. The girls would pull down their pants and take turns applying cotton balls and cotton swabs to each other's private parts. While Duomi experienced pleasant sensations from their activities, her friend Lili did not seem to feel or understand anything. And, anyway, Lili soon moved away with her parents, which put an end to their games. As she grew older, Duomi learned to be ashamed of what she had done. She wanted to forget the incident and so repressed all memory of it. Nandan's passionate pursuit caused the memory to resurface. It put Duomi in touch with herself once again, but it also awakened deep-seated anxiety in her.

Duomi says, "I was terribly frightened that I might be a congenital homosexual [*tiansheng de tongxinglianzhe*]. My worry was a chronic disease. Like a heavy, dark curtain, it set me apart from the normal crowd for good" (55). A subtle distinction is drawn here. As Duomi puts it, it is not her desire for other women that separates her from the crowd but rather her anxiety about that desire. Had society not perceived homosexuality as shameful, she might not have developed such a strong sense of categorical difference from others.

Unable to overcome her fear of being labeled a homosexual, yet naturally attracted to and attracting other women, Duomi suffers from internal conflicts. This pitiable state of self-contradiction, that is, the internal war that she is conducting against her own true nature, is one of the wars to which the novel's title alludes. Her self-denial is well illustrated by the outcome of her relationship with Nandan. A passionate letter from Nandan scared her and precipitated their separation. As Duomi describes it,

Nandan's letter was full of fervent praise for love between people of the same sex [*tongxing zhi ai*]. Her words danced in front of me as if they were grotesque flames. Like invisible eyes with piercing light, they also looked right through me and saw inside my heart. I did not read her letter twice. I put it in my pocket as if hiding a secret. During the break at work I sneaked back to my dormitory. There was only one thought in my head: destroy the letter right away. Her words were like demons coming from somewhere unknown, which nevertheless corresponded to the natural enemies in my head. My only thought was to kill them.

The relationship between Nandan and me ended at that instant. Now, at this moment, as I wrote down that sentence, I saw pieces of gray ash flying in front of my eyes like butterflies. They were the remains of the letter. (They were once full of a young woman's juice of life and solid affection.) Their fragile gray faces touched me, and I could feel their tiny particles, like powder. Meanwhile, I heard the sound of a heart breaking in the distance, coming through the cracks between the doors of the past. It made me contemplate for a long while. (56–57)

In a nostalgic and remorseful voice, Duomi confesses that, because of her attempt to escape, Nandan accused her of lacking inner strength, that is, the courage to face her own inner reality. Gradually, they drifted apart. Duomi's recollection of their ill-fated love affair ends in her speculation about Nandan's whereabouts. She says, "Nandan once said to me she would definitely go to the United States in the future, for only there could she find the life that she wanted. . . . She must be in the United States" (57). In an oblique way, Duomi comments on the social discrimination against homosexuals in China. She knows perfectly well that the association of homosexuality with shame is not universal and that, in the United States, people like Nandan have won the right to lead a lesbian lifestyle. Yet her realization does not help her. Duomi is too much of a coward to disregard social opinion where she is.

## Conclusion

At the juncture of censure and mass voyeurism, *One Person's War* manages to provide a complex view of homophobia in the sense of internalized social discrimination. Before Duomi has learned the ways and categories of the world, she is unaware that there is anything wrong with the way in which she and Lili play together. As she grows up, she learns to be afraid of her own attraction to other women as something abnormal, filthy, and shameful. Even though Lin Bai does not explicitly advocate homosexual rights in China, her protagonist's suppression of homoerotic desire at the expense of her own happiness provides a preparatory platform from which to launch a more direct and confrontational critique of a dehumanizing society. Admittedly, Duomi's reconstruction of her own originary but repressed homoerotic desire has an exceedingly essentialist strain, but the essentialism might be understood as a tactic to challenge the prevalent and recalcitrant modern medical stereotypes in China that classify homosexuality as an aberration of nature, a perversion, a mental disorder.[58] The essentialism nestled in *One Person's War* is, in other words, an example of the "necessary fiction" that operates as a reverse discourse to legitimate homosexuality as natural.[59]

Characteristic of Lin's style are the recurring strategies to represent lesbian eros through displacement and to construct the lesbian identity through explicit negation. By displacing homoerotic desire into feverish dreams and children's games, Lin minimizes the severity of her breaching of sexual taboos and maximizes the representability of female homoeroticism in the present heterosexual regime of the PRC. Furthermore, by making her protagonist, Duomi, explicitly articulate her chronic fear that she "might be a congenital homosexual," Lin establishes the salience of that identity through the persistence of fear. There would not have been the need for repeated negation if there were not an obdurate homosexual nature, which, paradoxically, is precisely an effect produced by the repetition of negation. In a way, Lin illustrates how citationality might work apart from the conforming citation of a productive law, which Judith Butler argues is crucial to the coalescing of gender identity.[60] Duomi's repeated citation of a declaration of identity and its negation congeals into a performative homosexual identity, albeit a self-restraining one. More radically, Duomi's discomfort with identity may imply that Lin Bai's objective has never been simply to define a category, whether *the homosexual* or *homosexuality*. "I rely on my instinct to write," she emphasized during my interview with her.[61] The unfolding of half a lifetime through an extended and undulating narrative, in an imagistic diction rich with light, sound, odors, taste, and touch, is more humane and comes closer to her being than do taxonomic classifications. Her goal as an artist is not to collapse experiential plenitude into one identity category—and certainly not into identity politics. It would be unfair for readers outside China to disregard the social circumstances in which Lin writes and to blame her protagonists for succumbing to homophobia, not to mention chiding her for her seeming apoliticism. There are, after all, limits to the efficacy of global theory when it negotiates with local specificity.

# GENDER-TRANSCENDENT
# CONSCIOUSNESS AND *PRIVATE LIFE*

As we have seen, in China in the 1990s, not only have innovative fictional representations of female homoeroticism by women writers appeared, but so has a broadening social realm in which pluralistic (including feminist) interpretive practices are possible. To highlight the fact that such pluralism disrupts the hold of traditional morality and a voyeuristic consumer economy, I have described that broadening social realm as *the third space.* Even though to date most literary critical and cultural studies analyses produced in mainland China are generally feminist rather than specifically queer, I have attempted to demonstrate the lesbian signifying possibilities of Lin Bai's writing as it circulates transnationally and is encountered by the diasporic reader. And I have been anticipated to a certain extent by those nonprofessional readers of Lin's fiction whose specifically lesbian readings contest mainstream interpretations from the margins.[1] But the People's Republic of China (PRC) may now have reached a critical moment at which specifically queer analyses can enter elite and academic discourse, further broadening the third space.[2] To examine this possibility,

I turn in this chapter to the creative and theoretical work of Chen Ran. My approach to Chen Ran is not unlike my approach to Lin Bai.

Chen Ran is the central and most-discussed figure in the recent critical debate in China over "female writing" (*nüxing xiezuo*) and "individualized writing" (*gerenhua xiezuo*).[3] Her daring representation of female sexuality, including female-female love relationships, has frequently invited comparison with Lin Bai. And, as have Lin's, Chen's fictional works have both encountered moralist censure and been appropriated by the growing consumer culture. Even though the government has never banned her books, a thinly veiled moralism pervades the literary critical approach to her work. Critics writing in academic journals have accused her of *zilian* (narcissism) and *zibi* (narrowness, solipsism), that is, focusing too narrowly on the self and disregarding broader social issues. And her *Siren shenghuo* (Private life) has been written off as mere exhibitionism (i.e., the willing exposure of privacy)—as has Lin's *Yige ren de zhanzheng* (One person's war). Although a growing number of critics—mostly feminists—praise Chen as a significant writer, detailed textual analyses are surprisingly few.[4] I believe that Chen's works deserve a much closer reading than they are customarily given in academic journals in the PRC.[5] Her powerful imagination and honest philosophical inquiry challenge conventional wisdom about gender and sexuality and the current consumerist construction of desire. Among other achievements, she signifies female-female love anew.

Born in 1962, Chen is one of the most intriguing experimental writers of the post-Mao era. Her cryptic style ensured that her early works were marginalized in the literary marketplace as avant-garde. Such marginalization may, ironically, have helped her largely escape censorship subsequently. Her avant-garde artistic reputation may also have protected her, the official guidelines being far from clear-cut—banning "concrete descriptions of homosexual behavior and other perverse sexual behavior" as obscene but explicitly exempting "works of literary and artistic merit that contain some elements of obscene and pornographic content"[6]—and censors' reactions, therefore, unpredictable. Indeed, some of Chen's writing contains erotic elements just as unconventional as those in Lin Bai's *One Person's War,* yet her works are rarely barred from publication. The reason why Chen has escaped censorship may be precisely the difference between the two authors' representational styles. While Lin's vivid depictions of female autoeroticism and homoerotic relationships and of unfortunate encounters between men and women seem true to life and therefore provoke a response from the censors, Chen's enigmatic plots and highly eccentric language seem too divorced from reality to be either graphic sexual description or pointed social criticism. In fact, Chen's work is so far removed from classical realism, which purports to delineate action and events objectively, that Zhou Ke has proposed the term *xinli xianshi zhuyi xiaoshuo* (fiction of psychological realism) to describe it.[7]

The obscurity and extreme stylization of Chen's texts facilitate a wide variety of interpretations, including the possibility that some engage in a coded discussion about lesbian desire and the frustration by society of its free expression in China today. Even though Chen has insisted that the richness of her style as well as the philosophical complexity of her ideas defy interpretation, she freely admits that one of the dimensions of her writing is the exploration of women's same-sex relationships. In fact, in her writing, both fiction and nonfiction, she adamantly defends the rights of all minorities, of the individual, not just women, against the oppression of the majority. And, in real life, Chen candidly sympathizes with a group of lesbian-identified young women in Beijing who run a non-profit telephone hot line that handles questions about sexual orientation and who started the underground lesbian newsletter *Tiankong* (Sky) in March 1999.[8]

### Gender-Transcendent Consciousness

In a 1998 interview with me, Chen Ran stated:

> For a long time I've been concerned about the question of homosexuality. No matter what my own sexual orientation is, I feel it is my responsibility to form an independent opinion on this issue and to contribute to human freedom and rights in this regard. I am embarrassed to say that so far I have done almost nothing because, in this country, mainstream opinions and judgments put one under intolerable pressure. If I speak loudly in public for the rights of the homosexual population—as feminists in other countries do—it will instantly become a major incident in the literary circle here and even entangle me unknowingly in some "politics." I do not like to be involved in this manner. Exploring homosexuality as a question of humanity through literature is the mild way, which I prefer.[9]

Much as Chen denies having made any public statement in support of homosexual rights, among her published work are a theoretical essay on surpassing heterosexuality that came out in 1994 and quite a few fictional works exploring intense friendship and attraction between women, including the short stories "Kungxinren dansheng" (The birth of a hollow man; 1990), "Wuchu gaobie" (Nowhere to say good-bye; 1991), "Qianxing yishi" (A hidden matter; 1992), "Maisuinü yu shouguaren" (The wheat woman and the widow; 1993), "Ji'e de koudai" (A hungry pocket; 1993), "Ling yizhi erduo de qiaoji sheng" (The sound of another ear knocking; 1994), and "Pokai" (Breaking through; 1995) and the novel *Siren shenghuo* (Private life; 1996). It is no exaggeration to say that, among writers in the PRC, Chen most persistently and creatively explores issues related to lesbianism.

A talk sensationally entitled "Chaoxingbie yishi yu wode chuangzuo" (Gender-transcendent consciousness and my creative writing) given at universities in England in 1994 (and later published) alerted critics to Chen's affirmation of same-sex love (*tongxing zhi ai*). But her definition of *gender-transcendent consciousness* (*chaoxingbie yishi*) in fact straddles two distinct notions. One is the notion of *transcending gender*, which refers specifically to the ability to choose a partner of one's own biological sex instead of being limited by the social imperative to procreate and, hence, to choose a partner of the opposite sex. The other is the notion of a radical indifference to anatomical sex and social gender that downplays sex/gender altogether.[10] When Chen does foreground the significance of sex/gender, she theorizes about major gender differences between men and women under the present Chinese social, economic, and political structures, all dominated by men. According to her, because of their hegemonic roles in Chinese society, men are trained to be aggressive, cruel, and dishonest. By contrast, women are trained to be much more genuine and sincere. "I believe that, because of the difference in psychological structure and ambitions, it is extremely difficult for men and women in this world to have real communication and to reach mutual understanding," she declares.[11] She thus proclaims that, in present-day China, some women (and some men) have no choice but to seek romantic comfort from members of their own sex. Furthermore, she idealizes same-sex love (*tongxing zhi ai*), considering it to be closer to pure art than heterosexuality (*yixinglian*) is. Heterosexuality has, Chen feels, held sway in the world, and especially in China, for thousands of years because of people's essential utilitarianism. It is reproduction, not real spiritual communication between the sexes, that has made heterosexuality the social norm.

In spite of her pessimism about ever finding "a noble and fatal [i.e., all-consuming] love" between the sexes,[12] Chen does not entirely idealize same-sex relationships. In fact, elsewhere she laments, "Between women—even the most extraordinary intellectual women—building a deep and lasting friendship is the most difficult thing in the world. I once had sincere and even sentimental friendships with other women, but the relationships all fell apart before long. The problem is the fine line between mutual admiration and jealousy. This line in the female sex is constantly sliding back and forth, especially among those in the same profession. Therefore, friendship is difficult to maintain."[13] That Chen frankly admits that she is writing about her own experience is impressive. And her observation rings true: in some women's relationships like-mindedness and mutual attraction coexist with competitiveness.

Tellingly, in Chen's fictional world homosexual desire does not rule out heterosexual desire. Typically, her female protagonists attract both men and women and may be seeking a deep, fulfilling connection with lovers of either sex, and the difficulties of love are present in both kinds of relationships. Rather than glorify a homosexual orientation, which prescribes the biological sex of one's object choice, Chen is more comfortable positing a romantic consciousness that does not hold sex/gender to be the primary concern. She proclaims:

My female protagonist [in "Wuchu gaobie" (Nowhere to say good-bye)] has realized that love and lovemaking are two related but different things. Love is much higher than sex. It encompasses the soul, mind, and body. It is love, not sex, that people have an insatiable longing for. Only love can truly excite the body and mind of a modern woman.

Where does love come from, then? It can certainly happen between the opposite sexes, and it is also possible between people of the same sex. This is understandable—sometimes it is easier for people of the same sex to form an understanding and an affinity. The bond is natural and effortless, like water understanding fish or the air comprehending human beings. Of course, not all people of the same sex can communicate well.

I believe that real love surpasses gender the same way that real literature and art are independent of politics. They are not utilitarian. They are pure art and offer no practical benefits.

As love sets itself further and further apart from the primitive purpose of procreation, and as love distances itself from relationships of economic dependence, and when love can finally become as pure as art and is no longer mixed with any purpose other than itself, . . . the hegemony of heterosexuality will collapse. A consciousness transcending gender will arise from its ashes.[14]

In the space of a few sentences, Chen oscillates between a preference for homosexual love and what might be called a *bisexual sensibility* as she theorizes about a yearning for love that cannot be reduced to the selection of sex/gender. The tension between homosexual identity politics and fluid romantic longing is further played out in her short stories. Lesbianism is sometimes idealized in her fiction as preferable to heterosexuality since the former avoids exposure to the crassness and insensitivity of men, but she does not always make such a schematic distinction. Most of the female protagonists in her urban stories are bisexual, meaning that they can be interested in both men and women, whether simultaneously or sequentially, and that they can also be disappointed by relationships with either sex. Even an extreme case—for example, "Kungxinren dansheng" (The birth of a hollow man), which describes the satisfying romantic bond between two women in a small village in contrast to the horrid, abusive marriage in which one of the women is trapped—subtly undermines the rigid boundaries of (biological) sexual difference. The love relationship between the female characters is observed through the eyes of the son of the unhappily married woman. Despite his biological sex, the little boy is enchanted by the warmth and beauty of feminine bonds and comes to identify strongly with his mother and her female friend. At the end of the story, he becomes a "hollow man" in that part of him dies together with his mother, who commits suicide because of an unwanted pregnancy that results after she has been humiliatingly raped by her husband. What Chen envisions as love is, in short, inseparable attachment and unselfish caring. As such, love occurs primarily between two women. However, a young boy can also be allowed to participate (playing, of course, a nonsexual role in the relationship).

Chen's impulse to define love as something independent of biological sex is at odds with her equally strong desire to essentialize lesbianism as superior love. The uneasy tension between bisexual openness and lesbian identification is reminiscent of some of the anxieties that bisexuality has aroused in lesbian communities. A large percentage of Paula Rust's lesbian subjects (all from the United States), for example, are either critical of or ambivalent about bisexuality.[15] Similar attitudes are found among lesbians in transnational China. For example, in their magazines Taiwanese lesbians have discussed at length their love-hate relationship with bisexual women.[16] *Tiankong* (Sky), the underground lesbian community newsletter in Beijing, also published members' contradictory opinions (affirming as well as hostile ones) of bisexuals.[17] Even at a theoretical level, major disagreements still exist among American social scientists' approaches to bisexuality. While some theorists conceptualize bisexuality as a combination of homosexuality and heterosexuality, that is, as an appetite for both masculinity and femininity, others understand bisexuality as a blindness to biological sex. Rust reports, for example, that some researchers have conceptualized bisexuals as "individuals for whom biological sex is a comparatively minor consideration in choosing sexual partners, in contrast to heterosexuals and homosexuals," who "have succumbed to social pressures to adopt an exclusive and stable sexual orientation."[18]

In this light, Chen seems in "Chaoxingbie yishi yu wode chuangzuo" to be advocating a similar blindness to biological sex and, by extension, social gender (since, in most circumstances, it is really by looking at a person's overall gender appearance, not his or her genitalia, that we tell his or her sex). Chen proclaims, "When a person of great character observes other people, he or she sees others in their respective individual essence detached from their sex. Quite often, a powerful character's admiration for another person is sexless. To perceive merely 'that is a woman' or 'that is a man' when looking at a person is too shallow."[19]

Chen's ideal is probably closest to a genderless utopia. But that positions her in an uneasy relation to the logic of fixed sex and gender choices in lesbian orientation. It also positions her in an uneasy relation to the logic of transgenderism.

Transgenderism implies, in simplified terms, an unconventional alignment between anatomical sex and social/performative gender that is exemplified by cross-dressing, passing, and the anatomical and psychological intersexualism in sex-reassignment surgery.[20] The word *transgenderism* suggests border crossing, instability, transitivity and, at the same time, the consolidation of a new gender identity through the bodily enactment and inscription of a conglomeration of gender signifiers. Indeed, the common claim that transgenderism exceeds a binary schema of gender should not obfuscate the fact that most transgender individuals are interested in embodying a certain distinctive gender (whether it be numbered as the third, fourth, or *n*th gender) rather than an amorphousness that is utterly unintelligible. The proliferation of transgender categories— such as female-to-male, male-to-female, invert, androgyne, the third sex, queen, butch, drag king, she-male, he-she, transvestite, among others— signifies, in itself, the need to name gender variance and to inhabit gendered subject positions. I argue, therefore, that transgender individuals are characterized by an investment in carving out and embodying new genders rather than an inchoate absence of gender.[21]

It appears that Chen Ran's idea of surpassing sex/gender does not particularly valorize the reification of one's sex/gender. For Chen, a transgenderist's radical enactment of a nonconforming but nonetheless recognizable and readable social/performative gender—such as an anatomical female's heavy investment in masculine accoutrements, cross-dressing, passing as a man, or hormonal/surgical adoption of masculine embodiment—might mean putting too much emphasis on gender identity and not enough on other ways in which to manifest and conceptualize personal qualities.[22]

In sum, that Chen justifies the love between women or between men (*tongxing zhi ai*) in terms of an existential need that traverses sex boundaries instead of in terms of the preoccupation with certain sex/gender traits may have arisen from her need to protect herself against the charge of advocating homosexuality in the PRC. In this regard, one might believe that she has intentionally blurred the issues of unconventional sex/gender identities and of sexual orientation, thereby depoliticizing them. At the same time, her claim may signify a genuine disagreement with the emphasis on sexual orientation and identity that is endemic to certain global discourses and gay liberation movements. Instead of theorizing about the predisposition of a sexual minority, Chen characterizes same-sex love as a pure art that transcends reproduction and may be practiced by anyone whose wisdom has surpassed utilitarianism. One PRC critic asserts: "What Chen Ran wants to say is that, because the world is such a solitary and isolating place, one should treasure the bonding between two individuals and care little about the conventions of civilization. It is the general discourses of 'defying solitude' and 'love' that justify the love between people of the same sex. . . . The primary concern for Chen has always been mankind's universal spiritual predicaments, such as the questions of freedom versus order, love versus solitude, and wall versus door. Gender is only one of the means for representing the general theme of surpassing."[23]

### Private Life

A theory without a practice is nothing but a theory. Ultimately, Chen is more interested and invested in exploring the myriad faces of eroticism through fiction than in proselytizing about gender transcendence. *Siren shenghuo* (Private life), her most intricate work to date, reveals through a series of love scenarios the fluid desire that does not take sex/gender as its primary condition.

*Private Life* is a life story recollected and told in the first person by Ni Aoao, a young woman whose name means "stubborn." As befits someone so named, Aoao shows a strong streak of individuality even as a young child. Caught in her parents' tempestuous marriage, Aoao gives all her sympathy to her mother and resents her tyrannical, self-centered father. One bright summer morning, observing her mother steam-ironing a pair of wool pants for her father, she feels an uncontrollable surge of anger and, when her mother is not looking, picks up a pair of scissors and makes a cut in one of the pant legs. Through this and other similar acts, Aoao sabotages paternal authority. The situation at school is not any easier for Aoao. The child believes that her teacher, Mr. T, is hostile to her and that her classmates shun her. They are "familiar strangers" to her.[24]

For several years, Aoao's only friend is a young widow living across the courtyard whom she calls Rice. The morning on which Aoao cuts her father's pants, she runs away from home and wanders through the streets, expecting uncertain punishment and experiencing hallucinations. Fatigued, she turns to Rice's home to seek respite because Rice is fond of her. Rice is too weak to work at a regular job, and she lives on insurance, but she has witch-like charms. Aoao admires her aristocratic Manchu blood and refined air.

Rice is in her twenties when Aoao is eleven. The narrator—the adult Aoao—recollects their relationship and comments:

> Years later I realized that she had always been waiting for me to grow up. She began waiting right after my birth in the 1960s. She waited and waited until distant mountains grew higher and higher and got covered by dead vines like white hair. She waited until ivy multiplied like green curtains that hung from the edges of her roof. She waited for me to grow into an adult woman with an independent mind and the ability to act. The age gap between us, like the separation by hills, wastelands, city walls, mists, and taboos, blocked her sight with the same cruelty, impeding her desire. (50)

The obstacle of age is manifested by Aoao's lack of understanding about kisses and caresses as a child. The pleasure of Rice's gentle touch on her bare back makes her realize why her dog is always quiet and obedient when being touched by people, but nothing more. Her innocence makes Rice cry. Rice invites Aoao to kiss her, to which the child responds, "Where would you like me to kiss?" Deeply frustrated, Rice's need for the ignorant child's affection intensifies. The narrating Aoao reminisces further and describes the scene:

> Rice held me to her bosom and started sobbing.
> I said, "Don't cry. I'll kiss you."
> I pressed a kiss on her here and there. I said, "Your bosom looks like my mom's. It's very different from mine."

"Aoao, when you grow up, it'll be the same."

She panted. Then she said, "Do you want to kiss it?"

I didn't say anything. I was afraid. Mr. T got furious about my classmates' circulating pictures that depicted private parts. I did not know whether seeing her bosom would be a mistake, too.

At that moment, Rice pulled up her shirt and loosened the button on her bra. Two breasts like transparent white peaches hopped out. They felt like silkworms ready to spit out silk, cool and fragile to the touch.

"Kiss it, Aoao."

I put it into my mouth, pretending that I was sucking my mother's milk when I was small, wriggling my lips.

I sucked like this for a long time, and gradually I heard her breathing become heavy.

I looked up and saw her tightly shut eyes. One of her hands was moving in between her thighs.

I became alarmed. I said, "Are you all right?"

She didn't reply but pressed me tightly to her bosom again.

We kept on playing like that. From time to time she said something that did not make sense or emitted a strange moan. We played until Mom called me home to have lunch.

My memory is always able to sift through the events of the past and retain those that I want to remember. Those rainy, dusky evenings, the ancient and grieving songs that came from afar, and Rice's blurry image in the dimly lit room all made firm imprints on my mind. (53–54)

That this passage was never banned because of its depiction of child molestation must be attributed to the constantly changing political climate in the PRC and the resultant frequent changes in censorship practice. Leniency may also have been shown Chen because of her reputation as an avant-garde author and, even more likely, because her work is approved by influential authors and critics, including Wang Meng, who served as the minister of culture at one time.[25] What is more, the censors may not have taken a scene like this between an adult woman and a little girl to be sexual in nature—or, like the child Aoao, they may have been feigning ignorance. Optimistically, one might argue that, by displacing adult eroticism onto a game between an adult and a child, Chen has succeeded in making the censors, who would otherwise have objected to a depiction of female homosexuality, tolerate the ambiguity and excitement of the same-sex encounter. More pessimistically, however, such tolerance might be construed as a sinister denial of the full sexual meaning of female-female contact. One cannot but wonder what would have happened had the passage in question depicted an adult male and a little boy kissing, sucking, and touching. Most likely, the official response would have been much more severe, the Chinese penal code recognizing (at least until 1997) forced man-boy contact—but not any woman-girl contact—as clearly sexual and abusive.[26]

For our purposes, more significant than Chen's success in dodging or, rather, manipulating the official censorship mechanism is the fundamental fact that she centers a bildungsroman on a diverse array of erotic relationships instead of the traditional grand themes (in the Chinese context at least) of the Communist Revolution and nation building. Furthermore, continuing the sexualizing trend in literature that started in the PRC in the mid-1980s, Chen takes the narrativization of desire to a new stage, where heterosexual love and sex prior to or outside monogamous marriage are no longer posited in the text as the primordial, vigorous human nature that must be reclaimed from the sexual repressiveness of the Maoist state. In other words, her text challenges, not only the Maoist state's prescription of heterosexual monogamous marriage as the only lawful context for sex, but also the dominance of heterosexual liberation in post-Mao China. Here, the initiation into sex and love in all variety of circumstances propels Aoao's narrative of growth forward, and desire is revealed to have multiple dimensions and modalities. Aoao's experiences bring forth many paradoxes: Heterosexuality and homosexuality are not necessarily mutually exclusive. Love and sex are not necessarily coincident. And solitude and romantic satisfaction are not necessarily contradictory. At the end of the story, it is through fantasy rather than any single concrete love object that Aoao gains the ultimate erotic experience. Combining the elements of her qualitatively different relationships with various people—both men and women—in her imagination, she gives herself perfect love and pleasure alone in the bathtub of her apartment. Her journey has been one of learning about desire and love, but it has also led to disappointment, separation, death, grief, and the disintegration of her sense of self. After her tumultuous experiences of both love and heartbreak, Aoao chooses solitude in spite of the refrain from a popular song that is broadcast day and night in the postrevolutionary city: "The season for love has come. Everyone should be in someone else's arms. . . . Those who remain in solitude are shameless" (233).

Prior to retreating into solitude, Aoao maintains an openness to all sorts of erotic encounters. Her desire traverses many boundaries. As a little girl, she embarks on the discovery of sensual pleasure with Rice. Three years later, she experiences vicarious excitement to the point of nausea while secretly watching a precocious female classmate and her boyfriend engage in intercourse. At eighteen, she matures into an attractive woman and is seduced by a former schoolteacher, Mr. T, who she had thought hated her. Like a distant observer, the narrating Aoao describes what passed through her mind the moment he penetrated her:

> She saw the man in front of her showing pain from the torture by longing, and she was touched. That brief moment allowed her hostility to slip away through her fingers like elapsed time. Besides that, she had no other romantic feelings for him. All she felt was that a certain desire in her body was awakened. She wanted to discover the mysterious pleasure that she had never fully experienced. She liked the pleasure more than the man. It was because she wanted to be intimate with the secret of sex that she became entwined with the man in front of her. Her desire at that instant was more intense than her repulsion in the past. She fell into the situation unprepared. At that moment, her body and her heart were alienated from each other; she was another person beside herself. She was a body manipulated by sardonic pleasure. (133)

Aoao succumbs to curiosity and pure physical sensation without much concern about love. Afterward, she visits Rice and enjoys a special romantic dinner that Rice prepares for her. As is often the case between them, they are eager to share with each other thoughts on Chinese and foreign writers; literature is their common love. Stimulated by wine, Rice recites to Aoao a poem by the contemporary female poet Yilei:

> Inlay me in your skin;
> I want to bloom to the fullest with you.
> Let my lips grow into your petals;
> Let your branches grow into my fluffy hair.
> I inhale your yellow
> And glow transparently among all things of creation. (139)

Rice is frank about her love for Aoao, but Aoao is preoccupied with what has just happened between her and Mr. T. She wants to unburden herself by telling Rice about the affair and seek the older woman's insight. She also wants to confess to Rice that for many years she has loved her. Aoao is thankful that Rice took loving care of her when she was young. Their emotional intimacy has increased with time. She does not need anyone else to cut into her life and body. She does not know how she could have let herself get entangled in such a mess with Mr. T.

Aoao compares her relationship with Mr. T with her relationship with Rice:

> T and I merely offered some body parts, some organs, to each other. It meant no more than performing labor in the fields.
>
> But Rice was a house built with mirrors that belonged to my heart. I could see myself in it from any angle. All the blank space on her body was my silence; her delight was always reflected by my smiles. During the years that she tirelessly watched me grow up, no sooner did she tighten her grasp on the thorns of life with her slender hands than pain rushed through my palms and blood oozed from my fingers. (141)

This sense of emotional, intellectual, and even bodily connectedness is missing from Aoao's relationship with Mr. T.

Analyzing the sexual relationships in another text by Chen Ran, "Ling yizhi erduo de qiaoji sheng" (The sound of another ear knocking), Wendy Larson has observed that desire in Chen's fiction is "mildly robotic, manipulated, and functional to the extent that it enacts itself to promote itself." Larson argues that, "far from the motivating, repressed, yet powerful and subtly invigorating desire of Sophia or the mother in 'Love Must Not Be Forgotten' ['Ai shi buneng wangji de']," the desire of Chen's female protagonist is without a possible object and antithetical to the humanistic love of both the May Fourth era and the immediate post–Cultural Revolution era.[27] This nondesire is, for Larson, indicative of Chen's postmodern play with surface and refusal of depth. I would agree with Larson that Chen has engendered a discourse depleting the depth and idealism of desire, but only insofar as we specify Chen's cynicism as targeted especially at the myth of a liberating and fulfilling heterosexuality. It is worth noting that, although disillusioned with their sexual liaisons with men, Chen's female characters still beseech an all-absorbing and motivating desire between women as their final hope for salvation, attainable or not. Her most forceful declaration of the life-redeeming power of women's love in a floating world is to be found, as Dai Jinhua points out, in the story "Pokai" (Breaking through), which recalls for Dai the May Fourth writer Lu Yin's wish for an all-woman paradise in the 1920s.[28] In the story, Chen's female protagonist cries out to her girlfriend at the end of a trying but enlightening journey: "I want you to come home with me! I need a sense of homeland! I need someone to face the world with me!"[29] The protagonist's fantasies about women's superior culture and a utopian woman's nation, combined with her critique of the unreasonable physical restraint between close female friends, constitute de facto a feminist-lesbian manifesto.

*Private Life* further challenges the supremacy of heterosexuality by presenting a female protagonist who, trapped in a mindless, passionless sexual relationship with a man, is neither contented with it nor affirming of it but instead deeply ambivalent about it. Her comparison of loveless sex with Mr. T to laboring in the fields smacks of detachment and contempt. Even more overt criticism of the mass-produced images and sounds of heterosexuality as a symptom of the postmodern malaise in China appears at the end of *Private Life,* where Aoao chooses to be "shamelessly" different and remain alone. She can almost hear the accusation: "Elite culture is passé; 'the postmodern revolution' pursues light-hearted entertainment and superficiality. You pretend to be deep—what a fool—you are shameless!" (237) Far from a sign of paralysis and aimless drifting, Aoao's solitude is an arduous but necessary and purposive act of resistance to the postmodern consumerism of (heterosexual) desire. Aoao is a social anomaly who puts up a lonely fight against the rampant proliferation of binary gender stereotypes and consumer (hetero)sexuality that Mayfair Yang, among others, identifies in the popular culture of post-Mao China.[30] Meanwhile, Aoao's gesture is by no means a return to Maoist puritanism. Rather, it is a decided departure from Mao's denigration of love and bourgeois individualism because it is precisely love that Aoao idealizes as the sustenance for her soul and precisely the uniqueness of Rice as an individual that bewitches and inspires Aoao.

The orgiastic—or, in Larson's words, "robotic" and "functional"—physical experience with Mr. T cannot satisfy Aoao spiritually. But she is flexible enough to learn from her sensations and to see that something may have been missing from her emotional intimacy with Rice. That night, after she returns home from the romantic dinner at Rice's place, she dreams of dancing with Rice and being undressed by her. Their naked bodies mirror each other beautifully. As soon as they start kissing, the familiar scent and curves of Rice's body return to Aoao's consciousness from afar—from her childhood memory. She feels guilty, as if she had betrayed and hurt Rice by being with Mr. T. Then she can no longer stand the intensity of her excitement and quickly thrusts herself forward to meet a mysterious "third hand" that grows toward her. As they dance, a whirlwind of sensations melts her and numbs her. After she relaxes and recovers from the fatigue, she suddenly sees that her partner is no longer Rice but a man. Aoao is shocked. A dialogue ensues:

> I was taken aback and asked, "What happened?"
> He laughed.

I said, "I don't need you."

He said, "Your desire needs me."

I blushed. I said, "My heart does not need you."

He said, "You don't know yourself. What you need is actually me."

I looked around anxiously for Rice. I felt fooled.

I struggled to get free from the man and told him in a loud voice: "I don't need you, not even a bit. . . ." (146–47)

Through the substitution and condensation characteristic of dreams, Aoao combines her two relationships and experiences them simultaneously. The dream scene can, apart from being read as Chen's attempt to make a distinction between heterosexuality and lesbianism, also be interpreted as her strategy for describing lesbian sex in a language that is acceptable to the heterosexist society and state.

Curious to learn how her description of lesbian eroticism would be different in a stress-free environment, I asked Chen when I interviewed her, "If you were to live in a country where lesbianism is perfectly acceptable and treated equally as heterosexuality, how would your writing be different? Would your description of women's love relationships become more straightforward, unfettered, and unabashedly sexual?" She replied: "Sometimes love's sweetness and fortitude come from the intensity of other people's objection to it and attempt to destroy it. Rebelliousness is part of lovers' psychology. By the same token, there is more than one possible answer to your question. If I were in a completely open environment, the process for expressing my ideas would definitely be more relaxed. But, at the same time, the challenge from the environment would also be weaker, and I might lose some enjoyment. [*Laughs.*] For, although the difficulties in work create hindrances, they also provide pleasure—I take pleasure in overcoming obstacles."[31]

Earlier in the interview, Chen had been straightforward about the necessity of supporting homosexual rights and social diversity. She even maintained that the world would be a very different place if from a young age children were told that one may choose any companion regardless of gender; choosing a same-sex partner would then be just as natural and ordinary as the fact that people have to eat.[32] Yet, when the discussion turned to the topic of artistic freedom, Chen denied that the lack of social inhibition would automatically stimulate and elevate the production of homoerotic writing. It is difficult to tell whether this is just the self-compensating thought of a writer who has no choice but to operate under social restrictions. But, if it is, indeed, more than just a rationalization of the status quo, Chen may be pointing out an important antithetical relation between the directness of speech and an artist's craft. For Chen, the pleasure of artistic creation resides in elaboration and ingenious transformation; hence, getting the (hypothetically) simple truth across in the most obvious and skeletal manner is not the artist's utmost concern. What is more, she asserts a fundamental difference between social freedom and the freedom of the imagination. Through a variety of characteristic exercises—displacement, condensation, metaphorization, and so forth—imagination can circumvent social control even where action cannot.

Aoao's life takes a dramatic turn shortly after her affair with Mr. T ends. She meets Yin'nan, a handsome, refined poet and fellow student at her university, and falls in love with him. Yet, in quick succession, several accidents take place and shatter her world. First, Rice is killed in a fire caused by her malfunctioning refrigerator. Then a stray bullet hits Aoao's left leg as the police quell a riot in the city in unbearable summer heat. All of a sudden, her poet lover must flee the country, and it is insinuated that his flight is necessitated by the police's crackdown on the "child-like crowds that had filled the streets" (195). (Here, the poetic images that Chen conjures up of the riot and police violence are evocative of the Chinese students' prodemocracy movement and the massacre in Tian'anmen Square in 1989, and the entire section may well be a disguised critique of the state's thwarting of the people's political will in that brutal summer.) The final blow is the death of Aoao's mother due to a heart problem. A breakdown ensues: Aoao begins hallucinating and having paranoid fantasies; she denies that her mother is dead and talks compulsively to her mother's clothes; she incessantly writes words down on paper, fragments characterized by free association and no logical connection whatsoever; she believes that she has become "Miss Zero" and has disappeared into nonexistence; she thinks that all the familiar people around her are strangers in a masquerade. Eventually, she is institutionalized.

It is not until Aoao returns home from a several months' stay in the mental hospital that she finally comes to terms with her mother's death and with the fact that the two people dearest to her—Rice and Yin'nan—are gone from her life forever. For months she was daydreaming in an attempt to forestall waking up to reality, but now she is past grieving. She describes "a woman's gentle singing . . . drifting toward [her] from a neighbor's window":

It was a song that Rice used to sing—

"Pushing open the gray window, I cannot but want to weep
Take me away, or else bury me

Oh, please open the door for me; I am knocking on the door in tears
Time has passed but I am still here"

I shut my window. I didn't want to hear that song at all. It had already
melted away in my body together with the countless white, pink, and blue
pills in the hospital. All grief and despair have already been cleansed from
my lungs and bones. (224)

Speaking like a doctor of the human spirit, Aoao concludes: "When a person finds herself in a broken world, if she cannot retune her inner harmony and wholeness in time, she will step toward collapse together with the world. She will be shattered into pieces herself. Every mental disorder, just like the symptoms of physical illness, is the result of the violent conflict between the body's inner reality and the reality of the outside world. It shows the struggle that a healthy character puts up to fight the external influences that damage health" (225).

The novel ends in scenes of Aoao alone in her apartment, especially in her bathtub. She elaborates a philosophy of the bathtub. Since the death of her mother and Rice and the desertion of Yin'nan, only her bathtub remains. One day, as she is soaking in the tub to let the heat and energy envelope her and dispel her nameless loneliness and fatigue, she suddenly feels like a beloved lying in the tub's embrace. In the empty apartment, only the bathtub hugs her tightly, helps her forget everything in the past, and makes her believe in the possibility of sharing. She puts her head quietly on the rim of the tub like a dried-up plant that, soaking in water, is coming back to life.

Aoao finds the bathtub such a soothing spot that she not only takes baths but also sleeps in the tub. One night she dries it and spreads her bedding in it "like a bird building a nest." After tucking herself in it comfortably, Aoao does something to herself, something that can be accomplished through sheer imagination. She describes it in a parodic poetic language, in a tone of self-mockery:

When I was doing this wonderful thing, two people whom I had loved
dearly in my life flashed through my mind: the fatally beautiful Rice and the
soulful, pure Yin'nan.
   This marvelous combination or confusion of genders was achieved in
two steps: front and back, up and down.
   When my fingers caressed my own round breasts, they had turned into
Rice's fingers in my consciousness. It was her long, delicate fingers that were
touching my skin, fondling my two velvety spheres. . . . White feathers were

flying and dancing. . . . Rose petals were sweet and pleasing. . . . Crimson cherries burst open. . . . Autumn maple leaves were encircling my lips and neck. . . . My breathing quickened, and the blood in my veins was set ablaze.

Then, a hand approached like a train with the whistle and clack of the wheels. It followed a set rail and ran slowly toward a platform covered by fragrant grass. When it reached the edge of an abyss covered by leaves, Yin'nan suddenly stood there upright. He was adventurous and pierced precisely and deeply into my breath. . . .

The aesthetic experience and the fulfillment of desire were perfectly united. (239)

Probably one of Chen Ran's most detailed descriptions of a woman's sexual fantasy, the depiction constructs a desire that is both sexual and aesthetic and that transcends the boundaries of sex/gender. Aoao's fantasy lover is a chameleon hermaphrodite that possesses both Rice's and Yin'nan's charming qualities.

Yet, if *Private Life* were meant to show only Aoao's desire for a hermaphrodite lover, which illustrates the concept of gender transcendence, the book would not be so interesting. The densest and most intriguing part of the narrative is, ultimately, the entire final third, which depicts the shattering of Aoao's world and her self and the process of her convalescence. Why does love end in death and separation and Aoao in solitude? The novel argues that love is a difficult bond in this world and that, no matter whom—man or woman—Aoao falls in love with, the difficulty is the same. Gender is overshadowed by other issues affecting human bonding—the fragility of life, the unpredictability of fate, the intrusion of state violence into private lives, and the vulnerability of the human spirit.

### Sexuality and Humanity

It may be for this reason—that gender is not the only thing that determines human bonding—that, when I asked Chen whether same-sex desire was the secret key for unlocking the meaning of her often-evasive and dense texts, she denied it:

My works touch on themes much broader than same-sex love [*tongxing'ai*]. It is only a small part, not the totality, of my concern. . . . What interests me is human nature itself. In fact, there is only one love in this world—whether you are in love with someone of the opposite sex or of the same sex, the meaning of being in love is the same. The problems that lovers face in everyday life are the same in both cases—they are all questions of human nature.

Later in the interview, I responded:

> Well, as a researcher, I feel conflicted about it. If I call a novel a representa-
> tion of homosexuality, [in the present circumstances in China] others will
> tend to think of the novel in very reductive terms. However, if I take the risk
> and call it such, perhaps I can prove that homosexual literature is very rich.
> In other words, this is another strategy—to try to expand the meaning of ho-
> mosexual literature. Those who love members of their own sex or choose a
> same-sex lifestyle are of course human. No one can presume that they are
> simply compelled by some biological factor and have never thought very
> deeply about love, life, or the world. It is, therefore, only to be taken for
> granted that the literature about these individuals has very wide-ranging
> themes and explores very profound and complicated aspects of human na-
> ture. The one does not exclude the other.

Chen answered:

> You're right. The problem right now is that society, including ourselves,
> holds prejudices against homosexual culture and literature [*tongxing'ai*
> *wenhua he wenxue*]. Still, I believe that homosexuality constitutes only a
> fraction of the subject matter of my creative writing. It is not everything. I
> wish to give it such a place. I am timid.[33]

The key Chinese term used throughout this exchange was *tongxing'ai,*
the meaning of which oscillated ambiguously between "same-sex love,"
in the sense theorized by Chen, and "homosexuality," in the popular
medical/clinical sense. What surfaced at the end of this exchange was
the question, How broad a semantic scope can one give to the term *tong-*
*xing'ai wenxue* (the literature of same-sex love, or homosexual literature)
before it loses specificity? What is the relation between sexuality and
humanity? Is sexuality a tiny part of humanity? Or is sexuality a prism
through which all the colors of humanity are refracted and magnified?

These basic questions are also evoked by Chen's powerful short story
"Jiaose leizhui" (Redundant roles; 1989). The narrator and protagonist of
the story complains about having to perform various roles and put on an
array of masks in daily life. She pretends to be psychologically ill and
hides in a mental asylum, finding relief only among the mentally ill, who
do not know how to hide their real thoughts and feelings and so behave in
an utterly honest manner.

Among the mental patients are two women who are lovers and are constantly kissing and caressing each other. Even though these characters are
not central to the story, their presence cannot be more thought provoking,

implying that homosexuality is still considered by society at large to be a mental disorder.[34] Society itself, however, is false and full of pretense. Only in the mental asylum, where masks are removed, can people be honest with themselves and display love for members of their own sex without restraint.

If such a parable about everyday pretense and performance can be described as a comment on lesbian existence—even though the story contains very little description of lesbian eros per se—then lesbianism and its masquerade as something other than itself in society must be understood as constituting the core of the narrative. Otherwise, such "passing" must be seen as only one of the many examples of everyday pretense on which the story touches; the issue does not provide an anchor that fixes the meaning of the text.

In the brief 1998 essay "You yizhong ku'nan yusheng julai" (There is a kind of suffering that comes with birth), Chen writes in a riddle-like fashion but expresses her sympathy (and identification?) with unprecedented clarity:

Do you know "the sorrow of the century" [*shiji de kuqi*]?

Like a person's genes, blood type, skin color, and race, there is a kind of suffering that comes with birth. It is not caused by material poverty, neither does it derive from spiritual crisis. But there it is—a real and secret existence. It is like a "virus" that hides in the body and cannot be told. Those who carry it keep their mouths tightly shut like a bottle, and the sadness of their whole lives ensues.

They call it "the sorrow of the century."

Regular people have no way of detecting it. The onlookers are unaware or look without seeing. Even if they see it through blurry eyes, they will at first reject it as incredible and then attack it violently. For regular people have a regular logic, and a regular logic means "reason"—it is like reasonable trees and flowers, prosperous and lush, pervading heaven and earth. But the "virus carrier" is like a strange and queer plant, excluded and forced to disappear into the wilderness. This inborn "existence" is like a type of skin that hangs on their bodies and faces. It is like a mark, inlaid deeply in their large, sorrowful, and helpless sockets. They acknowledge one another by recognizing the shocking desolation and grief buried in the eyes of one another. Only they themselves can secretly observe, understand, and provide comfort to one another.

This kind of inborn "existence" forces them to be like so many experienced "underground spies." Their words are always ambiguous and their faces forever indistinct. At every moment, they must live, anxious and fatigued, in lies. They have no choice but to stay alert and on guard against people at all times so as to prevent others' prying and detection during a moment of lapse. They have acquired many internal injuries. The dim shadows of their bodies are invisible among the bright and transparent crowds. They constantly force themselves to be passersby, for they avoid lingering in any place where their inner secret might be exposed. Their hearts wander adrift, are constantly on the run, and cannot find a permanent dwelling. Day after day, self-warnings, guardedness, concealment, and contradiction turn them into flighty birds that fear the bows, utterly exhausted and in despair.

There is a still deeper and more painful aspect of their struggle: they have no choice but to wage an everlasting secret and undeclared battle against those figures who think they have the authority to make demands on and interfere with their lives. (Such people are often their closest kin, like parents). . . .

Their suffering permeates the entire twentieth century.

I have a deep understanding of it. I see tears rush into their eyes in the dark. I am neither mute nor dumb, yet I cannot cry out for them. For this I despise myself!

The day will come when I write a book called *The Sorrow of the Century* for these suffering brethren.[35]

Although Chen Ran never identifies it explicitly, it is almost certain that the phrase *the sorrow of the century* refers to homosexual orientation. The images of inborn difference, the bottled-up truth, invisibility, and the telling look between persons carrying the same secret inside are all classic, if distressing and by now stereotypical, images of the closeted homosexual. The everlasting secret battle against parents is an especially poignant characteristic of the homosexual in the Chinese context, for parents' authority and their expectations that their children marry and reproduce remain strong in China (and other Chinese societies), and the relationship to the family is a serious source of worry among gay persons.[36] More so than her fictional works, Chen's personal essays can be quite straightforward in criticizing the injustice of homosexuals' plight in China.

Chen Ran insists that her fictional works have a strong political consciousness (*zhengzhi secai, sixiang juewu*).[37] *Private Life,* I argue, shows an ambition, not so much to comment on private matters in themselves, as to unravel the dialectics between private matters and public affairs. Her interweaving the surreal horror and bloodshed of the Tian'anmen incident with the abrupt disintegration of Aoao's personal life and her sanity amounts to a critical statement on the existing inescapable links between public and private in the PRC. In this context, Aoao's ultimate decision to stay home (especially in her bathtub) and refusal to take a job can, to paraphrase David Der-wei Wang, hardly be equated with defeat, withering agency, and total withdrawal. Her desire for seclusion must be read instead in terms of radical defiance of a state that has long encroached on private lives to the point of eliminating the private sphere.[38] In other words, Aoao's pursuit of privacy takes on, inevitably, the significance of a public act of resistance.[39]

Like Aoao, Chen Ran prizes solitude, independent thinking, and the sanctity of her own private space. What is more, Chen believes that her desire to maintain her privacy is consistent with taking meaningful public action through writing and publishing. As a writer, she has intervened in public culture with her individualistic voice and, simultaneously, guarded her own privacy jealously. She objects to inquisitive readers who naively equate her fiction with her personal life. Protesting to the critic Xiao Gang, she declared: "I do not agree when you call my works self-narratives [zixushi]. I like to write in the first-person voice, but that does not mean that my fiction is the autobiographical account of my personal life. People experience reality through two (or more) means. Certain details that you find in my fiction may be based on my real experience in the physical world, but, more commonly, they reflect only my psychological experience."[40] Chen's project is, therefore, vastly different from the hordes of "truthful records of people's oral confessions about love and sex" (qinggan koushu shilu) that appeared in China in the wake of the commercial success of Private Life.[41] Her book does not claim to have laid bare personal privacy, exhibitionist style.

Nevertheless, might we say that, by revealing her inner experience, Chen has laid bare something even more private than the mundane details of her tangible physical existence? To claim that by revealing only her inner experience she has managed to conceal her life from public view, she must rely on the untenable assumption that inner experience represents a distortion and an obfuscation of reality instead of being what it in fact is: a reality that is as valid as, if not more powerful than, the physical world. Perhaps, it is precisely because of the all-too-real nature of interiority that female same-sex desire in Chen's texts is, ultimately, not just an empty signifier that stands for antistate defiance, individualism, or anti-collectivism. Rather, Chen's exploration of female relationships is sincere on an experiential—if only psychological—level: it emanates an intensity of emotional investment, a seriousness of intellectual engagement, and a rare exhilaration that is typical of cherished fantasies. At the same time, her writing does not isolate the issues of sexual orientation and the oppressiveness of heterosexual supremacy from all other social problems. Female same-sex desire informs all the big questions about life and society that Chen wants to pose, but it is only one part of the enigma of human nature and existence for her.

FOUR :: **TAIWAN AFTER MARTIAL LAW**

# LESBIAN ACTIVISM IN THE MEDIATED PUBLIC SPHERE

After the Chinese Communists won the civil war against the Nationalist army and gained control over China in 1949, the United States provided life-sustaining military, political, and economic backing for Chiang Kai-shek's Nationalist regime in Taiwan for several decades, as part of the American geopolitical deployment meant to block the advance of world communism. As a result, postwar Taiwanese society developed a strong American orientation, although ambivalence toward American imperialist dominance or outright nativist resistance also surfaced.[1] Even after Nixon's normalization of diplomatic relations between the United States and Communist China (completed in 1979) at the expense of ties with Taiwan, American culture has continued, in both its popular and its elite guises, to be one of the defining forces shaping contemporary Taiwanese culture, including certain academic/intellectual practices and oppositional politics.[2]

For complex historical reasons, then, American lesbian and gay identity politics and queer discourses—reincarnated as *tongzhi yundong* (lesbian and gay movement) and *ku'er lunshu* (queer discourses), with, understandably, some modifications—have found avid emulators in late-twentieth-century Taiwan. One example of local modification is the Taiwanese manner of coming out (*xian shen, chu gui*). With some exceptions, such as those young people, now in their mid-teens to mid-twenties, who have self-identified as lesbian or gay since the rise of the activist movement in the 1990s, few lesbian and gay persons in Taiwan are comfortable coming out to parents or in the workplace. Coming out is, therefore, usually an anonymous, collective process, one utilizing pseudonyms and masks—a purely public gesture—rather than an individual process.[3] Generally, however, recent developments evince in Taiwan, more than in any other Chinese-speaking society, what Dennis Altman has termed *the Americanization of the homosexual* and *the globalization of sexual identities*.[4] The final part of this book examines, then, the formation of lesbian identity in Taiwan.

My approach is not an anthropological one. Pioneering anthropological studies of Taiwanese lesbians since the early 1990s have emphasized fieldwork in subcultural communities and tended to focus on gender as a central issue in lesbian subjectivity. Yengning Chao, for instance, observes the existence of three basic gender categories among lesbians in Taiwan: *T* (tomboy), *po* (wife), and *bufen* (undifferentiated).[5] Zheng Meili reports similar findings.[6] It is argued, moreover, that North American studies of the butch-femme dyad—such as Sue-Ellen Case's interpretation of the butch-femme aesthetic and the "seduced-and-abandoned" theme, Judith Butler's writing on gender as parody, and Esther Newton's notion of *compound drag*—shed significant light on T-po role-playing in Taiwan.[7] Jian Jiaxin takes the matter of lesbian genders a step further and devises her own classification system, cataloging dozens of varieties of Ts and pos on university campuses. She documents the direct link between college-educated lesbians' deconstruction of the traditional T-po role-playing popular in the T-bars and their exposure to and belief in Western feminism.[8]

The differing (but mutually infiltrating) lesbian subcultures of the T-bar and the university campus are, indeed, important. But I am more concerned with the issue of lesbian self-representation in public—how lesbian-identified persons and groups have in recent years striven to carve out a public space for themselves through representation. Among other things, I am interested in how the category *the lesbian* as a personal identity has penetrated and is signified through preexisting discourses in the public sphere—such as the discourse of feminism and that of autobiographical writing. The lesbian identity is, I argue, ineluctably lived through "mainstream" discourses as well as in the semienclosed spaces of the T-bar and the liberal university campus.[9] And certain lesbian collectives and individuals in Taiwan have directly confronted and contested old stereotypes and attempted to fashion new lesbian subject positions. In the process, they not only treasure the new possibilities for public identity and visibility but also reflect critically on the limitations and liabilities of identity and visibility in the current Taiwanese public sphere, limitations and liabilities due, for example, to the colossal power of the mass media to generate seductive, hypnotizing versions of reality.

In terms of immediate local circumstances, the formation of new social movements in Taiwan during the last decade was directly linked to the abrogation of martial law (which Chiang Kai-shek's Nationalist government had imposed in 1949). Since 1987, government control of print and electronic media has relaxed. Meanwhile, demonstrations and similar public gatherings became legal. Homosexuality came to occupy a prominent place in the new public territory of representability, debate, and activism.[10] A new women's resistance movement, linked to yet independent of the traditional women's movement, thus arose in the Taiwanese public sphere: lesbian activism (*nü tongzhi yundong*). Through a variety of discursive practices ranging from community magazine publishing and academic theorizing to public protests, lesbians—at times in coalition with gay male activists but mostly independently—engage in the project of self-definition, challenging rigid modern classifications and stereotypes of female homoerotic feelings, practices, and relationships.

Taiwanese lesbians' search for identity and community through public communication is a counterhegemonic discourse on multiple levels. In the most apparent sense, it is a striking example of what Foucault calls "a reverse discourse"—one in which homosexuality begins "to speak in its own behalf, to demand that its legitimacy and 'naturality' be acknowledged, often in the same vocabulary, using the same categories by which it was medically disqualified."[11] Many of the popular stereotypes in Taiwan concerning female same-sex love originated in late-nineteenth- and early-twentieth-century European male-authored medical literature on sex, which sought to catalog sexual perversions and described same-sex desire, including female same-sex desire, in terms of pathology, psychological abnormality, and gender confusion affecting only a minority. These stereotypes have acquired global significance because of the hegemony of Western science and popular culture in the twentieth century. Lesbian activist discourse also runs counter to traditional Confucian family values. Many lesbians must, therefore, exile themselves from the patriarchal family in order to find the space to be themselves. Recent Taiwanese lesbian activist publications further engage in battle with the sensationalist but politically conservative mass media, which, on the one hand, propagate stereotypes and, on the other, pry into and capitalize on the eroticism of a formative urban lesbian scene.

Insofar as lesbian activism is a counterhegemonic practice that defies patriarchal control of women's gender and sexuality, it is intimately linked to feminism. The connection between the two "women's movements" in Taiwan deserves a close inspection. Indeed, local female activists and academics have debated extensively the linkages and tensions between feminism and lesbian sexuality since the early 1990s, which is in stark contrast to the situation in the People's Republic of China (PRC), where female scholars have thus far subsumed widely divergent understandings of femininity and gender under one paradigmatic term—*nüxing yishi* (female consciousness)—without attempting to sort out and articulate the differences systematically.[12] Overall, Taiwanese lesbian activist discourse is ineluctably indebted to contemporary Western feminist and lesbian/gay theory, activism, and art. Modernization, from the introduction of homophobia to the borrowing of its counterdiscourse on a large scale, has come a full circle. What may be new is a viable, productive lesbian identity that Chinese women in Taiwan have never before been free to choose.

To understand the relation between lesbian activism and feminism in Taiwan, one might begin by analyzing the disgrace of lesbianism in Taiwan as a recent historical construct rather than as a long-standing Chinese cultural legacy or a universal given. As I have argued in my discussion of Republican China in part 2 of this study, the stigmatization of female same-sex love that took place in early-twentieth-century China was unprecedented, and that it developed along lines strikingly similar to those previously established in advanced industrialized/capitalist societies in the West and Japan can be meaningfully analyzed as a modality of male defense. In an age in which wage labor and urbanization expanded, upper- and middle-class women entered the workforce, and, consequently, patriarchal kinship lost considerable control over these women. For fear of New Women's autonomy and separatism, anxious men adopted/invented a new system of sexual ethics that, in the name of science, theorized heterosexuality as women's *sexuality*, that is, as their natural desire, pleasure, and orientation rather than as simply their duty. This system cast female-female love and desire as perverse. The regimentation of desire caused tangible anxiety among some intellectual women of the May Fourth generation. More than half a century later, the return of the concept of psycho-biological abnormality to popular sexual discourse in the PRC once again assists the patriarchy in maintaining control over women by dividing them and punishing those who form their primary relations with other women rather than with men.

In the light of the recurring confluence between modern sexology and traditional patriarchal values in regulating female-female intimacy in capitalist/industrializing societies since the early twentieth century, the recent emergence of Taiwanese lesbian voices and activism in the mass media, alternative publishing, campus meetings, street demonstrations, and so on does not simply indicate the political struggle of a sexual minority for public space and legitimacy. It has significance as feminist practice. Indeed, many lesbians in Taiwan are feminists, and many dedicated participants in feminist organizations are lesbians. Just as many feminist organizations have given vocal support to the lesbian and gay movement throughout the 1990s, the feminist leanings of lesbians are most apparent in the lesbian organization Women zhi jian (Between Us), whose members are mainly college-educated lesbians. In *Nü pengyou* (Girlfriend), the magazine published by Between Us, many contributors explicitly describe themselves as radical feminists (*jijin de nüxing zhuyi zhe*) or as participants in feminist study groups on university campuses. The tension between a fledgling lesbian identity politics and an already powerful women's movement in the Taiwanese public sphere erupted into heated debates in the early to mid-1990s and has far-reaching consequences to this day. The question whether feminism can embrace a variety of constituents and allow diversity to thrive will no doubt continue to inform relations among lesbians and feminists.

As lesbian activists enter the Taiwanese public sphere to advance a radical critique of the supremacy of the patriarchal nuclear family and to demand public legitimacy for lesbianism, they cannot afford to neglect the fact that one of the major characteristics of the public sphere in capitalist societies is that it is mass mediated and that face-to-face communication has come to play a limited role in it. Unlike the PRC, where the recent conversion from a Communist to a market economy is associated with the opening up of the public sphere,[13] Taiwan is a mature capitalist society in which the mass media threaten to reduce both the public and the private spheres to little more than media effects. Jürgen Habermas champions the public sphere of budding capitalism but is extremely critical of the public sphere of advanced capitalism. For him, the advanced capitalist mass media, hand in hand with parliamentary politics, hinder rather than encourage society's critical, rational thinking: "Critical publicity is replaced by manipulative publicity."[14] The capitalist mass media have been described in equally bleak terms by Jean Baudrillard, who believes that the masses are trained to consume rather than to respond and that media simulacra have replaced reality.[15] These bleak pictures do not describe the entire relation between the mass media and their audiences in Taiwan, but they point out inherent dangers in the communication structure.

Lesbian activism must confront the fact that the capitalist mass media monopolize communication, reproduce dominant values and ideologies, and distort the public sphere, transforming what was once a space of critical thinking and communication into little more than an arena in which public opinion is manipulated. Although public, face-to-face communication, such as lectures, group discussions, street demonstrations, guerrilla theater, public hearings, and debate in the legislature, is possible in present-day Taiwan, and although in recent years lesbians and feminists have created many such events, they realize that the mass media (television, radio, film, newspapers, and commercial magazines) are crucial fields of social warfare in that they reach a much wider audience. In recent years, feminist and gay/lesbian activities and agendas have succeeded in attracting some media attention. However, they constantly run the risk of being sensationalized, used by media preoccupied with profit making and attracting the largest audience possible to spice up what is otherwise safe, prepackaged content. And they will never be genuinely embraced. At present, therefore, lesbian activists and feminists rely on low-cost alternatives—publishing books and magazines and establishing a web presence—to promote critical discourse. At the very least, a prosperous capitalist economy combined with a democratizing government has ensured that it is not difficult for radical groups in Taiwan to raise funds sufficient to disseminate their opinions (by whatever means), even though such ventures are rarely profitable.[16]

The public sphere in Taiwan has become a site of contestation among different discourses: quasi-scientific normativization (i.e., pseudoscientific discourses that create notions of sexual normality vs. deviation), patriarchal family values, sensationalism, feminist and queer academic theories, and the liberatory self-representation of a new imagined community of lesbians. These discourses serve multiple and dissimilar functions: consumption, relaxation, profit making, control, information generation, scholarship, provocation, dissension, and identity formation. In this terrain, lesbian self-representation is the category that has the most difficulty making its presence known. Perceiving the mass media to be in-hospitable to radicalism and unworthy of trust, most lesbians choose to publish their self-representations in lesbian and feminist magazines, whose circulation is limited. Moreover, owing to the fact that revealing one's homosexual identity still has (predictable and unpredictable) adverse consequences in Taiwan, most lesbian authors protect themselves by using pseudonyms. Yes, lesbian self-representations have entered the public sphere, but the spaces that they occupy are not large and are often isolated.

Nevertheless, there are signs warranting optimism about the future growth and vitality of a critical lesbian-feminist public sphere in Taiwan and, more generally, the transnational Chinese-speaking world. One encouraging example is that, while feminists and lesbian activists have had difficulty getting their message across uncorrupted in the traditional media, the Internet has emerged as a powerful new public medium and forum. It has proved remarkably effective in supporting nonprofit feminist and antihomophobic publishing as well as open, well-circulated discussion under relatively safe and anonymous conditions. Such decentralization of mass communication greatly contributes to the proliferation of lifestyles, and vice versa.

### Existing Institutional Forces of Discrimination

In part 2 of this study, I documented the initial translation of sexology into the Chinese language and its dissemination through the urban periodical press. I pointed out that, beginning in the May Fourth era, "sexual science" gradually established itself as the chief language of or rationale for discrimination against homosexuality in modern Chinese urban culture. Moreover, the introduction of a medical discourse pathologizing homosexuality went hand in hand with reforms in the structure of opposite-sex courtship, marriage, and the family, love-based heterosexual monogamy and the nuclear family becoming the ideal.[17] The legacy of Republican Chinese modernity was to some extent transported to Taiwan when the Nationalist government fled there in 1949, bringing with it large numbers of intellectuals and students as well as troops.[18] The influx of Republican mainland culture and the infusion of postwar American culture intermingled with preexisting Chinese, colonial Japanese, and aboriginal heritages in the making of postwar Taiwanese culture. Into the twenty-first century, the sexual psychology that flourished in Europe, America, Japan, China, and elsewhere for the major part of the twentieth century has been discredited in many ways by new research in many disciplines. And the Taiwanese psychiatric establishment has in theory followed the lead of the West and depathologized homosexuality. However, in everyday parlance, outdated sexology continues to function as a powerful language that rejects homosexuality as abnormal.

At this point, it is crucial to remark that the medical profession is by no means the only social institution fostering homophobia in contemporary Taiwan. On the contrary, the Confucian patriarchal family transfigured by the influence of the modern nuclear family continues to prescribe and privilege a particular alignment between biological sex, culturally defined gender behavior, and romantic/erotic desire. This regime of gender and sexuality dictates that, to be considered normal, a woman accept a male spouse, join his family, and fulfill her reproductive destiny. The modern heterosexual regime works against women's same-sex desire, not only by denouncing and prohibiting it, but also by silencing it, erasing it, rendering it unthinkable, invisible, and insignificant. An analysis of the simultaneous demonization and erasure of lesbianism by major social institutions in Taiwan is, therefore, in order.

The typical reaction on discovering that a family member is homosexual is to reject that individual, to punish her, or to "fix" her. And traditional family values—such as the marriage imperative for women examined in part 1 of this study—are reinforced by medical authority. The family has been an especially tension-fraught zone for Taiwanese lesbians. In a publication by the lesbian student group "Taida Lambda" (the Society for the Study of Lesbian Culture at National Taiwan University), lesbian college students discuss the issue that most concerns them: coming out to family. Almost all the women who participated in the discussion fear coming out to their parents. Very few have tried. They observe: "For parents, the greatest expectation they have of a daughter is that she find a good man to marry." And they recount various coming-out horror stories: a father beating his daughter to make her admit her mistake and promise to reform; a mother begging her daughter to get counseling or a sex-change operation; parents threatening to sever family ties or even to commit suicide if the daughter does not "return to normal"; etc.[19] In the few instances in which parents show tolerance, it is because they have had time to get accustomed to a long-time partner as a friend first and only later as a lover.

As the analysis by Taida Lambda points out, the label *tongxinglian* (homosexual) evokes deep-seated negative associations and stereotypes, and using it during the coming-out process turns the lesbian daughter into a freak and causes her parents to react irrationally and violently.[20] In other words, the medical category that originated from sexual psychology is almost beyond reclamation. A later study by the anthropologist Zheng Meili of Taiwanese lesbians' relationships with their families confirms these patterns: family tension and extreme difficulty gaining parents' acceptance.[21] It might be added that a fear of parental disapproval is shared by lesbians and gays in mainland China.[22]

Beyond the family, the school, the workplace, and the state have, as the most important social institutions after the family, also functioned in various capacities in the attempt to demonize and erase lesbianism in Taiwan. Demonization and erasure work hand in hand. The Taiwanese educational system is structured in such a way that, in elementary and secondary schools, students are closely supervised by their teachers. However, teenage girls are often encouraged to develop same-sex friendships and to avoid boys. It is, thus, not unusual that they are able to keep same-sex love affairs secret from teachers as well as parents. Of course, teachers have been known to interfere. Suspecting that the boundaries of friendship have been exceeded, they will interrogate girls about their relationship and, if dissatisfied with the results of the interview, send them to the school's "counseling office" (*fudao shi*) and also notify their parents to keep an eye on them.[23]

A recent incident that received wide media coverage is especially revealing of the forces that work against female-female intimate relations in the schools. In July 1994, two girls identified as gifted in the most competitive girls' high school in Taipei committed suicide together in a hotel room. Media speculation about why they did so began immediately, and some suspected a homosexual relationship. This upset the girls' classmates, who wrote to a major newspaper proclaiming, "They were very close friends, but they were definitely not homosexuals!"[24] When students asked the school principal to give her opinion on homosexuality, she replied, "In an age when everything has gone into confusion, human beings should follow the example of nature and procreate."[25] Meanwhile, the school issued a pamphlet telling students that "same-sex love is not homosexuality" (*tongxing ai bu shi tongxinglian*), attempting to make a distinction between platonic love and sexual love.

The reaction of both the students and the teachers was based on tautologous logic and a demonization of homosexuality: Homosexuality is dirty and pathological, but these girls' love was pure and normal; therefore, their relationship was not homosexual. As the media frenzy escalated, psychologists and medical authorities, not surprisingly, intervened, restating the sexological distinction between "genuine homosexuality" and "pseudohomosexuality." A professor of counseling education and a psychiatrist both told reporters that real female homosexuality is rare and that most female homosexuality in adolescence does not count.[26] No doubt, the medical professionals have observed the "scientific truth" handed down by Havelock Ellis and the like. Theirs is a teleological view of sexuality, and heterosexuality is the default destination. They would never consider adolescent heterosexual love to be "situational," "temporary," or "pseudo"—or anything but true passion.

In 1998, a series of articles in *Nü pengyou* further point out that, although the word *homosexuality* has gained wide currency among students and teachers in primary and secondary schools because of the catchy media coverage of the local lesbian/gay subcultures since the early 1990s, it still carries very negative connotations. Some children in primary schools now use it to attack others.[27] More distressing, *Xuesheng fudao* (Students' counseling), the most influential monthly in counseling-education circles, a publication to which the majority of secondary schools subscribe, continues to attribute teenagers' homosexuality to broken families, improper gender identification, and temporary confusion.[28]

Even as adults, Taiwanese lesbians are not free from homophobic institutional demonization and erasure. At the workplace, a lesbian must hide her sexual identity. If her sexual preference is revealed, most likely she will become an object of intense gossip. Although not all outed lesbians lose their jobs, there is no law protecting workers from dismissal based solely on sexual preference.[29] Also, harassment by coworkers is likely to become intolerable, leading to voluntary resignation. In lesbian magazines, advice like the following abounds: "The name of one's workplace, like one's phone number at home, is something a lesbian should never give away at a lesbian bar."[30] Lesbians are urged to take the utmost care in hiding their sexual identities at work as well as at home and protect themselves from blackmail or indiscreet callers. One of *Nü pengyou's* "Eight Principles for Maintaining a Happy Lesbian Life" (*Nü tongzhi ba da susheng fa*) concerns precisely safety at work: "At the workplace, do all you can to camouflage your sexual preference. Protect yourself because your personal life has nothing to do with making a living."[31] At the state level, to date no antidiscrimination legislation protects lesbians and gay men.[32] Moreover, marriage is defined as being between a man and a woman. Lesbian couples are not accorded rights taken for granted by opposite-sex couples: adoption, in vitro fertilization, spousal benefits, joint tax filing, eligibility for family housing, and so on. In state-sanctioned textbooks, male homosexuality does not exist, much less female homosexuality. Homoerotic literature and art are either ignored or purposively misinterpreted. National history is passed on to future citizens of the state as unquestionably heterosexual.

## Lesbian Activism and Feminism

It is against this pervasive grid of modern medical stigmatization and demonization superimposed on traditional demonization and erasure that lesbian activism arose in the Taiwanese public sphere. Its symbolic beginning can be dated to 1990, when the first Taiwanese lesbian group, Between Us, formed and went public.[33] Since 1990, fresh, revisionist articulations of women's romantic, erotic bonds have become an important political project. Equally important, the negative stereotype of a monstrous, unfeminine lesbian body is being resignified in the urban T-bar, reclaimed and celebrated by *T-po* (tomboy-wife) lesbians as a victory in the battle against an oppressive ideology of gender—that is, a set of limiting definitions of women's roles that must be challenged.[34] Moreover, the negative discourse about a minority of women pathologically attracted to their own sex is being transformed, much like the word *queer* in the West, into a foundation on which to build a distinctive, empowering collective lesbian identity.

Since the Taiwanese mass media "discovered" lesbians in 1990, they have largely imagined lesbianism as a sexual perversion parallel to male homosexuality. So linked by the "enemy," Taiwanese lesbians and gay men have been further encouraged by Western queer activism and the notion of sexual orientation to form a queer political front across the gender divide. This wave of concerted queer activism is commonly called *tongzhi yundong*.

Feeling that *tongxinglian* (the homosexual)—the medial category that originated from sexual psychology—is almost beyond reclamation, lesbian and gay activists in Taiwan and Hong Kong have in recent years appropriated the term *tongzhi* (comrade, cadre) as the common denominator for people whose sexual preference is for those of the same sex, and the term is slowly gaining currency among young gays in major cities in mainland China as well. The Hong Kong sociologist Chou Wah-shan, whose publications in Chinese have greatly contributed to the popularity of the term *tongzhi* in Hong Kong, Taiwan, and Beijing in the last decade, has theorized that *tongzhi* is an umbrella term that includes not only lesbians and gays but also bisexuals, transgender persons, S/Mers, and other queers, including straights who are critical of heteronormativity.[35] However, in current everyday usage in Taiwan, *tongzhi* designates predominantly gays and lesbians, especially when the word is used alone, unmodified. Bisexuals, for instance, are usually called *shuangxing'lian tongzhi* (bisexual comrade), and drag queens are called *banzhuang tongzhi* (drag comrade). In contrast, gay men are called simply *tongzhi* (comrade) or *nan tongzhi* (male comrade), lesbians simply *nü tongzhi* (female comrade).

Many Taiwanese lesbians and gays prefer the new term, *tongzhi,* to the old, *tongxinglian,* for they believe that, wrested from twentieth-century Chinese political history, *tongzhi* is capable of suggesting the elements of choice and political activism in sexual identity. Paradoxically, another reason why the word *tongzhi* has become popular as the common denominator for lesbians and gays is precisely because the first character in the compound—*tong*—retains the specificity of the clinical term *tongxinglian* (homosexual). In fact, lesbians in Taiwan have used *tong* to create another name for themselves—*tongnü* (homo girl)—on the basis of a similar logic.[36] In other words, *tongzhi* denotes something more specific than "comrade," which is nonsexual if not antisexual. *Tongxinglian* is the half-spoken, partially negated history of *tongzhi.*

Certainly, many lesbians in Taiwan consider themselves allied with gay men as citizens of a queer nation. For instance, lesbian and gay activists have jointly claimed the Duanwu jie (the May Festival) traditionally dedicated to Qu Yuan's memory to be Xiaoyuan tongxinglian ri, Gay and Lesbian Awakening Day (GLAD).[37] The ancient poet and politician Qu Yuan wrote deeply affectionate and sorrowful poems when he fell out of favor with his king, comparing himself to beauties and fragrant plants, before drowning himself in the Miluo River. Orthodox Chinese hermeneutics never encouraged any interpretation of the homoeroticism inherent in Qu Yuan's writings, emphasizing rather that they are metaphoric and that Qu's sentiments are purely patriotic, even though there in fact exists no reliable historical record pertaining to Qu Yuan.[38] By celebrating GLAD, lesbians join gay male activists in reclaiming queer history from the hands of homophobic historians, carousing in the name of queer pride.

On the other hand, some Taiwanese lesbians and feminists have explored lesbianism as a specifically *female* counterhegemonic practice. As such, lesbianism is linked closely to feminism. A fledgling lesbian identity politics has positioned itself in a dialogic relation to the stronger, more established women's movement in Taiwan. Not only will examining the doubling and delicate boundaries between them enrich our understanding of the extent to which feminism dares take a militant and anti-institutional stance in the Taiwanese public sphere. It will also illuminate how lesbianism as a category has been created and signified as a form of feminism.

The marginalization of and hostility toward lesbians in feminist groups have occurred in many places in the United States and Europe in the 1960s, the 1970s, and even the 1980s.[39] A similar pattern is playing itself out in contemporary Taiwan. The similarity across space and time may indicate that patriarchy and women's resistance often play out the same structural dynamics around the issue of women's sexuality in different cultures. On the other hand, it may also mean that, as a developed capitalist society, Taiwan is highly Westernized in its cultural forms, such as medicine, academic theory, and the popular media. The extent to which it has assimilated Western cultural forms is proportionate to the extent to which it is integrated into the global capitalist system. Discourses first developed in advanced Western capitalist societies—such as homophobic sexual science, feminism(s), and gay/lesbian activism—are reproducing themselves in contention with one another in Taiwan. While some of the terms of the debate may appear familiar and, indeed, derivative and dated to queer activists and theorists in the West today, it is worth bearing in mind that they may very well be pertinent to the local reality of Taiwan and, hence, politically necessary and efficacious.

To be sure, there has been no lack of feminist theories advocating women's gender transgression and sexual freedom in Taiwan. Many feminists denounce the male conspiracy of regulatory theories of female sexuality, and they theorize about lesbian sex as a liberated use of the female body.[40] Yet, in actual political practice, even feminists in the most radical women's organization have questioned the legitimacy of lesbian agendas in the women's movement. For these feminists, lesbianism is the orientation of a particular minority, and the issues that arise from such particularism cannot be prioritized in the women's movement. Moreover, fearing guilt by association, these feminists wish to set up a boundary between their cause and lesbianism. They argue that the rights of lesbians should be advocated by all-lesbian or lesbian and gay activist groups and that a feminist organization may play at best a secondary, supporting role.[41]

This reasoning has surfaced in many forms. One is the argument that feminists should not speak for lesbians, that lesbians should speak for themselves on lesbian issues. Inherent in this argument, however, is a division between lesbians and feminists, as if feminists cannot be lesbians and lesbians cannot be feminists. Historically, such a heteronormative assumption has meant that, for many years, dedicated lesbian activists have been working for women's rights within Taiwanese feminist organizations with the implicit understanding that they put aside their own specific needs and visions as lesbians.

Who are lesbians? Are they self-assertive, defiant, and women-loving women who, nonetheless, do not qualify as feminists? Is same-sex desire not integral to women's alliance? Is same-sex desire really something that few women have experienced or can relate to? Who can patrol the borders of feminism? Is it all right for lesbians to march for heterosexual women's rights under the flag of feminism, but not vice versa?

A series of articles on the theme "Neibao nüxing zhuyi" (Imploding feminism) that appeared in 1995 in the journal *Funü xinzhi*—the journal of the most active feminist organization in Taiwan, the Funü xinzhi jijinhui (Awakening Foundation), a nongovernment organization staffed by both paid employees and volunteers—first exposed the fact that homophobia and heterosexual privilege are common within the Taiwanese feminist constituency as well as in society at large.[42] Through much of the 1990s, lesbian feminists were among the most dedicated activists at the Awakening Foundation, yet the assumption that the only respectable feminists were heterosexual or celibate[43] forced them to remain closeted, not only in public, but within the organization itself. Similarly, lesbian agendas—such as promoting homoeroticism as a valuable sexual and emotional resource for all women and lobbying for legislation allowing lesbians to marry, adopt children, etc. and outlawing workplace discrimination based on sexual orientation—were either marginalized or ignored in the women's movement.[44] The debate exposed the heterosexism that pervaded the feminist movement. It was significant, not only because it explored different ideological and political orientations among feminists and seriously questioned whether feminism in Taiwan could in the future be a pluralistic, democratic practice with multiple agendas, but also, and more important, because it represented serious collective feminist thinking about the implication of lesbianism for the women's movement as a whole. For the first time in the Taiwanese public sphere it was maintained that lesbianism resides at the heart of feminism rather than on the margins.[45] These reflections were possible because the traditional agenda of the women's movement—equal rights for men and women—had already entered the mainstream in Taiwan.[46] Thus, it was high time that feminists challenge the technology of gender on a deeper level: the structuring of gender norms through sexuality.

The debate was ostensibly ignited by Yuxuan Aji, the editor of the lesbian magazine *Nü pengyou*. In an article published simultaneously in *Nü pengyou* and *Funü xinzhi* in February 1995, Yuxuan attacks the Awakening Foundation for reinforcing compulsory heterosexuality and neglecting lesbian and gay human rights: "Even the most progressive feminist organizations have not tried to challenge the existent structure of the family. They merely pursue through legislation 'equality between the sexes' as classified by the heterosexual system. . . . In their proposal for revising the marriage law, they continue to define marriage as between a man and a woman."[47] In response to Yuxuan's criticism, in July 1995 *Funü xinzhi* put out an issue with feature articles on the relation between feminism and lesbian activism, the slogan "Yixinglian/tongxinglian: Dou shi/dou bushi" (Heterosexuality/homosexuality: Both/neither) displayed prominently on the cover. However, tension had long been pent up in the Awakening Foundation itself, tension that exploded in the next five issues of its magazine.

In its initial response to Yuxuan Aji, the Awakening Foundation defends itself by claiming that it is just as dedicated to challenging conventional family values as lesbian and gay activists are:

> When we were pushing the civil law movement, what we did was more than demanding that the legal codes [on marriage and family] be revised. . . . We promoted the notions that divorce is not one's fault, that adultery should be decriminalized, that domestic labor deserves pay, and that women's choice not to marry should be affirmed. We hoped to deconstruct and redefine marriage and family. . . .
>
> We hoped to open up women's space in marriage and to create women's possibilities outside marriage. Marriage will become one of women's choices, rather than the single, required path.[48]

Meanwhile, the same issue of *Funü xinzhi* published four other essays reflecting on the relation between lesbian activism and feminism. The first is a translation of the influential 1970 manifesto "The Woman Identified Woman" by the American group Radicalesbians. The following statement by Radicalesbians, in particular, is highlighted: "As long as the label 'dyke' can be used to frighten women into a less militant stand, keep her separate from her sisters, keep her from giving primacy to anything other than men and family—then to that extent she is controlled by the male culture. Until women see in each other the possibility of primal commitment which includes sexual love, they will be denying themselves the love and value they readily accord to men, thus affirming their second-class status."[49]

Hu Shuwen, the editor of *Funü xinzhi,* concurs with Radicalesbians:

> Equality between the two sexes—I am awfully tired of this phrase. What feminism and the women's movement want to change is not just the power relation between men and women; we must give more thought and heart to women themselves, that is, reflect on what kind of "same-sex" relationship women want to create. . . .
>
> The opposition between heterosexuality and homosexuality, or the difference between good women and bad women, is defined by male hegemony. Women are defined by the kind of relationship they . . . have with (heterosexual) men. If we do not challenge this kind of classification as well as the violence and oppression that it creates, women's power will be subject to division and erosion by the logic of heterosexual patriarchy, and the women's movement will have no way of being more than a tamed movement of "good women."[50]

Taking the division between "heterosexual women" and "homosexual women" to be the product of male supremacy and oppression, Hu Shuwen urges all feminists to take same-sex relations more seriously and face the challenge that lesbian activism poses. In another article, by contrast, Hsiao-hung Chang, an influential feminist scholar popular with the mass media, is primarily concerned with how the feminist and the lesbian activist can "see each other in tension" and "form coalitions on specific issues."[51] Gu Mingjun, another feminist, criticizes Chang, however; she feels that what feminists must face first is the lesbian closet in the feminist camp: "For some reason, . . . [Chang] seems to forget that lesbianism may be one variety of feminism and that feminism may be one variety of lesbianism. The possibility of coalition or mutual seeing does not have to be abstract or like a mutually beneficial foreign relation. On the contrary, it can mean the abolishment of policing and a concrete 'coming out' in one's own territory. . . . Why is feminism presumed 'heterosexual a priori'? . . . Rather than *seeing others,* . . . feminists should first see the possibility of further liberating gender within the feminist camp itself" (emphasis added).[52]

According to Gu, a homophobic ambience has led lesbian feminists in the Awakening feminist group to keep silent about both their sexual identities and their disagreement with the agendas and strategies of the women's movement. She believes that this silence has led to a kind of "alienation" (*yi hua*). In a subsequent roundtable discussion, the feminists Hu Shuwen, Gu Mingjun, Wang Ping, Zhang Juanfen, Ji Xin, Su Qianling, and Ding Naifei reached the consensus that the women's movement needs lesbian feminists and that the women's movement must do more for lesbians. Meanwhile, Hsiao-hung Chang raised the objection that, if there are not enough lesbians in the feminist collective, the women's movement's advocacy of lesbian rights will be "hollow."[53]

Hu Shuwen's response to Chang's assumption that feminists are primarily heterosexual was severe:

> Perhaps for "heterosexual feminists" there is an unbridgeable gap between lesbianism and heterosexuality. Therefore, when the women's movement begins to face and practice lesbian activism, they think that it is probably just a "gesture" on the part of "heterosexual" (what an assumption!) women out of "moral anxiety." . . .
>
> When we are actively thinking about and promoting a women's movement with a lesbian perspective, we have already come out. You keep worrying that this will be a hollow movement, that it will be a ghostly movement without a subject. You do not know that the subject has already faced you but you do not see it.[54]

Hu Shuwen argues that Hsiao-hung Chang unthinkingly takes her own orientation and outlook to be representative of feminism. Chang has not realized that what is happening is precisely that lesbians are demanding that power be redistributed in the women's movement. The women's movement does not belong to heterosexual women alone. Hu further implies that there exists a broad lesbian spectrum in the women's movement. By the very act of practicing lesbian activism, she and some other feminists have already formed lesbian identification. Lesbian identification is either already inside or growing out of committed feminism. Clearly, Chang's assumption that heterosexuality is the default position for feminists neglects the fact that, for women, the predominance of heterosexuality has never been just a matter of desire. It is implicated in the unequal distribution of power and economic resources between men and women. Feminists, of all people, should not as critics of male domination overlook the elements of choice and political resistance in lesbian identities.

As "women's bonding," the continuum and rupture between feminism and lesbianism is captured by the following story that Yuxuan Aji tells about herself, once an active participant in feminist organizations, including the Awakening Foundation, but now alienated and dedicating her energy to the lesbian group Between Us. She addresses her remarks to her onetime sister feminists:

> Isn't it strange? While we were advocating the ideas that women should identify with women and that women should love women, I fell in love with a real woman of flesh and blood, but I did not become a heroine as a consequence. Instead, I automatically withdrew from you and disappeared. When I turned from a "progressive heterosexual woman" into someone who practices lesbian eroticism and makes lesbian identification, the gigantic stigma of homosexuality became a fate that I could not dodge. Feminism and Western queer theory at best have kept me from drowning. I must find my way to survive, with other lesbians.[55]

Lesbianism may simply be an intense, concrete form of women's alliance, which feminists advocate, but this logical realization or consummation of women's alliance has become a disgrace. Homophobia opens a violent rift between homosociality and homosexuality, feminism and lesbianism. As Yuxuan trespasses on embodied love, she finds feminism in Taiwan no longer her home. It is the split, not the continuum between lesbianism and feminism, that requires explanation.

Yuxuan believes that, "in theory, lesbian activism can and must be integrated with the feminist movement." But, given the homophobic atmosphere of the women's movement in reality, a lesbian movement that is separate from the women's movement must be established. Lesbians must build their own collective identity and politics. Yuxuan maintains:

> Although lesbians are subject to the oppression of the male-female gender hierarchy, for them that oppression is not as pressing as the oppression of sexual orientation. Moreover, some lesbians (especially Ts [tomboys or butches]) resist female identity. They have always fought against the institutional violence of heterosexuality with their individual bodies. They do not identify as women as defined by the heterosexual institution. It is difficult for these lesbians to subscribe to feminism's principle that women identify with women. . . .
>
> Although the lesbian movement . . . does not consider itself part of feminism, as lesbians grope for the ways women may love each other and treat each other equally another kind of feminism is growing out of the subjectivity of lesbians.[56]

On the one hand, Yuxuan upholds *sexual orientation* as a fundamental category of difference that sets lesbians apart from other women. On

the other, Yuxun does not deny that *feminism* can be redefined and rein-
vented by lesbians. In one reading, it might even seem that she momentarily brings up the existence of certain Ts who do no identify as women
only quickly to suppress that presence in order for her own version of
lesbian feminism to emerge.[57] Nevertheless, as Yuxuan's overall position
privileges the experience of those lesbians who do not identify either as
women or with the women's movement as it currently exists, she under-
plays the fact that there are many lesbians for whom feminism is important and who are trying to transform the women's movement from within.
Indeed, the recent effort that Awakening feminists made toward challenging homophobia in the feminist camp represents a new tactic; that is,
rather than reify a minority sexual identity, they seek to deconstruct the
classification and particularization that established female homoeroticism as a localized phenomenon in the first place.

While feminists debate whether lesbianism is internal to themselves,
for lesbians "feminism or not" has also been a source of disagreement. Besides what Yuxuan points out about Ts, at Taida Lambda, for example,
some lesbians have raised the issue of why lesbian activism is often discussed in connection with feminism. This kind of discursive practice
signals to them the assumption that, unless it is packaged as feminism,
lesbianism has no legitimacy in itself. Other lesbians, who believe that
feminism is important for lesbians, respond: "Feminism fights against . . .
the inequality between men and women. Queer activism aims at disman-
tling the stratification of sex (in which husband-wife monogamous sex
is at the top and 'perverse sex' at the bottom). The two movements are
fundamentally different. Nevertheless, feminists must face the question of
sex. And queer activists cannot avoid the issue of gender because gender
is the overall framework. Feminism and queer activism take different
routes, but the two should maintain a dialogue."[58]

Lambda feminist lesbians aptly summarize the connection between
women's identity and sexual practice. Insofar as lesbianism defines itself
as women's same-sex eroticism and union, gender is already part of the
definition. Whether lesbians are enamored of femininity, attempting to
break down conventional notions of femininity, or simply forming life
partnerships and support groups with other women, the dynamic is not
located outside gender. Feminism's critique of the straitjacket that is conventional femininity as well as its attempt to empower women can be appropriated by lesbians for self-empowerment. Fundamentally, homophobia does not work the same way against women as it does against men

in a patriarchal society. The presence of lesbianism is uncomfortable for patriarchy when it represents women's potential for independence and strength.

Further, Lambda feminists confirm that it would be a great oversight for feminists to confront gender oppression as if it did not manifest itself through erotic practices, cultures, and institutions. Men's stigmatization of female-female intimacy and women's masculinity intensified in the capitalist, industrialized West in the early twentieth century as women began to call for emancipation, and Taiwanese feminists might benefit from contemplating this history. Compulsory heterosexuality may be men's final means of exercising control over women's relationships, women having otherwise gained the right to pursue an education, practice a profession, and participate in the political process. As Hu Shuwen insists, the stigmatization of lesbianism must be analyzed from women's point of view. If, after examination, there can be found no fundamental reason why any self-respecting woman should consider same-sex attraction unnatural, Taiwanese feminists can no longer hesitate to embrace lesbian activism as an integral part of women's collective struggle for autonomy.

Not long after the 1995–96 debates over the place of lesbian agendas in the women's movement, the prolesbian feminists Wang Ping and Ni Jiazhen were fired from their jobs at the Awakening Foundation. This move was unfortunate in that it indicated a move toward the mainstream instead of maintaining a radical, oppositional stance in full support of lesbian activism.[59] Wang Ping subsequently founded Xingbie renquan xiehui (the Gender/Sexuality Rights Association) in 2000, an organization dedicated primarily to lesbian and gay issues.[60] While the number of specifically lesbigay organizations that operate independently of major feminist organizations may have increased, the question that activists battling for lesbigay rights in Taiwan must ultimately confront is whether such organizations can avoid ghettoization and rally a sufficiently broad population base to effect change through democratic processes, something that they can do only if they guard against identity essentialism and compartmentalization and forge coalitions with other grassroots social movements.[61] It is, undoubtedly, both necessary and healthy to articulate differences, such as those between heterosexual feminist and lesbian feminist priorities, between butch-femme (*T-po*) lesbians and undifferentiated (*bufen*) lesbians, and even between butches and femmes. Nonetheless, if the articulation of differences automatically leads to particularized identities and never to mutual respect and empathy, it is to be expected that there will be damaging political ramifications—diluted energy and the impossibility of forming a powerful collective.

The dialogues among female activists (some of whom are academics) examined above are important because they had immediate consequences for the direction taken by the political programming of lesbian and feminist organizations. The growth of these organizations throughout the 1990s in Taiwan is emblematic of the vitality and strength—unique in the contemporary Chinese-speaking world—of the lesbian and feminist movements on the island. Lesbian organizing in mainland China is, as mentioned earlier, in a nascent phase. Although since the late 1990s there have begun to appear some group discussions (including academic ones) of female same-sex issues, the absence of formal channels for social movements in China has dictated that they adopt an apolitical stance and moderate rhetoric.[62] Most female literary critics' discussions of women's homoerotic literature in the PRC are, as indicated in part 3, couched in terms of *female consciousness* and *sisterhood,* calling little or no attention to the questions of nonconforming gender and sexual preference. By contrast, the 1990s in Taiwan witnessed, not only serious efforts on the part of the lesbian movement to signify itself through, and thus radicalize, a relatively established women's movement from within, but also soul-searching dialogues analyzing sexual differences among feminists, dialogues through which a militant lesbian feminist collective distinguished itself from heterosexist feminism and thrust itself into public view. That militant lesbian feminist collective deserves our attention partly because such a confrontational constituency was never visible in May Fourth China and still has limited visibility in post-Mao China, despite the many fictional representations of female same-sex love and eroticism during the two periods. To wit, the Taiwanese militant lesbian feminist persona is not just a new lesbian identity. It is an unprecedented public female identity, at least as far as the Chinese-speaking world is concerned.

As Mayfair Yang argues with regard to women's public spheres in transnational China, state and administrative boundaries have so far largely isolated mainland Chinese, Hong Kong, and Taiwanese feminists. At the same time, it is also apparent that such borders are becoming increasingly porous as the Greater China region becomes integrated economically, socially, culturally, and, to some extent, politically.[63] In the foreseeable future, intraregional interactions and alliances among feminists will increase. For example, Dai Jinhua, a major feminist literary and film scholar at Beijing University, held a visiting professorship in Taiwan in 1998 and participated in many local feminist debates.[64] We are left, then, with an intriguing question indeed—whether the pointed critiques of the structuring of gender norms, differences, and hierarchies that Taiwanese lesbian feminists have advanced on the island for over a decade can catalyze similar developments on the mainland in the near future.

### The Mass Mediatization and the Commercialization of Homosexuality: Will Lesbian Activism Be Different?

Although a public sphere in which lesbian rights and radicalism may be openly discussed or promoted has come into existence in Taiwan, it remains debatable to what extent lesbian interests and viewpoints have been adequately represented in it without either domesticating lesbianism or marking it as the inferior other of society. Although largely autonomous of the state, what the media produce in present-day Taiwan is often dictated by commercial interests. A consideration of lesbian feminist practice in the public sphere would, thus, be incomplete without, first, analyzing representations of lesbian and gay issues in the capitalist media and, second, illuminating the relation that a radical lesbian and feminist stance may have to the commercial media. Generally speaking, despite the almost overwhelming influence of the commercial media, lesbian activist discourse in Taiwan has resisted sensationalism and wholesale commodification and striven to engage in lesbian cultural production and give visibility to lesbian viewpoints beyond the commercial media.

The mass media in Taiwan in the 1990s take a schizophrenic approach to gay and lesbian issues. On the one hand, newspapers and television stations seem friendly to gay and lesbian activism. They carry many translated reports from the West on gay/lesbian pride parades, AIDS activism, same-sex marriages, and the like.[65] The popular press publishes a considerable number of articles submitted by academic writers and other private observers on queer genders, politics, literature, art, film, and so on. A number of newspaper columns and radio programs have even been devoted to the discussion and sharing of gay and lesbian experiences and problems. When gay and lesbian activists organize events protesting homophobia, it is common for them to notify the gay-friendly media so that the events will be covered and publicized. For instance, all the major media reported the first government-sponsored Taibei tongwanjie (Taipei Lesbian and Gay Festival) in September 2000.[66] Indeed, it looks as if the Taiwanese mass media are interested in promoting social change and human rights (including the free choice of sexual preference).

On the other hand, the Taiwanese media continue to reproduce the stereotype of homosexuality as abnormal and gender inversion. Most often, it is through the media rather than medical or psychiatric treatises that the public learns about outdated sexological ideas. It is through the media that medical classifications are disseminated and vulgarized. During the aforementioned Taipei Lesbian and Gay Festival in 2000, for example, the media coverage was highly mixed in quality. As the lesbian reporting staff of *Nü pengyou* notes, although some television stations and newspapers took the enlightened position that lesbians' and gay men's human rights should be protected, others were content to focus on the spectacle of the drag queens.[67]

Furthermore, the media associate homosexuality with sexual excitement and the criminal underworld. Since the beginning of the 1990s, the media have—with an eye toward profits—been intent on turning the homosexual subject into an erotic-exotic object for the popular gaze, giving queer sexualities problematic visibility. Sensational tabloid magazines such as *Dujia baodao* (Exclusive reports) and *Shibao zhoukan* (Times weekly) as well as a horde of other soft-core pornographic magazines have turned out story after story about lesbian/gay promiscuity, sexual techniques, cruising parks and bars, crimes, murders, and suicides. Some of these reports are voyeuristic; many are plainly fantastic. They portray gays and lesbians as stealthy, alien creatures whose secrets the reporters can pry into and reveal to satisfy the curiosity of the general public, the "normal" people.[68] This is especially pronounced in the case of lesbians. Unlike gay men, lesbians as a community were little known to the public until the late 1980s. The media's excitement at discovering lesbians was tremendous. It was predominated by a craving for observing lesbian sex and seeing spectacular transgender types. Lesbians' political struggle to make their erotic preference visible and legitimate thus comes dangerously close to the pervasive hypersexualization of women in the commercial media. The label *lesbian* all too easily reduces women to one-dimensional beings in the popular imagination, reinscribing hierarchical power relations between men and women as well as between heterosexuals and homosexuals.

The schizophrenic or hybrid character of the Taiwanese mass media alerts us to the possibility that theories of the relation between the mass media and social liberation that are either wholly laudatory or wholly derogatory capture only part of the truth. Mark Poster points out that, until recently, attempts to theorize the media followed the lines of a "broadcast model" and imagined communication as a process of "unidirectional speech," one in which there are very few production centers and a large number of recipients.[69] Moreover, most media theorists' characterizations of human subjectivity places it on one side of the autonomous/heteronomous divide. Working with the broadcast model, pessimistic theorists, such as Theodor Adorno, argue that the media impose a uniform false consciousness on the masses.[70] By contrast, optimistic theorists turn the broadcast model completely around. Hans Enzensberger, for example, claims: "For the first time in history, the media make possible a mass participation in a productive process at once social and socialized, participation whose practical means are in the hands of the masses themselves."[71]

If we observe the recent disarray of media representations of gay/lesbian sexuality in Taiwan, however, it seems that there is no straightforward correlation between the ideological character of the media and a monopoly on either capital or the means of production. The best example is the *Zhongguo shibao* (China times) media conglomerate. The same enterprise can issue a report on a gay pride parade in New York in its daily paper, carry an article on the subversive nature of queer gender performativity by the Taiwanese feminist scholar Hsiao-hung Chang in its evening paper, put out a fabricated, highly eroticized and scandalous story on a crime involving lesbians or gays in its weekly magazine, and still bring out avant-garde novels dealing positively with gay or lesbian themes through its book-publishing division. In other words, a monopoly on the means of production has not prevented ideological diversity. The media give the masses, not one choice, but many. At the same time, the masses are in no position to dictate what will and will not be published.

The relation between the media and their audience in Taiwan's capitalist economy should be reconceptualized as an interactive and mutually penetrating one. Despite their privileged position, the media cannot simply impose something on the masses. Rather, they must assess the market, attempt to determine what consumers want, how many different kinds of audiences are out there, and how large each audience is. And they are constantly modifying their product in the light of market response. The media also "develop markets" (*kaifa shichang*), offering innovative new products for public consumption.

Given this interactive model, if homosexuality has become one of the most trendy and best-selling topics in Taiwan, is it because lesbians and gays have become such a distinctive and powerful consumer group that their emotional needs and erotic interests must be catered to or because lesbian/gay sexualities have been domesticated and turned into curiosities that an audience that considers itself to be normal will find entertaining? It seems that both explanations are valid and that one need not preclude the other. If the many different kinds of homoerotic material produced by the *Zhongguo shibao* conglomerate suggest anything at all, it is the fact that, in a mature capitalist economy, the media must continually seek out new and different markets if they are to continue turning a profit and maintaining some semblance of credibility. But, because they must cater to so many different markets, they give the appearance of "schizophrenia," especially when what they are marketing is sexuality. To satisfy the demands of their audiences, the media must open avenues for critical discussion, intelligent analysis, rational reportage, and the latest information on gay liberation from "advanced" Western countries even as they capitalize on the scandalous side of homoeroticism.

Perhaps the fact that homoeroticism has been so successfully commercialized in Taiwan in recent years shows precisely that there is no easy, clear demarcation between the straight and the gay and that, although society at large may position itself as straight, it is heavily invested in queer pleasures. This is good news on one level. On another level, however, the amazing compatibility between capitalism and gay and lesbian sexualities is troubling. In contemporary Taiwan, other kinds of minority politics have made their presence felt in the public sphere. For example, the dire economic and cultural situation of aboriginal peoples (*yuanzhumin*) have caused some individuals of aboriginal descent to appeal for social justice, to rally for the restoration of their cultures, and to seek economic and political empowerment. Yet aboriginal identity politics proved to have no general, mass-market appeal and, hence, to be of limited value to the media. What, then, is it about gay and lesbian sexualities that makes them so media friendly? Do they pose only a limited challenge to the status quo?[72] Have they become mainstream within a mere couple of years because sex and love are what capitalism has always capitalized on and consumed?[73] If so, how can gay and lesbian identity politics be a truly progressive politics? How can it stop being assimilated by mainstream ideology? Does it want to? Is there any difference between lesbian politics and gay politics?

In June 1996, *G&L: Re'ai zazhi* (G&L: Love magazine), the first commercial gay and lesbian publication in Taiwan, was launched, a new business venture meant to "mainstream" gay and lesbian identities. If the mainstream ideology in Taiwan is represented by capitalism, this business venture attempted to carve out respectable gay and lesbian subject positions by signifying them through capitalist consumption. *G&L* is vastly different from earlier Taiwanese magazines devoted exclusively to queer sexualities and cultures in that it has a budget and a distribution network that make it competitive with mainstream commercial publications. In its first month alone, the beautifully made, glossy *G&L* sold more than fifteen thousand copies at the newsstand price of NT$200 (U.S.$8) a copy in Taiwan, and the publisher had to print a second run. The magazine envisions its readers to be "gays, lesbians, and all open-minded young gentlemen and ladies." In the inaugural issue of the magazine, the main editor, An Keqiang, predicted: "The time is ripe for creating a gay/lesbian magazine that provides tips on living, leisure, and consumption."[74]

The first issue of *G&L* at least is male centered and unabashedly consumerist. The magazine speaks to gay men, heterosexual women, and heterosexual men much more than to lesbians. Erotic images of half-nude men and other items of interest to gay men occupy 90 percent of the magazine. As readers' responses printed in the following issue point out, the first number had disappointingly little—only two pieces—to offer to lesbians.[75] The first piece, "Sharon yijing zhanchulai le," is a short interview with two Taiwanese lesbians, Sharon and Antonia, who have come out with pride; this piece constitutes the strongest political statement in the entire issue. The second, "Sange ren: Run," consists of a series of photographs of two feminine female models and a male model, all fashionably dressed, posing in different combinations, to show that "three is better than two" (see fig. 10). It is not difficult to see that these images advocating bisexuality reinscribe men's claims to lesbian bodies. The bisexual combination, two women plus a man, is remotely reminiscent of the traditional Chinese polygamous marriage. By making such an arrangement, the magazine shows itself fully aware of the difficulty involved in making lesbianism acceptable to mainstream society without introducing the notion of male privilege. Through their expressions and their attire, the female models affirm in every way society's ideal of delicate female beauty. Here, lesbianism means double visual pleasure for the male gaze.

*G&L* openly embraces consumerism. The main feature of the inaugural issue is a story about the gay and lesbian consumer culture in Taiwan that opens with an unqualified endorsement of capitalist consumer culture: "Our age is characterized by the motto, 'Business is guiltless, and consumption is right' [*Shangye wu zui, xiaofei you li*]. . . . The number of gay and lesbian consumers is large. They form an emerging market. They are a consumer group that businesses and advertising companies are eager to develop. Gay and lesbian issues are no longer serious agendas about human rights, dignity, and resistance. They can be sold as a commodity."[76] This introduction amounts to arguing that being queer or proqueer means

FIGURE 10 "Three Is Better Than Two." (*G&L: Re'ai zazhi*, no. 1 [1996]: 120)

no more than buying and using certain fashionable merchandise symbol-
izing good queer taste. It argues that gays and lesbians are, like everyone
else, just part of the highly capitalized society of Taiwan.

Certainly, there is more than a grain of truth to this position. If an as-
cription of queer identity is based solely on sexual preference, queers may
be very different from one another in matters other than sexual preference. Also, they may have much in common with nonqueers. Indeed, gays
and lesbians do not occupy any particularly disadvantaged and exploited
social stratum, at least not one defined in economic terms. Gays and lesbians should be treated like anyone else who has money to spend, the article argues. Money at once justifies and levels difference.

Nevertheless, the magazine's capitalist justification of homoeroticism
provokes questions. Is changing one's status in the consumer culture—
moving from being the object consumed by others to being the consuming
subject targeted by advertisers—the sign of liberation? If money is the
route to liberation, is the real distinction in society that between rich and

poor rather than between straight and gay? Is class the ultimate oppression? How can gays and lesbians who claim to resist oppressive social structures effortlessly embrace capitalist materialism and the economic class inequality that it entails? To whom does *G&L* primarily speak? Middle-class gay men interested in Guy Laroche perfume, Armani suits, gay porn videos, and tourist packages to Bangkok and San Francisco? If *G&L* perceives lesbians as having less purchasing power than gay men do or as being less interested in conspicuous consumption (as, indeed, the focus of the magazine's contents indicates), does this mean that lesbians deserve less respect than gay men do? A capitalist evaluation of people's worth and rights is problematic, to say the least.

Perhaps those who produce *G&L* magazine believe that there is no denying the fact that homosexual people are no more and no less concerned with universal social justice than are nonhomosexual people. Perhaps they believe that to say that homosexual people are different from mainstream society in any respect other than sexual preference would be untrue and oppressive in itself. My point, however, is that, claiming to serve gay men and lesbians, *G&L* has taken an ambiguous stance on gay and lesbian identities. It declares that, to end oppression based on erotic object choice, gay and lesbian identities must be demystified and shown to be absolutely ordinary. This move is important because, as long as there remains the discursive production of homosexuals as a social other, individuals whose sexual preference is thought to embody a multitude of insurmountable and inexplicable differences, homophobia and oppression persist. At the same time, *G&L* argues that gays' and lesbians' differences must be affirmed. And the way to affirm erotic difference is through capitalism. *G&L* perceives gays and lesbians as in need of custom-made entertainment and merchandise different from what is made available to straight society, and the magazine promises to provide what they need. *G&L* constructs gay and lesbian identities as the same as those of mainstream, heterosexual society in their need to consume but as different from the mainstream in terms of the objects consumed.

Perhaps aware of readers' criticisms, an attempt was made in later issues of *G&L* to increase content related to lesbians despite the fact that the editorial staff was all male. However, when asked by a reader who identified herself as a young T why the publisher had not put out a magazine devoted specifically to lesbian leisure needs, the editors replied candidly: "There are too few lesbian readers. We are worried that, if we publish a lesbian entertainment magazine, our lesbian friends won't show their support by purchasing it and our warehouse will end up filled with unsold copies!"[77] An attempt was also made to balance a consumerist orientation with activist agendas; the result was that coverage of protests against the intensified police harassment of gays in Taipei in 1997–98 and cogent analyses of candidates' attitudes toward gay rights during the Taipei mayoral election appeared alongside full-page reproduction of photographs of male nudes.[78] Ultimately, however, the editors were unable to find a successful mix of radical and mainstream content. Although the publisher succeeded in putting *G&L* in the magazine racks in convenience stores in Taiwan, he was forced to change his editorial policy in 2000 because the magazine was not profitable. *G&L* was made over to resemble it sister publication, *Ji'ai* (Glory), a thriving gay porn magazine that has no lesbian content.[79] In other words, unprofitable idealism was abandoned in favor of profitable pandering.

As we have seen, radical lesbian discourse apparently departs from such a consumerist, depoliticized interpretation of same-sex practice. Radical lesbianism challenges the existent power hierarchies in social institutions: in the patriarchal, heterosexual family, the normalizing pseudoscience of sexual psychology, the state's law on marriage and family, as well as the exploitation of lesbian gender and sex by the capitalist media. What it strives for is, not just the comforts and conveniences of a particular lifestyle, but also a systemic, structural change. It aspires to developing an ethics of love distinguished from coercion, violence, and exploitation. Recognizing the reality that lesbians are doubly oppressed as women and as homosexuals, lesbian activists cannot afford not to confront male domination even in a so-called free capitalist economy. The momentum of the radical lesbian movement comes from a critical, oppositional stance. What lesbian activism will do is precisely carry on serious agendas of "human rights, dignity, and resistance," which *G&L* had dismissed at the outset. Until society takes lesbian rights seriously, lesbians and feminists will continue to build a distinctively female imagined community on the basis of counterhegemonic writings by lesbians and feminists.

Because of their ambiguous and stupefying ideological effects, the commercial media will not likely be the major means by which radical lesbian feminist discourse maintains its momentum in the Taiwanese public sphere. Lesbian feminist discourse must find alternative ways of disseminating its message. Fortunately, the latest developments in communications technology have greatly facilitated access to public forums. And most important among such developments is the Internet. Taiwanese lesbian and feminist publications have traditionally been printed and have had only limited, local circulation, but recently there have emerged electronic feminist-lesbian journals able to reach large audiences on a global scale. One of the pioneers in this regard is *Hong peiji* (G-zine), an electronic journal featuring incisive feminist and lesbian activist commentary and purposefully "offensive" graphics.[80] The website is created and maintained by the Liangxing yu shehui yanjiushi (Gender and Society Study Group) at National Tsing Hua University in Taiwan. While arguably academic and "ivory tower" in origin, the reach of *Hong peiji* easily transcends geographic locations because of the World Wide Web, and its appeal is potentially populist given its dramatic visual presentation. Its democratic potential is illustrated by the fact that e-mail responses to it have been received across a variety of borders from nonacademic Chinese readers in North America, Hong Kong, and mainland China as well as from within Taiwan itself. After *Hong peiji,* many other lesbian websites (*lawang*) have become popular.[81]

Similarly, since the mid-1990s the Chinese electronic BBS (Bulletin Board System) has come to play an important role in the public discussion of homosexuality in Taiwan. Many young people, especially college students, meet others of similar sexual preferences as well as argue with their opponents on the net. According to a listing in 1996, there were more than forty BBS domains set up by students in different universities in Taiwan that had bulletin boards called "Members of the Same Sex" (MOTSS). The number has continuously grown, to the point of being uncountable. BBS communication has many characteristics conducive to the formation of a critical public sphere. Internet communication is decentralized and interactive. It can be either one-on-one or group oriented. Access to it is unrestricted and depends on neither capital nor social position. Thus it allows a freer exchange of opinion than do the traditional media. Finally, Internet communication is extremely private as well as public. An Internet user's on-line speech is not censored, and it is available to anyone who has access to and knows how to use a computer. It is somewhat paradoxical that the postmodern Internet corresponds in many ways to Habermas's nostalgic, humanistic ideal of the public sphere of modernity: "audience-oriented privacy."[82] If the Internet continues to maintain its autonomy, radical movements in Taiwan such as lesbian activism and feminism are likely increasingly to employ it for carving out and maintaining a critical public sphere. We have reason to hope that, as opinions become contested and liberalized in cyberspace, transformations in this emerging domain of the cultural imaginary will catalyze changes in the material conditions of the so-called reality as well.

# THE AUTOBIOGRAPHICAL LESBIAN

In the previous chapter, I have argued that, in post—martial law Taiwan, lesbian activism has sought to signify itself through a relatively established women's movement, radicalizing that movement from within. Meanwhile, some lesbian activists have set themselves apart from homophobic strains of feminism, thus projecting a militant lesbian feminist constituency into public view. The previous chapter has also examined the commercialization of homosexuality and the media attention devoted to it as the topic enters Taiwan's capitalist public sphere. Although lesbian activists have hoped to gain public recognition for lesbian sexualities and even worked with the mass media with some success, they have nonetheless shown considerable resistance to co-optation by the traditional mass media and, through utilizing new and alternative media, have tried to create spaces for the exchange of opinion and for lesbian cultural production. These characteristics suggest that, as the lesbian identity inserts itself into public culture and demands recognition, it has striven to maintain radical difference and nonconformity in self-representation.

To explore the issue further, I now take a close look at lesbian self-representation in Taiwan's avant-garde literature. The questions that the militant lesbian movement as a whole has posed about homophobia, identity, and the mediated character of Taiwan's public sphere are confronted by individual writers as well. While lesbian activists explicitly discuss these issues from a radical feminist perspective, one that consciously distinguishes itself from mainstream feminism, Qiu Miaojin, the lesbian writer whom I shall read as a prime example of Taiwan's new queer writers, is fascinating, not so much for her defiance, as for the intensity of her anguish. Amid society's rush toward a great variety of identity formations and politics, she is one of the first in post–martial law Taiwan to explore the costs of identity politics and heightened visibility. She attacks, with smoldering anger and wry humor, the mass media's overbearing desire to *see* dissident sexual subjects. Doubting the notions of authenticity and truthful confession, moreover, she calls into question the ontological and/or epistemological status of sexual identity.

### An Overview of Female Homoerotic Fiction in Taiwan

In part 3, I have argued that, more than any other writers in post-Mao China, Lin Bai and Chen Ran have persistently explored female same-sex desire in their fiction. However, in Lin's homoerotic plots, the female protagonists have internalized societal discrimination against homosexuals, restrain themselves from pursuing lesbian relationships, and woefully lament their own inability comfortably to inhabit the lesbian identity, whereas Chen's female protagonists search restlessly for love among both sexes and refuse to be limited by such an identity. In form, both Lin and Chen have largely relied on short stories to explore female-female relations. Neither writer has to date devoted a full-length novel to female same-sex desire. In *One Person's War,* the narrator, Duomi, recounts abortive same-sex relationships interspersed with painful heterosexual relationships, while *Private Life* relates Aoao's adventures with lovers of either sex. In short, one cannot find in contemporary fiction from the People's Republic of China (PRC) a full-length work that unmistakably develops lesbian sexuality and subjectivity as its central theme.[1] To find such works, one must look outside the PRC—in Taiwan. The rise in Taiwan during the last decade of novels and whole collections dealing with the subject of lesbian eroticism and lesbian subjectivity—which occurred amid a burgeoning lesbian and gay identity politics and the general proliferation of queer discourses—distinguishes the cultural scene of Taiwan not only from that of the PRC but also from that of the former British colony Hong Kong or any other Chinese-speaking society.[2]

To be sure, the 1970s had seen in Taiwan the appearance of Xuan Xiaofo's *Yuan zhi wai* (Outside the perfect circle; 1976) and Guo Lianghui's *Liangzhong yiwaide* (Beyond two kinds; 1978), which portrayed "tomboys" who play masculine roles opposite their femme lovers. And Zhu Tianxin's youthful narrative (in diary form) of her high school days, *Jirang ge* (Singing and drumming on the ground; 1977), is full of descriptions of the romantic but nonphysical love between girls. Despite these early examples, novels and autobiographical narratives that elaborate female-female sexuality and lesbian subjectivity did not proliferate in Taiwan until the last decade of the twentieth century.

The trend might be said to have begun in 1990. A novice writer, Ling Yan, entered her first novel, *Shi sheng huamei* (The muted thrush; 1990), in a literary competition sponsored by the *Zili wanbao* (Self-independence evening post) and won the coveted top prize. *Muted Thrush* delineates the decline of the Taiwanese opera (*koa-a-hi*) in the countryside by examining the troubles of a traveling troupe, and among the novel's innovative features are naturalistic descriptions of the sexual relations between actresses.[3] In 1994, the young writer Qiu Miaojin further surprised the literary world with *Eyu shouji* (The crocodile's journal), the first novel published in Taiwan to depict in depth the psychological turmoil of a lesbian college student and pointedly to satirize society's homophobia. In 1995, Qiu completed another novel about female-female desire—*Mengmate yishu* (Last letters from Montmartre)—before committing suicide in Paris. Following her tragic death, her lesbianism was widely publicized in the Taiwanese mass media, and her two novels took on significance as autobiographical narratives and won praise as milestones in Taiwanese lesbian self-representation. Another female writer who came out as lesbian during the mid-1990s was Chen Xue, who published two collections of short stories exploring female homoeroticism and mother-daughter desire—*E nü shu* (The book of an evil woman; 1995) and *Mengyou 1994* (Sleepwalking in 1994; 1996). Also lesbian identified is Lucifer Hung (Hong Ling), who takes pleasure in depicting lesbian vampirism and sadomasochism in a futuristic universe.[4] If we consider other relevant female writers who do not necessarily claim to be lesbian or queer, the list can be expanded to encompass Zhu Tianxin, Cao Lijuan, Du Xiulan, and many others.[5]

As can be seen from this mere sketch, the difference between Taiwan and the PRC over the last few decades is substantial. Prior to the 1980s, homosexuality could not be mentioned in public in the PRC, yet explicitly lesbian novels were being published across the Taiwan Strait. Because of the availability of popular sexual psychology as well as exposure to postwar American popular culture, the concepts of both female homosexuality and male homosexuality were present, if not prominent, in public discourse. For example, in *Yuan zhi wai* and *Liangzhong yiwaide,* one encounters characters who discriminate against female homosexuals as psychobiological perverts, a plot choice that clearly exploits the sexological stereotype, made popular in postwar American pulp fiction about lesbians,[6] of the monstrous, mannish lesbian, secret lesbian circles in the big city, and women in violent, tragic relationships. These novels and others like them may also have been depicting certain tomboy communities in Taipei during the 1970s, communities that were partly shaped by the American presence in Taiwan.[7]

Throughout the 1990s and into the twenty-first century, a period of accelerating globalization in both the PRC and Taiwan, certain differences between the two societies remain pronounced. In Taiwan, the proliferation of female homoerotic fiction was partly propelled by the wave of Western, primarily American, queer theory that swept through the island during the early to mid-1990s.[8] Starting in late 1993, some academics housed in Departments of English at major universities began to churn out analyses of foreign and Chinese queer books and films, and the articles were eagerly published by newspapers, many with circulations over a million. The influence of academic theory on the writing of female homoerotic fiction was especially apparent in the cases of Lucifer Hung and Chen Xue, who were then students at, respectively, National Taiwan University and Central University, schools then on the rise as the two major centers for the study of gender and sexuality in Taiwan because of the publishing activities of individual faculty members.[9] More generally, the increased production of female homoerotic fiction occurred at a time when new social movements involving new identity formations became possible.[10] Fueled by imported queer theory, and encouraged by local lesbian and gay identity formations, Taiwanese fiction about lesbian and other queer sexualities has grown voluminous.[11] Moreover, this body of literature has been commented on profusely by local academic critics, who tirelessly cite Western queer theory.[12]

Given the sheer volume of this body of literature, which amounts to nothing less than an avant-garde movement, I cannot hope to do justice to it in a brief analysis. My rationale for discussing Taiwanese female homoerotic fiction here is specifically to examine how *the lesbian* has inserted herself as an autobiographical subject into the ongoing discourse of serious, avant-garde literature in Taiwan. I do provide a reading of one key text, a reading that both concurs and disagrees with the analyses of Taiwanese critics. I highlight, for instance, the epistemological questions that come to the fore when identity is defined in terms of visibility and representability. In short, my discussion of Taiwanese lesbian autobiographical writing is intended to be illustrative rather than exhaustive.

This literature has sprung up in a social and political context radically different from that prevailing in the PRC. It has been nourished by discourses that are American in origin and new, post−martial law social movements. Its hybrid cultural character and subversive intent distinguish it from mainland Chinese writers' personal explorations of female-female relations in a partly closed society, where information from abroad remains narrowly filtered and where the state continues actively to discourage organized protest movements.[13] On the mainland, no major female writer has as yet claimed a lesbian identity, in part because professing a nonnormative sexual orientation is considered too limiting, both personally and professionally. The public sphere in Taiwan, in contrast, offers many possibilities for action. Although pushing an act prohibiting discrimination against lesbians and gays through the Taiwanese legislature has proved difficult,[14] the efforts of lesbian and gay activists over the last decade have at least created a social space for artistic creation and interpretation that is much freer than it was before. The space is considerably more elastic than what I have described as the third space of interpretation and signification in the PRC.

By noting the contrast between Taiwan and mainland China, I by no means overlook the fact that the heavy importation of American elite and popular cultures to Taiwan has had its own attendant problems. Certainly, the importation has been embraced by many in Taiwan as cosmopolitanism, social progress, an inevitable part of globalization, or a deliberate strategy. Hsiao-hung Chang, arguably the one critic who has contributed the most to popularizing theories of gender and sexuality in 1990s Taiwan, unapologetically characterizes her own methodology as "the hybridization and miscegenation of theory and 'local' events [*lilun yu 'bentu' shijian de xianghu zajiao, zazhong hua*]."[15] The sentiment is shared by many other literary and cultural critics, including Liang-ya Liou, who exultantly declares:

It is noteworthy that the erotic fiction of 1990s Taiwan frequently cites Western and Japanese intellectual trends and literary masterpieces, fully displaying the character of a cultural hybrid. Traversing and crossing multiple cultures, these fictional writings, not only transmogrify sex and gender, but also put on and take off cultures as if they were clothes. Citation does not mean exact copying. Rather, through forwarding and translating, it is a ceaseless process of extending, allegorizing, decontextualizing, rewriting, and localizing. It opens up extra space for reference, self-reflection, dialogue, and imagining. To change one's cultural clothes is to engage in a serious yet jubilant dialectics of difference and sameness between cultures. To use Western literary theory to analyze these texts, therefore, is to further enrich interaction of this nature and to transgress the self-boundaries of cultures.[16]

Although Liou does not use the word *postmodernism,* it is apparent that both she and Chang celebrate certain qualities associated with the postmodern: hybridity, pastiche, decentering, decontextualization, surface, and play. Such are the understandings of the postmodern popular on the island since the late 1980s, despite the subtle theoretical differences among various local literary and cultural critics who debate the applicability of the notion of postmodernity in Taiwan.[17]

The justifications given for playful, parodic transpositions of queer discourses from abroad notwithstanding, there is little denying that the originality of Taiwanese cultural creation has been put at risk. The 1970s witnessed serious debates among Taiwan's writers and critics over the appropriateness of introducing Western modernist writing styles and tenets of criticism.[18] What in this light is striking about the recent transportation of queer theory to Taiwan is that there has been very little "nativist resistance" in literary and academic circles; in fact, some local queer theorists are so popular with readers and audiences that they have become media celebrities.[19] The society's current extreme openness to Euro-American and Japanese cultural products has something to do with the fact that, after several decades of industrialization, Taiwan has, indeed, become like other postindustrial societies, characterized by a high level of urbanization, the growth of a sophisticated consumer culture, and a decline in the manufacturing sector. Because of the proliferation of postindustrial, urban lifestyles, American discourses of sexuality fulfill a genuine need among especially the younger members of a population eager to explore options beyond the nuclear family.

Still, the importation of American queer theory and political strategy is not completely unproblematic. For instance, the latest call for a transgender movement put out by He Chunrui and others at the Workshop for Gender/Sexuality Studies at National Central University has been criticized by Wei-cheng Chu. Chu argues that, in the West, the agitation for a transgender movement came from self-identified transgender communities; that, in Taiwan, despite the popularity of drag shows, there are very few publicly self-identified transgender individuals; and that for university professors to agitate for a transgender movement in Taiwan is, therefore, both inappropriate and premature, simply a mindless mimicking of Western academic developments.[20] Bad enough, if, as Ta-wei Chi argues, to be queer is to defy authority and social convention,[21] then the uncritical parroting of the latest trends in First World queer theory is quite the opposite of being queer. Worse still, it might mean misdirecting valuable resources away from, rather than toward, the really challenging problems of local sexual and gender politics.

Despite these potential dangers, one must acknowledge that there are many jewels in the literature of lesbian and other queer sexualities that arose in Taiwan over the past decade. Qiu Miaojin (1969–95), for instance, had an exceptional talent. Her voice is assertive, intellectual, witty, lyrical, and intimate. Several years after her death, her works continue to command a huge following among college-educated lesbians in Taiwan, for she gave beautiful and soulful expression to the experiences of that community. As Yuxuan Aji and Zheng Meili observe, the protagonist of Qiu's *Eyu shouji*—and the author's alter ego—has become the focus of a great deal of lesbian identification, and *Lazi,* her nickname, has become a preferred method of address among Taiwanese lesbians.[22] While the popularity of *lazi* may be at least partly attributed to the fact that it sounds like *lez* (for *lesbian*), it is largely due to the extraordinary charisma of Qiu's persona.

### The Crocodile's Journal

*To write is almost my second nature. To transform the material in my life into words is almost my greatest enjoyment. . . . Before I die, I shall be concerned about expressing the most important spiritual material that I have experienced in a manner that is most personal to me. Because it is closest to me.*

QIU MIAOJIN, "Zi shu"

On 25 June 1995, Qiu Miaojin committed suicide in Paris by plunging a knife into her heart. She died instantly. When the news of her death was made public in Taiwan on 30 June, "it caused a wave of shock and rumors in the literary circle. And it quickly became a hot discussion topic in BBS [Bulletin Board System] on the Internet—her personality, life, friends, and all the knots she could or could not untie."[23]

Suicide was, thus, more than self-destruction. It was—intentionally or otherwise—the ultimate act of self-publicization. Acknowledged as promising while she was alive,[24] her work was honored with several prizes after her death. To pay tribute to Qiu's talent, *Lianhe wenxue* (Unitas), a prestigious literary monthly in Taiwan, published several of her personal essays and poems as well as her novel *Mengmate yishu* (Last letters from Montmartre).[25] But most popular by far, with critics and the public alike, was her novel *Eyu shouji* (The crocodile's journal), which had been published a year before her death. It was honored with the "Prize of Recommendation" by the judges of the *Zhongguo shibao* (China times) Literary Awards in December 1995.

Curious readers searched *The Crocodile's Journal* for signs of Qiu's self-hatred, for signs of a tendency toward self-destruction—in short, for signs of her rejection of her own lesbian orientation. On the basis of certain bleak moments in the novel, it is said that Qiu believed that her existence, mired in the desire for women, was guilt laden and at odds with society. Conspicuously, interpretations of Qiu's suicide stressing her ambivalence about lesbianism echo popular notions of lesbians—that their love is often unrequited and that they have low self-esteem and morbid personalities. On the surface, Qiu's suicide lends itself well to the media's trite idioms and favorite plotlines.

But Qiu's representation of her experiences and thoughts is in all her works more complex and subversive than media representation makes it out to be. Her confession before death, *Last Letters from Montmartre,* is a beautiful work of love, commitment, and sacrifice. It does not reduce passion to pleasure but instead approaches it as an issue of willpower, character, and spiritual awareness. It does not negate lesbianism; on the contrary, it is dedicated to the beloved, to herself, and to art.

To illuminate the political dimension of Qiu's self-representation, I focus here on her most widely read work, *The Crocodile's Journal.* I argue that, despite the fact that Qiu's suicide afforded the mass media the opportunity to reinscribe lesbians as morbid and pathological, *The Crocodile's Journal* defies the dehumanization of lesbians. While the novel takes the guilt and pain of the lesbian orientation as its starting point, its critique of the social mechanism that turns lesbianism into something akin to a crime is severe. The novel stands as a powerful political protest, not

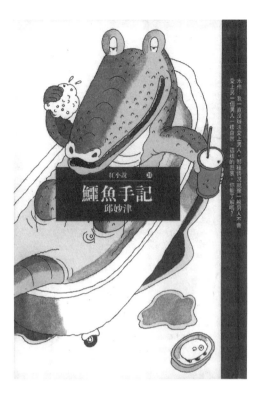

FIGURE 11 The cover of *Eyu shouji* (The crocodile's journal), by Qiu Miaojin (Taipei: Shibao wenhua, 1994).

for its optimism, but precisely for its painful, emotional engagement with the stigmatization of lesbianism in Taiwan.

Stylistically, the novel is a mix of realism and animal fable organized by the principles of montage and jump-cutting.[26] In the realistic portions, the first-person narrator—who most likely represents Qiu herself but who, because she never reveals her real name, is known only as Lazi, a nonsense nickname that some friends have given her—reminisces about her college days as she reconstructs them from her failing memory. These reminiscences revolve around tales of troubled same-sex relationships—those between an estranged younger female couple and between a gay male friend and his bisexual male lover as well as her own relationships with women—tales that are connected only because of her presence in all of them. In the animal fable portions, Lazi tells the life of a cartoon-like character called Crocodile, responding to rumors about the existence of "crocodiles" running loose on the island (fig. 11).[27] The novel alternates between the realistic and the animal fable portions, the two seemingly unconnected. However, on consideration, it becomes clear that, in both portions, Qiu is writing about herself. Crocodile is the reflection that Lazi sees of herself in the media mirror.[28] Rumors about "crocodiles" in the text mimic and parody the phobic and voyeuristic conjectures about lesbians and gay men in the Taiwanese media.[29]

The allegory of the crocodiles is probably one of the most subversive but also one of the saddest satires in Taiwanese literature. Through hyperbole, Qiu Miaojin demonstrates the process by which difference is produced, exaggerated, and deployed for creating a category of deviance as the object for discrimination, phobic fantasy, and patronizing sympathy. The target of her attack is the Taiwanese mainstream media, which "discovered" the T-bar subculture in Taipei in 1990 and started the craze for reportage about lesbians and renewed public interest in gay men. The media craze is exaggerated by Qiu to grotesque proportions. In her allegory, the objects that touch off mass voyeurism and the proliferation of pseudoknowledge are certain mysterious creatures called *crocodiles.* As soon as journalists report the discovery of crocodiles, readers inundate newspapers with calls, asking where they can see them. According to the journalists, crocodiles are difficult to detect because they wear tight-fitting human suits. Every day an eager public reads about the experts' latest discoveries, including such things as the crocodiles' favorite television shows and preferred brand of underwear.

According to research conducted by the Health Bureau, crocodiles are a variation of the human species, sharing 80 percent of their genes with humans. However, crocodiles are, not viviparous, but oviparous. A crocodile reproduces by laying eggs that, if attached to human skin, turn the affected person into a crocodile. This report instantly ignites public panic. Two organizations—the Association for the Extinction of Crocodiles and the Alliance for the Preservation of Crocodiles—engage in a televised debate. The former denounces the crocodiles as dangerous and declares that they must be jailed or eliminated before they turn the entire population into crocodiles. The latter maintains that, since they were once human, the crocodiles should be allowed to live—as a warning to the public—but confined to special zones, where tourists can visit them.

A certain shy, friendly creature named Crocodile is very flattered by all the attention. She yearns to come out and say hello to everyone. She sends a television station a video in which she takes off her body suit to show that she is, in fact, the same as everyone else—except her skin is greenish. She also assures everyone that she is not oviparous. In addition, she confesses that she is probably the only crocodile around. She was the one who called the *China Times* months ago to say that she had discovered "crocodiles." She did so because she yearned to be on television to talk to everyone. At the end of the video, she asks her imagined audience, "Is it true that, if I disappear, you will like me?" Then the scene cuts to a shot of the seaside, showing Crocodile drifting out to sea in a bathtub. Accompanying that image is voice-over by the director of the video, a character named after the British gay director Derek Jarman: "I have nothing to say. I wish you all happiness" (284).

In this allegory, Qiu Miaojin relentlessly attacks the media's invention of homosexuals as a mystical, biologically distinct species. The public, which is represented by the media, simultaneously asserts the crocodiles' alien difference and their ability to contaminate and convert others. Crocodiles' difference is at once fetishized and denied. Mimicry and ambivalence saturate the relation between the norm and the perverse, the oppressor and the oppressed, as Homi Bhabha asserts with regard to colonial discourse. Analyzing post-Enlightenment English mission discourse, Bhabha argues that the colonizer constructs the colonial subject as "almost the same" as the colonizer, "but not quite." The colonial subject is asserted, on the one hand, to be so human that its reform by civilized norms—its conversion—is necessary and, on the other, to be always only a mimicry of man.[30]

In Qiu's allegory of the crocodiles, the colonizer envisages conversion, but in the opposite direction. The "normal" public shows no apparent desire to convert crocodiles, that is, to "cure" crocodiles and bring them to its own "normal" or "superior" condition. The colonizer mainly fears being turned into a crocodile. Although the direction of conversion here is different than that in Bhabha's analysis, the colonizer's basic ambivalence—the assumption that crocodiles are "almost the same, but not quite"—and move both to erase difference and to reassert it are the same. Here, Qiu's strategy of parody—her exaggerated reinscription of mainstream imaginings of lesbians in dehumanizing, grotesque terms—may seem to border on self-humiliation. But it effectively exposes the power structure between subject and object in the production of knowledge. It also discloses the internal logic of identification and anxious repudiation in the so-called heterosexual majority's discourse about a so-called homosexual minority.

The media's fantastic construction of crocodiles as a collectivity obscures Crocodile's individuality. By creating a double for Lazi, called Crocodile in correspondence to the public category *crocodile,* however,

Qiu argues that the marginal subject's self-understanding is inflected or constituted in part by public terminology and definition. Dramatic tension exists in the uneasy, incongruous mapping between an individual self, a collective category, and the public's wild fantasies about that category. In the less-parodic portions of the novel, Qiu investigates in depth the issue of identity formation from the marginal subject's perspective. Much of Lazi's self-exploration depends on the exact same vocabulary that the hegemonic homophobic public discourse uses, such as the language of criminality and monstrosity. Yet that vocabulary is used to a different end. Specifically, Lazi relies heavily on the idea of an inconvertible, unchanging personal essence (*benzhi, tezhi*) in herself to justify her preference for women. The essentialism of her argument is, thus, yet another instance of the reverse discourse that deploys the sexological concept of congenital homosexuality for the purpose of naturalizing homosexuality.[31] More important, the novel debunks several myths about lesbianism current in Taiwan—for example, that the lesbian is a freakish, masculine woman who lures normal women astray or that adolescent girls' love, formed typically in single-sex middle and high schools, will not survive the transition to the coed college environment, where they will be free to meet men and experience "real" love—by portraying relationships between women that are lasting and that have true emotional depth.

The story begins in 1987, when Lazi graduates from Taipei First Girls' High School, passes the college entrance exam, and becomes a freshman at National Taiwan University. She lives alone in a tiny room. At midnight, she arises to read Kierkegaard, Schopenhauer, Dazai Osamu, and anti-KMT (Kuomintang) magazines until daybreak; then she returns to bed. Occasionally, she attends a meeting of the university debate society to show off her rhetorical skills "like a beautiful peacock" (14). But most of the time she lies in bed, paralyzed by a sense of helplessness and inexplicable sadness. An amorphous fear prevents her from seeking companionship. She says: "I don't want anybody. It's useless. It's unnecessary. I would get hurt and commit a crime" (13). The notion of crime is a central motif throughout her journal. Not only does Lazi dread her anticipated violation of the social order, but she also describes the world as having committed a horrible crime against her.

Later on, she reveals the source of her sadness and self-imposed isolation:

> I am a woman who loves women. Tears welled up and covered my face like egg white.

Time was soaked in tears. The whole world loved me, but it was useless because I hated myself. . . . How could the world be so cruel? When a person was still so young, she already had to be baffled by a strange feeling: "You are deserted by the world." "Your life is an offense," the judge's sentence said. Then the world rotates as usual as if nothing had happened and demands that you smile like a fortunate person. No knife pierced your chest. No one raped you, and you were not crouching on the sidewalk or locked up in a mental asylum. No one knew about your disaster. The world had already run away from the crime it had committed. (23)

Lazi secretly identifies with the lesbian subject deemed superfluous, defective, and offensive by society. Because of the private nature of desire, the wounds that her sexual feelings suffer from society's rejection are not apparent to others as other forms of social injustice or harm may be. Moreover, anxious to be in harmony with society, she assumes responsibility for guarding and punishing herself. Her tiny room becomes a symbol of the lesbian closet in which she hides. The rhetorical games played out at the debate society bespeak the shallow nature of the formal rules governing her interactions with others. No one can detect and condemn her love for women, for she has already suppressed it in anticipation of society's contempt. Later on in the journal, Lazi describes the heterosexual worldview as "poison" (154). Although part of her defies heterosexual supremacy, she has already been infected, "poisoned" by society's dominant ideology. Her self-analysis resonates with Louis Althusser's well-known remark that the most effective method of control is, not physical violence, but ideological hailing and interpellation.[32] Internalized heterosexism cannot but make Lazi fight her true nature.

As a result of self-negation, Lazi abstains from the love she longs for. However, she is forced to face her fear. At the university, she falls in love with Shui Ling, a delicate girl whom she met only three times in high school and has not seen for a year. Lazi forces her "woman-loving" essence to die, to become a mere apparition. But seeing Shui Ling again resuscitates that ghost. Lazi describes the resuscitation in symbolic terms: "Every Monday there was a ceremonial sacrifice to my soul. [Shui Ling] brought roses to make sacrifice to me. She wore white satin, floating with naked feet, dancing the dance of primordial eros. She closed her eyes, dizzied and drunk, and strewed the roses all over the grass. . . . In the roses, I seemed to see that I was still alive and so energetic that I could effortlessly jump up to snatch the roses away" (21–22). Shui Ling holds out the hope of revival to Lazi's fading soul. The two women are attracted to each other partly because of their differences. Shui Ling is delicate, elegant, hyperfeminine, while Lazi is a leader in student associations who dashes around in jeans on a bicycle. The situation here is not one of the tomboy Lazi seducing the good girl Shui Ling but one of Shui Ling offering Lazi her love.

Eventually, love overpowers Lazi, and she embraces Shui Ling, fondles and kisses her as if devouring her, all the time aware that her own consciousness has split in half "like a two-headed snake" (66–67). Soon afterward, Lazi runs away from the relationship. She feels that their physical intimacy has unleashed a monster within her, and that monster is too shocking for her. Lazi decides to leave so that Shui Ling can return to the so-called normal path, that is, meet a boy, fall in love, get married, and have children. She believes that Shui Ling loves with a "feminine maternal body" (155) that will easily adapt to the dominant, heterosexist system but that she herself is exiled forever from society by a freakish masculinity.

Lazi's self-loathing is an indication that she has fallen victim to the powerful myth of the mannish lesbian fated to surrender her femme lover to a man. The most well-known lesbian novel in the English-speaking world in which such dynamics are played out is Radclyffe Hall's *The Well of Loneliness,* published in 1928.[33] Influenced by Krafft-Ebing's theory of the link between female homosexuality and gender inversion, Hall created the male-identified lesbian Stephen Gordon as her protagonist. At the end of the story, the mannish Gordon allows a man to lure her young girlfriend away with an offer of marriage. The rivalry between an assertive, masculine woman and a man over a dependent, submissive girl is also common in Taiwanese fiction about female-female love. For example, it appears in Lin Daiman's "Bingdi lian" (Lotuses of one root; 1990) and Cao Lijuan's "Tongnü zhi wu" (The dance of a virgin; 1991). The fated triangle can, moreover, be traced back to Chinese fiction of the 1920s, to such texts as "Lishi de riji" (Lishi's diary) by Lu Yin and "Shuo you zhemo yihui shi" (Rumor has it that something like this happened) by Ling Shuhua (see chap. 5). In these stories, it is always the man, rather than the mannish woman, who wins the beautiful girl.

*The Crocodile's Journal* introduces a slight change into this standard situation. Lazi the tomboy is defeated, not by a man, but by a woman, by herself, by her own fear and doubt. A year after she runs away from Shui Ling, she learns, to her consternation, that, after she, Lazi, left, Shui Ling turned, not to a man, but to another woman. Lazi feels utterly humiliated, but she has also learned something that Shui Ling already knew—that love between women is neither shameful nor necessarily doomed. Shui

Ling did truly love Lazi, although Lazi could never believe it. And so Lazi runs away from what could have been the perfect love.

In the character Shui Ling, the story thus shows readers a determined feminine lesbian of a type that was difficult for early sexologists to theorize and that was inconceivable in the Taiwanese popular imagination. She loves women neither because she is mannish nor because she is seeking a temporary substitute for men. Sexual preference is distinct from gender identity. That Shui Ling repeatedly chooses women over men challenges, in fact, even perceptions prevalent in the Taiwanese T-po lesbian subculture. As the anthropologist Yengning Chao documents, it is common for Ts (tomboys) to presume that pos (femmes) are just ordinary women: "Ts consider themselves either more sexually authentic than men or at least rivals of them in winning 'women's' attention"; they perceive pos to be "'by nature' unapproachable, capricious, and difficult."[34] That is to say, Ts regard themselves as natural or predestined gender transgressors and pos as ordinary women who acquire deviant status only through their relationships with Ts. Ts' prejudice against feminine women has, according to Zhang Juanfen, led to a situation in which "femmes must constantly prove themselves [as lesbian]."[35] Shui Ling is, in this regard, exactly one such femme who has proved her tomboy lover's mistrust a dear mistake.

Lazi learns from this, her first love. In her second relationship, she loves with courage and determination, and she does not shy away from lovemaking. But the relationship falls apart because her lover, Xiaofan, who is engaged, is more emotionally involved with her fiancé than she is with Lazi. At the end of the novel, Lazi is determined to find the true love that will redeem both her social marginality and her cruel abandonment of Shui Ling.

*The Crocodile's Journal* explores the transition in young women's lives from an adolescent, same-sex environment to the coed, heterosexual university setting by telling a second story. Two younger female characters, Tuntun and Zhirou, confide their confusion and loss to Lazi. They were ardently in love with each other in high school. They slept in the same room, sang, played the guitar, studied, and took baths together. But their romance was shattered a month before the college entrance exam when Zhirou suddenly became anxious about their both being female and hid in the countryside from Tuntun. When she returned to the city a month later, she found that, seeking comfort, a despairing Tuntun had accepted the attention of a young man. At the university, the girls drift apart. They both become sexually involved with men, but they are not happy in any of these relationships. They miss their first love with each other. Yet they believe that things can never be the same again. Each thinks herself "no longer pure" (220). And "time" (178) is pushing them away from the love of women, pressing them forward along the heterosexual path.

This exploration of how girls' romantic school friendships change when they come of age and men enter the picture—especially of the women's sense that their most perfect love took place with other women in their youth and that such love is now destroyed, never to be replicated again—echoes a long line of representations in twentieth-century Chinese literature, representations that can be traced as far back as Ding Ling's "Shafei nüshi de riji" (Miss Sophia's diary; 1928) and Lu Yin's *Haibin guren* (Old acquaintances by the seaside; 1923) (see chap. 5). In contemporary mainland Chinese fiction, Liu Suola's "Lantian lühai" (The blue sky and ocean) is a compelling story of these motifs. In Taiwanese fiction, Zhu Tianxin's "Chunfeng hudie zhi shi" (Butterfly and spring air) and Cao Lijuan's "Tongnü zhi wu" (The dance of a virgin) are well-known contemporary examples.

In these stories, the women's sense of loss and nostalgia for their perfect love with other women is subversive, but their resignation to and acceptance of heterosexuality is self-limiting. Nevertheless, the experiences portrayed constitute an important part of the spectrum of lesbian desire. Early-twentieth-century male sexologists argued that women's "flames" or "raves" in schools had a sexual undercurrent but were not quite "homosexual." Havelock Ellis, for example, made his essay on girls' school friendships an appendix to his volume on sexual inversion rather than a full-fledged chapter. The male doctor's attempt was always to emphasize that these passionate friendships were passing, illusive, merely a nonserious game, a transitional phase that would eventually be replaced by heterosexual love. But, if we look at the aforementioned Chinese representations of girls' adolescent friendships by female authors, we immediately see that love between adolescent girls is often considered irreplaceable, such youthful romance remembered nostalgically. The emotional intensity with which such memories are invested is very different from the way in which men like Ellis would like to believe they are remembered.

The situation may be as Lazi describes:

I had a hypothesis meant to deceive myself and others: If I can fall in love with men, then my painful love for women will disappear. . . . In reality, however, the love for women and the love for men are two unrelated matters. If my desire for women has already been revealed, no matter whether it later disappears, and regardless of the form it takes in my memory, it is already in me. . . . Think of a jar of water. After black dye is added to it, if you add other colors, you may change its look, but you cannot cancel the fact that black is in the water. (152)

In another passage, she maintains about her tormenting relationship with Shui Ling: "Some grief and pain are so deep that they cannot be expressed. Some love is so deep that the same depth cannot be reached again. After it happened in the body, that part of the body became hollow. When you hark back, everything has fossilized" (189). Although the extraordinary love may not be repeated or reexperienced, its occurrence in the past cannot be eliminated from the body, either, because the body will always remember it through its own emotional death.

Lazi implies that the experience of deep love for another woman is not easily surpassed. Her insight challenges the common wisdom that women's love for one another must yield to their obligation to men. It also exposes the criminal character of compulsory heterosexuality, the forcing by patriarchal society of the role of wife and mother on all women.

Qiu's narrative helps us assess the possibility of a critical, dissenting lesbian discourse in a mass-mediated public sphere, a critical discourse, moreover, that is more individualistic than collective. *The Crocodile's Journal* belongs to an in-between space, one that is distinguished from the conservative mass media, on the one hand, and from radical feminist and lesbian activist discourses, on the other.[36] In spite of the fact that the novel contains an incisive critique of the media and the public, the dynamics between Qiu and the public is by no means simply confrontational. Although repulsed and alienated by a voyeuristic and prejudiced public represented by the media, both Lazi and Crocodile wish nonetheless to reach out to the public by making confessions of private, inner truth. Crocodile's irrepressible desire to have a videotape of herself broadcast on television suggests that, although the autobiographical lesbian resists the simulacra of the lesbian produced by the commercial media, yet she as a subject, including her sexual identity, has been conditioned in part by the scopophilia of the media.[37] Scattered remarks also reveal that the process by which Lazi composed her journal involved rewriting a set of diaries— some of which are lost—with the aim of producing a novel. In other words, despite the autobiographical lesbian's intention to present, through self-writing, the essence of her own subjectivity, her ontological truth is always already constructed by rhetoricity and fictionality. The lesbian autobiographical act is not exempt from the impulses of selective remembering and fictionalization to which all autobiographical acts are prone.[38] In the final analysis, autobiography may differ little from media simulacra.

Qiu's novel deconstructs a resilient lesbian self even as it creates it. From the outset, Lazi undermines her own story about her woman-loving essence by making the following confession:

> I used to believe that deep in every man there is an "archetype" about women. And the woman that he will love most in his life will be the one that most closely resembles his "archetype." Although I am a woman, the "archetype" deep inside me is also about women. An "archetypal" woman, like an illusion arising from the brink of death on a frozen, glacial peak, slips into my reality and escapes it again. I believed that such was the absolute beauty of the "archetype" in life. I believed so for four years. I spent the entirety of my university years—the most honest and courageous time in my life—on this belief alone.
>
> Now, I no longer believe it. The matter has become just an improvisation by a street artist, a small drawing hanging on my wall. When I, light-headed, no longer believe it, I begin to forget and sell off cheaply all the treasures stored in my house. Suddenly I also realize that it is time to write it down. The vial of memory will empty soon. Perhaps, after a nap, I won't even be able to locate the price list. (10)

Lazi's memoir is, therefore, meant to commemorate precisely a personal essence in which she no longer believes. Her journal captures a bygone truth. Her act of writing is also an act of peddling—cherished valuables are sold as dispensable merchandise. It is significant that, in the journal, she presents her nickname as having originated, not from the word *lesbian,* but from comic bantering between friends—she is good at recruiting new members for her student association; hence, Tuntun calls her the "recruit-er" (*la-zi*) (85–86). Identity is constantly improvised, and a randomly acquired name is just as good as any other.

Despite these details, which undercut the coherence and primacy of sexual identity, in most parts of the journal Lazi resists the public's tendency to trivialize lesbian subjectivity. One of the main ways in which mainstream society renders lesbianism palatable is precisely by commodifying it—turning it into a replaceable piece of merchandise rather than an irreplaceable ontology. Lesbian preference is made into a piece of titillating, scandalous news, a kind of chic or a fashion fad. Lazi's unchangeable masculinity and woman-loving essence does not lend itself to such lighthearted commercialization. Yet her narrative risks invoking another popular fantasy—the story of a sexual minority's inborn monstrosity and eventual self-destruction and excommunication. The risk is never far away no matter how self-conscious Lazi is in her self-referential commentary on the pitfalls of lesbian public self-representation.

Perhaps Qiu's novel is valuable precisely because it dramatizes the struggle between a lesbian individual's sense of self and the public discourses of lesbianism, including lesbian activist discourses. She reveals that an individual's experience of homophobia is much more painful than a radicalized community's joint political statement can ever indicate. For some Taiwanese queer theorists, Qiu's writing may not seem sufficiently combative.[39] Nevertheless, a dimension of social protest naturally arises from the individual's representation of personal pain because that representation jars with the public's mindless assumptions about the sexual dissident's lack of humanity. Afflicted personal writing has a political efficacy of its own.

It is because it is honest and questioning that Qiu's writing seems unique and especially affecting when compared with the more ideologically driven novels and short stories that certain queer theorists-cum-writers produced in 1990s Taiwan. The works of Chen Xue and Lucifer Hung—daring, scandalous, and subversive though they may be—cannot hide their deliberate agendas: assaulting the sedate bourgeois sensibility by describing incest, sadomasochism, insatiable sexual appetite and non-stop intercourse, and so forth.[40] And the impact of such works lessens with repeated exposure until what was initially shocking is rendered inoffensive. This is perhaps the paradox of the avant-garde. As Matei Calinescu argues, by the time aesthetic extremism has become a trend, it has been rendered an innocuous cliché. The initial euphoria quickly fades.[41]

Qiu is also unique among her generation of queer writers in her unsentimental criticism of the failure of the public sphere in Taiwan after martial law. In the early to mid-1990s, when society as a whole was experiencing exultation and a sense of liberation at the expansion of the public space that made room for new identity-oriented social movements, Qiu frankly expressed skepticism of the possibility of rational discussion and authentic self-representation in a public sphere where the mass media dominated communication and saturated everyday life so completely that media images became the truth—a hyperreality more powerful than any other reality. Further, she exposed identity, and, therefore, identity politics, as intrinsically reductionistic—inadequate to represent the complexity of human subjectivity. These reflections make *The Crocodile's Journal,* not only a landmark in the formative lesbian literary canon in

Taiwan, but also an insightful treatise on the structural problems of the mass-mediated public sphere in a developed capitalist economy.

:: 

The last two chapters of this study have taken as their focus a variety of lesbian self-representations in Taiwan's expanded public sphere after martial law. Beyond their open celebration of new lesbian identities and their contestation of trenchant gender and sexual biases, Taiwanese lesbian activists and writers have also felt threatened by the way in which the media have turned private life into a commodity to be marketed to a mass audience. Not uncommonly, they are also wary of the suppression of internal differences (within groups, within selves) involved in sexual identity formations. Similar questions about the boundaries of a variety of sexual identities will undoubtedly surface, with increasing intensity, in women's-group discussions and literary representations in the PRC as young urban women begin to explore object choice as a means of defining the self. It is, moreover, likely that there will be widespread concern among new cosmopolitan lesbian subjects about sensationalization if and when lesbian identities are commercially exploited by the mass media. So far, however, it is in Taiwan that the rewards and liabilities of a minoritized and radicalized lesbian identity have been articulated with particular clarity. Despite these palpable differences, women-preferring women on both sides of the Taiwan Strait share a common cause—the battle against patriarchy and compulsory heterosexuality. These emerging lesbians' attempts to undermine dominant familial and extrafamilial forces will have implications for women across transnational China.

# EPILOGUE

This study has traced the rise of sexuality in China in the twentieth century from a woman-centered perspective. During the period examined, a psychobiological discourse of heterosexuality as women's *sexuality*—that is, as women's inborn desire and healthy pleasure rather than their duty—came into being as one of the enlightenment discourses of the May Fourth era. Almost a century later, the discourse of women's heterosexual needs and inalienable rights operates as a powerful norm in the urban cultures of transnational China. Meanwhile, in an almost inverse relation to the rise of heterosexuality as women's sexuality, desire between women became identified and stigmatized as perverse. The taxonomy of female same-sex love was initially formed in the May Fourth era and gave rise to an intellectual debate. At the end of the twentieth century, female homosexuality has once again surfaced as a highly contested issue in transnational China.

Although cross-cultural comparisons can sometimes be contrived and can obscure more than they illuminate, I believe that Foucault's work does help us grasp the rise of sexuality in modern Chinese contexts. Influenced perhaps by Lévi-Strauss, Foucault argues that "relations of sex gave rise, in every society, to a *deployment of alliance:* a system of marriage, of fixation and development of kinship ties, of transmission of names and possessions." However, in the modern West, a new mechanism has been invented—the deployment of sexuality—for the production and distribution of power. The system of sexuality is, according to Foucault, "superimposed" on the system of alliance and "reduces its importance," although the former does not supplant the latter.[1] In examining modern Chinese contexts, I have found a somewhat similar situation. The discourse of sexuality has been deployed precisely to reinforce and reinvigorate the claims of the patriarchal family. Gender differences and hierarchies have been structured and maintained through normative heterosexuality. The system of sexuality has been in complicity with kinship.

While Foucault writes with seductive eloquence on the differences between various institutional, discursive practices and the shift from one mode to another, he never explains why power has been articulated especially through sexuality in the modern West.[2] He repeatedly insists that what is at stake are the relations of power created by the very invention of knowledge—in particular, the relations between those who study and those who embody sexual identities. He writes, "What [is] involved . . . [is] the very production of sexuality."[3] In other words, Foucault has not tried to explain why a system categorizing identities on the basis of sexual behavior has emerged at a particular historical moment as a means of either creating social stratification or maintaining social stability.

In comparison, some other historians have put forth analyses linking the emergence of gay and lesbian identity in the modern West to general social, economic change. John D'Emilio, for instance, holds that, in the United States over the roughly two-hundred-year period from the late eighteenth century to the 1970s, capitalism has, through its system of wage labor, undermined the household economy that creates interdependence among members of the nuclear family, allowing men and women the autonomy to develop identity and community through same-sex attraction. Medical theories about homosexuality—which so concern Foucault— "were an ideological response to a new way of organizing one's personal life," D'Emilio maintains.[4] Citing the contributions of not only D'Emilio but also Mary McIntosh, Randolph Trumbach, Richard Sennett, Jeffrey Weeks, Arnold Davidson, Thomas Laqueur, and others, David Halperin puts it succinctly:

I take it as established that a large-scale transformation of social and personal life took place in Europe as part of the massive cultural reorganization that accompanied the transition from a traditional, hierarchical, status-based society to a modern, individualistic, mass society during the period of industrialization and the rise of a capitalist economy. One symptom of that transformation, as a number of researchers (both before and after Foucault) have pointed out, is that something new happens to the various relations among sexual roles, sexual object-choices, sexual categories, sexual behaviors, and sexual identities in bourgeois Europe between the end of the seventeenth century and the beginning of the twentieth. Sex takes on new social and individual functions, and it assumes a new importance in defining and normalizing the modern self.[5]

In the light of the scholarly consensus to which Halperin alludes, what this study has reconstructed is, in fact, the lengthy and gradual process by which theories of women's sexuality produced in the West during the period of industrialization came to make an impact on and have relevance for the symbolic and material conditions of women in the urban cultures of industrializing and capitalizing China in the twentieth century. While I have highlighted in particular the translation of Western systems of sexual knowledge or "sexual science" into Chinese as an apparent and immediate catalyst spawning new sexual meanings in China, I have not lost sight of the institutional changes that have occurred in the social, economic, and political organizations of China as it pursues modernization. Western understandings of sexuality are pertinent to modern Chinese women's experience because—if for no other reason—a major dimension of the Chinese goal for progress since the late nineteenth century has been the approximation of the West. A considerable percentage of Chinese women's lives, especially in regions where and in periods during which the penetration of global capitalism has been deep, have been permanently reshaped because Western women's liberation has been taken as a model. For a good part of the twentieth century, Westernization was for urban Chinese women the basic constitutive principle of education, work, leisure, love, marriage, family, and citizenship, so much so that, in modern Chinese cultures, no aspect of women's same-sex desire has remained free of Western influence. Not only have Western theoretical paradigms of female same-sex desire been translated into the Chinese language, thus gaining public currency, but the structural transformation of Chinese societies has in itself mobilized new meanings of female same-sex desire.

In addition to seeing the complicity between the system of sexuality and that of patriarchal kinship in modern Chinese societies, one must also acknowledge that the discourse of sexuality has had diverse effects or ramifications. In its original form as psychopathology, the discourse of sexuality cataloged female same-sex eroticism (as well as certain other forms of erotic pleasure) as abnormal. Paradoxically, however, the taxonomy was promptly appropriated by some women to give a new name to their love for one another. In the May Fourth era, the neologism *female same-sex love* clearly had such appeal to certain women of the intellectual class. And, at the close of the twentieth century, the term *female homosexuality* continues to play contradictory roles: it functions as the basis for multiple reverse discourses that seek to naturalize and/or legitimate female same-sex desire at the same time as it continues to signal stigmatization and is wielded precisely to denigrate female same-sex desire.

The rise of sexuality as a widely disseminated discourse that contributed to large-scale changes in the discipline of the self in the modern industrial world should not be taken to mean that no sexual identity or personhood was possible in the premodern world.[6] Specifically, the classifying power of the modern taxonomy should not lead one to presume that, prior to its institution, no women in China preferred the company of women to that of men and to marriage. Indeed, as I have shown in my close readings of some late-imperial literary texts, especially Pu Songling's "Feng Sanniang," some late-imperial writers—men as well as women—imagined precisely an anomalous type of women who would fall in love with other women and adamantly reject men and marriage. In other words, while the current industrialist, capitalist, and urban organization of society may have enabled more Chinese women than ever before to cultivate a same-sex preference and to pursue a lifestyle based on that preference, capitalism or industrialization cannot, therefore, be singled out as the necessary condition for such an identity. Even in the most difficult times in the past, there were some women who courted death so as to be truthful to their own nonconformist preferences. Identifying the existence of the woman-preferring woman in late-imperial sources does not mean that I am venturing a theory about the biological determination of lesbianism across time and space. Rather, my claim is very specifically that, phenomenologically, the odd woman as observed or imagined by late-imperial writers exhibited preferences very similar to those of contemporary women who claim lesbian identifications. Late-imperial women's same-sex preferences may well have been contingent on circumstances and overdetermined—just as contingent, and overdetermined, as present-day sexual identities.

Having stated my argument, I believe that, if this book has interested readers, it is probably not because of any broad generalizations that they can bring away from it. Personally, what I have enjoyed the most in the process of writing are the particular imaginative flights enabled by the contemplation of the work of the creative writers examined here. None of their narrative acts can be predicted. I have enjoyed my encounters with Chen Ran's stubborn Aoao, with Qiu Miaojin's lyricism and satirical eloquence, and with Lu Yin's self-discovery in travel. Most of all, I have been fortunate to realize that late-imperial women left behind a rich and complex literary legacy. But that is the material for another writing adventure.

# THE THIRD FEMALE CHILD
# OF THE FENG FAMILY—
# A TRANSLATION OF PU SONGLING'S
# "FENG SANNIANG"

Fan Shiyiniang, daughter of the minister of education of Lu City, was a glamorous young lady with unusual poetic accomplishments.[1] Her parents loved her dearly and let her choose herself among those who proposed marriage. But she never approved of any.

It happened to be the fifteenth day of the seventh month [of the Chinese lunar calendar], the Zhongyuan Day.[2] Buddhist nuns in the Water-Moon Temple performed the ceremony of Yulanpenhui.[3] Throngs of women visited the temple, and Shiyiniang too went. As she looked leisurely at various things in the temple, another girl followed her and watched her face time and again, seeming desirous to speak with her. When Shiyiniang scrutinized the stranger, she found her to be a beauty around sixteen. Pleased by the stranger's appearance, Shiyiniang returned her gaze with a fixed, admiring look. The stranger said with a smile, "Aren't you Shiyiniang of the Fan family?" Shiyiniang answered yes. The stranger then said, "I've long heard about you; people's compliments have been truthful." In reply, Shiyiniang asked the girl her name and place of residence. The girl answered, "My family name is Feng; I'm called Sanniang because I'm the third daughter. I live in a nearby village." Arm in arm, they started a delightful conversation and offered many tender endearments to each other. They grew so enamored of each other that they could not bear separation. Shiyiniang asked, "How come you came without a companion?" "My parents died early," said Feng. "No one else lives with me except an old servant. She cannot come because she has to take care of the house." As Shiyiniang was going home, tears rushed into Feng's eyes. Shiyiniang also felt sad, so she invited Feng to go home with her. Feng said, "You are from a rich and significant family. Since I am not related to your family in the slightest, I am worried I will incur people's contempt. They will sneer at me." Shiyiniang insisted on her coming along, to which Feng replied, "Some other time." Then Shiyiniang took a golden hairpin out of her hair to give Feng. In return, Feng presented Shiyiniang with her green hairpin.

At home, Shiyiniang missed Feng passionately. She showed Feng's hairpin to her family. To their amazement, the hairpin was made neither of gold nor of jade but of something they did not recognize. Shiyiniang looked forward to her friend's visit every day; she never came. Disappointed, Shiyiniang fell sick. Her parents questioned her and discovered the cause. They sent people to look for Feng in nearby villages. However, nobody seemed to know her.

It was Double-Ninth Day.[4] Shiyiniang, listless and languid, asked her maid to help her walk into the garden for fresh air and the view. A quilted seat was set for her under the eastern fence. Suddenly a girl peeped over the wall. On a closer look, Shiyiniang recognized Feng. "Catch me!" shouted Feng. The maid obeyed, and Feng jumped off the wall. Shiyiniang was pleasantly surprised. She promptly stood up and made her friend sit down on her seat with her. She scolded her friend for not keeping her promise and asked where she had come from. Feng replied, "My house is far away. When I told you that I lived in a nearby village, I meant my uncle's house, which I visit quite often. After we parted, I missed you and suffered. However, we humble and poor people are not carefree when we make friends with the wealthy and noble. The prospect of being despised by the nobles' servants intimidates and shames one before one even sets foot in the door. That's what kept me from coming. A moment ago, as I passed by outside, I heard a young woman's voice. So I peeped hoping it would be you. It turned out to be you as I had wished." When Shiyiniang told Feng what caused her illness, Feng broke into tears. "The fact that I am here with you must be kept secret," said she; "I cannot bear the rumors that gossips might fabricate and spread." Shiyiniang promised. Both girls then went into Shiyiniang's room and lay down on the same bed. They poured out thoughts and feelings that had burdened their hearts. Shiyiniang's illness soon evaporated. They swore sisterhood, and each would wear the other's clothes and shoes. Whenever they saw people coming, Feng hid herself behind the curtains. This went on for about six months. Finally Shiyiniang's parents heard about it.

One day, as the girls were playing chess, Madame Fan came into the room unexpectedly. She stared at Feng and exclaimed, "Indeed my child has a friend!" Then she said to Shiyiniang, "It pleases us that you have a good friend at home. Why didn't you tell us earlier?" Shiyiniang told her mother about Feng's fears. Madame Fan looked at Feng and said, "We are very happy that a nice girl keeps our daughter company. Why did you hide from us?" Feng's face turned crimson. She played with her skirt bands without a murmur. After Madame Fan left, Feng bid farewell to Shiyiniang. It took Shiyiniang much effort to persuade her friend to stay.

Then, one evening, Feng ran into the room in great haste and fright. She cried, "I told you this is not the place for me to be. Now I've suffered a great insult!" Surprised, Shiyiniang queried the cause. Feng said, "Just now I went to the toilet. A young man came to harass me. Luckily I was able to escape, but how can I show my face around here without feeling shame in the future?" Shiyiniang made her describe the man's looks. Then she apologized. "You need not be alarmed," she said; "that was my silly brother. I will tell my mother about it immediately, and she will punish him with a flogging." However, Feng insisted on leaving. So Shiyiniang had to ask her to wait until dawn. Feng said, "My uncle's house is very close. Please lend me a ladder so that I can climb over the wall." Shiyiniang knew Feng could not be detained. She ordered two maids to climb over the wall to walk Feng home. After having walked half a mile Feng bid the maids farewell and went on by herself. When the maids returned, Shiyiniang cried bitterly on the bed as if she had lost her spouse.

A few months passed. One of Shiyiniang's maids went to the East Village on an errand. When she returned in the evening, she ran into Feng, who was accompanied by an old woman. The maid was glad to see Feng and asked how she was. Touched, Feng asked how things were with Shiyiniang. The maid grabbed her sleeve and said, "Miss Feng, please come over to our house. My lady is dying to see you!" "I miss her too," said Feng. "But I would not like her family to know about my visit. Open the door to the garden when you go home, and I will be there." The maid told

Shiyiniang so on her return. Shiyiniang was overjoyed. No sooner had they done what Feng had bidden than they found that Feng was already in the garden.

At their reunion, Shiyiniang and Feng told each other what had happened since their separation. Their conversation went on and on, and they did not sleep. After the maids were fast asleep, Feng got up and moved over to lie down on the same pillow with Shiyiniang. She whispered to Shiyiniang, "I know that you are not yet engaged to anyone. With your talent, beauty, and family status, you can easily have the son of a wealthy and noble family for a husband. However, young men of wealthy, noble families are often spoiled. If you want an excellent husband, please don't judge by material fortunes." Shiyiniang seconded her opinion. Feng continued, "The place where we met last year will host a ritual again this year. Please make a trip there tomorrow. I guarantee that you will see your ideal husband. I have studied the art of fortune-telling. I seldom make wrong judgments when I read people's faces." At the break of day, Feng left. They had agreed to meet later at the temple.

When Shiyiniang arrived there, Feng was already waiting. They walked around a bit. Then Shiyiniang invited Feng to leave in the same carriage with her. Hardly had they exited the gate hand clasping hand when they saw a young scholar, around eighteen, in a plain cotton robe. Without ornaments he looked handsome and magnificent. Feng pointed at him quietly. "He will be in the imperial academy," she said. Thereupon Shiyiniang gave him a glance. Then Feng told Shiyiniang, "You go home first. I'll come later."

At dusk, Feng came. She said, "I've got the details. He is Meng Anren of your neighborhood." Shiyiniang knew that Meng was poor, so she did not think he was suitable. Feng said, "Why, how could you follow the world's standards! If this person remains poor or insignificant for long, I will pluck out my own eyes and never again tell the capable men from the ordinary crowd!" Shiyiniang asked, "So what do you want me to do?" "Please give me some personal object so that I can effect your engagement with him." "You are rushing things!" cried Shiyiniang. "What if my parents don't agree?" Feng answered, "I am doing this precisely because I am afraid they will not agree. If you are determined, even death cannot change your mind." Shiyiniang decidedly refused. Thereupon Feng said, "The right marriage for you has already appeared on the horizon, but an obstacle of devilish enchantment is not yet cleared from your path. I am doing this to return the favor you have shown me in the past. Please allow me to take leave of you now. I will give him the golden phoenix hairpin you once gave me and pretend it is your gift to him." Before Shiyiniang could suggest that they discuss the matter further, Feng had gone out the door.

Meng, the young scholar, was poor yet very talented. He was selective about marriage, so he was not yet betrothed at eighteen. On that day he saw two striking beauties. When he went home, he started fantasizing about them. It was sometime before midnight when Feng Sanniang entered his room. He held up a candle to look at her and recognized her as one of the women he saw during the day. He was very pleased and questioned her. She said, "My surname is Feng. I am a companion to Miss Shiyiniang of the Fan family." In his exultation and eagerness, Meng did not care to find out more details, and he hurriedly advanced to embrace her. Feng rejected him, saying, "I come here not to recommend myself but to recommend someone else. Shiyiniang would like to be united with you forever. Please ask a matchmaker to arrange it." Her words astounded Meng, and he would not believe her. Then Feng showed Meng the hairpin, which made him wild with happiness. He swore, "I am deeply honored by her favor. If I cannot marry her, I will remain single all my life." Thereupon Feng left.

The following day Meng asked an old woman next door to go to see Madame Fan. Madame Fan thought that Meng was too poor to qualify, so she turned down his proposal flatly without consulting her daughter. When Shiyiniang learned about it, she was very disappointed. She was also upset that Feng had ruined her marriage prospects. Because it was difficult to retrieve the golden hairpin, Shiyiniang decided to die to keep the promise given by Feng on her behalf if necessary.

A few days later, a gentleman proposed for his son. He was afraid that Shiyiniang would turn down the offer, so he asked a local government official to be the matchmaker. The gentleman was very powerful at that time, and Sir Fan was afraid to offend him. He asked Shiyiniang's opinion, and Shiyiniang showed worry and displeasure. Her mother asked her what the matter was; she merely shed tears in silence. Afterward, Shiyiniang sent someone to tell her mother in secret that she would die rather than marry anyone other than Meng. Her father became furious on hearing this, so he promised the gentleman the marriage. Furthermore, he was suspicious that Shiyiniang had privately expressed love for Meng, so he wanted to hold the wedding ceremony as soon as possible. Vexed, Shiyiniang lay in bed day after day and refused to eat. On the eve of her wedding, she suddenly left her bed and sat in front of the mirror to make herself up. Her mother was pleased. A little while later a maid came running and informed her, "Miss has hanged herself!" It shocked everyone in the house to tears, but it was too late for regrets. Shiyiniang was buried within three days.

Meng had been indignant since his neighbor came back with Madame Fan's rejection. But he quietly gathered news about Shiyiniang in the hope that he could turn things around in his favor. When he learned that Shiyiniang's hand had been promised to another, rage burned inside him, and he gave up all hope. A few days later, when he heard that she had killed herself and was buried, he was thrown into grief and despondency, and he wished he had died with her. That evening he left his house to go to Shiyiniang's tomb to mourn for her. There at the grave he saw a person approach from afar. It turned out to be Feng Sanniang. She said to him, "Congratulations, your union can now be realized." He said in tears, "Don't you know that Shiyiniang is dead?" Feng answered, "That's exactly why I said it could be realized. Please ask your servants to dig open the tomb right away. I have an elixir that can revive her." Meng followed her directions; he had the coffin bared and opened and then the hole in the tomb covered again. He carried Shiyiniang's body home on his back, and Feng went with him. They placed the body on the bed, fed it the medicine, and in a moment Shiyiniang revived. When she opened her eyes, she saw Feng and asked, "Where am I?" "This is Meng Anren," Feng answered, pointing at him. When Feng told Shiyiniang what had transpired, Shiyiniang felt as if she had woken up from a dream.

Feng was afraid that Shiyiniang's parents would find out the truth, so she took Meng and Shiyiniang to a mountain village some dozens of miles away. Then Feng wanted to leave, but Shiyiniang wept and beseeched Feng to keep her company. Shiyiniang offered Feng a separate house to live in. She sold the jewelry her parents had put in her coffin, so they had enough money to live on. Feng always avoided Meng when he came near. As a result, one day Shiyiniang said in a magnanimous spirit, "My dear sister, we are as close as bone and flesh. It won't be easy, though, for us to be together forever unless we copy the sisters Nüying and Ehuang, who married the same man, Shun." Thereupon Feng said, "I once learned the secret for longevity. With respiratory techniques I can lengthen my life. That's why I do not wish to marry." Shiyiniang smiled and said, "Many people claim that they know the methods for longevity. But who has ever followed a method and found it effective?" Feng replied, "What I know is not known to the world. Fake methods have been circulating in the world. Only the 'Five Animal Pictorial' by Hua Tuo is the correct method, though. In general, inner alchemists aim at invigorating the circulation of their blood and vital force. Whenever I fall ill, no sooner do I pose like a tiger than my symptoms stop. Can you deny that it is effective?"

Then Shiyiniang plotted with Meng against Feng. She made him pretend that he had left on a trip to some distant place. That evening, she forced Feng to drink wine. After Feng fell drunk, Meng sneaked into her room and violated her. When Feng woke up, she lamented, "Sister, you've ruined me! If I had not breached the taboo against sex, I could have ascended into the primary heaven on my complete realization of the Tao [Way]. In an oversight I fell into your dirty trap. Such is my fate!" She got up immediately to leave. Shiyiniang sorrowfully begged for Feng's forgiveness, saying that she did so because she really wanted Feng to stay. Feng replied, "I must now tell you the truth—I am a fox. By chance I witnessed your beautiful face. At first sight I fell in love with you. I have let love hold me in its grip, like a silkworm enveloping itself in a cocoon. That's why a mistake like today's could happen. It was destined to happen because I was enchanted with love. My undoing was not caused by human efforts. If I stay, the spell over my emotions will multiply endlessly. You have a prosperous life ahead of you. Take care." With that Feng disappeared. Husband and wife remained astounded for a long time.

A year later, Meng succeeded in the exams for office. As Feng had predicted, he was appointed to the imperial academy. He went to the Fan residence with his name card and asked to see Sir Fan, but Sir Fan was ashamed and refused to see him. Meng insisted until he was granted a meeting. When admitted, he paid Sir Fan the respect due a father-in-law and kneeled on the ground to bow to him. Sir Fan was embarrassed and irritated, suspicious that Meng was being sarcastic. Then Meng asked to be alone with Sir Fan and told him what had happened. Sir Fan could not quite believe it, so he sent people to inspect Meng's house. When the report came back, he was truly amazed and happy. He bid Meng to keep the secret, for fear there would be disastrous consequences. Two years later, the powerful gentleman who once proposed marriage to the Fan family was discovered to be involved in bribery. Father and son were both exiled to the frontier in Liaohai. Shiyiniang was then able to visit her parents.

# NOTES

Unless otherwise noted, all translations are mine.

## Chapter 1

1. Although the word *Zhongguo* (Chinese) is not used on the page on which the pictures actually appear, this item is listed in the table of contents of the magazine as "Zhongguo meiren zhi xianqing (xuyu) (daiyue) (dushi) (douzhuang)." The images of Chinese beauties are followed by a few photographs of reclining Western beauties (*xifang meiren*).

2. The word *xu* literally means "catkin" or "cotton." *Xuyu,* or "catkin-like words," has the connotation of being soft-spoken, continuous, disorganized, airy, and free-flowing.

3. The inaugural manifesto (*Meiyu xuanyan*) emphasized that the magazine was published by a group of talented ladies (*caiyuan*). Four female staff members were introduced by their names and photographs: the editor in chief, Gao Jianhua, and the editors, Gu Renchai, Ma Simei, and Liang Guiqin. In addition, two men were introduced as assistant managers: Xu Xiaotian and Wu Jianlu. Gao Jianhua was married to Xu Xiaotian, a popular novelist in Shanghai in the 1910s, and it is commonly held that Xu played an important role in the magazine's development, helping edit it as well as writing for it. The magazine's manifesto addressed both male and female readers, and it is difficult to ascertain what percentage of its actual audience were women. Being one of the first

urban magazines featuring entertainment fiction by women, *Meiyu* was in some respects an innovative, pioneering effort. However, urban entertainment fiction in general would during the May Fourth era be ridiculed and criticized by elite intellectuals as frivolous and ideologically backward. For an analysis of the authors, readers, and ideological significance of urban popular fiction in the 1910s and 1920s, see Link, *Mandarin Ducks and Butterflies.*

4. Owing to traditional rules discouraging the appearance of gentry-class women in public, the Chinese women photographed and shown in magazines edited by men at the turn of the century were usually famous courtesans (*mingji*) and female students in missionary schools; they were rarely conservative women of the gentry class. *Meiyu* appeared later, so the models photographed for "Chinese beauties' activities of leisure" could be gentry women. Even if they were courtesans, their profession would not automatically render their behavior less elegant since high-class courtesans were expected to have mastered the refinement of genteel feminine demeanor. They were also regarded as exemplars of high urban taste. In Shanghai, the capital of Chinese prostitution in the late nineteenth century and the early twentieth, "the upper-class prostitute appeared in elite discourse as the embodiment and arbiter of sophisticated urbanity" (Hershatter, *Dangerous Pleasures,* 8).

Although no information is available on the exact circumstances under which the set of photographs captioned "Chinese beauties' activities of leisure" was taken, two scenarios seem more likely than others: (1) that several women were persuaded to pose for the camera with the explicit intention of producing photographs to print in the magazine; (2) that the magazine's editors solicited photographs from their female relatives and acquaintances, selected four, and printed them with the permission of the subjects. In the first scenario, some women models struck poses with the full intention of subjecting their performance to public view. In the second, the photographed women's consent to publication retroactively attributed the status of a public display to the postures in which they had been captured by the camera.

5. I wish to make it clear that I am a Han Chinese person of Taiwanese upbringing, with a fair amount of experience living as an adult in the United States. Considering that I may have been more Americanized than is usually the case for most Chinese women who have never lived in the United States, I do not claim that I am representative of all contemporary Chinese women in my awareness of lesbian sexuality as a category. However, this does not contradict my point: there are now a fair percentage of urban women in Taiwan and China who are sufficiently Westernized to find physical intimacy with other women signifying something more than friendship. Also, I believe that it is fair to say that, while holding hands or walking arm in arm in the streets is common among young women in Taiwan and the People's Republic of China, sitting in a female friend's lap and being hugged by her while having a tête-à-tête exceeds a common level of intimacy that can be comfortably shown in public. In present-day terms, the posture would not be regarded as an emblem of feminine refinement.

6. *Tugo* has been discontinued by its publisher. *G&L* carried both lesbian and gay content between 1996 and 2000; however, in 2000, the publisher transformed it into a gay-only magazine in order to keep it profitable.

7. In *G&L* and *Tugo,* only one sort of photograph showing several women in the same frame looks more explicitly sexual than "a long uninterrupted chat": those of nude female bodies captured from pornographic films that contain sex acts between women (see, e.g., the stills from the movie *Nühuan* [Female pleasures] in Yanping yingye gongsi, "Nühuan").

8. Hu, "Lun xiaoshuo ji baihua yunwen," 76.

9. Chen constructs two kinds of relations between the male elite and boy actors in the novel. The elegant type is animated by obsessional sentimentality and nonphysical

erotic love (*se er bu yin*), whereas the clownish type is characterized by naked lust and monetary exchange. Neither type of male-male relations precludes cross-sex marriage. For an analysis in English of the gender play in the novel and its praise of nonphysical love between males (modeled on the unconsummated love between Baoyu [male protagonist] and Daiyu [female protagonist] in the eighteenth-century classic *Dream of the Red Chamber*), see Wang, *Fin-de-Siècle Splendor*, 61–76.

10. Illuminating discussions of gender and/or male-female sexuality in Republican China are many. See, e.g., Witke, "Transformation of Attitudes towards Women"; Wang, *Women in the Chinese Enlightenment*; Dikötter, *Sex, Culture, and Modernity in China*; Hershatter, *Dangerous Pleasures*; Chow, *Woman and Chinese Modernity*; Zhang, *The City in Modern Chinese Literature and Film*; Barlow, ed., *Gender Politics in Modern China*; and Lu, ed., *Gender and Sexuality in Twentieth-Century Chinese Literature and Society*.

11. Among historians, Hershatter notes descriptions of sexual relations between courtesans in Shanghai guidebooks from the 1920s and 1930s and other sources such as Xu Ke's *Qingbai leichao*. Moreover, according to Hershatter, "public performances of lesbian sexual acts by prostitutes (featuring a dildo stuffed with wood-ear fungus, which swelled up when soaked in hot water) were described as an attraction in 1930s hotels" (*Dangerous Pleasures*, 118). Needless to say, there are major differences between the guidebooks' approach to sex between women as spectacle and the translated sexological theory about "female homosexuality." In my discussion of the Republican era, I am concerned primarily with educated New Women's same-sex relations as they surfaced in intellectuals' discussions of modern sexology and in May Fourth fiction.

The Chinese equivalent of the fin de siècle English term *New Woman*—*xin nüxing*—first surfaced in intellectual debate and fiction in the May Fourth era. Although its meaning was debated, the neologism in general signified "the modern woman." For a more detailed explanation of my use of the term in this book, see n. 63, this chapter, below.

12. Specific references are given in chap. 5. In general, critics' comments revolve around Lu Yin's "Lishi de riji" (Lishi's diary) and "Haibin guren" (Old acquaintances by the seaside) and Ding Ling's "Shafei nüshi de riji" (Miss Sophia's diary) and "Shujia zhong" (Summer break). Occasionally, Ling Shuhua's "Shuo you zhemo yihui shi" (Rumor has it that something like this happened) and female bonding in the stories of Feng Yuanjun and Bing Xin are mentioned. The fiction of Lu Yin and Ding Ling will be closely examined in chap. 5, together with such other texts as Lu Yin's personal essays on her encounters with women in Japan and the short stories concerning female same-sex love by the male writers Zhang Yiping and Yu Dafu.

13. For example, Xiaomingxiong, *Zhongguo tongxing'ai shilu*; Hinsch, *Passions of the Cut Sleeve*; and Chou, *Hou zhimin tongzhi*, and *Tongzhi*. These three influential authors all focus on male-male sexuality in discussing the transition from tradition to modernity.

14. See Foucault, *History of Sexuality*, 1:105–14.

15. Ibid., 101.

16. Merck, Segal, and Wright, eds., *Coming Out of Feminism?*

17. Evans, *Women and Sexuality in China*, 29.

18. Povinelli and Chauncey, "Thinking Sexuality Transnationally," 439.

19. See Liu, *Translingual Practice*. Barlow ("Zhishifenzi [Chinese Intellectuals] and Power") and Bergere (*The Golden Age of the Chinese Bourgeoisie*) point out that, in early-twentieth-century China, a new intellectual, bourgeois class arose that wielded tremendous social power by appropriating Western and Japanese ideas, forms, signs, and discourses. Elsewhere, Barlow (introduction to *Formations of Colonial Modernity in East Asia*, 6) argues that Chinese modernity can be understood in terms of "colonial modernity," which for her highlights the fact that "historical context is not a matter of positively defined, elemental, or discrete units—nation states, stages of development, or

civilizations, for instance—but rather a complex field of relationships or threads of material that connect multiply in space-time and can be surveyed from specific sites." Other than the aforementioned works, studies of transnationality in Chinese modernity are numerous (see, e.g., Lee, *Shanghai Modern;* Hu, *Tales of Translation;* and Shih, *The Lure of the Modern*).

20. See Povinelli and Chauncey, "Thinking Sexuality Transnationally," 443.

21. Boellstorff, "The Perfect Path," 480.

22. Rofel, "Qualities of Desire," 456, 457.

23. Ibid., 458.

24. I might add that outdated versions of psychiatric discourse, if not a fine-grained theory of psychological personality, furnish the daily vocabulary used by mainstream urban society in postsocialist China to talk about homosexuality, despite the fact that some cosmopolitan gays are now adopting new words from the contemporary West (e.g., the English word *gay*) and Hong Kong and Taiwan (e.g., the revamped Chinese Communist term *tongzhi,* or "comrade") to organize new sexual subjectivities and communities. What do the outmoded but widely circulated psychiatric terms do if not define and discipline same-sex sexuality?

25. Rofel (ibid.) argues that, in China, gay women feel freer than gay men to assert their wish never to marry. This is probably because the parental pressure on them to do so is not as strong. I suspect, nevertheless, that it also has something to do with the fact that, for women, marriages, even fake ones, mean subordination and a greater compromise of personal freedom. Therefore, gay women must be especially wary of entering marriages in which they are not emotionally invested.

26. Ibid., 464.

27. Berry, *A Bit on the Side,* 97.

28. There are, of course, major exceptions. Hershatter's monograph on prostitution in Shanghai from the late nineteenth century to the late twentieth, *Dangerous Pleasures,* is a brilliant piece of scholarship with a remarkable level of detail. Such serious attention to sex as a subject, however, is relatively rare among China historians.

29. The massive demolition in the last decade of premodern architecture all across China, including practically entire historic cities such as Beijing and Suzhou, physically illustrates this cold-blooded repudiation of the local/national past. Even with regard to the immediate revolutionary past, disavowal has occurred. For instance, Arif Dirlik ("Reversals, Ironies, Hegemonies") points out that, in an era in which global capitalism appears triumphant, many historians of modern China have found it difficult to affirm the Communist Revolution and have been quick to deny that a revolution ever occurred in a real sense (see also Dirlik, "Is There History after Eurocentrism?").

30. To date, the most ambitious monograph that examines the global sexual economy and culture by integrating information from around the world is probably Altman, *Global Sex.*

31. There were many dynastic changes and shifts in territorial claims throughout history. What is more, one might argue that the sense of unity of the modern Chinese nation-state is false (see Duara, *Rescuing History from the Nation*).

32. For analyses of the TB/G (tomboy/girl) community in Hong Kong, see Chou, *Tongzhi,* 213–48.

33. See Yang, introduction to *Spaces of Their Own.*

34. See Habermas, *The Structural Transformation of the Public Sphere,* 25, 81, 141–250.

35. See Huang, ed., "Symposium."

36. I second William Rowe's remarks on the late Qing and early Republican eras (see "The Public Sphere in Modern China," 314–15, 322–23).

37. Lee and Nathan, "The Beginning of Mass Culture."

38. Goodman, "Being Public," 45, 88. According to Goodman, far from acting against the state, "popular associations reformulated their structures in the context of a widely felt need to mirror the shape and spirit of the state" (47). This finding leads her to argue the importance of our paying greater attention to the specific features of the Chinese public arena, instead of being guided and, therefore, limited by a public-sphere theory based on European historical experience.

39. Zhang, *Chinese Modernism in the Era of Reforms,* 3–4.

40. See Davis et al., eds., *Urban Spaces in Contemporary China.* On unofficial public culture, see Link, Madsen, and Pickowicz, eds., *Unofficial China.* Although the appearance of an unofficial social space in the PRC in the last two decades is clear, I would like to add a cautionary note against unreserved optimism. Developments since the late 1990s have begun to show the inordinate power of the profit-seeking mass media to mold mass culture and public opinion, along with a worrisome polarization of wealth and poverty among the population and extreme consumerism (the last of which is analyzed in Yan, "The Politics of Consumerism in Chinese Society"). The social landscape of the late 1990s may have departed significantly from the liberalizing and democratizing picture that China scholars identified in a capitalizing China during the 1980s and early 1990s.

41. Yang, introduction to *Spaces of Their Own,* 17. Yang explicitly asserts that a public sphere has emerged in the PRC during the era of reform. For a discussion of public spheres in other Chinese societies of the late 1980s and early 1990s, focusing especially on identity and culture, see Chun, "Discourses of Identity."

42. Yang, introduction to *Spaces of Their Own,* 17. Yang joins many European history specialists in pointing out that a public sphere defined in Habermas's utopian terms is an ideal yet to be fully realized anywhere.

43. Barlow, "Politics and Protocols of *Funü,*" 340.

44. Barlow, "Politics and Protocols of *Funü,*" 340. To give my understanding of the constructive or regulative effects of discourse more concretely: Besides the obvious subjectifying differences that certain categories make, the form in which a social agent/actor articulates her ideas of female-female relations—high art, a graphic sexual confession, a journalistic report, a sociological commentary, or a medical treatise—also positions her differently in relation to others in the field of symbolic and material exchanges. Moreover, the same kinds of enunciative positions and communicative structures have not been available to all persons at all times. The questions why certain enunciative positions have come into being at particular moments and who can occupy them are, therefore, intriguing.

45. Barlow, "Politics and Protocols of *Funü,*" 340.

46. Barlow, "Theorizing Woman," 265–68. Barlow acknowledges that, in late-imperial Chinese texts, the character *nü* is also used as an undifferentiated female category when it appears in a pair with *nan* (male) (ibid., 256).

47. Ibid., 267, 266.

48. Here, I use the words *homosocial* and *homoerotic,* instead of *homosexual,* to describe traditional Chinese practices to indicate that "preference," or the exclusive orientation toward one particular gender as object, was not necessarily involved in those practices. Also, no clear distinction is made between the emotional states of friendship and love, both of which fell in the late-imperial period under the category *feelings (qing).*

49. Zhang Jingsheng's attitudes came through strongly in the popular but short-lived (1927) magazine that he edited: *Xin wenhua* (New culture). They can also be garnered in his editorial comments on six sex confessions in the notorious 1926 volume *Xing shi* (Sex histories). For example, in the essay "Xing mei" (Sexual beauty), originally published in *Xin wenhua,* he criticizes Chinese men for not being man-like and Chinese women for not being woman-like (*nan bu nan, nü bu nü*). He writes, "Sexual beauty does not exist in the men and women of our country. What is worse, there is plenty of ugli-

ness because the male and female sexes have been reversed [*nan nü xing de daozhi*]. Men have been feminized, and thus big masculine men are turned into pale-faced scholars. Women have been masculinized, and thus smart, lively girls are turned into stupid and slow old women" (279). Zhang claims that the reversal of the genders resulted from bad conception in the womb, which was in turn a consequence of the lack of excitement, energy, and pleasure between men and women during sexual intercourse (ibid., 279–80). For further details, see chap. 4 below.

50. For Foucault in the first volume of *The History of Sexuality*, 1870 marked a moment of great epistemological change as the year in which the homosexual as a "species" was born; before that there had been only a class of sodomitic acts (see *History of Sexuality*, 1:43). Foucault's audacious assertions are widely construed by subsequent historians of sexuality as indicating a great paradigm shift, and various attempts have been made to locate that shift in Western Europe sometime in the last few centuries. For a particularly insightful discussion of Foucault's original passage, arguing that Foucault is postulating the difference between the law and psychiatry as that between two institutional, discursive practices rather than as what was/is possible on personal levels of self-understanding, see Halperin, "Forgetting Foucault." For another brilliant reinterpretation of volume 1 of *The History of Sexuality*, arguing that Foucault longingly invoked the medieval not so much to provide a truthful account of the Middle Ages as to celebrate the pleasure of acts on the surfaces of the body and to call for a politics premised on the "disaggregation" of identity, see Dinshaw, *Getting Medieval*, 191–206.

51. In the late-imperial era, besides being called *nanse* (male love/sex), male-male eroticism was also conceived as a mode, as in *nanfeng* (the southern mode) and *nanse yi dao* (the way of male love). For seventeenth-century Chinese conceptions of homoeroticism, see Vitiello, "Exemplary Sodomites" (1994), 28–39; and Volpp, "The Male Queen," 16–57.

52. For instance, Dai Jinhua, a major feminist critic in the PRC, uses *jiemei qingyi* (sisterhood) and *jiemei zhi bang* (the nation of sisters) to analyze female bonding in Lu Yin's short stories from the 1920s as well as in the fiction by Chen Ran from the 1990s. The female-female relations depicted by these two novelists have been frequently described by other critics as examples of same-sex love (see Dai, "Chen Ran"). For further details, see chaps. 5 and 8.

53. Foucault, *The Archaeology of Knowledge*, 173.

54. The desire to superimpose newer concepts on previous ones is also evident in Euro-American studies of sexuality, in which there exists always the urge to discern whether this or that historical phenomenon or subject—such as the mollies in the eighteenth century—was "homosexual." Even the historians who render historical differences absolute in their writings seem to view their own research on previous sexual phenomena as relevant to contemporary dissident sexual subjects.

55. Chen, "Guanyu 'Guangdong de bu luojia he zishu'"; Pan, "Zhongguo wenxian," 538–40.

56. The ideology of separate spheres prescribed a general division of space and labor along gender lines. According to this ideology, men were to dominate in the outer sphere (which encompassed such sites as the state, markets, schools, religious establishments, literary societies, city streets, and rural fields), while women were to operate in the inner, domestic sphere. In practice, women occasionally crossed the boundary separating the two spheres. For instance, some women held jobs as low-end laborers and professionals, although, undeniably, the outer sphere was dominated by men, who monopolized the higher positions in it.

Because of the difficulty in accessing oral traditions that existed prior to the twentieth century, my examination of the premodern era is focused on texts, especially those written by the literati. Writing and publishing were largely male privileges in premodern China. Starting in the seventeenth century, an ever-increasing number of gentry women were educated in the literary arts and wrote (mainly poetry, but also some narratives and dramatic works). A small fraction of their writing was even published. However, owing to the ideology of separate spheres and the notion that women's words were not to circulate outside the inner chambers, many women's manuscripts must have perished together with their authors.

On the separate spheres in theory and practice in the seventeenth and eighteenth centuries, see Ko, *Teachers of the Inner Chambers;* and Mann, *Precious Records.* For a selection of premodern women's poetry, see Chang and Saussy, eds., *Women Writers of Traditional China.* For my discussion of female-female relations in late-imperial women's literature, see chap. 3 below.

57. Vitiello, "Exemplary Sodomites" (1994), 173.

58. The Chinese literary genre *biji* might be understood as notation books that contain casual jottings or miscellaneous notes. A literatus would write down his observations on a great variety of subjects, these casual jottings (which can be either subsumed under a unifying topic or completely unrelated) then being collected and published as a notation book. The language is classical. The content and style vary greatly from notation book to notation book. Some jottings are descriptions of people, places, and customs; others are narratives of events and happenings. The distinction between fact and fiction in this genre is often blurry.

59. Vitiello notes, "In Master Moon-Heart's story . . . lesbianism is included in the diagram of sexuality. . . . [L]esbianism is conceived as a sub-category of male homosexuality" (ibid., 173). The story by Master Moon-Heart to which Vitiello refers is the episode "The Country of the Holy Yin" in *Yichun xiangzhi* (Fragrant stuff from the court of spring), a work of late-Ming male homoerotica.

Sophie Volpp has identified another late-Ming text linking male homoeroticism with lesbianism: "Wang Jide's *The Male Queen* . . . features two male lovers but has a lesbian subplot." On the basis of this text, Volpp maintains, "[Bret] Hinsch's claim [in *Passions of the Cut Sleeve*] that love between men and lesbianism were viewed as 'completely separate forms of sexuality' is somewhat overstated" ("The Male Queen," 11). I would argue that the lesbian subplot that Volpp identifies in fact cuts short female homoeroticism, rendering women's same-sex attraction transient and inferior, not only to heteroeroticism, but also to male homoeroticism. The plot involves a princess falling in love with the king's beautiful new queen, who is actually a cross-dressed boy. When the princess discovers the queen's male identity, she is pleasantly surprised rather than upset. Loving the boy in the queen even more, the princess forces him to marry her in a secret ceremony.

60. Mann, *Precious Records,* 28–29. Prominent local administrators of the high Qing era wrote much didactic literature for women. See also the detailed discussion of the protocols of female behavior stipulated by Chen Hongmou in Barlow, "Theorizing Woman," 255–61.

61. Mann, *Precious Records,* 21.

62. Zito, *Of Body and Brush,* 223.

63. The capitalized term *New Woman* originated in English in the late nineteenth century. A translation, signifying "the modern woman," appeared in Japanese and Chinese in the early twentieth century.

In the Anglo-American context, readers of the English novel had begun to recognize the distinct figure of the New Woman by the 1890s. As Gail Cunningham notes, "Heroines who refused to conform to the traditional feminine role, challenged accepted ideals of marriage and maternity, chose to work for a living, or who in any way argued the feminist cause, became commonplace in the works of both major and minor writers and were firmly identified by readers and reviewers as New Women." The New Woman was intelligent, individualistic, defiant of social convention as a matter of principle, and essentially middle class (*The New Woman and the Victorian Novel*, 3, 10, 11). According to Ann Heilmann, "the term 'New Woman' was used in its capitalized form as early as 1865"; however, "the battle of words between Sarah Grand and Ouida, conducted in the *North American Review* in 1894, is often seen as a defining moment of the New Woman controversy" (*New Woman Fiction*, 22, 23). Beyond fiction and polemics, Esther Newton identifies the first generation of Anglo-American New Women as those born in the 1850s and 1860s, educated in the 1870s and 1880s, and flourishing from the 1890s through the First World War ("The Mythic Mannish Lesbian," 561; see also Richardson, ed., *The New Woman in Fiction and in Fact*).

In this book, *New Woman* in its capitalized form is reserved for women who were recognized as such in England and America from the fin de siècle through the early twentieth century, in early-twentieth-century Japan, and in May Fourth China.

64. For a controversial argument about male sexologists' antifeminism in Western Europe and America, see Faderman, *Surpassing the Love of Men*, 239–53. For an alternative point of view, see Newton, "The Mythic Mannish Lesbian." See also Halberstam, *Female Masculinity*.

65. I agree with Wang (*Women in the Chinese Enlightenment*, 17–20) that there were competing discourses regarding women in the May Fourth era. Although the Victorian sex binary, which typecast women as physically and intellectually inferior, was introduced in China, a contemporaneous feminist discourse argued that women were also human and that they had to have independent personhood (*duli renge*).

66. As mentioned already, female-female sex acts have never been criminalized, or, for that matter, mentioned, by Chinese law, traditional or modern. The legal discourse has not been a significant mode of control in the regulation of female-female relations. Nevertheless, there is unpredictable censorship of female homoerotic literature in post-Mao China (see chaps. 7 and 8).

67. Havelock Ellis, "Sexual Inversion in Women" (1895), cited in Newton, "The Mythic Mannish Lesbian," 568. Although this particular article by Ellis may not have been translated into Chinese, his other writings that were translated similarly put forth the model of sexual inversion and confuse sexual preference (which concerns object choice) with the issue of gender identity (which concerns the subject).

68. Esther Newton and George Chauncey have both argued that, historically speaking, male sexologists like Ellis were not entirely wrong about the masculinity of the early lesbian persona. Both critics maintain that masculine identification was a necessary strategy to adopt if early-twentieth-century British and American women were to make an outright statement about their physical desire for other women. See Newton, "The Mythic Mannish Lesbian," 561; and Chauncey, "From Sexual Inversion to Homosexuality," 117.

69. Ellis, "The School-Friendships of Girls" (for a Chinese translation, see Xie's "Nü xuesheng de tongxing ai"). Ellis's attempt to pronounce heterosexual love as more real than girls' school friendships is loaded with male anxiety and phallocentrism. Marjorie Garber has elegantly put forth a different interpretation of adolescent homoerotic love in boarding schools—no passion is ever false (see *Vice Versa*, 297–316, 324–34).

70. Pan, trans., *Xing xinli xue*, 325–26 n. 36.

71. Interestingly, physical contact and emotional ties between members of the same sex are more casually displayed than is opposite-sex intimacy in the films and other visual arts of the Maoist era. However, the eroticism of same-sex images from the Maoist era is usually ambiguous and unspoken rather than explicitly sexualized. Such images of same-sex intimacy evoke notions of homosexuality perhaps only unintentionally.

72. Evans, *Women and Sexuality in China*, 206. The erasure of the category from state-sanctioned materials about sex gives us little indication as to whether same-sex ac-

tivities lay just below the surface of official discourse. For further elucidation of this issue, see chap. 6.

73. The original passage in *Xiandai hanyu cidian* reads: "Tongxing lian'ai: nanzi he nanzi huo nüzi he nüzi zhijian fasheng de lian'ai guanxi, shi yizhong xinli biantai" (1029). The dictionary was completed, if not published, in 1965, before the Cultural Revolution.

74. On the valorization of gender difference by women scholars and popular consumer culture in the post-Mao era, see Honig and Hershatter, *Personal Voices;* Barlow, "Politics and Protocols of *Funü*"; Evans, *Women and Sexuality in China,* 26−32, 134−43, and passim; Wang, "Research on Women in Contemporary China"; and Yang, "From Gender Erasure to Gender Difference." More generally, on consumerism in 1990s China as a dominant and legitimating ideology, see Yan, "The Politics of Consumerism in Chinese Society."

75. Wang ("Research on Women in Contemporary China," 36) notes that, in public discussions in the PRC, the category *female consciousness* (*nüxing yishi*) stands for both femininity and feminist consciousness, which are as yet undifferentiated.

76. The notion of compulsory heterosexuality, famously formulated by Adrienne Rich (see her "Compulsory Heterosexuality and Lesbian Existence"), has been a major catalyst for lesbian feminism in Taiwan, where it is known as *qiangpo yixinglian jizhi.*

77. Wang Zheng, among others, has pointed out certain differences between the Women's Federation (the official women's organization) and women scholars (i.e., nonofficial, elite feminists) in post-Mao China. The former continues the Marxist emphasis on male-female equality in its "woman work," i.e., studying and solving women's problems, whereas the latter are fascinated with feminization as the recovery of women's human nature. However, there is to date very little discussion, in either group, of gender as a social construct as opposed to biological sex (see Wang, "Research on Women in Contemporary China," 12, 19, 35−36). Under these circumstances, the term *female consciousness,* which signifies the whole discourse of the rediscovery of femininity, has been used by many female and male literary critics to discuss the novelist Chen Ran's writings. This, in my view, shows that the fundamental difference between the dominant discourse of femininity and Chen's revolt against gender essentialism has been neither truly examined nor adequately articulated in the PRC.

78. Their apolitical stance can be gathered from the first Beijing lesbian newsletter, *Tiankong* (Sky), established in March 1999 and published without a government permit.

79. Halperin, *One Hundred Years of Homosexuality,* 15−40.

80. Hekma, "'A Female Soul in a Male Body.'"

81. Halperin, *Saint Foucault,* 62.

82. Halberstam, *Female Masculinity,* 51.

83. Liu, *Translingual Practice,* 27.

84. Rofel, *Other Modernities,* 13. Besides Rofel's *other modernities,* similar terms have been coined by other theorists to illuminate the persistence of heterogeneity and cultural difference among modernities. See, e.g., Nonini and Ong, "Chinese Transnationalism as an Alternative Modernity"; Appadurai, *Modernity at Large;* and Eisenstadt, "Multiple Modernities."

85. Furth, *A Flourishing Yin,* 48, 52. For an inspiring discussion of the impossibility of mapping the physiological knowledge of traditional Chinese medicine (as it is practiced in the PRC today) onto a modern anatomical body, see Farquhar, "Multiplicity, Point of View, and Responsibility in Traditional Chinese Healing."

86. These terms are categories of behavior, relations, or emotional/physical states; none of them automatically denote sexual orientation or identity for me. I am aware that some theorists have historicized the word *homosexuality* to such an extent that, for them, it signifies modernity and sexual identity. However, I believe that there has also

been an alternative usage among scholars in which *homosexuality* is conceptualized as a category of behavior and the category does not imply sexual orientation or identity by itself. To say that "X is a homosexual," however, is a different matter; used as a noun to refer to a person, the term *a homosexual* obviously denotes sexual identity.

## Chapter 2

1. The controversy over categories—or the question of what words to use to describe male-male or female-female relations in the past—is a familiar one in queer studies. David Halperin champions a strictly historicist approach and is critical of the use of modern terms as universal analytic categories in the writings of other historians such as John Boswell. For both sides of the argument, see Halperin, *One Hundred Years of Homosexuality,* and "Is There a History of Sexuality?"; and Boswell, "Revolutions, Universals, and Sexual Categories."

2. It must be noted that, although Pan was interested in eugenics, he did not subscribe to the nineteenth-century European sexological view (represented by Krafft-Ebing) that homosexuality was related to degeneration. In fact, in a study of the genealogy of Chinese actors, who, historically, as a class were involved in both male and female prostitution, Pan is interested in them as extraordinary "talents" (*rencai*) and is intent on investigating the role of heredity in determining their beauty and artistic ability. The idea could not be farther from Pan's mind that the actors' involvement in male prostitution caused hereditary defects and degeneration (see Pan, "Zhongguo lingren xueyuan zhi yanjiu").

3. Both Xiaomingxiong's and Hinsch's texts are popular among gay male readers in Hong Kong and Taiwan.

4. Altman, *Global Sex,* 86–105.

5. Sweeping claims about traditional Chinese sexual culture pervade such discussions among Chinese queer activists. For a sample, see Chou et al., "Zhongxi wenhua chayi yu huaren tongzhi yundong de fangxiang." See also Chou, *Tongzhi,* 13–58.

6. Rofel, "Qualities of Desire."

7. Sommer, *Sex, Law, and Society,* 114–65, 329–32. Both the Qing and the Ming had legislation concerning anal penetration between males. Since the Qing substatute was concerned predominantly with punishing males of marginal or mean status penetrating young males of good character/commoner status, it was not a categorical prohibition of male-male sex per se. As Sommer demonstrates, elite men could as a rule indulge their taste for boys without any trouble, although men of their station had wives, whether they desired women or not (ibid., 158). Vivien Ng's often-cited earlier study on Qing "sodomy" (*jijian*) law in terms of "homophobia," "Homosexuality and the State in Late Imperial China," does not adequately take the issue of status into account.

8. Volpp, "The Male Queen."

9. Vitiello, "The Dragon's Whim," and "Exemplary Sodomites" (1994).

10. Ko, *Teachers of the Inner Chambers,* 167, 266–74.

11. Hu, "Literary *Tanci,*" and "Jiafeng xuhuang/dianluan daofeng."

12. Hua, "Ming Qing funü juzuo." The plays analyzed by Hua Wei are *Yuanyang meng* (The dream of mandarin ducks) by Ye Xiaowan (1613–60?), *Fanhua meng* (The dream of prosperity and luxuriance) by Wang Yun (1749?–1819?), *Qiao ying* (The disguised image) by Wu Zao (1799?–1862?), and *Lihua meng* (The dream of pear blossoms) by He Peizhu (1819?–?). For Hua's related writings in English, see "The Lament of Frustrated Talents."

As a matter of fact, cross-dressing and other kinds of gender reversals occur frequently, to the point of being a stock situation, in the drama and fiction by men in the late Ming and the Qing. Maram Epstein argues that "gender inversion" and a fluid range of gender positions unconfined by binary biological distinctions are characteristic of the late-imperial imaginary. However, based on male-authored novels, Epstein also maintains that these works are ultimately self-referential: "Whether cast in the role of the dangerous 'other,' capable of destroying normative, patriarchal order, or of idealized self, the female characters in these novels . . . reflect a spectrum of male literati concerns related to issues of personal and social power" (*Competing Discourses,* 306). Epstein's argument resonates, by coincidence, with Hua Wei's observation of late-imperial women's plays: female dramatists use male characters and cross-dressing female characters, portrayed by actors specializing in *sheng* (young male) roles, to represent themselves.

13. Hua, "Ming Qing funü juzuo," 606.

14. Nietzsche, *On the Advantage and Disadvantage of History for Life.*

15. For exemplary readings of the specters of lesbian eroticism in literary texts, see Castle, *The Apparitional Lesbian.*

16. For a forceful argument against the use of the word *lesbianism* as a transhistorical analytic category, see Halperin, review of *Love between Women.*

17. Pflugfelder, *Cartographies of Desire.*

18. For various definitions of what constituted the May Fourth Movement, see Chow, *The May Fourth Movement.* The period from the mid-1910s to the mid-1920s is generally regarded as one of vital cultural rejuvenation and intellectual fermentation. I demarcate this era, named after the May Fourth incident of 1919, as the period between the founding of the intellectual magazine *Xin qingnian* (New youth) in 1915 and the Nationalist army's completion of the Northern Expedition and unification of China in 1927.

19. For an illuminating study of Liang Qichao's nationalistic as well as cosmopolitan outlook, see Tang, *Global Space and the Nationalist Discourse of Modernity.*

20. For an outline of the development of men's feminism, women's formal education, and the women's press at the end of Qing, see Wang, *Women in the Chinese Enlightenment,* 35–48.

21. Ibid., 14–15.

22. On the inchoate image of the new woman in late Qing fiction, which was heavily influenced by the translations of European fiction into Chinese, see Hu, *Tales of Translation.* As Hu points out, the ideal of the new woman was in the process of being constructed during the last decade of the Qing, although the term *xin nüxing* had not yet achieved currency (ibid., 4). Both Hu and Wang Zheng note that the category *new woman* did not become prominent in nationwide discussions until the May Fourth/New Culture era (see Wang, *Women in the Chinese Enlightenment,* 14–16). Therefore, I capitalize the term *new woman* only when discussing the May Fourth era, not when referring to women in the late Qing. See also my discussion of the origin of the capitalized, English version of the term in n. 63, chap. 1, above.

23. As Ko (*Teachers of the Inner Chambers,* 22–23) notes, the period spanning the late Ming and the early Qing has been treated by historians in Taiwan and Japan as a coherent historical epoch "in recognition of the many secular trends that transcended the dynastic transition," including the thriving development of women's culture. Ko's study of this epoch demarcates it as lasting from the 1570s to the 1720s. In defining the late-imperial era, therefore, I have chosen to date it as lasting from the late Ming onward. The end point is automatically set as 1911, the year in which the imperial system was overthrown.

24. Furth, "Androgynous Males and Deficient Females," 482.

25. Sommer, *Sex, Law, and Society,* 115. Sommer maintains, "The lack of legal references does not, of course, imply that women never formed erotic relationships with each other—there are plenty of references in *non*-legal sources. Nor does it mean that lawmakers were necessarily ignorant of such matters. Sex between women was simply not constructed as a crime. This interpretation makes sense, given the phallocentrism of

both law and social norms; if gender and power were keyed to a hierarchy of phallic penetration, then sex without a phallus would seem to undermine neither" (163). I find Sommer's analysis remarkably perceptive, although the nonlegal references to female-female sex that he mentions are far from numerous. His statement is thus less a well-supported argument than an intuitive insight.

26. Hinsch's *Passions of the Cut Sleeve* was for more than a decade the only monograph on Chinese homosexuality available in English and is cited frequently in the United States by China specialists and nonspecialists alike. Van Gulik's *Sexual Life in Ancient China* has been translated into Chinese and is a popular text in Taiwan and China.

27. Hinsch, *Passions of the Cut Sleeve,* 174–75. In fact, Hinsch's claim dramatizes the fallacy of a particular kind of approach—one that carries too strong a contemporary bias. From the outset, the object sought is lesbians of a late-twentieth-century sort: women who are economically independent, detached from men, with the freedom and mobility to meet other women in public spaces and form relationships. Owing to the difference between premodern Chinese social organization and postindustrial society, a search in the Chinese past for lesbians defined in late-twentieth-century terms is self-defeating. Perhaps out of the desire to find Chinese antecedents of modern lesbians, Hinsch has bypassed the opportunity to discover what forms of female same-sex bonds were in fact possible and permissible in premodern China. A different way of looking is required.

28. Ko shows that, in their poetry and prose, quite a few gentry women praised the feminine beauty of daughters, friends, and courtesans in sensuous terms. She coins the term *love-friendship continuum* to describe such homoeroticism (see *Teachers of the Inner Chambers,* 167, 266–74). In a shorter essay, Ko similarly argues that elite women's "homoerotic" poems indicate their privilege and relative freedom of expression in a gender system inflected by class (see "Same-Sex Love between Singing Girls and Gentry Wives"). Personally, I am not certain how we might go about comparing the amount of homoerotic liberty enjoyed by elite women who wrote with that enjoyed by those women, the vast majority, who left no written records.

29. See Chou, *Hou zhimin tongzhi,* 319–47; as well as Xiaomingxiong, *Zhongguo tongxing'ai shilu,* 7–14; and Hinsch, *Passions of the Cut Sleeve,* 163–71.

30. Van Gulik, *Sexual Life in Ancient China,* 48, 109, 163, 274, 302. The little material on which van Gulik bases his conjecture includes Li Yu's play *Lian xiang ban* (Women in love), which will be discussed later in this chapter, and a description of a sexual position involving two women and a man that appears in ancient sex manuals and erotic picture albums.

31. Van Gulik's claim implies that a woman's adultery was defined only in terms of sex with (the wrong) men. Considering the complete absence of female-female sex from the "illicit sex" (*jian*) section of traditional Chinese law, this assumption must certainly be considered accurate. See Sommer's discussion of the Qing legal regulation of illicit sex in *Sex, Law, and Society,* chaps. 3, 5–7.

32. Ko, *Teachers of the Inner Chambers,* 270.

33. Mann, *Precious Records,* 60.

34. Pan, "Zhongguo wenxian," 538.

35. Tompkins, *Sensational Designs.* Tompkins sees literary texts, "not as works of art embodying enduring themes in complex forms, but as attempts to redefine the social order"—they perform, in other words, "cultural work" (xi).

36. Patrick Hanan (*The Invention of Li Yu,* 15–16) opines that the female same-sex passion in the play forced Li Yu to flee the district where it was first performed because the audience took it as a lampoon of a real incident. Hanan's arguments are based on the preface by Yu Wei to *Lian xiang ban* in the Qing "Yishengtang" edition.

37. Among the stories in *Liaozhai zhiyi* containing female homoerotic bigamy are "Xiao Xie" (Miss Xiao Xie), "Lianxiang" (Lotus Scent), "Liancheng" (Miss Liancheng), "Qingmei" (Green Plum), "Shao nü" (Miss Shao), "Axiu" (Miss Axiu), "Chang'e" (Chang'e), "Xiangyü" (Fragrant Jade), and "Shen nü" (Goddess).

38. For a study of two-wife polygyny in the Qing beauty-scholar romance, see McMahon, "The Classic 'Beauty-Scholar' Romance," esp. 237–45.

39. A cursory look through the plot summaries provided in Tan and Tan, eds., *Tanci xulu,* will suffice to confirm this point.

40. Ko, *Teachers of the Inner Chambers,* 103–10. According to Ko, women's jealousy became an important public concern in the urban culture of seventeenth-century Jiangnan because the increase in companionate marriage between educated gentry women and men clashed with rampant concubinage. The principal wives, who in modern terms would be just "assertive women" insistent on their rights in the family, were chided as jealous and targeted for satire and censure.

41. Quoted in ibid., 105, in Ko's translation.

42. Li, *Lian xiang ban,* 7.

43. One can imagine several plot situations in which nontragic female same-sex preference and commitment is possible: e.g., two women escape from their husband's household, one of them dressing in men's guise so that they can pass as husband and wife; or two women retreat into uninhabited mountains; or widows or nuns might choose to live together. But it is difficult for me to imagine that these situations do not involve some kind of disguise, secrecy, or the semblance of a substitute practice. In other words, it is implausible that the two women would be known to the general society as lovers, by choice not bound to men.

44. Mann, *Precious Records,* 10.

45. Kai Shi, "Guangdong de 'bu luojia' he 'zishu,'" 938, 939.

46. Chen, "Guanyu 'Guangdong de bu luojia he zishu,'" 204.

47. Pan, "Zhongguo wenxian," 539–40. Pan mentions the lifting of a ban on sea trade but does not specify the year. In all likelihood he is alluding to developments during the Qing. In 1662, troubled by the Ming loyalist Koxinga's raids along the coast, the early Qing court ordered all ports closed to foreign trade. It lifted the ban in 1683 and opened customs houses at Canton as well as three other ports in 1685. In 1759, the court issued a decree limiting foreign trade to Canton, but elaborate restrictions were placed on the trading season, the physical movement of foreign traders while in Canton, which Chinese merchants were authorized to make transactions, etc. The Canton system of trade lasted until the end of the Opium War in 1842. In its treaty with the British, China was forced to abolish the single port system, to open five ports (including Canton) to trade, and to allow the British consuls and merchants and their families to live in those cities (see Hsü, *The Rise of Modern China,* 139–66, 190). Where Pan discusses the effect of foreign trade and foreign culture on Canton, he could be referring either to the period between 1759 and 1842, when Canton monopolized international trade, or to the period after 1842, when the contact between foreigners and the local people in Canton became less restricted than it had been before.

48. Stockard, *Daughters of the Canton Delta,* 48–89.

49. Siu, "Where Were the Women?"

50. Stockard, *Daughters of the Canton Delta,* 1–3. Stockard admits that similar practices can be found among ethnic minorities in Guangxi and Fujian Provinces, although she does not pursue the issue. For a study of late-twentieth-century literary and film appropriations of the delayed-transfer marriage and female-female bonding in the Huian area of Fujian, see Lee, "Cong *Shuang zhuo* de 'jiemei fuqi.'"

51. In this regard, I disagree with Cathy Silber. In a perceptive study of women's delayed-transfer marriage practices in the Jiangyong area in southern Hunan, where *nüshu*

(a script used only among women) recently attracted much curiosity from the outside world, Silber declares that the fact "that marriage practices entailing a woman's pro-longed residence in, or enduring ties to, her natal home are now known to occur in Shandong, Guangdong, Guangxi, Guizhou, Fujian (Huian), Hainan, and Hunan, indicate[s] that it is time to stop looking at these as isolated exceptions, even when they are identified as non-Han practices" ("From Daughter to Daughter-in-Law," 48). I am puzzled by what Silber means by not being isolated. It seems quite clear from the references that she cites in her notes that delayed-transfer marriage occurs on a limited geographic scale and that the locales where it is practiced are separated from one another by vast distances.

52. As Teri Silvio points out, "Historically, most Chinese regional theater has been performed by all-male or all-female casts, and the Chinese theater has long been associated with sexually unorthodox practices, including same-sex sexuality and prostitution." Discussing in particular outdoor-stage *koa-a-hi* (Taiwanese opera), in which women play all the leading roles, Silvio observes, "It is a commonsense assumption in Taiwan that many *koa-a-hi* actresses have their primary sexual and emotional relationships with women, either other actresses or fans" ("Reflexivity, Bodily Praxis, and Identity in Taiwanese Opera," 585). However, neither the Ts and the pos—tomboys and femmes (*po* is the Chinese word for *wife*)—in the urban T-bar subculture nor college-educated lesbian and gay activists identify strongly with this performance tradition, as urban lesbians generally have Western tastes and outlooks.

53. See Yu, "Manman chang lu." *Ai bao* (The love journal)—in which the Yu article appeared—was the first lesbian newsletter in Taiwan. The picture of two Chinese women dancing in a Shanghai dance hall on p. 21 of the second issue and the picture on the cover of the third issue are both copied from calendar posters popular in early Republican China (see Zhang, *Lao yuefenpai guanggao hua*, 2:102, 123). For the images reproduced in *Ai bao*, see my figures 7 and 8.

54. By using the word *fantasy*, I am by no means suggesting that contemporary Chinese gay men's belief in belonging to a Chinese homoerotic tradition is self-delusional. I am merely pointing out that, in psychoanalytic terms, identification is phantasmatic. There is a great gender disparity in the amount of phantasmatic resources available to contemporary Chinese gay men and women in premodern Chinese records. Alien to lesbians, the idea that there existed a great homosexual tradition in premodern China is running strong among gay male communities in Hong Kong, Taiwan, and mainland China. For an English treatment of the thesis of the great tradition, see Hinsch, *Passions of the Cut Sleeve*, which echoes the approach of Xiaomingxiong's *Zhongguo tongxing'ai shilu*. (*Zhongguo tongxing'ai shilu* was reprinted recently to meet popular demand among gay male readers in Hong Kong and Taiwan. Moreover, the commercial gay and lesbian magazine *G&L*, based in Taipei, published excerpts from it in the late 1990s.) On 1990s Beijing gay men's yearning to belong to the Chinese cultural tradition, see Rofel, "Qualities of Desire."

55. Sommer, *Sex, Law, and Society*, 163.

56. Volpp, "The Male Queen," 111–55. Volpp points out that, although literati such as Chen Weisong were the very ones who created the courtesan cult of the seventeenth century, their poems in tribute to famous boy actors argue "for the superiority of the femininity of the male sex" and "perpetuate the competition between the homoerotic and the heteroerotic" (112).

57. For an extensive study of the legend of Xiaoqing, see Widmer, "Xiaoqing's Literary Legacy."

58. Pan, "Zhongguo wenxian," 538.

59. Zhu, *Mingzhai xiaoshi*, 3360.

60. Pan, "Zhongguo wenxian," 538. Although Pan argues that Xiaoqing was a real person and that some stories about her were truthful biographies (see Pan, *Feng Xiaoqing*

*xing xinli biantai jiemi,* 69–80), whether these two accounts were based on real people or actual incidents cannot be determined. Ellen Widmer observes of the original biographical narratives and the fictional and dramatic literature about Xiaoqing: "Whoever [Xiaoqing] may have been, her shadowy life was quickly overwhelmed by legend. Some have questioned whether she in fact ever existed in the flesh" ("Xiaoqing's Literary Legacy," 112–13). And, since *Mingzhai xiaoshi* belongs to the genre *biji* (casual notes), a hybrid of history and invention, and since personal names are not used in the account itself, it is especially difficult to determine whether the second story has any basis in reality.

61. Tan and Tan, eds., *Tanci xulu,* 64.

62. Changbai, *Yingchuang yicao,* 4959.

63. It should be clear by now that my discussion concerns itself with the broader issue of female-female relations instead of being narrowly focused on female-female sex acts. In premodern Chinese literature, explicit descriptions of sex between women typically appear only in erotic or pornographic fiction. As McMahon (*Misers, Shrews, and Polygamists,* 145–46) points out, the scenes of sex between women function as a prelude to sex between a man and a woman. Most women in these scenes appear automaton-like and starved for sex. Of course, that they should be given dignity or psychological depth is out of the question. On the use, in late-imperial Chinese erotic fiction, of female-female sex as a means of seduction that leads to a woman's illicit sex with a man, see also Kang, *Chong shen fengyue jian,* 222–24. Kang rightly observes that adultery in late-imperial Chinese fiction is defined solely within the context of male-female sex. In Ming stories such as *Jiang Xingge chong hui zhenzhu shan* (A pearl-sewn shirt), a basically virtuous married woman agrees to female-female sex as an appropriate substitute for sex with her husband while he is away from home, only to discover that her female companion has aroused her with extended foreplay so as to lure her to have intercourse with a male stranger.

64. Translation taken from Rexroth and Chung, trans. and eds., *The Orchid Boat,* 73, and modified with reference to Hua, "The Lament of Frustrated Talents," 35.

65. Hua, "The Lament of Frustrated Talents," 35.

66. Quoted in Ko, *Teachers of the Inner Chambers,* 272, in Ko's translation.

67. Ibid., 272.

68. Ibid., 272–73.

69. Besides the poems analyzed by Ko in *Teachers of the Inner Chambers,* many other examples are to be found in Chang and Saussy, eds., *Women Writers of Traditional China.*

70. Hu, "Jiafeng xuhuang/dianluan daofeng," 1–3, and "Literary *Tanci,*" 238–71.

71. Hu, "Yuedu fanying yu tanci xiaoshuo de chuangzuo." Chen Duansheng's unfinished *Zai sheng yuan* was highly acclaimed among gentry women in her time, and another woman writer, Liang Desheng (1771–1857), wrote three additional chapters to give it closure. Unlike the radical Chen, Liang was a conformist with regard to the dominant ideology of gender roles. For a brief discussion in English of *Zai sheng yuan,* see Hu, "Literary *Tanci,*" 70–84.

72. For details about the situation in medieval and early modern Europe, see Brown, *Immodest Acts.*

73. Furth, "Androgynous Males and Deficient Females," 480, 481.

### Chapter 3

1. For Foucault's painstaking efforts to "suspend" the "unity" of discourses, see *The Archaeology of Knowledge,* 21–30.

2. All citations of *Liaozhai zhiyi* are taken from Pu, *Liaozhai zhiyi huijiao huizhu huiping ben,* with both chapter and page numbers from this edition given in the text.

3. For example, a graphic description of orgasmic sex between women appears in chap. 22 of the seventeenth-century *Gelian huaying* (Shadows of flowers behind the screen), in which two girls imitate copulation between an adult man and a woman (see Guben xiaoshuo jicheng bianweihui, ed., *Gelian huaying*, 1:382–84). Another example can be found in *Xiuta yeshi* (The unofficial history of events on an embroidered mat), in which a woman makes love to another woman so as to seduce her into having sex with her male lover (see Qingdian, *Xiuta yeshi*, 10–19). Note that, in these scenes, women are portrayed as having either loose morals or a bodily weakness. Their sex with women either is interspersed with or precedes illicit sex with men. It does not happen that a truly virtuous woman has genital sex with another woman—virtue and genital activity between women are mutually exclusive in Ming-Qing pornography. For a description of two female-female sex scenes in *Xinghua tian* (The sky of apricot flowers), a Qing erotic beauty-scholar romance, see McMahon, *Misers, Shrews, and Polygamists*, 145–46. McMahon comments: "Scenes of women having sex together are relatively rare in Chinese fiction but typically follow this example in that the relationship is not portrayed as sufficient in itself but instead as a temporary replacement for or prelude to sex with a man" (145–46).

4. On the diverse attitudes toward sex among American lesbians of the baby-boom generation, see Stein, *Sex and Sensibility*, 139–47.

5. Some stories in the collection were inspired by earlier classical tales or folklore. The story "Feng Sanniang," to be discussed in detail, seems to be one of those stories that Pu Songling invented himself. At least, I have not found any mention of classical or folklore precursors for the story in the reference books on *Liaozhai*'s source material.

6. McMahon reminds us that "polygamy was a matter of privilege and means," available only to powerful or wealthy men (*Misers, Shrews, and Polygamists*, 2). Monogamy was the predominant form of marriage.

7. The analytic concept *compulsory heterosexuality* is eloquently articulated in Rich, "Compulsory Heterosexuality and Lesbian Existence." Here, I invoke Rich's powerful phrase to suggest the subservience required of women in premodern China to act as sex objects for men. At the same time, insofar as *heterosexuality* is a modern invention that gains its meaning through difference from *homosexuality* in the sexological discourse, it may be that *compulsory sexual service, compulsory marriage,* and *compulsory chastity* are more apt than *compulsory heterosexuality* as descriptions of premodern Chinese women's situation. On this, I will have more to say later.

8. Freud, "The Uncanny."

9. Zeitlin, *Historian of the Strange,* 222 n. 15.

10. By contrast, in Pu's stories about male-female relationships, it is common for the female of a nonhuman species to become integrated into the human world through marriage and the raising of sons.

11. Freud, "Fetishism"; Lacan, "The Signification of the Phallus," 290.

12. For a complete translation of "Feng Sanniang," see the appendix.

13. The Chinese text actually reads "Shangyuan" (i.e., the fifteenth day of the first month). Judging from later parts of the narrative, however, scholars generally think that the text should read instead "Zhongyuan" (i.e., the fifteenth day of the seventh month).

14. See, e.g., Tang, "Lüe tan *Liaozhai zhiyi* zhong de aiqing xiaoshuo," 106; and Ye, *Liaozhai zhiyi zhong guihu gushi de tantao,* 32.

15. Lei, *Liaozhai yishu tonglun,* 95.

16. The quotations of Feng Zhenluan and He Shouqi are taken from Pu, *Liaozhai zhiyi huijiao huizhu huiping ben,* 610 and 617, respectively. Some reference material indicates that "Feng Sanniang" was adapted into a Sichuan opera entitled *Zuizhong yuan* (Affinity in drunkenness). I have not been able to locate a script of this opera to find out the adapters' take on the female-female relationship in the story, when the adap-

tation was done, and how popular this opera was. See Zhu, ed., *Liaozhai zhiyi ziliao huibian,* 720.

17. For a useful but incomplete survey that lists the translations of *Liaozhai* in various languages, see Wang, "*Liaozhai zhiyi* de minzu yuwen banben he waiwen yiben."

18. Zeitlin, *Historian of the Strange,* 259 n. 60.

19. In a discussion of lesbianism in traditional Chinese literature, Xiaomingxiong excerpts "Feng Sanniang" and gives a minimal (one-sentence) analysis (*Zhongguo tongxing'ai shilu,* 276–77). Note that Xiaomingxiong's book is not a scholarly study of *Liaozhai* but rather a revisionist gay history by a nonspecialist. It is part of the gay activist discourse in Hong Kong emergent since the 1980s.

20. Lee ("Cong *Shuang zhuo* de 'jiemei fuqi,'" 18) charts the recurrence of separation as the ending in modern Chinese fiction about lesbians. Radclyffe Hall's *The Well of Loneliness* readily comes to mind as a well-known English text that concludes with the lesbian's self-abnegation, surrendering her lover to a man and marriage. Although there are striking structural similarities between the story of Stephen Gordon (Hall's masculine heroine) and that of Feng Sanniang, here I shall refrain from too anachronistic and voluntarist an interpretation of Feng Sanniang in terms of butch sexuality and identity. Among other reasons, there is a kind of doubling between the feminine physical appearances of Feng and Shiyiniang that betrays the male author's desire for twofold visual pleasure. I am interested, therefore, less in uncovering the hidden presence of a certain butch-like subjectivity in the male-authored text than in a better-historicized question: What are the textual strategies that the male literatus Pu uses both to open up and to delimit the possibility of a woman-preferring woman?

21. According to Laura Mulvey, modern culture has equated woman with image and man with bearer of the look; for her analysis, which is based on classic Hollywood cinema, see *Visual and Other Pleasures,* 14–26. Pu Songling's story, of course, predates modern visual culture. Mulvey's insight might not, therefore, necessarily be pertinent to an analysis of Pu's emphasis on the gaze.

22. Li, *Lian xiang ban,* 18–22.

23. Ibid., 22. The nun says, "Not only can beauty enchant, but talent also charms. It was to avoid such attachments that I decided not to pursue the art of poetry."

24. Bernhardt, *Women and Property in China.*

25. For a theoretical reflection on the traffic in women in kin-based systems of social organization, see Rubin, "The Traffic in Women."

26. Li, *Lian xiang ban,* 86.

27. It is difficult to say whether Pu had *Women in Love* in mind when he composed "Feng Sanniang." My guess, however, is that he did not.

28. Laplanche and Pontalis, "Fantasy and the Origins of Sexuality."

29. Terry Castle (*The Apparitional Lesbian,* 66–91) makes a similar argument about Sylvia Townsend Warner.

30. Sedgwick, *Between Men.*

31. For one, Judith Butler (*Bodies That Matter,* 57–92) has demonstrated the repression of the transferability of the phallus in Freud's and Lacan's theories, which take the penis as the fixed reference point.

32. Deleuze, *Masochism,* 267.

33. Here, I refer to J. L. Austin's notion of *the performative* in language. When a speaker effects something (such as a promise, a marriage contract, refusal) in and/or by the articulation of words, the utterance is performative. Austin set up three categories— the locutionary, the illocutionary, and the perlocutionary—to specify three types of action in a speech act. For definitions, see Austin, *How to Do Things with Words,* 94–108.

34. I borrow from Langton's "Speech Acts and Unspeakable Acts" the example of the actor to illustrate illocutionary disablement.

35. See, e.g., Robinet, *Taoist Meditation*, 48. Of course, there are many other Taoist longevity techniques besides the sexual—running the whole gamut from meditation, visualization, alchemy, talismans, recitations, and respiratory techniques to gymnastics.

36. Furth, "Rethinking Van Gulik," 133.

37. Van Gulik (*Sexual Life in Ancient China*) provides detailed discussions of these points. See also Robinet, *Taoist Meditation*, 88–90.

38. I borrow the term *sexual vampirism* from van Gulik (*Sexual Life in Ancient China*, 316), who is critical of the debasement of the bedchamber arts in later historical periods (e.g., in Ming erotic novels).

39. For a lengthy citation of the legend of the Queen of Western Paradise from a text on the bedchamber arts, *Yufang neijue* (Secret skills for the inner chamber), see van Gulik, *Sexual Life in Ancient China*, 158.

40. Ge Hong's *Baopuzi* (The master who embraces simplicity; A.D. 317) distinguishes three kinds of immortals: the heavenly, the earthly, and those of the underworld. The heavenly are the highest type, and achieving this state requires of the adept the most sublimation and refinement of the body (see Robinet, *Taoist Meditation*, 45–46).

41. Robinet, *Taoist Meditation*, 90. Robinet refers to the Taoist *Zhen Gao* as a text that puts forth this position.

42. Engelhardt, "Qi for Life," 284.

43. Sun Bu'er (1119–?), an accomplished female adept of the northern school of Taoism, also warned against pregnancy and emphasized the purification of thoughts and desires as women's key to the successful cultivation of the Tao (see Xu, *Daojiao zongheng*, 88–91).

44. For a summary of the Ming pornographic novel *Zhaoyang qushi* (1621), which features a sex-vampirish female fox, see van Gulik, *Sexual Life in Ancient China*, 316–17.

In Pu's collection, fox spirits are diverse in gender, age, and personality, not generic or stereotypical. Basically, they are realistic humans. As Lu Xun (*Zhongguo xiaoshuo shilue*, 211) observes, Pu's plant and animal spirits "have ordinary human feelings; they are so amicable that the reader often forgets that they are a different species. Only occasionally do they show eccentricity and ignorance in their understanding of the world to remind us that they are not humans."

45. By contrast, it is quite common in *Liaozhai* stories for the female of a different species to settle down in a human community provided that she is open to involvement with a man and agrees to marriage. Typically, after marriage she gives birth to sons, who grow up to become important officials, bestowing worldly honor (i.e., a final stamp of societal approval) on their mother. The examples are numerous, but see, in particular, the story "Chang'e" (The fairy Chang'e), in which the fairy is involved in a love triangle (with a man and a woman). While the fairy sternly chastises a female fox spirit's erotic feelings for her, she is willing to bear children for a human male even though she is beyond desiring him physically. Eventually, the fairy raises sons who honor her with official titles, and the story ends without the slightest mention that she does not belong to the human world. In other words, the fairy has fulfilled the wifely duties and is, therefore, fully accepted and integrated into the human world.

46. Changbai, *Yingchuang yicao*, 5042.

47. By this I do not mean to suggest that, in Pu Songling's tales, the alien species always symbolically or allegorically represents some unusual trait.

48. In "Chang'e," which is not quite about women's love surpassing the love of men, Pu Songling bares and then interdicts one woman's carnal desire for another. When the fox spirit Diandang tries to seduce the female immortal Chang'e, the latter thwarts as well as condemns the attempt. This tale makes it clear that Pu is interested in sensual desire between women and that perhaps he is more sympathetic to sentiment than to sex between women.

49. Qiu, *Bi sheng hua,* 1062, 1068, 1073.

50. The last line is "yuan jie sansheng su you yin" (ibid., 192). The English translation is Hu's ("Literary *Tanci,*" 245–46), with minor modifications.

51. Hu, "Literary *Tanci,*" 246.

52. For a detailed analysis of the relation between unconventional women's power and men's authority in *Bi sheng hua,* see ibid., 247–52.

53. Rich, "Compulsory Heterosexuality and Lesbian Existence," 229.

54. Mann, *Precious Records,* 34, quoting Telford, "Covariates of Men's Age at First Marriage," 32.

55. Sommer, *Sex, Law, and Society,* chap. 2, esp. 64–65.

56. To be sure, there are some stories from the May Fourth era in which a female character who prefers same-sex love to marriage simply dies of heartbreak and/or illness and, thus, provides resolution to the conflicts expressed in the stories; Lu Yin's "Lishi de riji" (Lishi's diary) is the best example. At the same time, however, there are also other stories that do not make female characters involved in same-sex relationships die or disappear; see Ding Ling's "Shujia zhong" (Summer break) and Ye Shaojun's "Bei wangque de" (The forgotten), in which the relationships between female teachers continue on at the end of the story instead of being terminated. In contemporary nonliterary discussions of female same-sex love, some commentators sounded genuinely alarmed by, rather than unconcerned about, women's independence and same-sex love relationships. For details, see the next part of this book.

57. A well-known autobiography from the Republican period, Xie Bingying's *Yige nübing de zizhuan* (The autobiography of a woman soldier), mentions the "trouble of same-sex love" during the author's adolescence, not adulthood (see Xie, *Yige nübing de zizhuan,* 95–107).

### Chapter 4

1. Xiaomingxiong, *Zhongguo tongxing'ai shilu,* 7–8, 252; Hinsch, *Passions of the Cut Sleeve,* 167–69; Chou, *Hou zhimin tongzhi,* 339–47.

2. Chou, *Tongzhi,* 49–50; Dikötter, *Sex, Culture, and Modernity in China,* 137–45. Dikötter's cited sources consist of four sex-education pamphlets that contain brief mentions of homosexuality: Cheng, *Renlei de xing shenghuo;* Gui, *Nüren zhi yisheng;* Wang, *Qingchun de xing jiaoyu;* and Levy, trans., *Sex Histories.* Dikötter's discussion of Republican elites' view of homosexuality commits the error of overgeneralization, in that he makes totalizing assertions about modernizing Chinese intellectuals' attitudes solely on the basis of middlebrow medical sources and gives very few examples. He does not refer to any of the translated articles in intellectual journals, which discuss homosexuality at length (these are discussed later in this chapter), much less the fictional representations by May Fourth writers. Fundamentally, Dikötter denounces Republican Chinese sex-education material in a surprisingly harsh tone and refuses to recognize the influence of Western sexological prejudices on such material.

3. In an autobiographical sketch that Hirschfeld wrote for the *Encyclopaedia Sexualis* shortly before he died in 1935, he described the Nazis' persecution of him: "After the [First World] War, when the Nazi movement gripped Munich and spread in ever larger circles throughout Germany, Hirschfeld's name was placed on a proscription list. After delivering a popular scientific lecture in Munich, he was brutally attacked in the streets. Unconscious, he was taken to the Surgical Clinic, where his injury was diagnosed as a fracture of the skull. . . . The Nazis persecuted Hirschfeld, not only on account of his 'non-Aryan' extraction, but also because of his open acknowledgement of pacifistic and socialistic tendencies, and his work in sexual science" ("Magnus Hirschfeld," 320). These were the circumstances when, in November 1930, he accepted invitations to

deliver lectures in the United States, from New York to San Francisco. Later, invitations from Japan, China, Java, India, Egypt, and other countries eventually took him around the world. In May 1933, while in exile in Switzerland, Hirschfeld learned that the Nazis had destroyed his institute in Berlin, consigning the greater part of his scientific work and twelve thousand volumes in the library collection to flames (ibid., 321).

4. Hirschfeld, *Men and Women*, 65.

5. By using the term *the urban public*, I mean to suggest that the discourse of same-sex love definitely did not reach the entire Chinese population in the Republican period. We are likely safe in assuming that, since translations and adaptations of sexual psychology appeared in well-known urban periodicals and other popular publications, the discourse of same-sex love circulated widely among young, educated people interested in modern culture and learning. But, since during the 1920s and 1930s that particular subgroup was by and large concentrated in the cities and represented only a small portion (under 10 percent) of the population as a whole, that discourse was unlikely to have moved beyond the cities. (The percentage is my own estimate, based on the demographic figures and information on the student population and periodical circulation in early twentieth-century China cited in Lee and Nathan, "The Beginning of Mass Culture.")

6. Liu, *Translingual Practice*, 26.

7. The linguistic comparisons that I make will be both synchronic and diachronic: I examine the Chinese rendering of contemporary foreign sources in detail, an examination that leads me to an exploration of the continuity and rupture between new and old/existing Chinese categories.

8. In the late nineteenth century and the first quarter of the twentieth, hundreds of Japanese *kanji* (Chinese-character) translations of European words were adopted by Chinese intellectuals; these loanwords, which were once neologisms, are now part of the mainstream vocabulary of modern Chinese (see Liu, *Translingual Practice*, 17–18). Although linguists have not identified *tongxing ai* (read as *doseiai* in Japanese) as one such loanword, it almost certainly is. Republican articles to be discussed in this chapter show that the Japanese *kanji* translation of *homosexuality* had entered Chinese translations of European and Japanese sexological texts by the early 1920s.

9. On the history of Japanese translation of European sexology and the formation of a Japanese discourse of *doseiai* (same-sex love) from the 1890s through the early twentieth century, see Pflugfelder, *Cartographies of Desire*, 248–85. According to Pflugfelder, the first Japanese translation of Richard von Krafft-Ebing's *Psychopathia Sexualis* was published under the auspices of the Japanese Forensic Medicine Association in 1894, but it was promptly banned as obscene. In 1913, another translation of the influential work was published, this time without incident (ibid., 249). Some Republican Chinese authors were exceedingly familiar with the development of sexology in Japan as well as in Europe and America. Zhang (*Xing kexue*, 50–51), e.g., mentions that the importation of German sexology to Japan began early in the twentieth century and reached its peak between the two world wars.

10. Of the three terms, *tongxing lian'ai* is longer and more prosaic, while *tongxing ai* and *tongxing lian* are succinct with a terminological ring.

I have found only two Chinese authors using *tongxing lian* in the 1920s. The first is Feng Fei, according to whom, although both *lian* and *ai* denote "love," *lian* is more specific and narrow than *ai* in connotation and also seems to indicate a more active state (Feng, *Nüxing lun*, 102). The second is Chen Dongyuan, who, in both *Zhongguo funü shenghuo shi* and "Guanyu 'Guangdong de bu luojia he zishu,'" uses *tongxing lian* to discuss Cantonese women's same-sex unions. Judging from these texts, Chen assumed that his readers could comprehend the word without difficulty.

In the 1940s, Pan Guangdan chose *tongxing lian* over *tongxing ai*, as did Jingqu Houren. Jingqu shows extreme familiarity with the writings of Freud, Krafft-Ebing, Ellis,

Hirschfeld, Bloch, and one Japanese sexologist, Tanaka Yukichi (see Jingqu, *Shu yan lie qi lu,* 51–59). According to Jingqu, Tanaka's *Kinsei hoigaku* (Modern forensic medicine) was translated into Chinese, yet another example of the importation of Japanese sexology to Republican China. But I have not been able to find this Chinese translation.

In the late twentieth century, both *tongxinglian* and *tongxing'ai* are standard translations of *homosexuality.* In this book, I use the spelling *tongxing ai* (or *tongxing lian,* or *tongxing lian'ai*) in discussions of the Republican era (to reflect the relative fluidity of the term and its semantic instability at that time) and the spelling *tongxing'ai* (or *tongxinglian*) in discussions of late-twentieth-century materials (to reflect the term's unambiguously clinical ring and hypothetical equivalence to the English *homosexuality*).

11. Meng, *Mencius,* 160–65.

12. Morohashi, ed., *Dai kanwa jiten,* 4410. Here, one of the usages of *sei* (the same character as *xing*) is defined as the Japanese translation of "sex" in the sense of gender. According to Zhang (*Xing kexue*), it was not until the Meiji Restoration that Japanese intellectuals began to use *sei* to mean "sex."

13. The Japanese used the classical Chinese expression *lian'ai* to translate *love* when used in a romantic sense in Western languages. Chinese intellectuals adopted the usage. Some even went so far as to assert that there had been no Chinese term corresponding to the concept of romantic love until *lian'ai* was adopted (see, e.g., Zhang, ed., *Xin xing daode taolun ji,* 92). (Zhang Xichen served as the editor of two important women's journals in the 1920s, *Funü zazhi* [The lady's journal] and *Xin nüxing* [New woman]. He was also the founder of the influential Kaiming [Enlightenment] Bookstore.)

14. See Roxane Witke's documentation of the May Fourth discourse of love as well as marriage reform in her "Transformation of Attitudes towards Women." See also Zhang, ed., *Xin xing daode taolun ji.* The May Fourth idealization and promotion of male-female love paralleled the breaking free of Victorian repression that occurred in England and America in the 1910s and 1920s. Chinese intellectuals saw much merit in such texts as Edward Carpenter's *Love's Coming of Age* (1896) and Marie Stopes's *Married Love* (1918). The Chinese translations of these texts were popular and played a significant role in shaping the ideal of heterosexual love for urban middle-class Chinese youths.

15. The sources are too numerous to list (see, for starters, Zhang, ed., *Aiqing dingze;* and almost any issue of *Xin nüxing*).

16. "Same-sex sexual desire" would be *tongxing xingyu.* "Same-sex sexual intercourse" would be *tongxing xingjiao.* Neither of the two appeared as equivalents for the category *homosexuality.* The first phrase is awkward and has never been used; the second, however, can conceivably be used to talk about sexual intercourse between people of the same sex.

17. For instance, Feng Yuan, a minor male character in the eighteenth-century novel *Honglou meng* (The dream of the red chamber), is described as "ku ai nanfeng, bu xi nüse" (he was obsessed with boys and not interested in girls) (see Cao, *Honglou meng bashihui jiaoben,* 1:38). This line varies in some of the hand-copied and printed Qing editions of *Honglou meng.* Among other variations are "ku ai nanfeng, zui yan nüzi" (he was obsessed with boys and disliked women) and "ku ai nanfeng, bu shen jin nüse" (he was obsessed with boys and rarely touched girls).

18. Rumors about *mo jing dang* did not appear until the end of the Qing and were concentrated in Shanghai. For anecdotes, see Xu, *Qingbai leichao,* 38:114; and Tao, "Mo jing dang," 65–70. Gail Hershatter translates *mo jingzi* (equivalent to *mo jing*) as "mirror polishing," explaining that, according to a 1935 slang dictionary in Shanghai, "the term derived from the old custom of using a smooth copper mirror to polish another copper mirror, with no protrusions on either surface" (*Dangerous Pleasures,* 118). While Hershatter's translation of *mo jing* is no doubt more accurate in uncovering the term's origin, I have rendered it as *mirror rubbing* to convey its sexual innuendo.

19. John Boswell argues that, unlike English, "many languages fail to distinguish in any neat way between 'friend' and 'lover'" (*Same-Sex Unions*, 4). In the light of the discussion of Mao Yibo's argument that follows, I suspect that certain cultures' obsession with keeping separate the categories *friendship* and *love* is coextensive with homophobia and that challenging the distinction attacks homophobia at its heart.

20. The fascinating passage from the Chinese original reads, "Ren suowei liangxing jian de guanxi, zui miqie de youyi guanxi, ji suowei Sexual friendship, wo chengren na shi youde, erqie bu xianyu yixing de, tongxing jian you hechang meiyou yinle xinyang, xingqing, shiye dengdeng zhi xiang touhe er fasheng zui miqie zui qinre de guanxi de ne?"

21. Mao, "Zai lun xing'ai yu youyi," 1257–58.

22. For a detailed analysis of New Women's anxiety about same-sex desire as seen in May Fourth fiction, see the next chapter. Although no oral histories of women who during the early twentieth century chose same-sex lifestyles have ever been published, cohabiting intellectual female couples can easily be found in May Fourth fiction.

23. Hu ("Lun xiaoshuo ji baihua yunwen," 76) comments in 1918 that the author, Chen Sen, and characters of the Qing homoerotic novel *Pinhua baojian* (A precious mirror for classifying flowers) did not know that men's having sex with other men could be considered a bad thing. *Pinhua baojian,* which depicts Qing elite men's patronage of boy actors specializing in female operatic roles, is the best illustration of the level of sophistication at which male homoeroticism was socially institutionalized along class and gender hierarchies in Qing China. Hu's comment is a sobering indicator that, regardless of the class relation between sex partners or their respective symbolic gender roles, male-male intercourse had in modernizing China acquired a bad reputation and become viewed as deviant or morally questionable. About Qing attitudes, see also Sommer, *Sex, Law, and Society,* 114–65.

24. Jingqu, *Shu yan lie qi lu,* 51.

25. I am grateful to Sylvia Li-chun Lin for providing me with this article.

26. The pen name Shan Zai—the gender reference of which is unclear—is taken from the Buddhist term *shan zai,* often used as an exclamation or sigh. By signing thus, the author indicates that he disapproves of but feels powerless to change "female same-sex love."

Before the New Culturalists' advocacy of vernacular literature, some early women's periodicals had already opted for the colloquial language as their medium in order to reach a wider female audience since the average level of literacy among educated women was lower than that among men. *Beijing nübao* (Beijing women's newspaper; 1905–9) and *Nüzi baihua bao* (Women's newspaper in the vernacular; 1912–13) were two such examples. See Jiang et al., eds., *Beijing funü baokan kao,* 36, 99.

27. For example, Ellis and Symonds, *Das konträre Geschlechtsgefühl,* a translation of vol. 2 (*Sexual Inversion*) of Ellis's *Studies in the Psychology of Sex.* This German edition of *Sexual Inversion* appeared before the first English edition in Britain (1897). For a discussion of the initial collaboration between Ellis and Symonds and their later disagreement, see Bristow, "Symonds's History, Ellis's Heredity."

28. Shan, "Funü tongxing zhi aiqing," 36.

29. Vitiello, "Exemplary Sodomites" (1994), 28–39; Volpp, "The Male Queen," 16–57.

30. Shan, "Funü tongxing zhi aiqing," 36.

31. Ibid., 38.

32. Nirvard, "Women and the Women's Press," 47.

33. Shen, trans., "Tongxing ai yu jiaoyu," 22123.

34. Here I quote from the English original: Carpenter, *The Intermediate Sex,* 90–91.

35. Ibid., 105.

36. See Pan, trans., *Xing xinli xue.*

37. Ellis, *The Psychology of Sex,* 220–21.

38. As with Shan Zai, the author's gender cannot be determined from the pen name Yan Shi. Pen names were common in Chinese newspapers and periodicals during the early half of the twentieth century. It is probably not because the article deals with homosexuality that the author chose to use a pen name.

39. Yan, "Nannü de geli yu tongxing ai," 14–15.

40. The word *biantai* (perversion, abnormality) was beginning, in the early 1920s, to be used widely in Chinese translations of European and Japanese sexological and psychological writings. The word was adopted from *hentai* in Japanese sources.

41. Wei, trans., "Tongxing ai zai nüzi jiaoyu shang de xin yiyi," 1065. My English translation is based on the Chinese version. For an alternative interpretation of Furuya's essay, see Larson, *Women and Writing in Modern China,* 88–91. Larson detects the presence of a social prohibition on lesbian sex in the essay's denial of physical relationships among women.

42. For details, see, e.g., Peng, "Xing qimeng yu ziwo jiefang."

43. For Zhang's theory about the causal connection between female climax, ovulation, and perfect impregnation, see his "Disanzhong shui." For criticism of Zhang's theories as wild fantasy and Taoist superstition masquerading as modern science, see Zhou, "Xing jiaoyu yundong de weiji"; Zhou, "Ping Zhang Jingsheng boshi *Meide xingyu*"; and Zhang, "*Xin nüxing* yu xing de yanjiu." See also Pan, "*Xin wenhua* yu jia kexue." For objections to Zhang, ed., *Xing shi,* criticizing it as pornography, see Zhang, "*Xin nüxing* yu xing de yanjiu."

44. Zhang, "Xing mei."

45. In *Xing shi,* Zhang writes against male-male anal intercourse: "One can say that the slackness of the vagina indirectly encourages the fondness for sodomy [*zhuzhang hao nanse*]. However the anus is the faecal passage and is dirty. Moreover since there is neither vigorous activity nor electrical functioning, it ordinarily does not constitute a rival to the vagina. Therefore I should like to urge all of my . . . readers to note that through giving full consideration and research to the vagina not only can one bring about a perfection and completeness of intercourse between the sexes, but one can also exterminate the ridiculous game of sodomy [*houting baxi*], a game which is abnormal, dirty, meaningless, inhuman, and not even indulged in by the birds and beasts" (quoted from Zhang, *Sex Histories,* 90–91, with Levy's translation of *baxi* as "evil habit" modified to read "ridiculous game").

46. Zhang, "Xing mei," 279–81.

47. For a perceptive study of Chinese male intellectuals' "masculinity complex" (or "marginality complex") from the May Fourth era to the 1980s, see Zhong, *Masculinity Besieged?* (Zhong does not, it should be noted, mention Zhang Jingsheng as an example.) For Krafft-Ebing's writings on homosexuality, sexual inversion, heredity, and degeneration, see his *Psychopathia Sexualis.* For a study of John Addington Symonds's and Havelock Ellis's respective engagement with Krafft-Ebing's theory of heredity, see Bristow, "Symonds's History, Ellis's Heredity."

48. Ellis, "The School-Friendships of Girls," 373.

49. Ibid., 374.

50. Ibid., 379.

51. I have labeled Furuya's article *affirmative,* but some interpret it differently. For Larson, the essay's insistent claims that women's same-sex relationships are pure and nonsexual are evidence that the mere possibility of physical lesbian love breached moral ideology. Larson also cites two essays by Chinese intellectuals in the 1920s strongly criticizing women's remaining single as damaging women, men, and society (*Women and Writing in Modern China,* 88–91). I agree that there is an avoidance of female-female sex

by Furuya, an avoidance that may reflect Chinese moral ideology or, even more likely, Japanese moral anxiety. Nevertheless, insofar as she strives to justify a form of strong romantic love between women that exceeds ordinary friendship, I would like to acknowledge her article as encouraging female same-sex love within certain limits. At the least, cross-sex marriage and female same-sex love are not considered to be mutually exclusive.

52. Qiu, trans., "Tongxing lian'ai lun," 526.

53. For an example of Pan Guangdan's reputation as a forerunner in the study of homosexuality in China, see Yang, preface to *Tamende shijie* (*Tamende shijie* is the first in-depth sociological-anthropological study of gay men in contemporary mainland China). Only Pan is mentioned by Yang as a precursor in researching Chinese homosexuality and translating Western sexology.

I have come across very few scholarly references to the 1920s translations of Western sexology. Exceptions are the discussion of Xie's translation of Ellis in Peng, "Xing qimeng yu ziwo jiefang," 130, and the discussion of Wei's translation of Furuya in Larson, *Women and Writing in Modern China*, 88−89.

54. Ellis, *The Psychology of Sex*, 235.

55. Pan, trans., *Xing xinli xue*, 325−26 n. 36.

56. It was common for 1930s Chinese sex-education manuals to include brief passages on homosexuality, describing it as sexual perversion. See, e.g., Yi, *Xing dian*, 66. See also the four sex-education pamphlets cited in Dikötter, *Sex, Culture, and Modernity in China*, 137−45.

Ellis's popular authority in China may have been linked partly to his relative forth-rightness in describing sex and partly to his prominence in America in the first part of the twentieth century. In 1900, Ellis had transferred the publication of *Studies in the Psychology of Sex* (1897−1928) to the United States to avoid Britain's conservative obscenity laws (Carpenter, by contrast, continued to publish in the United Kingdom and was, in consequence, constrained in subject matter). By the mid-1930s, Ellis's seven-volume work had become "one of the most comprehensive accounts of sexual physiology and behavior," and Ellis himself "had [in the United States] become a household name where the study of sex was concerned" (Bristow, "Symonds's History, Ellis's Heredity," 80). Because of Ellis's prestige in America, *Studies in the Psychology of Sex* was available at major university libraries and some foreign-language bookstores in China in the 1920s and 1930s, which helped catalyze intellectuals' interest. For example, Pan Guangdan, who studied at Qinghua University (which was funded with the Boxer Rebellion indemnity that the United States returned to the Chinese government), first discovered *Studies in the Psychology of Sex* (then six volumes) in the Qinghua library in 1920. Studying the work of Ellis became one of his lifelong passions, which led him to work on a translation of Ellis's *Psychology of Sex* between 1939 and 1942 (see Pan, "Yi xu," 2). Ellis's relatively explicit descriptions of sexual feelings and behavior were probably what made the Chinese translations of his work attractive beyond intellectual circles, that is, to ordinary middle-class readers. In other words, factors other than interest in gender and sexual concepts—such as availability and explicitness—may have played a role in the global circulation of sexological discourse.

57. In a theoretical rumination, Ann Stoler (*Race and the Education of Desire*) argues that Foucault was one of the first to point out the importance of the colonial discourse of race for the modern discourse of sexuality. Not only have those with a preference for members of their own sex been construed as a racial minority, but they have also been construed as a gender minority; Magnus Hirschfeld's theory of "the third sex" is an early example of such thinking. Recent scientific studies searching for the gay gene or the gay brain stem from similar ways of thinking, which seek either to racialize or to assign a

nonstandard biological sex to gay men. The overall assumption is that the homosexual orientation is produced by a biological factor found in only a minority of the general population. For an example of a high-profile biological study of sexual orientation, see LeVay, *The Sexual Brain*. And, for an in-depth critique of studies like LeVay's, see Murphy, *Gay Science*.

58. Dikötter, *Sex, Culture, and Modernity in China*, 143.

59. Fuss, *Essentially Speaking*; Weeks, "Values in an Age of Uncertainty," 397.

60. Dikötter, *Sex, Culture, and Modernity in China*, 139.

61. See Bland and Doan, eds., *Sexology in Culture*. See also n. 57, this chapter.

62. Katz, *Gay American History*, 129–207.

63. D'Emilio, *Sexual Politics, Sexual Communities*, 35, 37. Among cultures that privilege heterosexuality over homosexuality, the degree of acceptance of bisexual behavior nonetheless varies. Sources from the early Republican period suggest that the attitude in China toward bisexual behavior (at least male bisexual behavior) was more lax than that in Anglo-American cultures.

64. Related to this discussion is the fact that the reconceptualization of sexual behavior in terms of acts instead of essential identity has already proved to be a fruitful tactic for queer politics in the United States. In *Getting Medieval*, Carolyn Dinshaw notes current queer resistance to identity politics in preference for an acts-centered model of coalition politics: "Such an acts-centered model is politically efficacious in particular circumstances, countering the persecution of already marginalized identity-based groups—efficacious when, for example, the concept of 'high-risk acts' in AIDS activist discourse counters the phobic, racist, and misogynist concept of 'high-risk groups'" (204). Dinshaw points out that many queer theorists and activists have been particularly inspired by Foucault's preference for acts in volume 1 of *The History of Sexuality*.

65. According to Foucault (in the widely cited first volume of *The History of Sexuality*), prior to the birth of *homosexuality*, what existed were a wide variety of illicit sexual acts—*sodomy*—and that not until the proliferation of "scientific" discourses on human sexuality in the nineteenth century did there emerge the category of a special type of person—the embodiment of a unique nature—the homosexual. However, he says contradictory things about when the shift in epistème occurred. In one place, he chooses the year 1870 because that is when Westphal published his theory of "contrary sexual sensations." At other times, he identifies the seventeenth and eighteenth centuries as the turning point, in that during that period there began to be a "confessional" soul-searching subject in the matter of sex (see *History of Sexuality*, 1:43, 58–61, 63).

Many Foucault-influenced studies of sexuality set out with the thesis that the binary conceptual system of heterosexuality vs. homosexuality as well as the notions *sexual identity* and *sexual orientation* have their specific histories as cultural productions. Halperin recently argued, however, that, rather than positing wholesale historical changes, Foucault is specifically drawing a distinction between two modes of institutional, discursive practice: premodern European legal definitions of *sodomy* and nineteenth-century psychiatric definitions of *homosexuality* ("Forgetting Foucault," 93–120).

66. See Sedgwick, *Epistemology of the Closet*, 44–48.

67. On the ideal of the nuclear family in Republican China, see Glosser, *Chinese Visions of Family and State*.

68. Even in Wilhelmine Germany, where identity categories such as *the invert, the third sex*, and *the homosexual* were first coined and became popular, the novels and short stories of that period show that the new medical taxonomic system did not entirely dominate people's erotic imagination and self-understanding (see Jones, *"We of the Third Sex,"* 143–71).

## Chapter 5

1. As Wang Zheng notes, the May Fourth term *funü wenti* was originally a rendition of the English phrase *the woman question* (*Women in the Chinese Enlightenment*, 3n). I feel that it is best to translate *funü wenti* back into English as "the woman question," instead of "the woman problem," as Wang suggests, to make it clear that, in the 1920s, rather than treating women as a problem or even a burden on the nation, Chinese feminist magazines seriously explored the question of changing female identity.

2. By considering the gender and sexual discourse in fiction, my approach to the question of culture differs significantly from that in Dikötter's *Sex, Culture, and Modernity in China,* which takes medical discourse (the main component of which was sex-education material) as the sole indicator of the Chinese modernizing elites' view of sex. Granted that Republican intellectuals strongly advocated science, it is still a crude simplification to attribute absolute hegemony to prescriptive medical discourse at the expense of other types of discourses when considering the questions of culture and modernity in Republican China. On the inadequacies of Dikötter's approach, see n. 2, chap. 4, above.

3. Zhao, "Zhongguo xin wenyi yu jingshen fenxi," 21–22.

4. Zhao, "Tongxing lian'ai xiaoshuo de chajin."

5. Zhou, trans., "Zeng suo huan." Zhou bases his translation and comments on Wharton, *Sappho,* 64–71.

6. John Fairbank (*China,* 255–56) opines that, because of the weakness of the state during the warlord era (1916–27), there was considerable "civil growth" from the mid-1910s to the 1920s and that the intelligentsia could freely debate many significant cultural issues.

7. On the enormous growth of the media and popular fiction in the late Qing and beyond, see Lee and Nathan, "The Beginning of Mass Culture." On the new possibilities for writing in the late Qing, see Huters, "A New Way of Writing," 243–77. On experimentation with new roles for and images of women in late Qing fiction, see Hu, *Tales of Translation.* On the role of fictional writing in the making of a modern national imaginary in the late Qing and Republican eras, see Wang, *Xiaoshuo Zhongguo,* and *Ruhe xiandai, zenyang wenxue?*

8. The bookstores in different cities that carried *Xin nüxing* were listed inside the back cover of the magazine.

9. Chen, "Guanyu 'Guangdong de bu luojia he zishu,'" 206.

10. Chen, *Zhongguo funü shenghuo shi,* 300.

11. Zhang, "Disanzhong shui."

12. Among others, Audre Lorde ("The Use of the Erotic") posits that, between women, the erotic has the potential to inspire the subversion of the incipient and the conventional.

13. French feminists have theorized extensively about the liberatory potential of the unconscious for women's writing, postulating that women can better release their creativity in a language that is metaphoric and poetic, as opposed to rational and grammatical. As an example of this practice, Luce Irigaray creates lesbian pleasures in fluid metaphors (see her *This Sex Which Is Not One,* 205–18).

14. Larson, *Women and Writing in Modern China,* 157.

15. Peng, "The New Woman," 281, 290.

16. Wang, *Xiaoshuo zhongguo,* 305. Besides Peng and Wang, Ying-ying Chien, writing in the context of the lesbian and gay movement in 1990s Taiwan, claims that "Lishi's Diary" is the "first work in modern Chinese literature that is narrated from the perspective of a female homosexual [*nü tongxinglianzhe*] about female homosexual love, gender transgression, and the problems of heterosexual marriage." According to Chien, "The May Fourth stories about female same-sex bonding [*nüxing tonxing qingyi*] could be con-

sidered a subgenre. Although the subgenre disappeared after the May Fourth era and was forgotten by commentators, it transformed into an undercurrent, which has resurfaced in mainland China, Hong Kong, and especially Taiwan in the 1990s and moved from the margins to the center [of the literary scene]" (*Hechu shi nüer jia,* 23, 33).

I have not found Chien's comments particularly useful because they show an untheorized assumption of the existence of an organic and continuous tradition of modern Chinese literature, a tradition predicated on a linear, developmental view of literary creation. Her remarks also presume that the meaning of female same-sex love in the 1920s was exactly the same as the meaning of female homosexuality or lesbianism in Taiwan in the 1990s, for she makes no attempt to historicize Lu Yin's interest in female same-sex love and to situate it within the contemporary discourse on same-sex love. It is, moreover, inaccurate to suggest that, between the 1920s and the 1990s, there were no fictional representations in Chinese exploring what Chien—somewhat amorphously—calls *female same-sex bonding.*

17. Larson, *Women and Writing in Modern China,* 162. For Larson's insightful discussion of marriage resistance in early-twentieth-century Canton, a discussion based on the work of Janice Stockard and Marjorie Topley, see ibid., 160–63. For my analysis of the same local practices in Canton, focusing on May Fourth male intellectuals and late-twentieth-century Chinese lesbians' relations to them, see chap. 2.

18. Meng and Dai, *Fuchu lishi dibiao,* 96.

19. In her more recent writings on the representations of female-female relations by 1990s Chinese women writers, Dai Jinhua still prefers to use *sisterly bonding* (*jiemei qingyi*) rather than *homosexuality* as an analytic category (see Dai, "Chen Ran").

20. Meng and Dai, *Fuchu lishi dibiao,* 91.

21. Newton, "The Mythic Mannish Lesbian," 561. Newton defines the first generation of New Women in the West as those "who were born in the 1850s and 1860s, educated in the 1870s and 1880s, and flourished from the 1890s through the First World War" (561). For an analysis of the conventions and dynamics of women's same-sex love in English boarding schools, see Vicinus, "Distance and Desire."

22. On the development of education for women in China through 1911, see Burton, *The Education of Women in China.* For the growth of women's elementary, secondary, and higher education in the Republican period and statistics on female student populations, see Chen, "Min'guo chuqi funü diwei de yanbian," 19–33.

23. For an account of the social and cultural characteristics of university students in the Republican period (most of whom were men), see Yeh, *The Alienated Academy.*

24. Lu, *Lu Yin xuanji,* 2:150. Volume and page numbers for quotations taken from *Lu Yin xuanji* are hereafter given in the text.

25. Witke, "Transformation of Attitudes toward Women."

26. Newton, "The Mythic Mannish Lesbian," 564, 567; Faderman, *Surpassing the Love of Men,* 239–53.

27. Mao, "Lu Yin lun," 7.

28. Meng and Dai, *Fuchu lishi dibiao,* 100.

29. Lu Yin and her classmates were the first women to attend an all-female normal college in China (Beijing nüzi shifan xuetang) in 1917.

30. The lesbian subtext is not as overt in *Old Acquaintances,* the term *tongxing de ai* (love of the same sex) being used instead of *tongxing de ailian.* For example, one of Lusha's classmates, Yunqing, comments of her best friend: "Lingyu used to tell me that there is no difference between the love of the same sex [*tongxing de ai*] and the love of the opposite sex. When I told her she was wrong, she got all agitated and cried. But what about now?" (2:157).

31. According to Zhang (*Psychoanalysis in China,* 86), Freud's *Interpretation of Dreams* was not translated into Chinese until 1932, but, as early as 1920, his dream

theory had been introduced by the psychologist Zhu Guangqian. For an argument about Chinese writers' use of psychoanalysis, not as a metatheory of the human mind, but rather as "a translingual mode of representation," see Liu's illuminating reading of Shi Zhicun in *Translingual Practice*, 133–43.

32. For a discussion of dream symbolism in the fiction of Guo Moruo and Lu Xun, see Zhang, *Psychoanalysis in China*. Zhang maintains that the use of dreams in Chinese literature to indicate characters' states of mind predated the introduction of Freud's theory. However, the emphasis on the sexual nature of dreams and the detailed theorization of the mechanisms of "dreamwork"—condensation, displacement, symbolization—are unique to Freudian interpretation of dreams.

33. Although masculinization may have been historically necessary for women to assert their physical desire for women, that desire is of course not inherently male. In other words, masculinization is historically contingent. On the masculinity of the early lesbian persona, see n. 68, chap. 1, above.

34. Judging from her *Lu Yin zizhuan* (Autobiography; 1934) and her *Dongjing xiaopin,* apparently Lu Yin was unskilled in such household matters as cooking, cleaning, and gardening.

35. That Lu Yin's homoerotic desire finds release in her interest in prostitutes is interesting when we consider that, in the West, prostitutes as hypereroticized objects for sexual service have figured prominently in novelistic representations of lesbian eroticism. See, e.g., Faderman's discussion of "lesbian evil" in nineteenth-century French literature (*Surpassing the Love of Men*, 282–84).

36. My assumption is that, if discovered in male drag in a brothel, Lu Yin might be suspected either of being in the sex trade herself or of homoeroticism.

37. In the 1920s and 1930s, the rubric *New Woman* was applied to a wide variety of unconventional women with divergent attitudes toward sex. At one end of the spectrum was the seriously minded intellectual dedicated to social revolution but conservative in sexual matters (i.e., monogamous and heterosexual). At the other end was the fashionably adorned and uninhibited glamour girl, who might or might not be as intellectual and reform minded. For examples of the former type, see the intellectual career women profiled in Wang, *Women in the Chinese Enlightenment*. For literary constructions of the latter type, see the fiction of the Xin ganjue pai, the New Perceptionists, who were active in Shanghai in the late 1920s and 1930s. For an analysis of the image of the hypereroticized New Woman in 1930s Shanghai, see Peng, "'Xin nüxing' yu Shanghai dushi wenhua: Xin ganjue pai yanjiu."

38. The question is not completely resolved in my mind whether in the 1920s and 1930s a woman who had taken a female lover would perceive herself as indecent. There may not be a neat, simple answer. I would like to think that opting for a same-sex lifestyle then—especially choosing to be sexual as well as affectionate with a girlfriend—required great courage and a determination to control one's own destiny. Such a self-identity would, therefore, be ideologically complex, carrying the double meaning of social deviance and revolutionary bravery.

39. While in China public baths for men were common, women usually took their baths in private at home.

40. It could be argued that, because of her loyalty, as a married Chinese woman, to her husband, Lu Yin avoided observing the unclothed Japanese male body closely. Even if she had been able to observe it, she would not have felt free to write about it—at least not in any public forum. However, my sense is that she was simply less attracted to the male than to the female body.

41. Evidently, Yang wrote his story in a great hurry, pressed by a deadline imposed by the editor Xu Zhimo. On its publication in the *Beijing chenbao fukan* (Beijing morn-

ing newspaper supplement), the story dissatisfied all Yang's friends. Therefore, he asked Ling Shuhua to rewrite it. (See Ling, "Shuo you zhemo yihui shi," 89 [Yang's note].)

42. Yang, "Ta weishenmo huran fafeng le," 13.

43. Ling Shuhua, "Shuo you zhemo yihui shi," 97.

44. Ding, "Shujia zhong," 153.

45. Ibid., 152.

46. Ibid., 176–77.

47. Liu, *Translingual Practice*, 172–79.

48. In this regard, *Ta shi yige ruo nüzi* is not unlike Yu's most celebrated short story, "Chenlun" (Sinking; 1921), in which the male protagonist's sexual frustration is attributed to national impotence. Both stories deploy individuals' sexual/gender disorders as an allegory for national weakness.

49. Zhang Yiping is usually classified by literary historians as a member of the Jing pai (the Beijing School). He began his career as a writer in 1924, contributing short stories, personal essays, and poems to the then newly established journal *Yu si* (Threads of talk). He gained instantaneous fame in 1926 on the publication of his collection of short stories *Qingshu yishu* (Love letters).

50. In *Qingshu yishu*, the title of Blake's print is erroneously given as *The Meeting of Soul and Body*. Following the reproduction is an epigraph in English taken from a poem by Sarojini Naidu called "Ecstasy": "Cover mine eyes, O my Love! / Mine eyes that are weary of bliss / As of light that is poignant and strong. / Oh, silence my lips with a kiss, / My lips that are weary of song! / Shelter my soul, O my Love! / My soul is bent low with the pain / And the burden of love, like the grace / Of a flower that is smitten with rain; / Oh, shelter my soul from thy face!"

51. The twelve illustrations of "The Grave" were designed by Blake and executed with a method combining etching and engraving by Louis Schiavonetti. They first appeared with Blair's text in an 1808 edition. For reproductions and a detailed study, see Essick and Paley, *Robert Blair's "The Grave."*

52. Ibid., 70.

53. The temporal setting for the reunion seems to have been the Final Judgment.

54. The idea of a lovers' embrace is implied by Blair's description of the body as the soul's "partner," although it seems unlikely that he meant anything overtly sexual. According to some Blake scholars, in creating the image, Blake was also influenced by a line from Hervey's *Meditations:* "And O! with what cordial congratulations, what transporting endearment, do the soul and body, those affectionate companions, re-unite" (ibid.).

55. This purely hypothetical image might, in fact, be in consonance with certain elements of the Christian tradition. In that tradition, it is not unusual for a lover to compare the object of his affections to his own soul. The operative gender ideology is, however, ambiguous since the comparison was utilized in both same-sex and opposite-sex situations. For example, in the oldest story of paired saints, David and Jonathan, from the Jewish scripture, it is written: "It came to pass . . . that the soul of Jonathan was knit with the soul of David, and Jonathan loved him as his own soul" (1 Sam. 18:1, cited in Boswell, *Same-Sex Unions*, 137). In *Same-Sex Unions*, Boswell is interested in paired saints as models of abiding affection and union between people of the same gender.

56. Wendy Larson argues that, in the late 1920s and 1930s, leftist "critics and writers called for a new literature of social commitment that denied the validity and importance of individual experience and emotion, substituting for it social and class awareness, knowledge, and especially action. Although these critics usually did not directly attack 'women's literature,' they rejected the traditional characteristics of women's writing and described women writers as prone to the error of writing in the traditional way." According to Larson, most women writers active in the 1920s simply stopped writing in the

1930s; a few, such as Ding Ling, succumbed to the leftist literary ideology: "Ding Ling best exemplifies the shift in the late 1920s . . . from delving into subjective, interior consciousness to representing a bleak outside reality to be altered through revolutionary action" (*Women and Writing in Modern China*, 180, 188).

In this regard, Lydia Liu (*Translingual Practice*, 198–213) has provided an alternative interpretation. In Liu's reading, fictional texts by leftist women writers, such as Xiao Hong's *Shengsi chang* (The field of life and death; 1935) and Ding Ling's "Wo zai Xiacun de shihou" (When I was in Xia Village; 1940), showed ambivalence toward nationalism even in the 1930s and 1940s. A further examination of the relation between women and male-dominated theories of writing in Republican China, I suggest, should take into account as many women writers active in the 1930s and 1940s as possible, such as Bai Wei, Zhang Ailing, Su Qing, Shi Jimei, and Mei Niang.

57. Xie, *Yige nübing de zizhuan*, 95.

58. It is not made clear in the text how old Xie Bingying (1906–2000) was when she attended normal college. We do know, however, that she was eleven when she began elementary school, which would mean that she was probably in her late teens when she began normal college. And she remained in school until 1926, the year she joined the army. See ibid., 81–121.

59. Ibid., 96, 99.

60. Ibid., 165, 166. On the "unisex" ideal of the Wuhan Central Military and Political Institute, where Xie matriculated in January 1927 and received her military training, see Gilmartin, *Engendering the Chinese Revolution*, 189–90.

61. Prior to the appearance of Xie's autobiographical account, "Dr. Sex" Zhang Jingsheng had during the 1920s solicited sexual histories, including same-sex experiences, from his readers, publishing the results in the collection *Xing shi*, which prints six of the histories thus elicited. Inspired by Havelock Ellis's case studies, Zhang placed an ad in the Beijing newspaper *Jingfu* asking Chinese young people to respond to such questions as, "Have you ever been in love with people of your own sex (i.e., men with men, women with women)? Did you have genital contact? What form did that contact take? Or did you see it as a kind of spiritual love? Do you still have such predilections?" (*Xing shi*, 111). In the volume, one of the six respondents—the only woman—described the prevalence of same-sex sexual behavior in school (see ibid., 5–14). It is unclear whether Xie's inclusion of her own romantic/sexual awakenings in her autobiography was influenced by *Xing shi*.

62. Guo, *Wode younian*, 95, 95, 98.

63. I am not alone in making this assessment. Wang Qingning ("Qin'aide XXX") observes that the vitality and confrontational tactics of the Taiwanese lesbian movement are envied by some Hong Kong and mainland Chinese lesbians. At the 1998 conference of Chinese *tongzhi* (an umbrella term for gay, lesbian, bisexual, and transgender persons) held in Hong Kong, which was attended by Chinese persons from more than a dozen countries in and outside Asia, the female representatives from Taiwan included lesbian feminists, lesbian novelists, and academic queer theorists—a constituency far more versatile and politically experienced than the Chinese lesbian representatives from other parts of Asia (such as Hong Kong, mainland China, Malaysia) or North America. Chou Wah-shan, one of the key figures in queer activism in Hong Kong and mainland China, also marvels at the explosive growth of an American-style lesbian and gay identity politics in 1990s Taiwan (see Chou, *Tongzhi*, 141).

64. Yang, introduction to *Spaces of Their Own*. Instead of stretching the category *transnational China* to include all Chinese the world over, Yang has defined *transnational China* as consisting of mainland China, Hong Kong, and Taiwan, a grouping that has also been dubbed *Greater China* by other scholars.

## Chapter 6

1. Evans, *Women and Sexuality in China,* 206.

2. Zhang, *Xing kexue.*

3. For an excellent collection of posters and innovative analyses thereof from various vantage points, see Evans and Donald, eds., *Picturing Power in the People's Republic of China.*

During the Cultural Revolution (1966–1976), public performances of only a limited number of Chinese operas and other works were allowed. Between 1949 and 1965, the government had repeatedly tried to tighten its control over opera repertory. By late 1966, only five operas and three nonoperatic works (two ballets and one symphonic suite) were being performed. These works, on contemporary and revolutionary themes, were called *yangbanxi* (model theater), meaning that they would serve as the model for other works. By the early 1970s, several new models had been created. For most of the Cultural Revolution, the models and their adaptations were the only works staged (see Yung, "Model Opera as Model," 146–48).

4. Chen, "Growing Up with Posters in the Maoist Era," esp. 111–12.

5. *Yige ren de zhanzheng* is discussed at greater length in the next chapter.

6. For an analysis of *Nüer lou* that self-consciously posits itself as "Western feminist," see Kaplan, "Problematizing Cross-Cultural Analysis."

7. At the end of the collection, the editors attach an announcement soliciting further submissions. The only requirement is that the stories be about "real people and incidents" (*zhenren zhenshi*) (see Zhang and Yue, eds., *Zhongguo zhiqing qinglian baogao,* 3:458–59).

8. Diamant, *Revolutionizing the Family,* 192 (on the pervasiveness of out-of-wedlock births), 224 (quotation), 193–94 (on the women's sexual relationship). The women's coworkers objected only to the fact that a Party member was encouraging divorce, not discouraging it.

9. On liberal feminism in the May Fourth era and its significance as a historical precedent for the rise of unofficial feminism in the PRC since the mid-1980s, see Wang, *Women in the Chinese Enlightenment,* esp. the introduction.

10. Wan, "Fulu," 176, 171.

11. An, *Hong taiyang,* 26–27. The men whom An interviewed purportedly participated in the activity surrounding popular gay cruising grounds. In addition to conducting interviews, An also distributed questionnaires, of which more than five hundred were returned completed. An claims that his interest in conducting interviews face-to-face differed from previous studies on homosexual men by PRC sociologists, which relied predominantly on questionnaires, focused on statistics, and made little effort to represent the local characteristics of each city (ibid., 26).

In contemporary Taiwan, as in post-Mao China, there is no law criminalizing homosexuality per se. However, male-male sexual or cruising behavior in public has been frequently subjected to police harassment and prosecuted as *fanghai fenghua zui* (the crime of impairing cultural propriety) or *fanghai shanliang fengsu* (a threat to decent social customs).

12. The category *hooliganism* existed in the Chinese criminal code that was in effect between 1980 and 1997. It encompassed, among other items of behavior, certain instances of male-male sodomy (*jijian*): "men's sodomizing children, sodomizing male minors by force, or repeated sodomy by force and threat" (see Liu, ed., *Zhongguo xingfa shiyong daquan,* 556).

13. *Xiandai hanyu cidian,* 1029.

14. Evans, *Women and Sexuality in China,* 167–88.

15. Liu et al., *Zhongguo dangdai xing wenhua,* 201–8.

16. Chou, "Shi tongxing ai, bushi tongxing bing."

17. An, *Hong taiyang,* 53–57.

18. An email message circulated by API Queer Women and Transgender Coalition in the San Francisco Bay Area in early 2001 reported: "*The Chinese Classification of Mental Disorders Third Revision* (CCMD-3), forthcoming in April 2001, will delete homosexuality from the list of mental disorders, but still retain 'Ego-Dystonic Homosexuality,' source from Chinese Psychiatric Association (CPA) said. CPA stressed that this decision was based on their own empirical findings as well as those from their counterparts in other countries. In 1996, CPA set up a special task force to assess the mental status of lesbians and gay men. From the sample of 54 persons, six of whom had approached psychiatrists for 'change,' researchers considered that some still showed signs of mental problems. In the past few years, both American Psychiatric Association and American Psychological Association have sent letters to CPA, urging the deletion of homosexuality as a mental disorder. CPA sent members to attend the annual conference of American Psychiatric Association in 2000. Suggestions from both pro- and anti-depathologization sides were solicited, in addition to International Classification of Diseases 10th Revision (ICD-10) issued by World Health Organization. The standing committee of CPA elected to pass the resolution of depathologization of homosexuality for CCMD-3 recently." I thank Tamara Chin for forwarding this message.

19. The deletion of hooliganism from the criminal code is generally favored by gay men, according to the openly gay male writer Cui Zien (telephone interview by author, 15 December 1998). Lisa Rofel opines that the PRC government excised hooliganism, or "activities that involved 'roaming' beyond appropriate social borders or relations," "partly . . . because of its associations with socialism but also because sweeping social activity out of public space no longer makes sense" ("Qualities of Desire," 459).

20. Li and Wang's total sample was forty-nine gay men. Because of the difficulty obtaining a random sample, they had to rely on a "snowballing method," whereby the first few interviewees introduced their friends to Li and Wang and those friends in turn introduced other friends (*Tamende shijie,* 24). Initially, no publisher on the mainland would accept *Tamende shijie;* therefore, the book appeared first in Hong Kong. Later that same year, 1992, Li and Wang convinced a mainland publisher, the Shanxi People's Publishing House, to reissue it. Because the topic proved popular, a slightly modified version was put out by Li Yinhe as *Tongxinglian yawenhua* in 1998.

21. For instance, to offset her previous focus on gay men, Li Yinhe included a brief discussion of female homosexuality in a later study. The discussion consists mainly of excerpts from her interviews with a few women who have had sexual experiences with other women (see Li, *Zhongguo nüxing,* 207–24). Because Li reports her data in the form of a fragmented narrative—interviews are not presented as continuous wholes, and subjects are not even assigned names—the size of her sample cannot be determined, and, therefore, neither can the significance of her study. The study's lack of methodological clarity undermines its usefulness.

22. Chin, "Translingual Tongzhi," 6.

23. I thank Tamara Chin for informing me about this incident.

24. Chou (*Hou zhimin tongzhi,* 360–69) has argued that *tongzhi* is not equivalent to *homosexual, gay, lesbian, queer,* or any other term denoting sexual identity as constituted in the West. I find, however, that, in practice, it is essentially equivalent. In the PRC, where, during the Maoist era, *tongzhi* was the most common and politically correct form of address between people, the term can function as a euphemism for *lesbian* and *gay* in that it sounds less derogatory, and much more normal and acceptable, than does *tongxinglian.* Moreover, because the vast majority of the population is still unaware of the new meaning of *tongzhi,* it can function as a trendy code word whose meaning is rec-

ognizable only to those privy to information about the new urban middle-class cosmopolitan culture.

25. The convention is reported in "Diyici dalu nü tongzhi huiyi zhaokai."

26. Shi Tou and four other lesbian-identified women, conversation with the author, Beijing, 16 December 1998.

27. Among other initiatives meant to stimulate discussion and awareness of sexual orientation, a telephone hotline has been set up by Shi Tou and some of her friends (both male and female) to answer questions about sexual orientation. Displayed on the front of the hotline's business card is a sketch of two smiling, identical-looking young women (both with long hair), a telephone number, and the hotline's hours of operation. Printed on the back is this message: "We are a group of female/male comrades [nü/nan tongzhi] who have clear understandings of our own sexual orientation [xing qingxiang]. If you or your friends would like to discuss questions concerning same-sex orientations [tongxing qingxiang], we welcome your call to our hotline. We will sincerely exchange opinions with you."

28. Reported by the gay activist Wan Yanhai on his website "Aizhi" (Love and knowledge). To see a transcript (in Chinese) of this "Talk It Easy" episode, visit http://www .aizhi.org.news.hnws.htm. According to Wan, about eighty persons called HNST the morning after the program aired. Most calls concerned Cui Zien.

29. See Zi, "Xiang ai rongyi xiang shou nan"; and Xiao, "Menghuan rensheng."

30. See Zhang Jie, "Fangzhou" (The ark); Liu Suola, "Lantian lühai" (The blue sky and ocean); and Wang, Dixiongmen (Brothers). For comments on female relationships in PRC women's literature from the 1980s, see Liu, "The Female Tradition in Modern Chinese Literature."

31. During the 1980s, it was not unusual for writers to deny that their work had anything to do with homosexuality, a word that still carried negative medical connotations. For example, the male writer Lu Zhaohuan declares that his well-known novella Shuang zhuo (Double bracelets) is about "something that is like homosexuality but definitely is not homosexuality [leisi tongxinglian, que jue fei tongxinglian]" (cited in Lee, "Cong Shuang zhuo de 'jiemei fuqi,'" 12). Lu emphasizes that his story is about "superstition" and the "sexual repression" of women in the Huidong region of Fujian Province. He wants to "light a lamp in the dark, enclosed mind of [these] women" by exposing the "self-deception" and "the series of psychological abnormalities" that women develop when they "do not have love [aiqing]" (Lu, Shuang zhuo, 89–91). Lee ("Cong Shuang zhuo de 'jiemei fuqi,'" 9, 12) criticizes Lu for defining love only in heterosexual terms.

Women writers of the period, such as Zhang Jie, Wang Anyi, and Liu Suola, never linked the female friendships that they described to homosexuality. Sensitive to the writers' tendency to reject sexual categories as irrelevant, Lydia Liu does not use the word lesbian to discuss the female bonding in this earlier body of literature. She explains, "The word 'female bonding,' rather than homosexuality, is used here to describe the range of female relationships explored. . . . In choosing not to pin down the meaning of those relationships, I intend to emphasize the fact that identity politics, which seems to be the main thrust of the current debate on homosexuality in the United States, is not the way in which my Chinese authors deal with sexual relationships in their works, and I see no reason why I should fix identities (gay, lesbian, bisexual, or straight) on their characters" ("The Female Tradition in Modern Chinese Literature," 43). The situation shifted slightly in the 1990s in that both Lin Bai and Chen Ran, whose works I shall analyze, did on occasion use the words tongxing zhi ai (same-sex love) and tongxinglian (homosexuality)—which had become more familiar generally—to describe characters and situations in their stories.

# Chapter 7

1. For a discussion of Chinese debates on literary subjectivity, see Wang, *High Culture Fever,* chap. 5.

2. On Chinese avant-garde novelists' rejection of aesthetic humanism since 1987, see Chen, *Wubian de tiaozhan.* On intellectuals' dystopianism and loss of hegemony in the age of popular culture, see Wang, *High Culture Fever,* chaps. 5–7. For another wideranging interpretation of the desires for modernism and postmodernism in post-Mao China, see Zhang, *Chinese Modernism in the Era of Reforms.* For optimistic evaluations of the expanding unofficial social space in China from the 1980s through the early 1990s, see Davis et al., eds., *Urban Spaces in Contemporary China;* and Link, Madsen, and Pickowicz, eds., *Unofficial China.* On consumerism as a dominant ideology in 1990s China, see Yan, "The Politics of Consumerism in Chinese Society."

3. Rather than describe every sex scene in detail, what Jia often does is insert at those points in the text where sex scenes are anticipated a parenthetical remark like the following: "(here 103 words have been deleted)." (Of course the number of words indicated varies.) Such authorial interpolations poke fun at the censorship (including authors' self-censorship) of erotica in China.

4. For a journalistic account of the scandal that Jia's novel caused in China in the early 1990s, see Zha, *China Pop,* 129–64.

5. *Zhonghua dushu bao* does not function simply as the official mouthpiece of Xinwen chuban shu. Rather, in recent years, the review's editorial staff has deliberately tried to maintain an open forum by soliciting different views on controversial topics. According to Yu Hongmei—who, working under the feminist scholar Dai Jinhua, received a master's degree in comparative literature from Beijing University in the mid-1990s—several graduates of the comparative literature program at Beijing University have joined the review's editorial staff of late and have been intent on enlivening its pages by publishing diametrically opposed opinions (Yu Hongmei, conversation with the author, Eugene, Oreg., April 2001). When tempestuous debate ensues, government attention is usually attracted. This is not necessarily a problem, however, because, even if the publication in question is banned, the usual result is stimulated sales. Such was the case, e.g., with *Shanghai baobai* (Shanghai baby), whose young author, Wei Hui, was catapulted to international fame when it was banned in April 2000.

6. For disparaging reviews of *One Person's War,* see Ding, "Nüxing wenxue ji qita," and "Wo xiangxin jiandan pusu zhi li." For reviews defending Lin Bai, see Xu, "Yinwei chenmo tai jiu"; Wang, "Yishu yu guanhuai ruoshi zuqun"; and Yidian, "Jiannan de miandui." I thank Lin Bai for providing me with these articles. Xu Kun's response to Ding Laixian has been reprinted in her *Shuangdiao yexingchuan,* 66–71. The publication history of *One Person's War* has been gathered from the following two sources: Lin Bai, interview by author, Beijing, 13 December 1998; and Lin, "Houji."

7. Lin, interview by author.

8. I take the notion of a hierarchy of sex from Rubin's "Thinking Sex." Rubin's examples are drawn primarily from the United States.

9. To be sure, the publication regulations put into effect by the Xinwen chuban shu in 1988 stipulate that "obscene, concrete descriptions of homosexual behavior and other perverse sexual behavior" fall into the category of obscenity (*yinhui*) and must be banned. However, explicitly exempted are "works of literary and artistic merit that contain some elements of obscene and pornographic content." And nowhere is it stated that an author's gender matters. Of course, the Xinwen chuban shu has the authority to interpret the regulations as it sees fit; it also has the final say in determinations of obscenity. See Fawubu diaochaju, ed., *Zhonggong zhongyao fagui huibian,* 126–27.

10. Ding, "Nüxing wenxue ji qita."

11. Xu, "Yinwei chenmo tai jiu"; also in Xu, *Shuangdiao yexingchuan,* 70.

12. Ding, "Nüxing wenxue ji qita."

13. Lin Bai, interview by author. The reader should note that I have never seen the cover of the Gansu edition, which is now difficult to find. I am, therefore, unable to judge whether it would be considered pornographic by Western standards. I did show Lin the cover of the Taiwanese lesbian writer Chen Xue's *E nü shu* (The book of an evil woman), which features a double image (one a mirror reverse) of a female nude. And she clearly envied its appealing, artistic design and exclaimed that she would not have minded to have something as tasteful grace the cover of her own novel.

14. Translations of the writings of French feminists such as Hélène Cixous were introduced to China in the early 1990s. Especially influential is Zhang, ed., *Dangdai nüxing zhuyi wenxue piping,* which presents a representative sampling of the work of several authors. Cixous's notion that women may develop a fresh language by returning to the body and the unconscious has inspired Chinese critics to create the phrases *yong shenti xiezuo* (to write with the body) and *shenti xushi* (narration of the body). Xu Kun, e.g., celebrates *shenti xushi* in her study of Chinese women's writing in the 1990s (*Shuangdiao yexingchuan,* 62–64). The ambiguous Chinese phrases have sometimes been propagated in 1990s China as a directive urging women to write about their bodily experience above all else.

15. Dai, "Rewriting Chinese Women," 204. Xu Kun describes an especially horrific cover for *Wode qingrenmen* (My lovers) by Hai Nan: "Sitting in a photograph in a lower corner of the cover is the author herself. Above her are the lower bodies, legs, and feet of several big, rough men. One of them even holds in his hands an iron staff and ropes for applying violence. The vulgarity makes one automatically suspect that the book is in bad taste, so all literary critics who consider themselves serious have avoided mentioning it" (*Shuangdiao yexingchuan,* 50).

16. Metz, *The Imaginary Signifier,* 59.

17. Metz theorizes cinema spectatorship as the quintessential form of voyeurism among all forms of arts spectatorship. He writes, "The cinema only gives [spectacles and sounds] in effigy, inaccessible from the outset, in a primordial *elsewhere,* infinitely desirable (= never possessible), on another scene which is that of absence and which nonetheless represents the absent in detail, thus making it very present, but by a different itinerary." He argues that voyeurism in theater remains linked to exhibitionism in that theater spectatorship rests on the fiction of the actor's active consent and exhibitionism. By contrast, the cinema spectator sits in darkness and obscurity and watches the film as if in a situation of "*unauthorised* scopophilia," for "the cinema's voyeurism must (of necessity) do without any very clear mark of consent on the part of the object." Moreover, those who attend a cinema screening are isolated from one another and do not, as in theater, constitute a true audience: "Despite appearances, [they] more closely resemble the fragmented group of readers of a novel" (ibid., 61, 63, 64). Metz's writing on the voyeuristic nature of the experience of seeing a film provides the basis for my reflections on the voyeuristic nature of the experience of novel reading. My argument departs from Metz's, however, in that I agree with Silverman (*Male Subjectivity at the Margins*) that the voyeur's mastery may be a "compensatory" fiction.

18. Silverman, *Male Subjectivity at the Margins,* 164–65.

19. The Chinese term *si xiaoshuo* was originally a loan word from Japanese, where it was introduced as a rendering of the Western literary term *the I-novel.* However, as it has circulated in the PRC, *si xiaoshuo* has lately acquired the meaning of "novels about the author's privacy." Chinese journalists and literary critics have, in the course of discussing women's writing in the 1990s, coined such other terms as *yinsi wenxue* (literature about privacy), *siyu* (private talk), *geren xiezuo* (personal writing), *gerenhua xiezuo* (individualized writing), and *sirenhua xiezuo* (privatized writing). As Xu Kun points out, there is plenty of conceptual confusion in this jumble of terms; many critics fail to

differentiate between descriptions of private experience and an individualistic narrative style or voice (see her *Shuangdiao yexingshuan*, 41–48). Agreeing with the perceptive male critic Wu Liang, Xu also points out that, five years after the controversy over Lin Bai's *One Person's War*, "publishers are mass producing and reproducing, for the market, a great number—practically whole series—of 'female autobiographies,' the private character of which is questionable" (ibid., 46).

20. Foucault has problematized the repressive hypothesis and theorized the productive and diffuse forms of power in the field of force relations (*History of Sexuality*, 1:101–2). Mayfair Yang argues that, in Maoist China, unlike Victorian Europe, repression and an emptying out of the public discourse of sex were genuinely at work. However, with regard to the proliferation of sexual discourse in the post-Mao era, Yang agrees with Foucault's insight about productive power: "In this new formation of state biopower and market normalization and masculinization of sexuality, 'we must not think that by saying yes to [women's] sex, one says no to power'" ("From Gender Erasure to Gender Difference," 62).

21. Evans, *Women and Sexuality in China*, 213.

22. Yang, "From Gender Erasure to Gender Difference," 50.

23. This crisis of masculinity has surfaced yet again in the uproar over the female writer Wei Hui's novel *Shanghai baobei* (Shanghai baby), which Wei claims is "semi-autobiographical." The plot contrasts the female protagonist's two relationships—one with an emasculated, impotent Chinese man, the other with a hypermasculine and phallic German man. Chinese men have found the novel highly offensive, criticizing it, ironically, for its "worship of the phallus" (*yangwu chongbai*). One cannot but wonder whether the same criticism would have been heaped on the novel had the Chinese love interest been a paragon of virility. The book was banned a few months after its publication, but it is estimated that several million pirated copies have been sold within China since then. Moreover, an authorized Chinese edition has been issued in Taiwan, and foreign-language editions have appeared in Japanese, English, German, and Dutch.

24. For male critics' accusations of Lin Bai's narcissism, see Xue, "Fuchu lishi dibiao zhi hou"; Xiao, "Jiushi niandai Zhongguo wenxue," esp. 108; and Zheng, "Nüxing jinji yu hou xinshiqi nüxing xiezuo," esp. 36.

At least one female critic, Xu Shan, is wary of the neurotic connotation that the term *zilian* (narcissism) can occasionally carry in contemporary Chinese studies of women's literature of the 1990s. She too, in fact, uses *zilian* in discussions of such women writers as Chen Ran and Lin Bai, but she tries to redefine the term before applying it: "[Chen's female characters'] self-admiration is often linked to female narcissism. But this kind of narcissism is not just a repetition of the mode of narcissism defined by psychology or medical pathology. Rather, narcissism is a gesture that women actively take in the present circumstances. It is motivated completely by their spiritual affirmation of the self. It is a way for women to express love for themselves" ("Nuola," 42). Another—and otherwise incisive—woman critic has not tried to unpack the psychoanalytic baggage carried by the term *zilian*. She simply equates *zilian* with *ziwei* (autoeroticism, masturbation), which she theorizes as women's spontaneous pleasure and arduous fight against sexual surveillance (Xu, *Shuangdiao yexingchuan*, 75–84).

25. Freud characterizes femininity in terms of narcissism, among other things. He claims that women are more narcissistic than men because they need to compensate for their castrated state or genital lack: "We attribute a larger amount of narcissism to femininity, which also affects women's choice of object, so that to be loved is a stronger need for them than to love. The effect of penis-envy has a share, further, in the physical vanity of women, since they are bound to value their charms more highly as a late compensation for their original sexual inferiority" (Freud, "Femininity," 132). I doubt that most

Chinese critics read Freud voraciously, but Freudian terminology certainly has become trendy.

26. Irigaray, *This Sex Which Is Not One*, 196.

27. The division of spaces here works only as a figure of speech because, technically speaking, even diametrically opposed responses to the novel can very well be complicit with each other and share the same basic principles. For example, both moral censure and mass voyeurism can be predicated on the assumption that certain forms of sexuality are deviant.

28. Herdt, "Third Sexes and Third Genders"; Garber, *Vested Interests*, 9–13; Anzaldúa, *Borderlands/La Frontera*, 3, 11; Bhabha, *The Location of Culture*, 36–39. Marjorie Garber writes that the third term enables our "moving from a structure of complementarity or symmetry to a contextualization, in which what once stood as an exclusive dual relation becomes an element in a larger chain" (*Vested Interests*, 12). My formulation of the third space is not directly related to the China historian Philip Huang's theorization of "the third realm between state and society," by which Huang means, first and foremost, a realm where the gentry class of late-imperial China cooperated with the state and semiautonomously provided public services, e.g., water control, famine relief, defense, dispute resolution (outside the formal legal system), etc. (see "'Public Sphere'/ 'Civil Society' in China?"). My formulation of the third space is also remote from the urban space theorist Edward Soja's concept of "thirdspace" as "a fully *lived space*, a simultaneously real-and-imagined, actual-and-virtual, locus of structured individual and collective experience and agency" (*Postmetropolis*, 11).

29. I am, of course, borrowing words from Gayatri Spivak. It should be noted that Lin Bai's position as a subaltern—if one insists on viewing her as such—is not without ambiguity. Foucault's thoughts on power, confession, and knowledge in volume 1 of *The History of Sexuality* may be pertinent here even though his discussion of the entangled relation between power and knowledge tackles primarily the discourses of sexuality in pedagogy, medicine, and economics (i.e., demography and eugenics) and is not concerned with the literary discourse of sexuality. It seems to me that, by dint of confession, not only does Lin Bai subject her sexual history to public scrutiny and surveillance and assume the tactical position of the dominated, but she also produces the effect of her artistic mastery as well as her authority as the one who possesses knowledge about sex.

30. Dai, "Rewriting Chinese Women," 204.

31. Yang, "From Gender Erasure to Gender Difference," 63. In contrast to her focus on elite women writers' agency and neglect of the role of women readers, Yang has, with regard to visual popular culture, affirmed the necessity of retheorizing women's spectatorship. She writes, "Recent feminist theories of female spectatorship suggest that Laura Mulvey's thesis [in *Visual and Other Pleasures*] of the male gaze was too 'totalizing' and that a female audience can assume an active subject position in their consumption of popular culture" (63).

32. While I stress that the third space cannot be carved out by creative women writers (or their works) alone but requires innovative readers as well, my purpose in discussing it is not to theorize about the phenomenology of interpretation in general. Rather, what interests me is the specific question whether there are formative discourses in China that are moving the meaning of, e.g., *One Person's War* beyond a monolithic or dualistic bind. Evidence of the third space can be concretely identified in the emergence of such discourses.

33. Xu, *Shuangdiao yexingchuan*, 45–46.

34. Disparaging criticism aside, much praise for *One Person's War* can be found in the writings of male and female critics alike, but especially female critics. Some of these, such as Dai Jinhua, prefer to use the terms *jiemei qingyi* (sisterly bonding) and *jiemei zhi*

*bang* (sisters' nation) rather than *nüxing tongxinglian* (female homosexuality) when discussing female-female relations. Those who speak of "female homosexuality" do so only briefly and perfunctorily. In commenting on *One Person's War,* women critics in China rarely provide detailed, close readings of the novel. Rather, they pursue general lines of inquiry and group Lin with other innovative women writers of the 1990s, considering their works to be examples of women's autobiographical writing and "individualized/private" writing (*gerenhua xiezuo* or *sirenhua xiezuo*) meant, they believe, to subvert male-dominated grand historical narratives and inscribe women's experience into history. See, e.g., Dai, "Qiyu yu tuwei"; Xu, "Nuola"; and Xu, *Shuangdiao yexingchuan,* 64–90. Xu Kun's reading is the most detailed that I have thus far encountered in mainland Chinese criticism of *One Person's War.*

35. Evans, *Women and Sexuality in China,* 112, 218.

36. Authorized editions of *One Person's War* meant to circulate outside mainland China were issued in 1998 by Tiandi Publishing House in Hong Kong and Maitian Publishing House in Taiwan.

37. I identify my diasporic relation to both Taiwan, my native place, and mainland China, my ancestral land.

38. Chow, *Writing Diaspora,* 15.

39. Chen, "Yuwang ru shui," 139, 139, 141.

40. Both novelists informed me during interviews that, despite their artistic differences, they were often mentioned in the same breath for their exploration of female-female relationships. For example, Dai Jinhua ("Rewriting Chinese Women," 204) mentions Lin Bai, Chen Ran, and Xu Xiaobin as having authored representative fictional works expressing "the fear of and longing for sisterhood and lesbian relationships."

41. Some sociologists in the PRC have tried to investigate female homosexuality, but their attempts have been largely frustrated by lesbians' reluctance to come forward. Fang Gang, e.g., an ambitious journalist, also had difficulty finding female informants despite being known for having produced a very popular account of homosexuals in China. For a few excerpts from the sociologist Li Yinhe's interviews with women who have had same-sex sexual experiences, see Li, *Zhongguo nüxing,* 207–24.

42. Chen Ran, interview by author, Beijing, 13 December 1998 (a published version of this interview has appeared as Chen, "Chaoxingbie yishi yu tongxing'ai"). Chen's remarks arose when I asked her how she felt about the fact that, in the fairly perceptive essay "Chen Ran," the feminist critic Dai Jinhua analyzed the female-female relations in her fiction in terms of sisterly bonding (*jiemei qingyi*) and consistently avoided using the word *homosexuality* (*tongxinglian*). Chen replied that Dai had informed her that the choice of the more general category *sisterly bonding* was deliberate, meant to protect Chen from the stigma of homosexuality. It seems that, even if Dai herself is not homophobic, she thinks it best to avoid an open discussion of the topic. While in her earlier writings Dai occasionally associates homosexuality with perversion and gender inversion, she seems lately to have modified her opinion about gay and lesbian sexualities, probably as a result of her recent experiences abroad as a visiting professor at several universities, most notably Fu Jen University in Taiwan. In Taiwan, she associated with such leading Taiwanese feminists and queer theorists as Hsiao-hung Chang (Dai Jinhua, interview by author, Beijing, 15 December 1998).

43. I am referring here to Lin Bai's "Mao de jiqing shidai" (The passionate days of the cat) and "Zhiming de feixiang" (A flight of fatality).

44. The *huilang* of the title is a sort of interior balcony, furnished with immovable benches that also function as railings, that runs along all sides of the upper floor of a building, overlooking the inner courtyard.

45. Chen, "Lin Bai lun," 252.

46. Chen, "Yuwang ru shui," 139.

47. Lin, "Huilang zhi yi," 199. Page numbers for subsequent citations will be given in the text.

48. In reconstructing and recounting her experiences in Shuimo, the narrator neither observes chronological order nor cites her conversations with the old woman in the mansion directly, thus making no attempt to give the impression that her narration consists of straightforward facts. Furthermore, her mention of falling ill in Shuimo, running a high fever, and waking from delirious dreams in the hostel calls the reliability of her memory of her experiences—and, therefore, her narrative—into question. Even if we accept that the narrator has had an encounter with an old woman in the mansion, it is still far from clear what part of the story about Zhu Liang and Qiye comes from the old woman and what part is the narrator's own fantasy.

49. Pan, "Zhongguo wenxian," 538.

50. Evans, *Women and Sexuality in China,* 27.

51. Butler, *Gender Trouble,* 133.

52. Foucault, *History of Sexuality,* 1:101.

53. When asked during my interview what relationship she herself bore to the character Duomi, Lin Bai claimed that *One Person's War* began as a record of her own life but that her imagination got the best of her and, charmed by her own words, she let Duomi take on a life of her own. Duomi's life is, thus, an imaginative reconceptualization of her own.

54. Cited in Ding, "Nüxing wenxue ji qita."

55. Ding, "Nüxing wenxue ji qita."

56. Lin Bai, *Yige ren de zhanzheng,* 2. Page numbers for subsequent quotations, which are from the 1997 Jiangsu wenyi chubanshe edition, will be given in the text.

57. Meng, "*Baimaonü* yanbian de qishi," 82–89.

58. At the repeated urging of the American Psychiatric Association and the American Psychological Association, in April 2001 the Chinese Psychiatric Association finally deleted homosexuality from its list of mental disorders.

59. Fuss, *Essentially Speaking;* Weeks, "Values in an Age of Uncertainty."

60. Butler, *Gender Trouble,* 134–41. Briefly, Butler's influential yet controversial claim is as follows: "Gender is an identity tenuously constituted in time, instituted in an exterior space through *a stylized repetition of acts.* The effect of gender is produced through the stylization of the body and, hence, must be understood as the mundane way in which bodily gestures, movements, and styles of various kinds constitute the illusion of an abiding gendered self" (140). Gender attributes are, not expressive, but performative. Through repeated enactment (a kind of "citation") of some ideal ("the law"), gestures and movements coalesce and produce the effect of gender identity on the surface of the body. Between the acts, however, lies the possibility of "a failure to repeat, a deformity, or a parodic repetition" (141) that subverts identity.

61. For Lin's writing philosophy, especially her interest in reconstructing personal experience through the memories of sensations, see her "Jiyi yu gerenhua xiezuo."

## Chapter 8

1. As mentioned in the preceding chapter, Lin Bai reports having frequently received admiring letters from self-identified gay women who feel that she has conveyed their experiences vividly (Lin Bai, interview by author).

2. Evidence that the third space may be broadening includes the fact that a conversation that I had with Chen Ran in Beijing in late 1998 about her representation of same-sex desire has since been published in China in a version edited by the novelist (Chen, "Chaoxingbie yishi yu tongxing'ai") in a collection of her interviews (see Chen, ed., *Buke yanshuo*). The possibilities for a diasporic reader to intervene in and contribute to

the third space in China are, indeed, open, and transnational queer reading tactics do have a chance to land and become localized in China. I thank Shen Rui for introducing me to the novelist.

3. The critical discussion of women's literature revolved around Chen Ran for several years, until the meteoric rise in the spring of 2000 of a group of younger writers (born in the 1970s) commonly dubbed *wanshengdai zuojia* (writers of the late-born generation). The representative figures are Wei Hui and Mian Mian.

4. One arguable exception is Dai's "Chen Ran," which contains some analyses of specific passages quoted from Chen's works; it is, nevertheless, dominated by a rigid framework of Freudian psychoanalysis and depends heavily on concepts such as the Oedipus complex. Xu Kun, another important woman critic, promises close readings but in fact delivers only broad generalizations about recurring motifs (see *Shuangdiao yexingchuan*, 36–40, 51–61, 82–84).

5. Discussions of contemporary writers in articles on women's literature of the 1990s are usually only cursory, such academic treatments tending toward broader, more general coverage instead of engaging one work or writer in detail.

6. Fawubu diaochaju, ed., *Zhonggong zhongyao fagui huibian*, 126–27. Also exempt are "art that shows the beauty of the human body" and "natural and social sciences that cover knowledge about the human anatomy, reproduction, disease prevention, sex, sexual morality, and the sociology of sex" (ibid., 127).

7. Zhou, "Jiliao er bu anfen de wenxue tansuo," 315.

8. On the exploration of women's relationships, see Chen, "Chaoxingbie yishi yu tongxing'ai," 131. On Chen's moral support for the hot line and the newsletter, see ibid., 115–16. Shi Tou, the young, openly gay woman painter who edits *Tiankong*, even invited Chen to write for the newsletter. But, at the time of my interview with her, Chen had not yet agreed to do so.

9. Ibid., 108–10.

10. The Chinese word that Chen uses to refer to anatomical sex, the social gender system, and psychological gender identity throughout the essay is *xingbie* (or its abbreviated form, *xing*, in compound words), which, by itself, does not distinguish between the various concepts. On some occasions, she implies that *xingbie* is a result of acculturation; e.g., she makes assertions about existing psychological differences between men and women and attributes these differences to the structure of male domination in the present society. On other occasions, she uses *xingbie* to designate anatomical sex without reference to social gender, especially when she describes love between those of the same sex (*tongxing*) as nonprocreative. Recent queer and feminist theories of gender in the United States have made such fine distinctions between and so effectively disjoined anatomical sex, social gender, and gender identity that rendering *xingbie* uniformly as any one word in English simply does not seem adequate to me. Without trying to give Chen's essay a theoretical precision that her original language does not have, I have translated *xingbie* alternately as "sex," "gender," or the nonspecific "sex/gender" depending on the context in which it is used.

11. Chen, "Chaoxingbie yishi yu wode chuangzuo," 106.

12. Ibid.

13. Chen, *A'er xiaowu*, 94–95.

14. Chen, "Chaoxingbie yishi yu wode chuangzuo," 106–7.

15. See Rust, *Bisexuality and the Challenge to Lesbian Politics*, 46–101.

16. See, e.g., "Aihen shuangxinglian."

17. See "Shuangxinglian luntan."

18. Rust, *Bisexuality and the Challenge to Lesbian Politics*, 34.

19. Chen, "Chaoxingbie yishi yu wode chuangzuo," 107.

20. While some theorists, such as Sandy Stone ("The *Empire* Strikes Back"), draw

lines between visible crossing and transsexuality, here I am using *transgenderism* as the umbrella term for cross-identifications of various forms, including crossing, passing, and sex reassignment. For recent debates on transgenderism that refine definitions of the term, see Stryker, ed., "The Transgender Issue."

21. On a theoretical level, in view of the necessity of synthesis in any cognitive effort I am dubious about the usefulness of multiplying the number of genders indefinitely as the future direction for gender theory. Judith Halberstam argues with Marjorie Garber's reliance on "thirdness," which Halberstam perceives as stabilizing the gender binarism that it is meant to disrupt. Halberstam believes that it is more fruitful to look specifically at the multiplicity of identities and vernaculars of masculine females rather than subsuming them under an umbrella term such as *the third gender* (see Halberstam, *Female Masculinity*, 27–29; responding to Garber, *Vested Interests*). While I applaud Halberstam's attention to specificity, it seems to me that a certain conceptual synthesis is still operative, and perhaps necessarily so, in Halberstam's own project, which is represented by her conceptual framework of "female masculinity" throughout. In other words, Halberstam cannot deny that her own theoretical productivity impinges on the fact that she has made female husbands, inverts, and stone butches readable and intelligible as one distinctive gender (or transgender), i.e., the masculine female.

22. This is, of course, strictly an analysis of Chen's concept of gender transcendence and does not represent my own view of transgender identities.

23. He, "Geti de shengcun jingyan yu xiezuo," 410.

24. Chen, *Siren shenghuo*, 59. Page numbers for subsequent quotations will be given in the text.

25. Wang Meng wrote an enthusiastic commentary on Chen Ran's works, which prefaces several selections of Chen's short stories (see Wang, "Mosheng de Chen Ran").

26. As mentioned already, between 1980 and 1997, the PRC government's relative awareness of male-male sexual behavior was reflected negatively in the category *hooliganism*. The law particularly disapproved of forced man-boy sexual contact. In contrast, female-female sexual activity—of any kind—has never been criminalized.

27. Larson, "Women and the Discourse of Desire in Postrevolutionary China," 216, 218. For an alternative reading of desire in Chen Ran's writing, see Huot, *China's New Cultural Scene*, 36–41, which focuses on same-sex love and Chen's female protagonists' attempt to break through the heterosexual matrix in "Pokai" (Breaking through). Although useful, Huot's reading is marred by a tendency to make authoritative-sounding assertions in an offhand manner that may not suit some readers.

28. Dai, "Chen Ran," 401; see also Huot, *China's New Cultural Scene*, 36–41. The association between Chen Ran and Lu Yin is made by literary historians/critics like Dai but not necessarily by Chen Ran herself. Chen's writing to date has not mentioned or alluded to Lu Yin. Therefore, the resonance between the two female writers should probably be understood more as a coincidence than as the later writer's conscious effort to reconnect to the May Fourth legacy.

29. Chen, "Pokai," 442.

30. Yang, "From Gender Erasure to Gender Difference," 47–51.

31. Chen, "Chaoxingbie yishi yu tongxing'ai," 119. I had forwarded my questions to Chen before the interview took place.

32. See ibid., 115.

33. Chen, "Chaoxingbie yishi yu tongxing'ai," 111, 131, 131.

34. The Chinese Psychiatric Association (CPA) did not remove homosexuality from its list of mental disorders until April 2001, almost thirty years after the depathologization of homosexuality in the United States. The CPA's *The Chinese Classification of Mental Disorders Third Revision* (CCMD-3) still retains "Ego-Dystonic Homosexuality" (see Zhonghua jingshen kexue hui, *Zhongguo jingshen zhang'ai fenlei yu zhenduan*

*biaozhun*). ("Ego-dystonic homosexuals" are those who hate their own sexual orientation and have sought professional help or medical treatment. Their self-hatred is perceived as a mental problem.)

35. Chen, "You yizhong ku'nan yusheng julai," 130–32.

36. Rofel, "Qualities of Desire," 460–64. On the basis of fieldwork conducted in mainland China between 1989 and 1991, Li Yihe and Wang Xiaobo found that the social imperative that adult men marry was so strong that almost all the gay men whom they interviewed were either already married or resigned to having to marry at some point. The vast majority of the forty-nine interview subjects had not revealed their real sexual orientation to those close to them in everyday life, including parents, siblings, spouses, coworkers, and supervisors (*Tamende shijie,* 151–52). Among the reasons cited by gay men for marrying are the obligation to make one's parents happy, pressure from neighbors and work units, eligibility for allocated housing (which is available only to married couples), having children, and "in order to get a divorce" (i.e., being divorced implies having been married and is, therefore, less suspect than staying single; it is "proof," if you will, of heterosexuality) (see ibid., 163–67).

37. Chen, "Chaoxingbie yishi yu tongxing'ai," 138.

38. Wang, "Gudude ren shi wuchide," v.

39. More generally, there has been a turn toward interiority and private living space in post-Mao China (see Tang, *Chinese Modern,* 295–315).

40. Chen, "Ling yishan kaiqi de men," 254–55.

41. The representative text in this genre, whose rationale is the direct opposite of Chen Ran's *Private Life,* is a best-seller: An's *Juedui yinsi.* The volume is presented as the author's truthful recordings of ordinary people's unembellished oral histories of love and sexual experiences.

### Chapter 9

1. In the 1970s and early 1980s, e.g., the nativist resistance appeared most notably in the form of literary debates. Certain critics championed nativist literature as opposed to Western-influenced modernist writing. Aside from exploring the pains of industrialization and urbanization in 1970s Taiwan, the so-called nativist realist literature often depicts ironic colonial power relations, critiquing American imperialism as well as Japan's economic dominance in Taiwan. See Sung-sheng Yvonne Chang's definitive study *Modernism and the Nativist Resistance,* esp. 148–76.

2. For instance, the Taiwanese higher education system has become increasingly Americanized over the last decade. In the realm of politics, dissidents opposing Taiwan's Nationalist government in the 1980s not infrequently went into self-imposed exile in the United States, where they were inspired by the operation of democracy. Some of them, such as Xu Xinliang, Peng Mingmin, and Chen Fangming, have returned to Taiwan in the late 1980s and 1990s to become major political figures in the Minjindang (Democratic Progressive Party) or public intellectuals. Japan's influence on Taiwan in the 1980s and 1990s has been largely in the realm of popular culture and the consumer economy, but it has also had its palpable effects on Taiwan's intellectual and political life.

3. For an analysis of the current difficulties that gays and lesbians in Taiwan face when revealing their sexual identify as well as a critique of both the epistemology involved in the notion *coming out* and the strategic value of coming out American style in Taiwan, see Qitian et al., "Shengli yingxiong huo zhanlue jia"; Wang, "Buyao jiaochu yaokong qi"; and Chao, "Chugui huo bu chugui." See also the discussion of the use of masks in Martin, "Surface Tensions."

4. See Altman, *Global Sex,* and *The Homosexualization of America.* To be fair, some Taiwanese queer theorists are well aware of the controversy over their adoption of

Anglo-American queer theory and have tried to justify their own roles in cross-cultural transactions. Kaweibo, e.g., argues, "There were [queer] seeds in the local environment of Taiwan, and that is why the foreign fertilizer has been effective in encouraging growth" ("Shemo shi kuer," 238).

5. Chao, "Embodying the Invisible," 137–41. In the early to mid-1990s, Chao observed that the Ts and pos active in the T-bars in Taipei were unfamiliar with the English word *lesbian,* whereas the undifferentiated type was commonly found among college-educated young women who identified with both North American feminism and the English category *lesbian* (ibid., 140–41). According to Chao, *T-bar* means essentially "lesbian bar" (ibid., 29). By the mid-1990s, more than thirty T-bars had been opened in Taipei, Taichung, and Kaohsiung, the three major—and the three most modern and Westernized—cities in Taiwan (ibid., 47). T-bars imitate the style of the Japanese hostess clubs. By contrast, "gay [male] bars are considerably 'Westernized.' This Western attribute is clear in the bilingual—Chinese/English—safe sex booklets circulated at the bar" (ibid., 51). The clientele at the T-bars is very young, generally between the ages of fourteen and twenty-three (ibid., 71).

6. Zheng, *Nüer quan,* 122–40.

7. See ibid., 137–39; and Chao, "Embodying the Invisible," 29–30, 128, 132–33, 156, 180–83. See also Case, "Seduced and Abandoned"; Butler, *Gender Trouble;* and Newton, "Baking Ziti for the Coronation." Chao cites many more American lesbian studies and queer theorists than Zheng does—perhaps owing to her extended academic training in the United States—but Chao is also more interested in critiquing American queer theory than Zheng is.

8. See Jian, "Huanchu nü tongzhi," 79–107.

9. The T-bar and the liberal university campus are neither self-contained spaces nor utopias. For instance, the youth consumerism of the T-bar has many elements in common with the overall youth-centered consumer culture in Taiwan, especially in its urban/cosmopolitan character (see Chao, "Embodying the Invisible," 88–117). And there is plenty of homophobia on the relatively liberal university campus, as evinced by the backlash against gays and lesbians during student elections at National Taiwan University in late 1995 and early 1996 (see Bai, "Wenhua yu zhengzhi de shuang quxian," 212–13).

10. On new identity-based social movements in post–martial law Taiwan, see Chun, "Discourses of Identity."

11. Foucault, *History of Sexuality,* 1:101.

12. The term *female consciousness* is conceptually vague enough that it can be used to describe both Chen Ran's desire to transcend feminine stereotypes and Lin Bai's glorification of sensual femininity (for details, see pt. 3). For situations beyond literary criticism, see Wang, "Research on Women in Contemporary China."

13. Yang, introduction to *Spaces of Their Own.* As mentioned before, although other social scientists studying China do not necessarily use the terminology of Habermas's public-sphere theory, like Yang many have put forth observations about the opening up of an unofficial social space in China during the 1980s and the early 1990s (see Davis et al., eds., *Urban Spaces in Contemporary China;* and Link, Madsen, and Pickowicz, eds., *Unofficial China*). Unfortunately, developments in the PRC since the late 1990s have begun to show the inordinate power of the profit-seeking mass media to mold mass culture and public opinion. The country has also become increasingly polarized economically, with scant middle ground between wealth and poverty, at the same time as crass consumerism has increasingly taken hold. The protests of the dispossessed have appeared in the unofficial social space, but they have yet to be taken seriously.

14. Habermas, *The Structural Transformation of the Public Sphere,* 177–78.

15. Baudrillard claims: "Simulation is no longer that of a territory, a referential

being or a substance. It is the generation by models of a real without origin or reality: a hyperreal." Elsewhere: "What characterizes the mass media is . . . noncommunication— if one accepts the definition of communication as an exchange, as the reciprocal space of speech and response, and thus of *responsibility*. . . . Now the whole present architecture of the media is founded on this last definition: they are what finally forbids response" (*Selected Writings*, 166, 207–8). For a concise account of optimistic as well as pessimistic theories of the relation between the media and social liberation, see Poster, *The Second Media Age*, 1–22.

16. For example, the feminist magazine *Funü xinzhi* (Women's awakening) was run on a deficit from 1982 to 1995 by Funü xinzhi jijinhui (the Awakening Foundation), which relies mainly on donations and grants. In June 1996, the foundation launched another women's journal, *Saodong* (STIR—Sisters in revolt), a trimonthly.

17. For a detailed study of the advocacy of the nuclear family (*xiao jiating*) in the Republican era, see Glosser, *Chinese Visions of Family and State*.

18. Currently, the mainlanders who migrated to Taiwan in the late 1940s and their descendants constitute about 12 percent of Taiwan's population (Chao, "Embodying the Invisible," 6).

19. Taida Lambda, *Women shi nü tongxinglian*, 60–71, 100–105, 155–65. It should be noted that quite a few Lambda members say that they find it easier to come out to siblings or nonlesbian close friends.

20. Ibid., 68–71.

21. Zheng, *Nüer quan*, 75–96.

22. For mainland echoes—especially the themes of secrecy and conflict with one's closest kin in Chen, "You yizhong ku'nan yusheng julai"—see chap. 8.

23. For Taiwanese lesbians' accounts of adolescent love affairs and their run-ins with school authorities, see "Feichang qingchunqi."

24. The letter is reprinted in its entirety in Xu, "Huan ju shouji," 4.

25. Cited in Xue, "Women shenshen xiang'ai, dan jue bushi 'zhenzhengde' tongxinglian?" 8.

26. Cited in ibid.

27. Xiao and Gou, "Guoxiao jiaoshi fang shilu."

28. See Xiao, "Zuozeide han zhuo zei."

29. For example, a teacher known to be lesbian might be fired because she is perceived as leading an immoral lifestyle and, therefore, as setting a bad example for her students. A real incident is related in Xiao and Gou, "Guoxiao jiaoshi fang shilu," 8.

30. Ye, "Nü tongzhi de ziwei zhi dao."

31. Xiao, "Jing, yin, ti, tou."

32. In 1993, the Taiwanese legislature held a public hearing on homosexual human rights, as a first step toward determining whether sexual orientation should be included, along with gender, in antidiscrimination legislation then being debated. To date, however, sexual orientation remains excluded from Taiwan's antidiscrimination law. For a record of the public hearing, see Tongzhi gongzuofang, ed., *Fan qishi zhi yue*.

33. The founding of Between Us in 1990 was reported in the radical magazine *Xin wenhua* (New culture), which also published autobiographical stories and political statements by members of the group. Later on, the Awakening Foundation declared support for the lesbian group from a feminist stance. Between Us garnered a great deal of publicity in 1992. The Taiwan Television Co. (TTV) broadcast voyeuristic videos of the Taipei lesbian scene, and Between Us issued a public statement denouncing such reportage as exploitative and detrimental. Armed with a letter signed by thirty writers, artists, and critics published in the newspaper *Zhongguo shibao* (China times), Between Us succeeded in making the National Press Council rule against TTV and force it to apologize. See the chronicle of events in Yu, "Manman chang lu," 8.

34. The resignifying project extends into print. See "T de shenti," which focuses on the meanings and pleasures of the bodies of tomboys.

35. Chou, *Hou zhimin tongzhi*, 360–65.

36. Among other Taiwanese neologisms that include the character *tong* as a short-hand for homosexuality or same-sex desire is *Tongwanjie*, which was coined by activists to name the lesbian and gay festival held in Taipei in 2000.

37. The first GLAD, which was marked by film screenings, performances, discussions, and candlelit lakeside conversation, was celebrated on the campus of National Taiwan University on 1 June 1995 (see Chi et al., "Xiaoyuan tongxinglian ri").

38. The first modern Chinese scholars to suspect that Qu Yuan was a sexual favorite of the Chu King's were Sun Cizhou and Wen Yiduo in the 1940s (see Wen, *Chuci yanjiu shizhong*, 3–16).

39. On the strife between mainstream feminism and lesbianism in the United States and Britain, see Wilton, *Lesbian Studies*, 87–109. For a brief outline of the marginalization of lesbians in the women's movement in France in the 1970s, see Rosenfeld, "Splits in French Feminism/Lesbianism."

40. I should note that, in addition to activists' discussions of the relation between the women's and the lesbigay movements, there have also been some academic discussions in Taiwan of the tension between feminist theory and queer theory. Such discussions are reminiscent of the debate in Anglo-American theoretical circles in the early 1990s over whether sexuality is best treated as an analytic category separate from gender. As Biddy Martin noted in 1992, one source of the tension was that there existed "a tendency among some lesbian, bisexual, and gay theorists and activists to construct 'queerness' as a vanguard position that announces its newness and advance over against an apparently superseded and now anachronistic feminism with its emphasis on gender" (*Femininity Played Straight*, 71). For a range of opinions on the relation between feminism and lesbian theory, see Merck, Segal, and Wright, eds., *Coming Out of Feminism?*

41. Hsiao-hung Chang is representative of this position. See her remarks in Hu et al., "Nü tongzhi yundong chu gui," 5–6. See also the discussion below.

42. The Awakening Foundation is but one of many women's organizations in Taiwan. Nevertheless, it is by far the most politically active and theoretically sophisticated. In my discussion in this section of the chapter, the words *women's movement* and *feminism* refer to what the Awakening leads and represents.

43. In Taiwan, although a woman's celibacy is not uncommonly interpreted by others as a sign of a lack of sex appeal and of a failure to get married, it also has the alternative implication of independence. Moreover, a strong-willed modern woman's practice of celibacy for ideological reasons is somewhat reminiscent of some women's rejection of marriage for religious reasons in traditional Chinese society (a fictional example of which is Feng Sanniang's rejection of sex with men because she is intent on cultivating her Tao [see chap. 3 above]).

44. See Hu et al., "Nü tongzhi yundong chu gui."

45. The relation between feminism and lesbianism has been explored in many feminist study groups (*nü yan she*) and lesbian groups on university campuses in Taiwan. However, unlike similar discussions, the debate at the Awakening Foundation reached a wider audience because it was published. Of course, with the development of the Internet, feminist groups generally have become increasingly effective in communicating with a wider public. The women's movement in Taiwan may, therefore, have made a transition to an era of diversification and dispersal, one in which no one organization can claim a leading position in terms of its ability to shape public opinion.

46. The feminist Hu Shuwen points out that the agenda of gender equality has been partially realized and largely accepted by mainstream society in Taiwan. She maintains

that feminists should start facing the more controversial issue of sexuality (see Hu, "Yi nü chu gui," 14).

47. Yuxuan, "Jiehun quan yu bu jiehun quan."

48. Xinzhi gongzuoshi, "Chai jie hunyin shenhua."

49. Radicalesbians, "The Woman Identified Woman," 19. A long excerpt of the article is published in Chinese translation in Zhang, trans., "Nüren rentong nüren."

50. Hu, "Yi nü chu gui," 13, 16.

51. Chang, "Zai zhangli zhong huxiang kanjian."

52. Gu, "Kanjian he banzhuang zhi wai, nüxing zhuyi zhe daodi neng zuo shemo," 11.

53. Hu et al., "Nü tongzhi yundong chu gui," 3.

54. Hu, "Zhuti zao yi miandui nimen, zhishi nimen kanbujian."

55. Yuxuan, "Xishou zhi qian, fenli, you qi biyao," 16.

56. Ibid., 17–18.

57. Since the debates in 1995–96, Taiwanese queer theorists have, in reflecting on the tension between local lesbian feminism and the T-po subculture, been informed by the historical discord between lesbian feminists and the butch-femme communities in the West (see Liou, "Zai xingbie de aimei jiaojie: Chao xingbie de dingyi, mailuo, yundong ji lunshu kongjian").

58. Taida Lambda, *Women shi nü tongxinglian,* 111. The idea of "the stratification of sex" is apparently borrowed from Gayle Rubin, who in "Thinking Sex" discusses, in a more detailed fashion than Foucault does, the deployment of sexuality as a system distinct from kinship in the social contestation of power. Rubin's article, regarded by some as foundational for gay and lesbian studies in the United States, is anthologized in a collection of essays popular in Taiwan among university students interested in sexuality studies during the 1990s: Abelove, Barale, and Halperin, eds., *The Lesbian and Gay Studies Reader.*

59. This was a view publicly presented by Wang Ping and Ni Jiazhen in Wang, Ni, et al., "Xingbie zhengzhi yu tongzhi yundong," 87–90.

60. I thank Ping-ying Chang for informing me about this development. Unlike many campus lesbigay study groups, Wang's organization is formally registered with the government, thus claiming state recognition.

61. Indeed, coalition politics has been crucial to the lesbigay movement from the start, and it is not limited simply to forming close ties to the women's movement during the early to mid-1990s. Lesbigay activists were strong supporters, e.g., of the legal sex workers whose work licenses were abruptly terminated by the Taipei city government in 1997 (Wang, Ni, et al., "Xingbie zhengzhi yu tongzhi yundong," 89).

62. Shi Tou and four other lesbian-identified women, conversation with author. Group discussions among young urban women in mainland China have so far occurred outside the purview of the mainstream media, unlike the situation in Taiwan, where lesbian and feminist organizations garnered considerable media coverage throughout the 1990s. For example, the first mainland Chinese lesbian conference (held in 1998) was reported in the underground Beijing lesbian newsletter *Tiankong* (Sky) but otherwise largely ignored. In fact, few mainland lesbians have actively sought media attention, Shi Tou being an important exception (see, e.g., Shi, "Shi Tou yishu zuopin xuan"). In Hong Kong, several lesbian organizations came into existence in the late 1990s, but their presence has not been as visible as has that of Taiwanese lesbian and feminist organizations. On the Hong Kong scene, see Chou, *Tongzhi,* 84–87.

63. Yang, introduction to *Spaces of Their Own,* 24–30.

64. Dai Jinhua, interview with author.

65. For example, in June 1994, the Taiwanese mass media was among the many in

the world to celebrate the twenty-fifth anniversary of the Stonewall riot. Coverage of the gay pride celebrations in the United States and elsewhere in the West appeared almost daily in Taiwanese newspapers. On the significance of the Stonewall riot as the symbolic beginning of the gay and lesbian liberation movement in the United States, see D'Emilio, *Sexual Politics, Sexual Communities,* 231–33.

66. Yuxuan et al., "Taibei tongwanjie zhuanti." There are many other examples of the media's coverage of lesbian and gay activism. For instance, Taida Lambda held a press conference on the publication in 1995 of their *Women shi nü tongxinglian.* The first GLAD at National Taiwan University in 1995 was also well publicized by the media. The wedding of gay male writer Xu Yousheng and his lover in late 1996 was another major media event.

67. Yuxuan et al., "Taibei tongwanjie zhuanti," 14–16.

68. Some of the earliest voyeuristic media reports on Taipei lesbians include Huang et al., "Tansuo nanren zhi bu de shijie"; and Su et al., "Nü tongxinglianzhe xing'ai biantai da jiemi." These reports generally focus on T-po role-playing in the T-bar. They stereotype Ts as *nanren po* (female men)—male impersonators—and femmes as normal women who are somehow weak or confused enough to be sexually exploited by the so-called *boli qingmo* (crystal sex demons). (*Boli,* or "crystal," is the Taiwanese slang for gays. Its origin is unclear.) The reporters' curiosity about lesbian sex centers on the question, How do they do it without a penis? Their language deploys puns and mock versions of classical idioms and romantic verses to ridicule lesbian sex, suggesting that it is just a substitute for or an imitation of heterosexual sex. The early reports conceived of "female homosexuals" as counterparts to male homosexuals, who used to be the only homosexuals about which the public had heard. For a while, lesbians were called *nü boli* (female crystals), a term derived from the Taiwanese slang *boli,* meaning male homosexuals. The lesbian bar was described as a new *boli leyuan* (crystal paradise). The traditional term for male homosexuality, *duanxiu* (cut sleeve), was also used to represent lesbianism.

69. Poster, *The Second Media Age,* 3–22.

70. Horkheimer and Adorno, *Dialectic of Enlightenment,* 120–67.

71. Enzensberger cited in Baudrillard, *Selected Writings,* 207.

72. Lauren Berlant's recent analysis of the relation between sex and citizenship in the United States raises certain questions that are close to what I have in mind. Among other complex arguments, she points out that the fact that sex became the focal point, for both the Left and the Right, of the debate over American identity during the Reagan era indicates a deflection of public attention from class and poverty (see *The Queen of America Goes to Washington City,* 7–10).

73. In *Global Sex,* 106–21, Dennis Altman gives a cogent overview of the increased commercialization of sex in the current phase of global capitalism.

74. An, "Prelude." In the United States, much has already been said about gay consumerism; for a succinct analysis, see Ingebretsen, "Gone Shopping."

75. See, e.g., *G&L: Re'ai zazhi,* no. 2 (1996): 12.

76. Li et al., "Taiwan tongzhi xiaofei wenhua," 19.

77. "Duzhe lai han."

78. "Tongzhi zhengjian da leitai"; Yulong, comp., "Tongzhi falü renquan zuotanhui."

79. I thank Ping-ying Chang for bringing this to my attention.

80. *Hong peiji*'s URL is http://r703a.chem.nthu.edu.tw/~rpgs/gzine/.

81. For a list of recommended Chinese lesbian websites, see Lü, "You kong qu guang lawang ba." Among other sites is TO-GET-HER Lez Cyberpub (http://www.to-get-her.org).

82. Habermas, *The Structural Transformation of the Public Sphere,* 51. For Habermas's discussion of "the bourgeois family and the institutionalization of a privateness oriented to an audience," see ibid., 43–51.

## Chapter 10

1. On p. 17 of his "Zhongguo tongxinglian shengtai baogao" (A report of homosexuality's state of survival in China), the gay film critic Cui Zien mentions that Gezi, a self-employed female writer, has published the first full-length novel in the People's Republic of China dedicated to the theme of lesbian love: *Miqing de rizi* (The days of bewildering love). I came across this reference too late to verify Cui's claim about this obscure novel and its little-known author. Investigation must await another occasion.

2. In Hong Kong, several lesbian (or sexuality-related) organizations such as Jiemei tongzhi (Queer Sisters) came into existence in the late 1990s (Chou, *Tongzhi*, 82–84). However, serious literary representations of lesbian sexuality and subjectivity are rare in the consumer culture of Hong Kong, despite the fact that the Hong Kong film industry produced in the late 1980s and early 1990s a good number of pornographic films containing female-female sex acts. The paucity of serious literary representations in Hong Kong in this regard forms quite a contrast to the proliferation of lesbian-themed avant-garde literature in Taiwan in the 1990s. For two interesting short stories about female-female love and desire by Hong Kong women writers, see Lee, "Shuangmei mo"; and Wong, "Ta shi nüzi, wo ye shi nüzi." I am unaware of significant lesbian-themed literature in Chinese published outside the Greater China region. There is some on the Internet, but the quality leaves much to be desired.

3. For an anthropological account of sexual relations among *kao-a-hi* actresses, see Silvio, "Reflexivity, Bodily Praxis, and Identity in Taiwanese Opera."

4. See Hung, *Yiduan xixiegui liezhuan, Zhijie yishou, Yuzhou Aodisai,* and *Mogui biji.* See also Hung's discussion of her own fiction in "Leisi yu bianzi de jiaohuan."

5. See, e.g., Zhu, *Xiang wo juancun de xiongdimen,* and *Gudu;* Cao, "Tongnü zhi wu," and *Guanyu baifa ji qita;* and Du, *Ni nü.*

6. On postwar American pulp fiction about lesbians, see Zimet, *Strange Sisters.*

7. One example of this American influence is the singer Huang Xiaoning, active in Taiwan in the late 1960s and the 1970s. Huang, who performed in the pubs frequented by American military personnel stationed in Taipei, always dressed in men's three-piece suits and was open about her "TB" (tomboy) identity. And it is held among Taiwanese lesbians that she learned her butch style from "associating with American girls" and "cultural exchange" (Zheng, *Nüer quan,* 131).

8. See Chi and Lin, comps., "Taiwan tongzhi wenxue yu wenhua yanjiu shumu."

9. The representative figures were Hsiao-hung Chang, Huang Yuxiu, Liang-ya Liou, He Chunrui, and Ding Naifei, among others.

10. The recent sociological literature on new social movements around the world is voluminous. For a succinct discussion of new social movements as identity-oriented movements and of their significance in an era of global capitalism, see Sklair, "Social Movements and Global Capitalism." More specifically, the relaxation of press censorship and the annulment of martial law in 1987 spawned a new public sphere in Taiwan (see Chun, "Discourses of Identity"). As mentioned in chap. 9, among the new social movements that arose in the daily expanding sphere of public representation and activism was the lesbian movement, which was inaugurated symbolically by the founding of the lesbian organization Between Us in 1990. The movement grew as feminist and lesbian study groups mushroomed on university campuses and as social energy erupted into many other unprecedented activities. Public hearings and demonstrations protesting discrimination against gays were held. The T-po role-playing in urban T-bars was interpreted and resignified as gender trouble and performativity by academic feminists writing for newspapers. Experimental plays on homoerotic themes attracted large crowds, whether performances took place in the streets or in alternative theaters. Homoerotic films and videos were made. Last but not least, discussions of lesbian and gay cultures and issues multiplied on the Internet.

11. For a bibliography of contemporary Taiwanese homoerotic fiction through 1996, see Chi and Lin, comps., "Taiwan tongzhi wenxue yu wenhua yanjiu shumu," 274–77. For an extensive study in English of Taiwanese homoerotic fiction, see Tan, "Re-Negotiating Transcultural Sexuality." Tan's study is valuable, but, because it attempts to cover almost all known Taiwanese texts about same-sex love and eroticism published between 1960 and 1997, the analyses of individual works are often lacking in depth. Another flaw is that Tan speaks in an undefined way about writers' strategies to cope with the prejudices against homosexuality, which often conflates authors with their fictional gay characters without sufficiently investigating the historical/factual background.

12. For example, Liang-ya Liou has published theory-informed essays on the works of the lesbian and gay writers Lucifer Hung, Chen Xue, Qiu Miaojin, and Ta-wei Chi (see *Yuwang gengyishi*).

The reader should note that I do not object to the use of Western queer theory in interpreting Taiwanese literature per se. The usefulness of critical theory must, in my view, be judged on a case-by-case basis. One cannot know beforehand whether a theoretical framework has explanatory power for a particular work. I am concerned, however, when certain Taiwanese critics do not seem interested in examining in depth the theories that they use—i.e., when authority is automatically attributed to theory without any questioning and recontextualizing.

13. The PRC government tries to filter even communication on the Internet; many websites in the West or Taiwan are banned on the mainland.

14. The difficulty has something to do with the election culture in Taiwan. Because lesbians and gays constitute a minority of voters, few candidates for seats in the legislature champion gay rights. The latest improvement in relations between the Taiwanese government and lesbians and gays is that the operations of certain nongovernment organizations promoting human rights for lesbians and gays are officially sanctioned.

15. Chang, *Yuwang xin ditu*, 75. What Chang means by *theory* is Western theory, especially that which is written/available in English.

16. Liou, *Yuwang gengyishi*, 10.

17. Theorists of the postmodern introduced to Taiwan run the whole gamut from Jean-François Lyotard, Ihab Hassan, and Andreas Huyssen to Fredric Jameson and many others. For the most recent scholarship assessing the applicability of postmodern theory to Taiwan's literature and culture, see Chou and Liu, eds., *Shuxie Taiwan*. Not all critics collected in the volume embrace postmodern theory. For Chen Fangming, e.g., the pluralization of writing styles in the post–martial law era is best understood in terms of postcolonialism instead of postmodernity (see his "Houxiandai huo houzhimin"). For a counteropinion advocating the investigation of "translated postmodernity" in Taiwan and other Chinese societies, see Liao, "Taiwan."

18. See Chang, *Modernism and the Nativist Resistance*. While Chang focuses on the debates surrounding fictional writing, Michelle Yeh has attended to the tension between modernist poets and nativists in postwar Taiwan (see her *Modern Chinese Poetry*, 117 and passim).

19. Hsiao-hung Chang, He Chunrui, Ta-wei Chi, and Lucifer Hung readily come to mind as examples of this media celebrity.

20. Chu, "Kua xingbie yundong de Taiwan sisuo."

21. Chi, "Kuer lun."

22. Yuxuan and Zheng, "Xingfu zheng zai bijin," 218. The word *lazi* has been used in the Taiwanese lesbian magazine *Nü pengyou* (Girlfriend) since the mid-1990s. It is interchangeable with several other terms designating "lesbian": *tongnü* (lit. homo girl), *nü tongxinglian* (female homosexual), *nü tongzhi* (lit. female comrade), and *leisibian* (a transliteration of *lesbian*).

23. Chu, "Qianyan," 15.

24. Early on in her career, Qiu Miaojin's short fiction won two major literary prizes. Her early short stories are collected under the title *Gui de kuanghuan* (Hedonist ghosts). She was also interested in filmmaking and produced a video, also entitled *Gui de kuanghuan.*

25. The essays and poems appeared in the September 1995 issue and *Mengmate yishu*—in four installments—in the December 1995–March 1996 issues of *Lianhe wenxue.*

26. *The Crocodile's Journal* is a self-referential work. Lazi, the narrator, constantly refers to her own narrative as a novel in progress. Her creative process involves rewriting a set of old diaries—some of which she can no longer find—that she kept in college. Her narrative is, thus, a reconstructed journal, consisting entirely of loosely linked episodes of Lazi's life in college. At intervals, snippets of the story about Crocodile are inserted into this journal. Because the story about Crocodile is not integrated with the story of Lazi's relationships, the juxtaposition of the two stories invokes the techniques of montage and jump-cutting.

27. Liang-ya Liou points out that there is a cartoon-like quality about the character Crocodile—humorous and exaggerated. See Liou, *Yuwang gengyishi,* 130–31.

28. Crocodile goes by the name Genet at a party, suggesting that Qiu identified with the French writer Jean Genet and that the title *The Crocodile's Journal* pays tribute to Genet's autobiographical novel *The Thief's Journal,* whose protagonist is a homosexual and a criminal (see Qiu, *Eyu shouji,* 159; page numbers for subsequent quotations will be given in the text).

29. The voyeurism of the Taiwanese mainstream media is exemplified by the following two incidents. In 1992, Qu Meifeng, a reporter for Taiwan Television (TTV), dressed herself as a T to sneak into a T-bar. Using a hidden camera, she videotaped the patrons of the bar without consent, and the tape was broadcast. The lesbian organization Between Us strenuously protested this violation of individuals' privacy, issuing a strongly worded statement over the signatures of more than thirty writers and artists. In 1998, history repeated itself. Two reporters from Chinese Television (CTV) videotaped the customers in a T-bar with a camera hidden in a bag and broadcast the tape without obtaining permission. Again, Between Us issued a public statement opposing the violation of individuals' rights. This time the organization solicited one thousand signatories on its website. See Women zhi jian et al., "Kangyi Huashi zhuanji."

30. Bhabha, "Of Mimicry and Man."

31. Foucault, *History of Sexuality,* 1:101. Compare the discussion in chap. 7 above of Lin Bai's creation of a reverse discourse in *One Person's War.*

32. Althusser, *Lenin and Philosophy.*

33. Most of my analysis of *The Crocodile's Journal* in this chapter, including my comparison of Qiu and Hall, first appeared in my "The Emerging Lesbian." Liang-ya Liou (*Yuwang gengyishi,* 112) also notes the similarity between Qiu's novel and Hall's.

34. Chao, "Embodying the Invisible," 131, 132.

35. Zhang, "Nütong shequn de rentong yu zhanyan."

36. Although it was not serialized anywhere before being published in book form, *The Crocodile's Journal* is nevertheless still tied—ironically—to the mass media. Because of its nonlinear, montage style and unusual subject matter, and despite its criticism of the mass media, it first appeared in a series of experimental novels called Hong xiaoshuo (Red Novels)—"a series that most aptly captures the essence and tempo of our time," according to the books' covers—published by a division of the *Zhongguo shibao* (China times) conglomerate, which issues one of the two largest newspapers in Taiwan. This means that the novel is well distributed through a commercial network unavailable to alternative lesbian and feminist magazines. *The Crocodile's Journal* is, in short, bound to the media conglomerate in concrete economic terms.

37. On scopophilia (the desire to see; pleasure in looking), see Metz, *The Imaginary Signifier,* 58, 63. See also my discussion of Lin Bai in chap. 7. Yengning Chao has analyzed the popularity in Taiwan of Hong Kong–made pornographic films containing female-female eroticism in terms of scopophilia; she links it to the Taiwanese public's desire for authenticity and representability as a nation-state (Chao, "Embodying the Invisible," 186–212).

38. Lejeune, *On Autobiography.* Lejeune claims: "Most autobiographies are inspired by a creative, and therefore fictional, impulse to select only those events and experiences in the writer's life that go to build up an integrated pattern" (155).

39. Ta-wei Chi, e.g., calls Crocodile's act of floating into the sea at the end of the novel "a retreat from battle" (cited in Liou, *Yuwang gengyishi,* 136).

40. However, for positive appraisals of the works of Lucifer Hung and Chen Xue, see Liou, *Yuwang gengyishi,* 57–82, 83–110; and Martin, "Chen Xue's Queer Tactics."

41. Calinescu, *Five Faces of Modernity,* 120–25.


## Epilogue

1. Foucault, *History of Sexuality,* 1:106 (and see generally 105–14). See also Butler, "Sexual Traffic," 85.

2. Connecting knowledge, power, and sexuality as a discourse, Foucault writes, "[The deployment of sexuality] has been linked from the outset with an intensification of the body—with its exploitation as an object of knowledge and an element in relations of power" (*History of Sexuality,* 1:107).

3. Ibid., 105.

4. D'Emilio, "Capitalism and Gay Identity," 105. D'Emilio maintains that capitalism elevates the family in theory while undermining it in reality. His argument can be summarized as follows: Although it has reduced the economic necessity that binds the nuclear family together, capitalism is nevertheless invested in the production of the next generation of labor through the nuclear family. Moreover, because psychological insecurity accompanies the socialization of production under capitalism, the family has become idealized as a place where individuals can obtain emotional support and happiness. It is not surprising that the right wing of an advanced capitalist society such as America promotes family values. When attacked for undermining the family, gays and lesbians merely serve as a scapegoat for the entire capitalist society.

5. Halperin, "Forgetting Foucault," 96. Others cited by Halperin in support of this assertion are George Chauncey, Jonathan Ned Katz, Carolyn J. Dean, and Estelle Freedman.

6. Halperin makes this claim with regard to premodern European history (see "Forgetting Foucault," 97). In the case of premodern China, certain understandings of male-male eroticism in terms of sexual identity or personhood (rather than in terms of sex acts) obviously existed. For instance, those who had a particular taste for boys could easily be described as such (*hao nanse*), regardless of their marital status. That is to say, ordinary language distinguished between men whose intense desire for boys led to this being their major sexual outlet and men who were involved in male-male behavior only occasionally.


## Appendix

1. The name Fan Shiyiniang means, literally, "the eleventh female child of the Fan family (or clan)." The name of the eponymous heroine, Feng Sanniang, means, literally, "the third child of the Feng family (or clan)."

2. Ordinary people worshiped ancestors on the Zhongyuan Day. Taoist priests held ceremonies to set all beings (such as hungry ghosts) free from pain. Buddhist temples

held the Yulanpenhui ceremony (see n. 3, this chapter, below), in which pious believers made offerings to the Buddha, the truth, and the monks (or nuns) to repay parents for the favors of life and nurturing and to save them from the sufferings of being hung upside down or of hunger in the underworld.

3. Yulanpenhui: a ceremony to save one's parents from the sufferings of hunger in the underworld.

4. Double-Ninth Day (Chongjiu) is the ninth day of the ninth month on the Chinese lunar calendar. On this folk holiday, people would hike up a mountain or walk up to the top floor of a tall structure to enjoy the view and avoid evil spirits. In "Feng Sanniang," Shiyiniang seems to have small, bound feet and to be incapable of long walks.

# SELECT GLOSSARY OF CHINESE NAMES AND TERMS

*Ai bao* 愛報
aiqing 愛情
*Aizhi jianbao* 愛知簡報
Aizibing jiaoyu yu teshu xingwenti yan-taohui 愛滋病教育與特殊性問題研討會
"Axiu" 阿繡
"Aying" 阿英

bai xiangzhi 拜相知
banzhuang tongzhi 扮裝同志
Baoyu 寶玉
"Bei wangque de" 被忘卻的
benzhi 本質
bi xiongdi gurou jian de qinggan hai yao qinmi 比兄弟骨肉間的情感還要親密
bianchang 變常
biantai 變態
biji 筆記
bing he 病鶴
Bing Xin 冰心
bu jia dang 不嫁黨

bu luojia 不落家
bu zhi nanse wei eshi 不知男色為惡事
bufen 不分

caiyuan 才媛
"Chang'e" 嫦娥
chaoxingbie yishi 超性別意識
Chen Weisong 陳維崧
"Chenlun" 沈淪
chu gui 出櫃
chungong 春宮
ci 詞
ci su de neimu, ju wo kan guanyu tong-xing lian yi fangmian duo xie 此俗的內幕,據我看關於同性戀一方面多些

Daiyu 黛玉
dajia xiang'ai 大家相愛
"Dapo lian'ai meng" 打破戀愛夢
duan xiu 斷袖
duli renge 獨立人格
dushen zhuyi nüzi 獨身主義女子

341

Fan Shiyiniang　范十一娘
"Fangzhou"　方舟
*Fanhua meng*　繁華夢
*Fei du*　廢都
fei peng　飛鵬
feng　風
"Feng Sanniang"　封三娘
Feng Yuan　馮淵
Feng Yuanjun　馮沅君
Feng Zhenluan　馮鎮巒
fengqi　風氣
fu　婦
fu nü yu nü tongxing zhi xiang lian'ai shi
　　tongyu nanzi zhi hao nanse　夫女與女
　　同性之相戀愛實同於男子之好男色
fudao shi　輔導室
fuke　婦科
*Funü shibao*　婦女時報
"Funü tongxing zhi aiqing"　婦女同性
　　之愛情
funü wenti　婦女問題
*Funü xinzhi*　婦女新知
*Funü zazhi*　婦女雜誌
"Fuqin"　父親

Gao Jianhua　高劍華
gaoxiao　高小
geminghua de tongzhi ai　革命化的同
　　志愛
gerenhua xiezuo　個人化寫作
gu　蠱
Gu Renchai　顧紉苣
guang gun　光棍

"Haibin guren"　海濱故人
hao nanse　好男色
He Peizhu　何佩珠
He Shouqi　何守奇
huai fenzi　壞份子
huangse　黃色
hunyin zhidu bu liang　婚姻制度不良

"Ji nü"　績女
jia　家
jia feng xu huang　假鳳虛凰
Jia Pingwa　賈平凹
jian　姦
Jiang Dehua　姜德華
"Jiang Xingge chong hui zhenzhu shan"
　　蔣興哥重會珍珠衫
Jiangzhu Nüshi　絳珠女史

"Jiaonuo"　嬌娜
"Jiaose leizhui"　角色累贅
*Jiaoyu zazhi*　教育雜誌
jibing　疾病
"Ji'e de koudai"　飢餓的口袋
jie tongxing ai de niyou　結同性愛的膩友
jiemei　姐妹(姊妹)
jiemei qingyi　姐妹情誼
Jiemei tongzhi　姊妹同志
jiemei zhi bang　姐妹之邦
jijian　雞姦
*Jin ping mei*　金瓶梅
jindai　近代
jing　精
jing pai　京派
jinghua　淨化
jinlan hui　金蘭會
*Jinshi fayixue*　近世法醫學

kaifa shichang　開發市場
Kaiming shudian　開明書店
koa-a-hi　歌仔戲
"Kongxinren dansheng"　空心人誕生
ku ai nanfeng bu xi nüse　酷愛男風不
　　喜女色
kuer lunshu　酷兒論述
kunhuo　困惑

lawang　拉網
lazi　拉子
leisibian　蕾絲邊
leisipin　累斯嬪
li　禮
Li Bo　李白
"Liancheng"　連城
Liang Guiqin　梁桂琴
"Lianxiang"　蓮香
*Lihua meng*　梨花夢
Lin Duomi　林多米
"Ling yizhi erduo de qiaoji sheng"　另一
　　隻耳朵的敲擊聲
lingrou heyi　靈肉合一
"Linju"　鄰居
"Lishi de riji"　麗石的日記
"Liudao zhi yipie"　柳島之一瞥
liumang xingwei　流氓行為
Lu Qingzi　陸卿子
Lu Yin　廬隱

"Maisuinü yu shouguaren"　麥穗女與
　　守寡人

meili de duyao　美麗的毒藥
*Meiyu*　眉語
"*Meiyu* xuanyan"　眉語宣言
Meng Anren　孟安仁
Meng Lijun　孟麗君
*Menglan suobi*　夢闌瑣筆
Ming　明
mingji　名妓
mo jing dang　磨鏡黨
mo jingzi　磨鏡子
"Muyu"　沐浴

nan bu nan nü bu nü　男不男女不女
nan nü xing de daozhi　男女性的倒置
nan tongzhi　男同志
nan xianggong　男相公
nanfeng　男風
nanfeng　南風
nannü zhi lian'ai　男女之戀愛
nanren po　男人婆
nanse　男色
nanse yi dao　男色一道
nei/wai　內／外
Ni Aoao　倪拗拗
nü　女
nü boli　女玻璃
nü nanzi　女男子
*Nü pengyou*　女朋友
nü tongxing'ai　女同性愛
nü tongxinglian　女同性戀
nü tongxinglianzhe　女同性戀者
nü tongzhi　女同志
Nü tongzhi huiyi　女同志會議
nü tongzhi yundong　女同志運動
nü yan she　女研社
nüxing si xiaoshuo　女性私小說
nüxing yishi　女性意識
nüzi tongxing lian'ai　女子同性戀愛
nüzi zhi tongxing lian　女子之同性戀

ou duo qingzhang　偶墮情障

pi　癖

qi　氣
qiangpo yixinglian jizhi　強迫異性戀
　機制
"Qianxing yishi"　潛性逸事
qing　情
Qing　清
*Qing shi*　情史

qing wan　情玩
qinggan koushu shilu　情感口述實錄
qingjie zhi ai yan　情節之哀豔
qingkuang　清狂
"Qingmei"　青梅
qingyu zhi biantai　情慾之變態
qingyu zhi diandao　情慾之顛倒
"Qinjiliao"　秦吉了
qipao　旗袍
qite de fengsu　奇特的風俗
Qu Yuan　屈原
quanzili de ren　圈子裡的人

*Re'ai zazhi*　熱愛雜誌
rencai　人材
renlei　人類

san lian　三戀
se　色
se er bu yin　色而不淫
se xiang　色相
"Shafei nüshi de riji"　莎菲女士的日記
shangye wu zui, xiaofei you li　商業無
　罪，消費有理
"Shao nü"　邵女
shen jiao　神交
"Shen nü"　神女
shenfen zhengzhi　身份政治
shenglai jiu you nanxing de xingge　生來
　就有男性的性格
*Shengsi chang*　生死場
*Sheyang zhenzhongfang*　攝養枕中方
shi buzu weixun de bimo　是不足為訓
　的筆墨
shiji de kuqi　世紀的哭泣
shuangxinglian tongzhi　雙性戀同志
sixiang juewu　思想覺悟
Song　宋
"Songluo shan xia"　松蘿山下

T-po　T婆
"Tai yi"　胎異
Taibei tongwanjie　台北同玩節
tanchu　探觸
tanci　彈詞
Tao　道
tezhi　特質
*Tiankong*　天空
tongnü　同女
tongxing　同性
tongxing ai (tongxing'ai)　同性愛

tongxing ai de jiufen 同性愛的糾紛
tongxing de ai 同性的愛
tongxing de ailian 同性的愛戀
tongxing jian zhongqing qilai le 同性間
　　鐘情起來了
tongxing lian (tongxinglian) 同性戀
tongxing lian'ai 同性戀愛
tongxing lianren 同性戀人
tongxing zhi ai 同性之愛
tongxing zhi lian 同性之戀
tongzhi 同志
*Tugo zazhi* 土狗雜誌
tuifei 頹廢

Wang Jide 王驥德
Wang Yun 王筠
weixie 猥褻
Wenxue yanjiu hui 文學研究會
"Wo zai Xiacun de shihou" 我在霞村
　　的時候
Women zhi jian 我們之間
Wu Jianlu 吳劍鹿
*Wu nü yuan* 五女緣
"Wuchu gaobie" 無處告別

xian 仙
xian shen 現身
xiandai zhishi jieji de nüzi 現代知識階
　　級的女子
"Xiangyu" 香玉
Xiao Hong 蕭紅
xiao jiating 小家庭
Xiaoqing 小青
*Xiaoshuo yuebao* 小説月報
"Xiaoxie" 小謝
Xie Xucai 謝絮才
Xie Xuexian 謝雪仙
xifang meiren 西方美人
Xin ganjue pai 新感覺派
Xin guixiu pai 新閨秀派
*Xin nüxing* 新女性
*Xin qingnian* 新青年
*Xin wenhua* 新文化
xin wenyi 新文藝
xing 性
Xing kexue 性科學
xingbie 性別

Xingbie renquan xiehui 性別人權協會
xingdaocuo yiyi shang de tongxinglian
　　性倒錯意義上的同性戀
Xinwen chuban shu 新聞出版署
Xu Xiaobin 徐小彬
Xu Xiaotian 許嘯天
Xu Yuan 徐媛
xunjing mei 馴靜美

yangwu chongbai 陽物崇拜
Ye Xiaowan 葉小紈
yi hua 異化
yichang 異常
*Yichun xiangzhi* 宜春香質
yifu yiqi zhi 一夫一妻制
yin 淫
yin yang 陰陽
"Yingning" 嬰寧
yinhui 淫穢
yixing 異性
yixing zhijian de ai 異性之間的愛
yixinglian 異性戀
you 友
yu 愁
yu 欲
*Yu si* 語絲
yuanzhumin 原住民
*Yuanyang meng* 鴛鴦夢

"Zeng Wumen Qinglin jiaoshu" 贈吳門
　　青林校書
zhaohuan 召喚
zhencao 貞操
zhengzhi secai 政治色彩
zhi 智
zhiguai 志怪
zhong gu 中蠱
*Zhonghua dushu bao* 中華讀書報
zhuzhang jingshen shenghuo 主張精
　　神生活
zibi 自閉
Zili nüxue 自立女學
zilian 自戀
zishu 自梳
zixushi 自敘式
ziyou lian'ai 自由戀愛

# SELECT BIBLIOGRAPHY

Abelove, Henry, Michèle Aina Barale, and David M. Halperin, eds. *The Lesbian and Gay Studies Reader.* New York: Routledge, 1993.

"Aihen shuangxinglian" 愛恨雙性戀 (Love hate bisexuals). *Nü pengyou,* no. 3 (1995): 7–15.

Althusser, Louis. *Lenin and Philosophy.* Translated by Ben Brewster. New York: Monthly Review Press, 1971.

Altman, Dennis. *The Homosexualization of America, the Americanization of the Homosexual.* New York: St. Martin's, 1982.

———. *Global Sex.* Chicago: University of Chicago Press, 2001.

An Dun 安頓. *Juedui yinsi* 絕對隱私 (Absolute privacy). Beijing: Xin shijie chubanshe, 1998.

An Keqiang 安克強. *Hong taiyang xia de hei linghun* 紅太陽下的黑靈魂 (Black souls under the red sun). Taipei: Shibao wenhua, 1995.

———. "Prelude." *G&L: Re'ai zazhi,* no. 1 (1996): 8.

Anderson, Benedict. *Imagined Community: Reflections on the Origin and the Spread of Nationalism.* Rev. ed. London: Verso, 1991.

Anzaldúa, Gloria. *Borderlands/La Frontera: The New Mestiza.* San Francisco: Spinsters/Aunt Lute, 1987.

Appadurai, Arjun. *Modernity at Large.* Minneapolis: University of Minnesota Press, 1996.

Austin, J. L. *How to Do Things with Words.* Cambridge, Mass.: Harvard University Press, 1962.

Bai Peiji 白佩姬. "Wenhua yu zhengzhi de shuang quxian" 文化與政治的雙曲線 (The double curves of culture and politics). In *Kuer qishilu: Taiwan dangdai QUEER lunshu duben*, ed. Ta-wei Chi, 211–18. Taipei: Yuanzun wenhua, 1997.

Bao Qin 抱嶔. "Bu jia hui" 不嫁會 (The refuse-to-marry party). In *Funü xianxing ji* 婦女現形記 (Women's true forms exposed), ed. Lankeshanqiao 爛柯山樵, 2:42–44. Shanghai: Putong shuju, 1919.

Barlow, Tani E. Introduction to *I Myself Am a Woman: Selected Writings of Ding Ling*, ed. Tani E. Barlow with Gary J. Bjorge, 1–45. Boston: Beacon, 1989.

———. "*Zhishifenzi* (Chinese Intellectuals) and Power." *Dialectical Anthropology* 16 (1990): 209–32.

———, ed. *Gender Politics in Modern China: Writing and Feminism*. Durham, N.C.: Duke University Press, 1993.

———. "Politics and Protocols of *Funü*: (Un)making National Woman." In *Engendering China: Women, Culture, and the State*, ed. Christina K. Gilmartin et al., 339–59. Cambridge, Mass.: Harvard University Press, 1994.

———. "Theorizing Woman: *Funü, Guojia, Jiating*." In *Body, Subject, and Power in China*, ed. Angela Zito and Tani E. Barlow, 253–89. Chicago: University of Chicago Press, 1994.

———. Introduction to *Formations of Colonial Modernity in East Asia*, ed. Tani Barlow, 1–20. Durham, N.C.: Duke University Press, 1997.

Baudrillard, Jean. *Selected Writings*. Edited by Mark Poster. Stanford, Calif.: Stanford University Press, 1988.

Bergere, Marie-Claire. *The Golden Age of the Chinese Bourgeoisie, 1911–1937*. Translated by Janet Lloyd. New York: Cambridge University Press, 1990.

Berlant, Lauren. *The Queen of America Goes to Washington City: Essays on Sex and Citizenship*. Durham, N.C.: Duke University Press, 1997.

Bernhardt, Kathryn. *Women and Property in China, 960–1949*. Stanford, Calif.: Stanford University Press, 1999.

Berry, Chris. *A Bit on the Side: East-West Topographies of Desire*. Sydney: EMPress, 1994.

Bhabha, Homi K. "Of Mimicry and Man." *October*, no. 28 (1984): 125–33.

———. *The Location of Culture*. New York: Routledge, 1994.

Bland, Lucy, and Laura Doan, eds. *Sexology in Culture*. Chicago: University of Chicago Press, 1998.

Boellstorff, Tom. "The Perfect Path: Gay Men, Marriage, Indonesia." *GLQ* 5, no. 4 (1999): 475–509.

Boswell, John. *Christianity, Social Tolerance, and Homosexuality*. Chicago: University of Chicago Press, 1980.

———. "Revolutions, Universals, and Sexual Categories." In *Hidden from History: Reclaiming the Gay and Lesbian Past*, ed. Martin Duberman, Martha Vicinus, and George Chauncey Jr., 17–36. New York: Meridian, 1990.

———. *Same-Sex Unions in Premodern Europe*. New York: Villard, 1994.

Bourdieu, Pierre. *Language and Symbolic Power*. Translated by Gino Raymond and Matthew Adamson. Cambridge, Mass.: Harvard University Press, 1994.

Bristow, Joseph. "Symonds's History, Ellis's Heredity: Sexual Inversion." In *Sexology in Culture*, ed. Lucy Bland and Laura Doan, 79–99. Chicago: University of Chicago Press, 1998.

Brome, Vincent. *Havelock Ellis, Philosopher of Sex: A Biography*. London: Routledge & Kegan Paul, 1979.

Brown, Judith. *Immodest Acts*. Oxford: Oxford University Press, 1986.

Burton, Margaret E. *The Education of Women in China*. New York: Fleming H. Revell, 1911.

Butler, Judith. *Gender Trouble: Feminism and the Subversion of Identity.* New York: Routledge, 1990.

———. *Bodies That Matter: On the Discursive Limits of "Sex."* New York: Routledge, 1993.

———. "Against Proper Objects." *Differences* 6, nos. 2–3 (1994): 1–26.

———. "Sexual Traffic." Interview with Gayle Rubin. *Differences* 6, nos. 2–3 (1994): 62–99.

———. *Excitable Speech: A Politics of the Performative.* New York: Routledge, 1997.

Calinescu, Matei. *Five Faces of Modernity: Modernism, Avant-Garde, Decadence, Kitch, Postmodernism.* Durham, N.C.: Duke University Press, 1987.

Cao Lijuan 曹麗娟. "Tongnü zhi wu" 同女之舞 (The dance of a virgin). In *Xiaoshuo chao* 小說潮 (The tide of fiction), ed. Ya Xian 瘂弦, 7–37. Taipei: Lianjing, 1992.

———. *Guanyu baifa ji qita* 關於白髮及其他 (About her white hair and other things). *Lianhe wenxue,* no. 145 (1997): 62–89.

Cao Xueqin 曹雪芹. *Honglou meng bashihui jiaoben* 紅樓夢八十回校本 (The dream of the red chamber, a collated edition of the first eighty chapters). Collated by Wang Xishi 王惜時. Proofread by Yu Pingbo 俞平伯. 2 vols. Beijing: Renmin wenxue chubanshe, 1993.

Carpenter, Edward. "Affection in Education." In *The Intermediate Sex.* London: Allen & Unwin, 1908.

———. "The Homogenic Attachment." In *The Intermediate Sex,* 39–82. London: Allen & Unwin, 1908.

———. *The Intermediate Sex.* London: Allen & Unwin, 1908.

———. *Love's Coming of Age.* 1896. Reprint, New York: M. Kennerley, 1911.

———. *My Days and Dreams: Being Autobiographical Notes.* 2d ed. London: Allen & Unwin, 1916.

Case, Sue-Ellen. "Seduced and Abandoned: Chicanas and Lesbians in Representation." In *Negotiating Performance: Gender, Sexuality, and Theatricality in Latina/o America,* ed. Diana Taylor and Juan Villegas, 88–101. Durham, N.C.: Duke University Press, 1994.

Cass, Victoria. *Dangerous Women: Warriors, Grannies, and Geishas of the Ming.* Lanham, Md.: Rowman & Littlefield, 1999.

Castle, Terry. *The Apparitional Lesbian: Female Homosexuality and Modern Culture.* New York: Columbia University Press, 1993.

Chang, Hsiao-hung (Zhang Xiaohong) 張小虹. "Zai zhangli zhong huxiang kanjian" 在張力中互相看見 (Seeing each other in tension). *Funü xinzhi,* no. 158 (1995): 5–8.

———. *Yuwang xin ditu* 慾望新地圖 (Queer desire: Gender and sexuality). Taipei: Lianhe wenxue chubanshe, 1996.

———. *Zilian nüren* 自戀女人 (Narcissistic women). Taipei: Lianhe wenxue chubanshe, 1996.

Chang, Kang-i Sun, and Haun Saussy, eds. *Women Writers of Traditional China: An Anthology of Poetry and Criticism.* Stanford, Calif.: Stanford University Press, 1999.

Chang, Sung-sheng Yvonne. "Chu T'ien-wen and Taiwan's Recent Cultural and Literary Trends." *Modern Chinese Literature* 6, no. 1 (1992): 61–81.

———. *Modernism and the Nativist Resistance: Contemporary Chinese Fiction from Taiwan.* Durham, N.C.: Duke University Press, 1993.

———. "Beyond Cultural and National Identities: Current Re-Evaluation of the Kominka Literature from Taiwan's Japanese Period." In *Modern Chinese Literature and Cultural Studies in the Age of Theory: Reimagining a Field,* ed. Rey Chow, 99–126. Durham, N.C.: Duke University Press, 2000.

Changbai Haogezi 長白浩歌子. *Yingchuang yicao* 螢窗異草 (Unusual grass by the firefly window). In *Biji xiaoshuo daguan* 筆記小說大觀 (A collection of the reprints of notation books), 19:4927–5060. Taipei: Xinxing shuju, 1960.

Chao, Yengning Antonia (Zhao Yenning) 趙彥寧. "Embodying the Invisible: Body Politics in Constructing Contemporary Taiwanese Lesbian Identities." Ph.D. diss., Cornell University, 1996.

———. "Chugui huo bu chugui: Zhe shi yige youguan heian de wenti" 出櫃或不出櫃：這是一個有關黑暗的問題 (Come out or not: This is a question concerning darkness). *Saodong*, no. 3 (1997): 59–64.

Chauncey, George, Jr. "From Sexual Inversion to Homosexuality: Medicine and the Changing Conceptualization of Female Deviance." *Salmagundi*, nos. 58–59 (1982–83): 114–45.

Chen Chaonan 陳超南 and Feng Yiyou 馮懿有, eds. *Lao guanggao* 老廣告 (Old advertisements). Shanghai: Shanghai renmin meishu chubanshe, 1998.

Chen Chongguang 陳重光. "Min'guo chuqi funü diwei de yanbian" 民國初期婦女地位的演變 (Changes in women's status in the early Republican period). Master's thesis, Wenhua University, 1972.

Chen Dongyuan 陳東原. "Guanyu 'Guangdong de bu luojia he zishu'" 關於「廣東的不落家和自梳」 (About "The delayed transfer marriage and sworn spinsterhood in Canton"). *Xin nüxing* 2, no. 2 (1927): 203–6.

———. *Zhongguo funü shenghuo shi* 中國婦女生活史 (The history of the lives of Chinese women). Shanghai: Shangwu yinshuguan, 1928; reprint, Taipei: Taiwan Shangwu yinshuguan, 1970.

Chen Duansheng 陳端生 and Liang Desheng 梁德繩. *Zai sheng yuan* 再生緣 (The destiny of another lifetime). Henan: Zhongzhou shuhuashe, 1982.

Chen Fangming 陳芳明. "Houxiandai huo houzhimin: Zhanhou Taiwan wenxue shi de yige jieshi" 後現代或後殖民：戰後台灣文學史的一個解釋 (Postmodern or postcolonial: An interpretation of postwar Taiwan's literary history). In *Shuxie Taiwan: Wenxue shi, houzhimin yu houxiandai,* ed. Ying-Hsiung Chou and Joyce Chi-Hui Liu, 41–63. Taipei: Maitian, 2000.

Chen Ran 陳染. *Zuichunli de yangguang* 嘴唇裡的陽光 (Sunshine between the lips). Wuhan: Changjiang wenyi chubanshe, 1992.

———. "Chaoxingbie yishi yu wode chuangzuo" 超性別意識與我的創作 (Gender-transcendent consciousness and my creative writing). *Zhongshan*, no. 93 (1994): 105–7.

———. *Chen Ran wenji* 陳染文集 (The works of Chen Ran). 4 vols. Nanjing: Jiangsu wenyi chubanshe, 1996.

———. *Chen Ran zuopin zixuanji* 陳染作品自選集 (The self-selected works of Chen Ran). 2 vols. Beijing: Guangming ribao chubanshe, 1996.

———. "Ling yishan kaiqi de men" 另一扇開啓的門 (Another open door). Interview by Xiaogang 蕭剛. In *Siren shenghuo*, by Chen Ran, 247–77. Beijing: Zuojia chubanshe, 1996.

———. "Pokai" 破開 (Breaking through). In *Chen Ran zuopin zixuanji*, 1:411–42. Beijing: Guangming ribao chubanshe, 1996.

———. *Siren shenghuo* 私人生活 (Private life). Beijing: Zuojia chubanshe, 1996.

———. *A'er xiaowu* 阿爾小屋 (The house of Arles). Beijing: Huayi chubanshe, 1998.

———, ed. *Buke yanshuo* 不可言説 (Beyond language). Beijing: Zuojia chubanshe, 2000.

———. "Chaoxingbie yishi yu tongxing'ai" 超性別意識與同性愛 (Gender-transcendent consciousness and same-sex love). Interview by Tze-lan Sang 桑梓蘭. In *Buke yanshuo*, ed. Chen Ran, 101–39. Beijing: Zuojia chubanshe, 2000.

———. *Sheng sheng sheng duan* 聲聲聲斷 (Broken sounds). Beijing: Zuojia chubanshe, 2000.

———. "You yizhong ku'nan yusheng julai" 有一種苦難與生俱來 (There is a kind of suffering that comes with birth). In *Sheng sheng sheng duan* (Broken sounds), 130–32. Beijing: Zuojia chubanshe, 2000.

Chen Sen 陳森. *Pinhua baojian* 品花寶鑑 (A precious mirror for classifying flowers). 2 vols. Beijing: Renmin Zhongguo chubanshe, 1993.

Chen Sihe 陳思和. "Lin Bai lun" 林白論 (On Lin Bai). In *Shuoba, fangjian,* by Lin Bai, 247–61. Taipei: Sanmin shuju, 1998.

Chen, Xiaomei. "Growing Up with Posters in the Maoist Era." In *Picturing Power in the People's Republic of China: Posters of the Cultural Revolution,* ed. Harriet Evans and Stephanie Donald, 101–22. Lanham, Md.: Rowman & Littlefield, 1999.

Chen Xiaoming 陳曉明. *Wubian de tiaozhan: Zhongguo xianfeng wenxue de houxiandaixing* 無邊的挑戰: 中國先鋒文學的後現代性 (Boundless challenge: The postmodernity of Chinese avant-garde literature). Changchun: Shidai wenyi chubanshe, 1993.

———. "Yuwang ru shui: Xingbie de shenhua" 欲望如水: 性別的神話 (Water-like desire: The myth of gender). *Zhongshan,* no. 85 (1993): 137–43.

Chen Xue 陳雪. *E nü shu* 惡女書 (The book of an evil woman). Taipei: Huangguan, 1995.

———. *Mengyou 1994* 夢遊一九九四 (Sleepwalking in 1994). Taipei: Yuanliu, 1996.

Cheng Hao 程浩. *Renlei de xing shenghuo* 人類的性生活 (The sexual life of mankind). Shanghai: Yadong shuju, 1934.

Chi, Ta-wei (Ji Dawei) 紀大偉. "Kuer lun" 酷兒論 (On queer). In *Kuer qishilu: Taiwan dangdai QUEER lunshu duben,* ed. Ta-wei Chi, 9–16. Taipei: Yuanzun wenhua, 1997.

———, ed. *Kuer qishilu: Taiwan dangdai QUEER lunshu duben* 酷兒啓示錄: 台灣當代 QUEER 論述讀本 (Queer archipelago: A reader of the queer discourses in Taiwan). Taipei: Yuanzun wenhua, 1997.

Chi, Ta-wei 紀大偉, and Lin Xiumei 林秀梅, comps. "Taiwan tongzhi wenxue yu wenhua yanjiu shumu" 台灣同志文學與文化研究書目 (A bibliography of Taiwanese lesbian and gay literature and cultural studies). In *Yuwang xin ditu,* by Hsiao-hung Chang, 247–81. Taipei: Lianhe wenxue chubanshe, 1996.

Chi, Ta-wei 紀大偉, et al. "Xiaoyuan tongxinglian ri" 校園同性戀日 (Gay and Lesbian Awakening Day on campus). *Funü xinzhi,* no. 158 (1995): 22–28.

Chien, Ying-ying (Jian Yingying) 簡瑛瑛. *Hechu shi nüer jia* 何處是女兒家 (Where is the home of daughters?). Taipei: Lianjing, 1998.

Chin, Tamara. "Translingual Tongzhi, 1998." University of California, Berkeley, Department of Comparative Literature, 1998. Typescript.

Chou Wah-shan (Zhou Huashan) 周華山, ed. *Beijing tongzhi gushi* 北京同志故事 (Stories of Beijing *tongzhi*). Hong Kong: Xianggang tongzhi yanjiushe, 1996.

———. "Shi tongxing ai, bushi tongxing bing" 是同性愛, 不是同性病 (It's same-sex love, not same-sex disease). In *Beijing tongzhi gushi,* ed. Chou Wah-shan, 9–37. Hong Kong: Xianggang tongzhi yanjiushe, 1996.

———. *Hou zhimin tongzhi* 後殖民同志 (Postcolonial *tongzhi*). Hong Kong: Xianggang tongzhi yanjiushe, 1997.

———. *Tongzhi: Politics of Same-Sex Eroticism in Chinese Societies.* New York: Haworth, 2000.

Chou Wah-shan 周華山, et al. "Zhongxi wenhua chayi yu huaren tongzhi yundong de fangxiang" 中西文化差異與華人同志運動的方向 (Differences between Chinese and Western cultures and the direction of the Chinese lesbigay and transgender movements, a panel discussion). In *Huaren tongzhi xin duben,* ed. Lu Jianxiong, 45–57. Hong Kong: Huasheng shudian, 1999.

Chou, Ying-Hsiung (Zhou Yingxiong) 周英雄, and Joyce Chi-Hui Liu (Liu Jihui) 劉紀蕙, eds. *Shuxie Taiwan: Wenxue shi, houzhimin yu houxiandai* 書寫台灣: 文學史, 後殖民與後現代 (Writing Taiwan: Literary history, postcolonial and postmodern). Taipei: Maitian, 2000.

Chow, Rey. *Woman and Chinese Modernity: The Politics of Reading between West and East.* Minnesota: University of Minnesota Press, 1991.

———. *Writing Diaspora: Tactics of Intervention in Contemporary Cultural Studies.* Bloomington: Indiana University Press, 1993.

———, ed. *Modern Chinese Literature and Cultural Studies in the Age of Theory: Reimagining a Field.* Durham, N.C.: Duke University Press, 2000.

Chow, Tse-tsung. *The May Fourth Movement: Intellectual Revolution in Modern China.* Stanford, Calif.: Stanford University Press, 1960.

Chu Anmin 初安民. "Qianyan" 前言 (Editor's preface). *Lianhe wenxue,* no. 131 (1995): 15.

Chu, Wei-cheng (Zhu Weicheng) 朱偉誠. "Kua xingbie yundong de Taiwan sisuo" 跨性別運動的台灣思索 (Reflections on the transgender movement in Taiwan). *Chengpin haodu,* no. 5 (2000): 8–10.

Chun, Allen. "Discourses of Identity in the Changing Spaces of Public Culture in Taiwan, Hong Kong, and Singapore." *Theory, Culture, and Society* 13, no. 1 (1996): 51–75.

Cui Zien 崔子恩. "Zhongguo tongxinglian shengtai baogao" 中國同性戀生態報告 (A report on homosexuality's state of survival in China). *Xiandai wenming huabao,* no. 119 (2002): 6–23.

Cunningham, Gail. *The New Woman and the Victorian Novel.* New York: Barnes & Noble, 1978.

Dai Jinhua 戴錦華. "Chen Ran: Geren he nüxing de shuxie" 陳染: 個人和女性的書寫 (Chen Ran: Individualized and female writing). In *Chen Ran zuopin zixuanji,* by Chen Ran, 2:382–402. Beijing: Guangming ribao chubanshe, 1996.

———. "Qiyu yu tuwei: Jiushi niandai nüxing xiezuo" 奇遇與突圍: 九十年代女性寫作 (Unexpected encounters and breaking out of a blockade: Female writing in the 1990s). *Wenxue pinglun* 1996, no. 5 (September): 95–102.

———. "Rewriting Chinese Women: Gender Production and Cultural Space in the Eighties and Nineties." Translated by Yu Ning with the assistance of Mayfair Yang. In *Spaces of Their Own: Women's Public Sphere in Transnational China,* ed. Mayfair Yang, 191–206. Minneapolis: University of Minnesota Press, 1999.

Dal Lago, Francesca. "Crossed Legs in 1930s Shanghai: How 'Modern' the Modern Woman?" *East Asian History,* no. 19 (2000): 103–43.

Davis, Deborah, Richard Kraus, Barry Naughton, and Elizabeth Perry, eds. *Urban Spaces in Contemporary China: The Potential for Autonomy and Community in Post-Mao China.* Cambridge: Cambridge University Press, 1995.

Deleuze, Gilles. *Masochism.* New York: Zone, 1991.

D'Emilio, John. "Capitalism and Gay Identity." In *Powers of Desire: The Politics of Sexuality,* ed. Ann Snitow, Christine Stanswell, and Sharon Thompson, 100–113. New York: Monthly Review Press, 1983.

———. *Sexual Politics, Sexual Communities: The Making of a Homosexual Minority in the United States, 1940–1970.* Chicago: University of Chicago Press, 1983.

D'Emilio, John, and Estelle B. Freedman. *Intimate Matters: A History of Sexuality in America.* 2d ed. Chicago: University of Chicago Press, 1997.

Diamant, Neil. *Revolutionizing the Family: Politics, Love, and Divorce in Urban and Rural China, 1949–1968.* Berkeley and Los Angeles: University of California Press, 2000.

Dikötter, Frank. *Sex, Culture, and Modernity in China.* Honolulu: University of Hawaii Press, 1995.

Ding Laixian 丁來先. "Nüxing wenxue ji qita" 女性文學及其他 (Female literature and other things). *Zhonghua dushu bao,* 20 December 1995.

———. "Wo xiangxin jiandan pusu zhi li" 我相信簡單樸素之理 (I believe in simple truths). *Zhonghua dushu bao,* 7 February 1996.

Ding Ling 丁玲. *Ding Ling wenxuan* 丁玲文選 (Selected writings by Ding Ling). Shanghai: Qizhi shuju, 1936.

———. "Shujia zhong" 暑假中. (Summer break). In *Ding Ling wenxuan,* 145–206. Shanghai: Qizhi shuju, 1936.

Dinshaw, Carolyn. *Getting Medieval: Sexualities and Communities, Pre- and Postmodern.* Durham, N.C.: Duke University Press, 1999.

Dirlik, Arif. *Revolution and History: The Origins of Marxist Historiography in China, 1919–1937.* Berkeley and Los Angeles: University of California Press, 1978.

———. "Is There History after Eurocentrism? Globalism, Postcolonialism, and the Disavowal of History." In *History after the Three Worlds: Post-Eurocentric Historiographies,* ed. Arif Dirlik, Vinay Bahl, and Peter Gran, 25–47. Lanham, Md.: Rowman & Littlefield, 2000.

———. "Reversals, Ironies, Hegemonies: Notes on the Contemporary Historiography of Modern China." In *History after the Three Worlds: Post-Eurocentric Historiographies,* ed. Arif Dirlik, Vinay Bahl, and Peter Gran, 125–56. Lanham, Md.: Rowman & Littlefield, 2000.

Dirlik, Arif, Vinay Bahl, and Peter Gran, eds. *History after the Three Worlds: Post-Eurocentric Historiographies.* Lanham, Md.: Rowman & Littlefield, 2000.

"Diyici dalu nü tongzhi huiyi zhaokai" 第一次大陸女同志會議召開 (The first mainland Chinese lesbian conference was held). *Tiankong,* no. 1 (1999): 18.

Du Xiulan 杜修蘭. *Ni nü* 逆女 (Rebel daughter). Taipei: Huangguan, 1996.

Duara, Prasenjit. *Rescuing History from the Nation: Questioning Narratives of Modern China.* Chicago: University of Chicago Press, 1995.

Duberman, Martin, Martha Vicinus, and George Chauncey Jr., eds. *Hidden from History: Reclaiming the Gay and Lesbian Past.* New York: Meridian, 1990.

"Duzhe lai han" 讀者來函 (A letter from a reader). *G&L: Re'ai zazhi,* no. 15 (1998): 5.

Eisenstadt, S. N. "Multiple Modernities." *Daedalus* 129, no. 1 (2000): 1–29.

Ellis, Havelock. *Studies in the Psychology of Sex.* 1st ed. Vol. 1, *The Evolution of Modesty; The Phenomena of Sexual Periodicity and Auto-Eroticism.* Philadelphia: F. A. Davis, 1900. Vol. 2, *Sexual Inversion* (with J. A. Symonds). London: Watford University Press, 1897. Reprint. Philadelphia: F. A. Davis, 1901. Vol. 3, *Analysis of the Sexual Impulse; Love and Pain; The Sexual Impulse in Women.* Philadelphia: F. A. Davis, 1903. Vol. 4, *Sexual Selection in Man.* Philadelphia: F. A. Davis, 1905. Vol. 5, *Erotic Symbolism; The Mechanism of Detumescence; The Psychic State in Pregnancy.* Philadelphia: F. A. Davis, 1906. Vol. 6, *Sex in Relation to Society.* Philadelphia: F. A. Davis, 1910. Vol. 7, *Eonism and Other Supplementary Studies.* Philadelphia: F. A. Davis, 1928.

———. "Appendix: The School-Friendships of Girls." In *Studies in the Psychology of Sex* (3d ed.), vol. 2, *Sexual Inversion,* 368–84. Philadelphia: F. A. Davis, 1920.

———. *The Psychology of Sex: A Manual for Students.* 2d ed. New York: Emerson, 1944.

Ellis, Havelock, and J. A. Symonds. *Das konträre Geschlechtsgefühl.* Translated by Hans Kurella. Leipzig: Georg H. Wigand, 1896.

*Encyclopaedia Sexualis: A Comprehensive Encyclopaedia-Dictionary of the Sexual Sciences.* Edited by Victor Robinson. New York: Dingwall-Rock, in collaboration with Medical Review of Reviews, 1936.

Engelhardt, Ute. "Qi for Life." In *Taoist Meditation and Longevity Techniques,* ed. Livia Kohn, 263–69. Ann Arbor: University of Michigan, Center for Chinese Studies, 1989.

Epstein, Maram. *Competing Discourses: Orthodoxy, Authenticity, and Engendered Meanings in Late Imperial Chinese Fiction.* Cambridge, Mass.: Harvard University, Asia Center, 2001.

Essick, Robert N., and Morton D. Paley. *Robert Blair's "The Grave."* London: Scolar, 1982.

Evans, Harriet. *Women and Sexuality in China: Dominant Discourses of Female Sexuality and Gender since 1949.* New York: Continuum, 1997.

Evans, Harriet, and Stephanie Donald, eds. *Picturing Power in the People's Republic of China: Posters of the Cultural Revolution.* Lanham, Md.: Rowman & Littlefield, 1999.

Faderman, Lillian. *Surpassing the Love of Men: Romantic Friendship and Love between Women from the Renaissance to the Present.* New York: William Morrow, 1981.

Faderman, Lillian, and Brigitte Eriksson, eds. *Lesbian Feminism in Turn-of-the-Century Germany.* Weatherby Lake, Mo.: Naiad, 1980.

Fairbank, John. *China: A New History.* Cambridge, Mass.: Harvard University Press, 1992.

Fang Gang 方剛. *Tongxinglian zai Zhongguo* 同性戀在中國 (Homosexuality in China). Changchun: Jilin renmin chubanshe, 1995.

———. *Zhongguo bianxingren xianxiang* 中國變性人現象 (The phenomenon of Chinese transsexuals). Guangzhou: Guangzhou chubanshe, 1996.

Farquhar, Judith. "Multiplicity, Point of View, and Responsibility in Traditional Chinese Healing." In *Body, Subject, and Power in China,* ed. Angela Zito and Tani E. Barlow, 78–102. Chicago: University of Chicago Press, 1994.

Fawubu diaochaju 法務部調查局, ed. *Zhonggong zhongyao fagui huibian, 1989–1990* 中共重要法規匯編 (An assemblage of the important legal regulations of the People's Republic of China, 1989–1990). Taipei: Fawubu diaochaju, 1991.

"Feichang qingchunqi" 非常青春期 (Extraordinary adolescence). *Nü pengyou,* no. 7 (1995): 6–14.

Feng Fei 馮飛. *Nüxing lun* 女性論 (On women). Shanghai: Zhonghua shuju, 1920.

Foucault, Michel. *The Archaeology of Knowledge.* Translated by A. M. Sheridan Smith. New York: Pantheon, 1972.

———. *The History of Sexuality.* Translated by Robert Hurley. Vol. 1, *An Introduction.* New York: Pantheon, 1978. Reprint, New York: Vintage, 1990. Vol. 2, *The Use of Pleasure.* New York: Pantheon, 1985. Reprint, New York: Vintage, 1990. Vol. 3, *The Care of the Self.* New York: Pantheon, 1986. Reprint. New York: Vintage, 1988.

Freud, Sigmund. "The Uncanny" (1919). In *The Standard Edition of the Complete Psychological Works of Sigmund Freud,* vol. 17, trans. James Strachey, 219–52. London: Hogarth, 1955.

———. "Fetishism" (1927). In *The Standard Edition of the Complete Psychological Works of Sigmund Freud,* vol. 21, trans. James Strachey, 152–57. London: Hogarth, 1961.

———. "Femininity" (1933). In *The Standard Edition of the Complete Psychological Works of Sigmund Freud,* vol. 22, trans. James Strachey, 112–35. London: Hogarth, 1964.

———. *The Standard Edition of the Complete Psychological Works of Sigmund Freud.* Translated by James Strachey. 24 vols. London: Hogarth, 1953–74.

Furth, Charlotte. "Androgynous Males and Deficient Females: Biology and Gender Boundaries in Sixteenth- and Seventeenth-Century China." In *The Lesbian and Gay Studies Reader,* ed. Henry Abelove, Michèle Aina Barale, and David M. Halperin, 479–97. New York: Routledge, 1993.

———. "Rethinking Van Gulik: Sexuality and Reproduction in Traditional Chinese Medicine." In *Engendering China: Women, Culture, and the State,* ed. Christina K. Gilmartin et al., 125–46. Cambridge, Mass.: Harvard University Press, 1994.

———. *A Flourishing Yin: Gender in China's Medical History, 960–1665.* Berkeley and Los Angeles: University of California Press, 1999.

Fuss, Diana. *Essentially Speaking*. New York: Routledge, 1989.

———, ed. *Inside/Out: Lesbian Theories, Gay Theories*. New York: Routledge, 1989.

Gallichan, Walter M. *The Psychology of Marriage*. New York: Frederick A. Stokes, 1917.

———. *A Textbook of Sex Education*. Boston: Small, Maynard, 1921.

Gao Mingxuan 高銘暄 et al., eds. *Zhongguo xingfa cidian* 中國刑法詞典 (A dictionary of the Chinese criminal code). Shanghai: Xuelin chubanshe, 1989.

Garber, Marjorie. *Vested Interests: Cross-Dressing and Cultural Anxiety*. New York: Harper Perennial, 1992.

———. *Vice Versa: Bisexuality and the Eroticism of Everyday Life*. New York: Touchstone, 1995.

Gezi 格子. *Miqing de rizi* 迷情的日子 (The days of bewildering love). Shenyang: Chunfeng wenyi chubanshe, 1999.

Gilmartin, Christina K. *Engendering the Chinese Revolution: Radical Women, Communist Politics, and Mass Movements in the 1920s*. Berkeley and Los Angeles: University of California Press, 1995.

Gilmartin, Christina K., Gail Hershatter, Lisa Rofel, and Tyrene White, eds. *Engendering China: Women, Culture, and the State*. Cambridge, Mass.: Harvard University Press, 1994.

Glosser, Susan. *Chinese Visions of Family and State, 1915–1923*. Berkeley and Los Angeles: University of California Press, in press.

Goodman, Bryna. "Being Public: The Politics of Representation in 1918 Shanghai." *Harvard Journal of Asiatic Studies* 60, no. 1 (2000): 45–88.

Grewal, Inderpal, and Caren Kaplan, eds. *Scattered Hegemony: Postmodernity and Transnational Feminist Practices*. Minneapolis: University of Minnesota Press, 1994.

Gu Mingjun 古明君. "Kanjian he banzhuang zhi wai, nüxing zhuyi zhe daodi neng zuo shemo?" 看見和扮裝之外女性主義者到底能作什麼 (What can feminists do besides "seeing" and "crossdressing"?). *Funü xinzhi*, no. 159 (1995): 8–11.

Guben xiaoshuo jicheng bianweihui 古本小說集成編委會, ed. *Gelian huaying* 隔簾花影 (Shadows of flowers behind the screen). 2 vols. Shanghai: Shanghai guji chubanshe, 1990.

Gui Zhiliang 桂質良. *Nüren zhi yisheng* 女人之一生 (A woman's life). Beijing: Zhengzhong shuju, 1936.

Guo Lianghui 郭良蕙. *Liangzhong yiwaide* 兩種以外的 (Beyond two kinds). Taipei: Hanlin, 1978. Reprinted as *Disan xing* 第三性 (The third sex) (Taipei: Shibao wenhua, 1987).

Guo Moruo 郭沫若. *Wode younian* 我的幼年 (My youth). Shanghai: Xin wenyi shuju, 1932.

Guo Yuwen 郭玉雯. *Liaozhai zhiyi de huanmeng shijie* 聊齋誌異的幻夢世界 (The fantasy world of *Liaozhai*). Taipei: Xuesheng shuju, 1985.

Habermas, Jürgen. *The Structural Transformation of the Public Sphere*. Translated by Thomas Burger. Cambridge, Mass.: MIT Press, 1991.

Halberstam, Judith. *Female Masculinity*. Durham, N.C.: Duke University Press, 1998.

Hall, Radclyffe. *The Well of Loneliness*. New York: Pocket, 1950.

Halperin, David M. *One Hundred Years of Homosexuality and Other Essays on Greek Love*. New York: Routledge, 1990.

———. "Is There a History of Sexuality?" In *The Lesbian and Gay Studies Reader*, ed. Henry Abelove, Michèle Aina Barale, and David M. Halperin, 416–31. New York: Routledge, 1993.

———. *Saint Foucault: Toward a Gay Hagiography*. New York: Oxford University Press, 1995.

———. "Forgetting Foucault: Acts, Identities, and the History of Sexuality." *Representations,* no. 63 (1998): 93–120.

———. Review of *Love between Women: Early Christian Responses to Female Homoeroticism,* by Bernadette J. Brooten. In "The *GLQ* Forum: Lesbian Historiography before the Name?" *GLQ* 4, no. 4 (1998): 559–78.

Hanan, Patrick. *The Invention of Li Yu.* Cambridge, Mass.: Harvard University Press, 1988.

He Chunrui 何春蕤, ed. *Xing/bie yanjiu de xin shiye* 性/別研究的新視野 (A new horizon in sexuality and gender studies). 2 vols. Taipei: Yuanliu, 1997.

He Guimei 賀桂梅. "Geti de shengcun jingyan yu xiezuo" 個體的生存經驗與寫作 (Individual existence and writing). In *Chen Ran zuopin zixuanji,* by Chen Ran, 2:403–12. Beijing: Guangming ribao chubanshe, 1996.

Heilmann, Ann. *New Woman Fiction: Women Writing First-Wave Feminism.* New York: St. Martin's, 2000.

Hekma, Gert. "'A Female Soul in a Male Body': Sexual Inversion as Gender Inversion in Nineteenth-Century Sexology." In *Third Sex, Third Gender: Beyond Sexual Dimorphism in Culture and History,* ed. Gilbert Herdt, 213–39. New York: Zone, 1994.

Herdt, Gilbert. "Introduction: Third Sexes and Third Genders." In *Third Sex, Third Gender: Beyond Sexual Dimorphism in Culture and History,* ed. Gilbert Herdt, 21–81. New York: Zone, 1994.

———, ed. *Third Sex, Third Gender: Beyond Sexual Dimorphism in Culture and History.* New York: Zone, 1994.

Hershatter, Gail. *Dangerous Pleasures: Prostitution and Modernity in Twentieth-Century Shanghai.* Berkeley and Los Angeles: University of California Press, 1997.

Hinsch, Bret. *Passions of the Cut Sleeve: The Male Homosexual Tradition in China.* Berkeley and Los Angeles: University of California Press, 1990.

Hirschfeld, Magnus. *Men and Women: The World Journey of a Sexologist.* Translated by O. P. Green. New York: Putnam's, 1935.

———. "Magnus Hirschfeld." In *A Homosexual Emancipation Miscellany, c. 1835–1952,* gen. ed. Jonathan Katz, 317–21. New York: Arno, 1975.

Hoagland, Sarah Lucia, and Julia Penelope, eds. *For Lesbians Only: A Separatist Anthology.* London: Onlywomen, 1988.

Hockx, Michel, ed. *The Literary Field of Twentieth-Century China.* Honolulu: University of Hawaii Press, 1999.

Honig, Emily, and Gail Hershatter. *Personal Voices: Chinese Women in the 1980s.* Stanford, Calif.: Stanford University Press, 1988.

Horkheimer, Max, and Theodor W. Adorno. *Dialectic of Enlightenment.* Translated by John Cumming. New York: Continuum, 1993.

Hsü, Immanuel Chung-yueh. *The Rise of Modern China.* 6th ed. New York: Oxford University Press, 2000.

Hu Mei 胡玫, dir. *Nüer lou* 女兒樓 (Army nurse). Beijing: August First Studio, 1985.

Hu Shi 胡適. "Lun xiaoshuo ji baihua yunwen" 論小説及白話韻文 (On fiction and vernacular verse). *Xin qingnian* 4, no. 1 (1918): 75–79.

Hu Shuwen 胡淑雯. "Yi nü chu gui" 異女出櫃 (Heterosexual women come out). *Funü xinzhi,* no. 158 (1995): 13–16.

———. "Zhuti zao yi miandui nimen, zhishi nimen kanbujian" 主體早已面對你們, 只是你們看不見 (The subjectivity did exist; it's you who didn't see it). *Funü xinzhi,* no. 163 (1995): 14.

Hu Shuwen 胡淑雯 et al. "Nü tongzhi yundong chu gui" 女同志運動出櫃 (Lesbian feminists come out—a talk). *Funü xinzhi,* no. 161 (1995): 9–15; no. 162 (1995): 1–7.

Hu, Siao-chen (Hu Xiaozhen) 胡曉真. "Literary *Tanci:* A Woman's Tradition of Narrative in Verse." Ph.D. diss., Harvard University, 1994.

———. "Cainü cheye wei mian—Qingdai funü tanci xiaoshuo zhong de ziwo chengxian" 才女徹夜未眠: 清代婦女彈詞小說中的自我呈現 (Self-representation in Qing women's *tanci* novels). *Jindai Zhongguo funü shi yanjiu*, no. 3 (1995): 51–76.

———. "Jiafeng xuhuang/dianluan daofeng—cong Qingdai nü xiaoshuojia tanqi" 假鳳虛鳳顛鸞倒鳳: 從清代女小說家談起 (Cross-dressing/lovemaking—a consideration beginning with Qing women novelists). Paper presented at the conference "Yuwang xin ditu: Wenxue, wenhua yu xingyu quxiang" (A new map of desire: Literature, culture, and sexual orientation), National Taiwan University, 20 April 1996.

———. "Yuedu fanying yu tanci xiaoshuo de chuangzuo" 閱讀反應與彈詞小說的創作 (Reader's response and the creation of *tanci* novels). *Zhongyang yanjiuyuan Zhongguo wenzhe yanjiu jikan*, no. 8 (1996): 305–64.

Hu Ying. *Tales of Translation: Composing the New Woman in China, 1899–1918*. Stanford, Calif.: Stanford University Press, 2000.

Hua, Wei (Hua Wei) 華瑋. "The Lament of Frustrated Talents: An Analysis of Three Women's Plays in Late Imperial China." *Ming Studies*, no. 32 (1994): 28–42.

———. "Ming Qing funü juzuo zhong zhi 'ninan' biaoxian yu xingbie wenti" 明清婦女劇作中之「擬男」表現與性別問題 (Male performance and the issue of gender in Ming-Qing women's dramatic works). In *Ming Qing xiqu guoji yantaohui lunwen ji* 明清戲曲國際研討會論文集 (The collection of essays of the international conference on Ming-Qing drama), ed. Hua Wei 華瑋 and Wang Ailing 王璦玲, 2:573–623. Taipei: Academia Sinica, Institute of Chinese Literature and Philosophy, 1998.

Huang Manying 黃曼螢 et al. "Tansuo nanren zhi bu de shijie" 探索男人止步的世界 (Exploring a world that shuts men out). *Shibao zhoukan*, no. 697 (1991): 32–45.

Huang, Philip C. C. "'Public Sphere'/'Civil Society' in China? The Third Realm between State and Society." *Modern China* 19, no. 2 (1993): 216–40.

———, ed. "Symposium: 'Public Sphere'/'Civil Society' in China? Paradigmatic Issues in Chinese Studies, III." A special issue of *Modern China*, vol. 19, no. 2 (1993).

Hung, Lucifer (Hong Ling) 洪凌. *Yiduan xixiegui liezhuan* 異端吸血鬼列傳 (The biographies of deviant vampires). Taipei: Huangguan, 1995.

———. *Yuzhou Aodisai* 宇宙奧迪賽 (The universe odyssey). Taipei: Shibao wenhua, 1995.

———. *Zhijie yishou* 肢解異獸 (Dismembering monsters). Taipei: Yuanliu, 1995.

———. *Mogui biji* 魔鬼筆記 (The devil's notebook). Taipei: Wanxiang, 1996.

———. "Leisi yu bianzi de jiaohuan" 蕾絲與鞭子的交歡 (The intercourse between lace and the whip). In *Leisi yu bianzi de jiaohuan: Taiwan dangdai qingse wenxue lun*, ed. Lin Yaode and Lin Shuifu, 91–124. Taipei: Shibao wenhua, 1997.

Huot, Claire. *China's New Cultural Scene: A Handbook of Changes*. Durham, N.C.: Duke University Press, 2000.

Huters, Theodore. "A New Way of Writing: The Possibilities for Literature in Late Qing China, 1895–1908." *Modern China* 14, no. 3 (1988): 243–77.

———. "Ideologies of Realism in Modern China: The Hard Imperatives of Imported Theory." In *Politics, Ideology, and Literary Discourse in Modern China*, ed. Liu Kang and Xiaobing Tang, 143–73. Durham, N.C.: Duke University Press, 1993.

Huters, Theodore, R. Bin Wong, and Pauline Yu, eds. *Culture and State in Chinese History: Conventions, Accommodations, and Critiques*. Stanford, Calif.: Stanford University Press, 1997.

Ingebretsen, Edward. "Gone Shopping: The Commercialization of Same-Sex Desire." *Journal of Gay, Lesbian, and Bisexual Identity* 4, no. 2 (1999): 125–48.

Irigaray, Luce. *This Sex Which Is Not One*. Translated by Catherine Porter. Ithaca, N.Y.: Cornell University Press, 1977.

Jameson, Fredric. *Postmodernism; or, The Cultural Logic of Late Capitalism*. Durham, N.C.: Duke University Press, 1991.

Jameson, Fredric, and Masao Miyoshi, eds. *The Cultures of Globalization.* Durham, N.C.: Duke University Press, 1999.

Ji Chen 寄塵. "Ga pengyou zhi exi" 軋朋友之惡習 (The evil habit of bonding with a friend). In *Shanghai heimu yiqianzhong* 上海黑幕一千種 (One thousand secret dealings in Shanghai) (4th ed.), ed. Wang Shubi 汪漱碧. Shanghai: Chunming shudian, 1939.

Jian Jiaxin 簡家欣. "Huanchu nü tongzhi: Jiuling niandai Taiwan nü tongzhi de lunshu xinggou yu yundong jijie" 喚出女同志: 九零年代台灣女同志的論述形構與運動集結 (Summoning lesbians: The discursive construction and mobilization of lesbians in 1990s Taiwan). Master's thesis, National Taiwan University, 1996.

Jiang Weitang 蔣緯堂 et al., eds. *Beijing funü baokan kao, 1905–1949* 北京婦女報刊考 (An examination of Beijing women's press). Beijing: Guangming ribao chubanshe, 1990.

Jingqu Houren 敬渠後人. *Shu yan lie qi lu* 書豔獵奇錄 (Writing about the erotic and hunting for the unusual). Shanghai: Fengxing chubanshe, 1940.

Johnson, David, Andrew J. Nathan, and Evelyn S. Rawski, eds. *Popular Culture in Late Imperial China.* Berkeley and Los Angeles: University of California Press, 1985.

Jones, James W. *"We of the Third Sex": Literary Representations of Homosexuality in Wilhelmine Germany.* New York: Peter Lang, 1990.

Kai Shi 慨士. "Guangdong de 'bu luojia' he 'zishu'" 廣東的不落家和自梳 ("Delayed transfer marriage" and "sworn spinsterhood" in Canton). *Xin nüxing* 1, no. 12 (1926): 937–42.

Kang Zhengguo 康正果. *Chong shen fengyue jian: Xing yu Zhongguo gudian wenxue* 重審風月鑑: 性與中國古典文學 (Reexamining the mirror of wind and moon: Sex and classical Chinese literature). Taipei: Maitian, 1996.

Kaplan, E. Ann. "Problematizing Cross-Cultural Analysis: The Case of Women in the Recent Chinese Cinema." In *Perspectives on Chinese Cinema*, ed. Chris Berry, 141–54. London: BFI, 1991.

Katz, Jonathan Ned. *Gay American History: Lesbians and Gay Men in the U.S.A.* Rev. ed. New York: Meridian, 1992.

Kaweibo 卡維波. "Shemo shi kuer—seqing guozu" 什麼是酷兒? 色情國族 (What is queer? an erotic nation). In *Kuer qishilu: Taiwan dangdai QUEER lunshu duben,* ed. Ta-wei Chi, 231–43. Taipei: Yuanzun wenhua, 1997.

Kazuko, Ono. *Chinese Women in a Century of Revolution, 1850–1950.* Stanford, Calif.: Stanford University Press.

Ko, Dorothy. "Same-Sex Love between Singing Girls and Gentry Wives in Seventeenth-Century Jiangnan." Paper presented at the conference "Women and Literature in Ming-Qing China," Yale University, 22–26 June 1993.

———. *Teachers of the Inner Chambers: Women and Culture in Seventeenth-Century China.* Stanford, Calif.: Stanford University Press, 1994.

Krafft-Ebing, Richard von. *Psychopathia Sexualis.* Translated by F. J. Rebman. New York: Rebman, 1906.

Lacan, Jacques. *Ecrits: A Selection.* Translated by Alan Sheridan. New York: Norton, 1977.

———. "The Signification of the Phallus" (1958). In *Ecrits: A Selection,* trans. Alan Sheridan, 281–91. New York: Norton, 1977.

Langton, Rae. "Speech Acts and Unspeakable Acts." *Philosophy and Public Affairs* 22, no. 4 (1993): 293–330.

Laplanche, Jean, and Jean-Bertrand Pontalis. "Fantasy and the Origins of Sexuality." In *Formations of Fantasy,* ed. Victor Burgin, James Donald, and Cora Kaplan, 5–34. New York: Methuen, 1986.

Laqueur, Thomas. *Making Sex: Body and Gender from the Greeks to Freud.* Cambridge, Mass.: Harvard University Press, 1990.

Larson, Wendy. "Women and the Discourse of Desire in Postrevolutionary China: The Awkward Postmodern of Chen Ran." *Boundary 2* 24, no. 3 (1997): 201–23.

——. *Women and Writing in Modern China.* Stanford, Calif.: Stanford University Press, 1998.

Leary, Charles Leland. "Sexual Modernism in China: Zhang Jingsheng and 1920s Urban Culture." Ph.D. diss., Cornell University, 1994.

Lee, Jien-mei (Li Jinmei) 李金梅. "Cong *Shuang zhuo* de 'jiemei fuqi' lun youguan nü tongxinglian zuopin de yuedu yu shuxie" 從《雙鐲》的「姊妹夫妻」論有關女同性戀作品的閱讀與書寫 (The "sisterhood marriage" in *Double Bracelets:* On the reading and writing of fiction about lesbians). Master's thesis, National Taiwan University, 1993.

Lee, Leo Ou-fan. *The Romantic Generation of Modern Chinese Writers.* Cambridge, Mass.: Harvard University Press, 1973.

——. *Shanghai Modern: The Flowering of a New Urban Culture in China, 1930–1945.* Cambridge, Mass.: Harvard University Press, 1999.

Lee, Leo Ou-fan, and Andrew J. Nathan. "The Beginning of Mass Culture: Journalism and Fiction in the Late Ch'ing and Beyond." In *Popular Culture in Late Imperial China,* ed. David Johnson, Andrew Nathan, and Evelyn Rawski, 360–95. Berkeley and Los Angeles: University of California Press, 1985.

Lee, Lilian (Li Bihua) 李碧華. "Shuangmei mo" 雙妹嘜 (Twin sisters). In *You seng* 誘僧 (The seduction of a monk), 109–24. Taipei: Huangguan, 1992.

Lei Qunming 雷群明. *Liaozhai yishu tonglun* 聊齋藝術通論 (A general study of the art of the *Liaozhai zhiyi*). Shanghai: Sanlian shudian, 1990.

Lejeune, Philippe. *On Autobiography.* Translated by Katherine Leary. Minneapolis: University of Minnesota Press, 1989.

LeVay, Simon. *The Sexual Brain.* Cambridge, Mass.: MIT Press, 1994.

Levy, Howard, trans. *Sex Histories: China's First Modern Treatise on Sex Education.* Yokohama, 1967. A translation of Zhang Jingsheng, *Xing shi* (Shanghai: Meide shudian, 1926).

Li Conghua. *China: The Consumer Revolution.* Singapore: Wiley (Asia), 1998.

Li Yinhe 李銀河. *Tongxinglian yawenhua* 同性戀亞文化 (The subculture of homosexuality). Beijing: Jinri Zhongguo chubanshe, 1998.

——. *Zhongguo nüxing de ganqing yu xing* 中國女性的感情與性 (Chinese women's love and sex). Beijing: Jinri Zhongguo chubanshe, 1998.

Li Yinhe 李銀河 and Wang Xiaobo 王小波. *Tamende shijie: Zhongguo nan tongxinglian qunluo toushi* 他們的世界: 中國男同性戀群落透視 (Their world: A penetrating look into gay male communities in China). Hong Kong: Tiandi tushu youxian gongsi, 1992.

Li Yixue 李怡學 et al. "Taiwan tongzhi xiaofei wenhua: Guke zhishang, tongzhi wansui" 台灣同志消費文化: 顧客至上, 同志萬歲 (Gay and lesbian consumer culture in Taiwan: The customer is always right; long live queers). *G&L: Re'ai zazhi,* no. 1 (1996): 19–28.

Li Youning 李又寧, ed. *Jindai Zhonghua funü zixu shiwen xuan* 近代中華婦女自敘詩文選 (A selection of modern Chinese women's autobiographical poetry and prose). Taipei: Lianjing, 1980.

Li Yu 李漁. *Li Yu quanji* 李漁全集 (The complete works of Li Yu). Edited by Xiao Xinqiao 蕭欣橋 et al. 20 vols. Hangzhou: Zhejiang guji chubanshe, 1990.

——. *Lian xiang ban* 憐香伴 (Women in love). In *Li Yu quanji,* ed. Xiao Xinqiao et al., 4:3–110. Hangzhou: Zhejiang guji chubanshe, 1990.

Liao, Ping-hui 廖炳惠. "Taiwan: Houxiandai huo houzhimin?" 台灣：後現代或後殖民？ (Taiwan: Postmodern or postcolonial?). In *Shuxie Taiwan: Wenxue shi, houzhimin yu houxiandai,* ed. Ying-Hsiung Chou and Joyce Chi-Hui Liu, 85–99. Taipei: Maitian, 2000.

Lieberman, Sally Taylor. *The Mother and Narrative Politics in Modern China.* Charlottesville: University Press of Virginia, 1998.

Lin Bai 林白. "Yige ren de zhansheng" 一個人的戰爭 (One person's war). *Huacheng,* no. 87 (1994): 4–80.

———. *Yige ren de zhanzheng* 一個人的戰爭 (One person's war). Taiyuan: Gansu renmin chubanshe, 1994.

———. *Yige ren de zhanzheng* 一個人的戰爭 (One person's war). Huhehaote shi: Nei Menggu renmin chubanshe, 1996.

———. "Houji" 後記 (Afterword [to *Yige ren de zhanzheng*]). In *Lin Bai wenji,* 2:293–96. Nanjing: Jiangsu wenyi chubanshe, 1997.

———. "Huilang zhi yi" 迴廊之椅 (The bench on the interior balcony). In *Lin Bai wenji,* 1:199–234. Nanjing: Jiangsu wenyi chubanshe, 1997.

———. "Jiyi yu gerenhua xiezuo" 記憶與個人化寫作 (Memory and individualized writing). In *Lin Bai wenji,* 4:293–96. Nanjing: Jiangsu wenyi chubanshe, 1997.

———. *Lin Bai wenji* 林白文集 (The collected works of Lin Bai). 4 vols. Nanjing: Jiangsu wenyi chubanshe, 1997.

———. "Mao de jiqing shidai" 貓的激情時代 (The passionate days of the cat). In *Lin Bai wenji,* 1:1–5. Nanjing: Jiangsu wenyi chubanshe, 1997.

———. "Pingzhong zhi shui" 瓶中之水 (Water in a bottle). In *Lin Bai wenji,* 1:235–78. Nanjing: Jiangsu wenyi chubanshe, 1997.

———. "Tong xin'aizhe buneng fenshou" 同心愛者不能分手 (Unable to be separated from the beloved). In *Lin Bai wenji,* 1:123–58. Nanjing: Jiangsu wenyi chubanshe, 1997.

———. *Yige ren de zhanzheng* 一個人的戰爭 (One person's war). In *Lin Bai wenji,* 2:1–225. Nanjing: Jiangsu wenyi chubanshe, 1997.

———. "Zhiming de feixiang" 致命的飛翔 (A flight of fatality). In *Lin Bai wenji,* 1:317–59. Nanjing: Jiangsu wenyi chubanshe, 1997.

———. *Shuoba, fangjian* 說吧，房間 (Speak, room). Taipei: Sanmin shuju, 1998.

———. *Yige ren de zhanzheng* 一個人的戰爭 (One person's war). Hong Kong: Tiandi tushu youxian gongsi, 1998.

———. *Yige ren de zhanzheng* 一個人的戰爭 (One person's war). Taipei: Maitian, 1998.

Lin Daiman 林黛嫚. "Bingdi lian" 並蒂蓮 (Lotuses of one root). In *Heibai xinqing,* 139–61. Taipei: Xidai, 1990.

———. *Heibai xinqing* 黑白心情 (Moods in black and white). Taipei: Xidai, 1990.

Lin Yaode 林燿德 and Lin Shuifu 林水福, eds. *Leisi yu bianzi de jiaohuan: Taiwan dangdai qingse wenxue lun* 蕾絲與鞭子的交歡：台灣當代情色文學論 (The intercourse between lace and the whip: Essays on contemporary Taiwanese erotic literature). Taipei: Shibao wenhua, 1997.

Ling Shuhua 凌叔華. *Ling Shuhua xiaoshuo ji* 凌叔華小説 (Collected short stories by Ling Shuhua). 2 vols. Taipei: Hongfan shudian, 1984.

———. "Shuo you zhemo yihui shi" 説有這麼一回事 (Rumor has it that something like this happened). In *Ling Shuhua xiaoshuo ji,* 1:89–101. Taipei: Hongfan shudian, 1984.

Ling Yan 凌煙. *Shi sheng huamei* 失聲畫眉 (Muted thrush). Taipei: Zili wanbao, 1990.

Link, Perry. *Mandarin Ducks and Butterflies: Popular Fiction in Early-Twentieth-Century Chinese Cities.* Berkeley and Los Angeles: University of California Press, 1981.

Link, Perry, Richard Madsen, and Paul G. Pickowicz, eds. *Unofficial China: Popular Culture and Thought in the People's Republic.* Boulder, Colo.: Westview, 1989.

Liou, Liang-ya (Liu Liangya) 劉亮雅. *Yuwang gengyishi: Qingse xiaoshuo de zhengzhi yu meixue* 慾望更衣室：情色小説的政治與美學 (Engendering dissident desires: The politics and aesthetics of erotic fictions). Taipei: Yuanzun wenhua, 1998.

———. "Zai xingbie de aimei jiaojie: Chao xingbie de dingyi, mailuo, yundong ji lunshu kongjian" 在性別的曖昧交界：超性別的定義、脈絡、運動及論述空間 (At the ambiguous borders of gender: The definition, historical context, movement, and discursive space of transgender). *Chengpin haodu*, no. 5 (2000): 5–7.

Liu Dalin 劉達臨 et al. *Zhongguo dangdai xing wenhua* 中國當代性文化 (Sexual behavior in modern China). Shanghai: Sanlian shudian, 1992.

Liu Fuchu 劉富初, ed. *Zhongguo xingfa shiyong daquan* 中國刑法適用大全 (A complete and practical guide to the Chinese criminal code). Hebei: Falü chubanshe, 1991.

Liu, Lydia H. "The Female Tradition in Modern Chinese Literature: Negotiating Feminisms across East/West Boundaries." *Genders,* no. 12 (1991): 22–44.

———. *Translingual Practice: Literature, National Culture, and Translated Modernity— China, 1900–1937.* Stanford, Calif.: Stanford University Press, 1995.

———, ed. *Tokens of Exchange: The Problem of Translation in Global Circulations.* Durham, N.C.: Duke University Press, 1999.

Liu Suola 劉索拉. "Lantian lühai" 藍天綠海 (The blue sky and ocean). In *Ni bie wu xuanze,* 142–92. Taipei: Xindi, 1988.

———. *Ni bie wu xuanze* 你別無選擇 (You have no other choice). Taipei: Xindi, 1988.

Liu Yisheng 劉逸生. *Liaozhai de huanhuan zhenzhen* 聊齋的幻幻真真 (The real and unreal in *Liaozhai*). Hong Kong: Zhonghua shuju, 1990.

Long Sheng 龍升. "Gebi e lian" 戈壁噩戀 (A nightmarish affair in the Gobi). In *Zhongguo zhiqing qinglian baogao,* ed. Zhang Dening and Yue Jianyi, 1:414–30. Beijing: Guangming ribao chubanshe, 1998.

Lorde, Audre. "The Use of the Erotic: The Erotic as Power." In *The Lesbian and Gay Studies Reader,* ed. Henry Abelove, Michèle Aina Barale, and David M. Halperin, 339–43. New York: Routledge, 1993.

Lu Jianxiong 盧劍雄, ed. *Huaren tongzhi xin duben* 華人同志新讀本 (A new reader on Chinese *tongzhi*: Essays and conference proceedings). Hong Kong: Huasheng shudian, 1999.

Lü Jing Bei 綠鯨背. "You kong qu guang lawang ba" 有空去逛拉網吧 (When you're free, go check out lesbian websites). *Nü pengyou,* no. 11 (1998): 33.

Lu, Tonglin, ed. *Gender and Sexuality in Twentieth-Century Chinese Literature and Society.* Albany: State University of New York Press, 1993.

Lu Xun 魯迅. *Zhongguo xiaoshuo shilue* 中國小説史略 (A brief history of Chinese fiction). Beijing: Beixin shuju, 1935. Reprint. Taipei: Gufeng chubanshe, n.d.

Lu Yin 廬隱. *Lu Yin zizhuan* 廬隱自傳 (Autobiography). Shanghai: Diyi chubanshe, 1934.

———. *Lu Yin xuanji* 廬隱選集 (Selected works of Lu Yin). Edited by Qian Hong 錢虹. 2 vols. Fuzhou: Fujian renmin chubanshe, 1985.

Lu Zhaohuan 陸昭環. *Shuang zhuo* 雙鐲 (Double bracelets). Taipei: Fengyun shidai chuban gongsi, 1989.

Luo Suwen 羅蘇文. *Nüxing yu jindai Zhongguo shehui* 女性與近代中國社會 (Women and modern Chinese society). Shanghai: Shanghai renmin chubanshe, 1996.

Mann, Susan. *Precious Records: Women in China's Long Eighteenth Century.* Stanford, Calif.: Stanford University Press, 1997.

Mao Dun 茅盾. "Lu Yin lun" 廬隱論 (On Lu Yin). In *Lu Yin xuanji,* ed. Qian Hong, 1:1–8. Fuzhou: Fujian renmin chubanshe, 1985.

Mao Feng 矛鋒. *Tongxinglian wenxue shi* 同性戀文學史 (The history of homosexual literature). Taipei: Hanzhong wenhua, 1996.

Mao Yibo 毛一波. "Zai lun xing'ai yu youyi" 再論性愛與友誼 (Yet again on sexual love and friendship). *Xin nüxing* 3, no. 11 (1928): 1248–58.

Martin, Biddy. *Femininity Played Straight: The Significance of Being Lesbian.* New York: Routledge, 1996.

Martin, Fran. "Chen Xue's Queer Tactics." *Positions* 7, no. 1 (1999): 71–94.

———. "Surface Tensions: Reading Productions of *Tongzhi* in Contemporary Taiwan." *GLQ* 6, no. 1 (2000): 61–86.

Mattelart, Armand. *Mapping World Communication.* Translated by Susan Emanuel and James A. Cohen. Minneapolis: University of Minnesota Press, 1994.

McMahon, Keith. "The Classic 'Beauty-Scholar' Romance and the Superiority of the Talented Woman." In *Body, Subject, and Power in China,* ed. Angela Zito and Tani E. Barlow, 227–52. Chicago: University of Chicago Press, 1994.

———. *Misers, Shrews, and Polygamists: Sexuality and Male-Female Relations in Eighteenth-Century Chinese Fiction.* Durham, N.C.: Duke University Press, 1995.

Meng Yue 孟悦. "*Baimaonü* yanbian de qishi" 白毛女演變的啓示 (The lesson of the transformations of *The White-Haired Girl*). In *Zai jiedu: Dazhong wenyi yu yishi xingtai* 再解讀: 大眾文藝與意識形態 (Reinterpretation: Mass arts and literature and ideology), ed. Tang Xiaobing, 68–89. Hong Kong: Oxford University Press, 1993.

Meng Yue 孟悦 and Dai Jinhua 戴錦華. *Fuchu lishi dibiao* 浮出歷史地表 (Voices emerging into the foreground of history: A study of modern Chinese women's literature). Taipei: Shibao wenhua, 1993.

Meng Zi 孟子. *Mencius.* Translated by D. C. Lau. New York: Penguin, 1970.

Merck, Mandy, Naomi Segal, and Elizabeth Wright, eds. *Coming Out of Feminism?* Oxford: Blackwell, 1998.

Metz, Christian. *The Imaginary Signifier: Psychoanalysis and the Cinema.* Translated by Celia Britton et al. Bloomington: Indiana University Press, 1982.

Min, Anchee. *The Red Azalea.* New York: Pantheon, 1994.

Morohashi, Tetsuji 諸橋轍次. *Dai kanwa jiten* 大漢和辭典 (Morohashi's Chinese-Japanese dictionary). 12 vols. Tokyo: Daishukan shoten, 1955–1960.

"Mulans" 木蘭. *G&L: Re'ai zazhi,* no. 15 (1998): 129–36.

Mulvey, Laura. *Visual and Other Pleasures.* Bloomington: Indiana University Press, 1989.

Murphy, Timothy. *Gay Science: The Ethics of Sexual Orientation Research.* New York: Columbia University Press, 1997.

Nestle, Joan, ed. *The Persistent Desire: A Femme-Butch Reader.* Boston: Alyson, 1992.

Newton, Esther. "The Mythic Mannish Lesbian: Radclyffe Hall and the New Woman." *Signs* 9, no. 4 (1984): 557–75.

———. *Cherry Grove, Fire Island: Sixty Years in America's First Gay and Lesbian Community.* Boston: Beacon, 1993.

———. "Baking Ziti for the Coronation: Homophobia, Sexism, and the Subordination Status of Lesbians in Cherry Grove." Paper presented at the annual meeting of the American Anthropological Association, Atlanta, 2 December 1994.

Ng, Vivien W. "Homosexuality and the State in Late Imperial China." In *Hidden from History: Reclaiming the Gay and Lesbian Past,* ed. Martin Duberman, Martha Vicinus, and George Chauncey Jr., 76–89. New York: Meridian, 1990.

Nietzsche, Friedrich. *On the Advantage and Disadvantage of History for Life.* Translated by Peter Preuss. Indianapolis: Hackett, 1980.

Nirvard, Jacqueline. "Women and the Women's Press: The Case of the *Ladies' Journal* (*Funü zazhi*), 1915–1931." *Republican China* 10, no. 1b (1984): 37–55.

Nonini, Donald M., and Aihwa Ong. "Chinese Transnationalism as an Alternative Modernity." In *Ungrounded Empires: The Cultural Politics of Modern Chinese Transnationalism,* ed. Donald M. Nonini and Aihwa Ong, 3–33. New York: Routledge, 1997.

———, eds. *Ungrounded Empires: The Cultural Politics of Modern Chinese Transnationalism.* New York: Routledge, 1997.

Pan Guangdan 潘光旦. *Feng Xiaoqing xing xinli biantai jiemi* 馮小青性心理變態揭祕 (Revealing Feng Xiaoqing's perversion in sexual psychology). Shanghai: 1927; Beijing: Wenhua yishu chubanshe, 1990.

———, trans. *Xing xinli xue* 性心理學. Shanghai, 1946; Beijing: Sanlian shudian, 1987. A translation of Havelock Ellis, *The Psychology of Sex: A Manual for Students* (London: William Heinemann Medical Books, 1933).

———. "Yi xu" 譯序 (Translator's preface). In *Xing xinli xue*, by Pan Guangdan, 1–7. Shanghai, 1946; Beijing: Sanlian shudian, 1987.

———. "Zhongguo wenxian zhong tongxing lian juli" 中國文獻中同性戀舉例 (Examples of homosexuality in Chinese documents). In *Xing xinli xue*, by Pan Guangdan, 516–47. Shanghai, 1946; Beijing: Sanlian shudian, 1987.

———. *Pan Guangdan wenji* 潘光旦文集 (The works of Pan Guangdan). Edited by Pan Naimu 潘乃穆 and Pan Naihe 潘乃和. 5 vols. Beijing: Beijing daxue chubanshe, 1994.

———. "*Xin wenhua* yu jia kexue—bo Zhang Jingsheng" 新文化與假科學——駁張競生 (*New Culture* and fake sexual science—a refutation of Zhang Jingsheng). In *Pan Guangdan wenji*, ed. Pan Naimu and Pan Naihe, 1:401–6. Beijing: Beijing daxue chubanshe, 1994.

———. "Zhongguo lingren xueyuan zhi yanjiu" 中國伶人血緣之研究 (A study of the genealogy of Chinese actors). In *Pan Guangdan wenji*, ed. Pan Naimu and Pan Naihe, 2:73–304. Beijing: Beijing daxue chubanshe, 1994.

Peng, Hsiao-yen (Peng Xiaoyan) 彭小妍. "Xing qimeng yu ziwo jiefang" 性啟蒙與自我解放 (Sexual enlightenment and self-liberation). In *Chaoyue xieshi* 超越寫實 (Beyond realism), 117–37. Taipei: Lianjing, 1993.

———. "The New Woman: May Fourth Women's Struggle for Self-Liberation" (in English). *Zhongyang yanjiuyuan Zhongguo wenzhe yanjiu jikan*, no. 6 (1995): 259–338.

———. "Wusi de 'xin xing daode': Nüxing qingyu lunshu yu jian'gou minzu guojia" 五四的新性道德：女性情慾論述與建構民族國家 (The 'new sexual morality' of the May Fourth era: Female sexuality and nation building). *Jindai Zhongguo funü shi yanjiu*, no. 3 (1995): 77–96.

———. "'Xin nüxing' yu Shanghai dushi wenhua: Xin ganjue pai yanjiu" 新女性與上海都市文化：新感覺派研究 (The "new woman" and Shanghai urban culture: A study of the new perceptionists). *Zhongyang yanjiuyuan Zhongguo wenzhe yanjiu jikan*, no. 10 (1997): 317–55.

Pflugfelder, Gregory M. *Cartographies of Desire: Male-Male Sexuality in Japanese Discourse, 1600–1950.* Berkeley and Los Angeles: University of California Press, 1999.

Poster, Mark. *The Second Media Age.* Cambridge: Polity, 1995.

Povinelli, Elizabeth, and George Chauncey. "Thinking Sexuality Transnationally." *GLQ* 5, no. 4 (1999): 439–49.

Pu Songling 蒲松齡. *Liaozhai zhiyi huijiao huizhu huiping ben* 聊齋誌異會校會註會評本 (The complete collated and annotated *Liaozhai's Records of the Strange*). Edited by Zhang Youhe 張友鶴. Rev. ed., 1978. Reprint, Shanghai: Shanghai guji chubanshe, 1983.

Qingdian Zhuren 情顛主人. *Xiuta yeshi* 繡榻野史 (The unofficial history of events on an embroidered mat). Reprint, Taipei: Tianyi chubanshe, 1993.

Qitian Xiaosheng 齊天小聖 et al. "Shengli yingxiong huo zhanlue jia" 牲禮英雄或戰略家 (A sacrificial hero or a strategist). *Saodong*, no. 3 (1997): 45–51.

Qiu Miaojin 邱妙津. *Gui de kuanghuan* 鬼的狂歡 (Hedonist ghosts). Taipei: Lianhe wenxue chubanshe, 1991.

———. *Eyu shouji* 鱷魚手記 (The crocodile's journal). Taipei: Shibao, 1994.

———. "Zi shu" 自述 (Self-narration). *Lianhe wenxue,* no. 131 (1995): 40–41.

———. *Mengmate yishu* 蒙馬特遺書 (Last letters from Montmartre). Taipei: Lianhe wenxue chubanshe, 1996.

Qiu Xinru 邱心如. *Bi sheng hua* 筆生花 (Flowers generated from the writing brush). 3 vols. Taipei: Heluo, 1980.

Qiu Yuan 秋原 (Hu Qiuyuan 胡秋原), trans. "Tongxing lian'ai lun" 同性戀愛論 (On same-sex romantic love). *Xin nüxing* 4, no. 4 (1929): 513–34; 4, no. 5 (1929): 605–28. A translation of Edward Carpenter's "The Homogenic Attachment."

Radicalesbians. "The Woman Identified Woman." In *For Lesbians Only: A Separatist Anthology,* ed. Sarah Lucia Hoagland and Julia Penelope, 17–21. London: Onlywomen, 1988.

Rankin, Mary Backus. "Some Observations on a Chinese Public Sphere." *Modern China* 19, no. 2 (1993): 158–82.

"Renshi tongxinglian" 認識同性戀 (Learning about homosexuality). *Xiwang* (Guangzhou) 1998, no. 6 (June): 51–73.

Rexroth, Kenneth, and Ling Chung, trans. and eds. *The Orchid Boat: Women Poets of China.* New York: McGraw-Hill, 1972.

Rich, Adrienne. "Compulsory Heterosexuality and Lesbian Existence." In *The Lesbian and Gay Studies Reader,* ed. Henry Abelove, Michèle Aina Barale, and David M. Halperin, 227–54. New York: Routledge, 1993.

Richardson, Angelique, ed. *The New Woman in Fiction and in Fact: Fin-de-Siècle Feminisms.* New York: Palgrave, 2001.

Robinet, Isabelle. *Taoist Meditation.* Translated by Julian F. Pas and Norman J. Girardot. Albany: State University of New York Press, 1993.

Rofel, Lisa. "Museum as Women's Space: Displays of Gender in Post-Mao China." In *Spaces of Their Own: Women's Public Sphere in Transnational China,* ed. Mayfair Yang, 116–31. Minneapolis: University of Minnesota Press, 1999.

———. *Other Modernities: Gendered Yearnings in China after Socialism.* Berkeley and Los Angeles: University or California Press, 1999.

———. "Qualities of Desire: Imagining Gay Identities in China." *GLQ* 5, no. 4 (1999): 451–74.

Rosenfeld, Marthe. "Splits in French Feminism/Lesbianism." In *For Lesbians Only: A Separatist Anthology,* ed. Sarah Lucia Hoagland and Julia Penelope, 457–66. London: Onlywomen, 1988.

Rowe, William T. "The Public Sphere in Modern China." *Modern China* 16, no. 3 (1990): 309–29.

———. "The Problem of 'Civil Society' in Late Imperial China." *Modern China* 19, no. 2 (1993): 139–57.

Rubin, Gayle. "The Traffic in Women." In *Toward an Anthropology of Women,* ed. Rayna R. Reiter, 159–66. New York: Monthly Review Press, 1975.

———. "Thinking Sex." In *The Lesbian and Gay Studies Reader,* ed. Henry Abelove, Michèle Aina Barale, and David M. Halperin, 3–44. New York: Routledge, 1993.

Rust, Paula C. *Bisexuality and the Challenge to Lesbian Politics.* New York: New York University Press, 1995.

Sang, Tze-lan Deborah (Sang Zilan) 桑梓蘭. "Cheng Dieyi: Yige quanshi de qidian" 程蝶衣：一個詮釋的起點 (Cheng Dieyi: Toward a queer reading of *Farewell My Concubine*). *Dangdai* (Taipei), no. 96 (1994): 54–73.

———. "The Emerging Lesbian: Female Same-Sex Desire in Modern Chinese Literature and Culture." Ph.D. diss., University of California, Berkeley, 1996.

———. "Feminism's Double: Lesbian Activism in the Mediated Public Sphere of Taiwan." In *Spaces of Their Own: Women's Public Sphere in Transnational China,* ed. Mayfair Yang, 132–61. Minneapolis: University of Minnesota Press, 1999.

———. "Translating Homosexuality: The Discourse of *Tongxing'ai* in Republican China (1912–1949)." In *Tokens of Exchange: The Problem of Translation in Global Circulations,* ed. Lydia H. Liu, 276–304. Durham, N.C.: Duke University Press, 1999.

———. "At the Juncture of Censure and Mass Voyeurism: Narratives of Female Homoerotic Desire in Post-Mao China." *GLQ* 8, no. 4 (2002): 523–52.

"Sange ren. Run" 三個人 Run (Three people. Run). *G&L: Re'ai zazhi,* no. 1 (1996): 120–29.

Sedgwick, Eve Kosofsky. *Between Men: English Literature and Male Homosocial Desire.* New York: Columbia University Press, 1985.

———. *The Epistemology of the Closet.* Berkeley and Los Angeles: University of California Press, 1990.

———. *Tendencies.* Durham, N.C.: Duke University Press, 1993.

Shan Zai 善哉. "Funü tongxing zhi aiqing" 婦女同性之愛情 (Same-sex erotic love between women). *Funü shibao* 1, no. 7 (June 1911): 36–38.

"Shanron yijing chulai le" Shanron 已經站出來了 (Shanron has already come out). *G&L: Re'ai zazhi,* no. 1 (1996): 78–80.

Shen Fu 沈復. *Six Records of a Floating Life.* Translated by Leonard Pratt and Chiang Su-hui. Harmondsworth: Penguin, 1983.

Shen Zemin 沈澤民, trans. "Tongxing ai yu jiaoyu" 同性愛與教育 (Same-sex love and education). *Jiaoyu zazhi* 15, no. 8 (1923): 22115–24. A translation of Edward Carpenter's "Affection in Education."

Shi Tou 石頭. "Shi Tou yishu zuopin xuan" 石頭藝術作品選. (Selected artworks of Shi Tou). *Xiandai wenming huabao,* no. 119 (2002): 50–52.

Shih, Shu-mei. *The Lure of the Modern: Writing Modernism in Semicolonial China, 1917–1937.* Berkeley and Los Angeles: University of California Press, 2001.

"Shuangxinglian luntan" 雙性戀論壇 (A forum on bisexuality). *Tiankong,* no. 2 (1999): 13–14.

Silber, Cathy. "From Daughter to Daughter-in-Law in the Women's Script of Southern Hunan." In *Engendering China: Women, Culture, and the State,* ed. Christina K. Gilmartin et al., 47–68. Cambridge, Mass.: Harvard University Press, 1994.

Silverman, Kaja. *Male Subjectivity at the Margins.* New York: Routledge, 1992.

Silvio, Teri. "Reflexivity, Bodily Praxis, and Identity in Taiwanese Opera." *GLQ* 5, no. 4 (1999): 585–604.

Siu, Helen F. "Where Were the Women? Rethinking Marriage Resistance and Regional Culture in South China." *Late Imperial China* 11, no. 2 (1990): 32–62.

Sklair, Leslie. "Social Movements and Global Capitalism." In *The Cultures of Globalization,* ed. Fredric Jameson and Masao Miyoshi, 291–311. Durham, N.C.: Duke University Press, 1999.

Soja, Edward W. *Postmetropolis: Critical Studies of Cities and Regions.* Oxford: Blackwell, 2000.

Sommer, Mathew. *Sex, Law, and Society in Late Imperial China.* Stanford, Calif.: Stanford University Press, 2000.

Spivak, Gayatri Chakravorty. "Can the Subaltern Speak?" In *Marxism and the Interpretation of Culture,* ed. Cary Nelson and Lawrence Grossberg, 217–313. Urbana: University of Illinois Press, 1988.

Stein, Arlene. *Sex and Sensibility: Stories of a Lesbian Generation.* Berkeley, Calif.: University of California Press, 1997.

Stockard, Janice E. *Daughters of the Canton Delta: Marriage Patterns and Economic Strategies in South China, 1860–1930.* Stanford, Calif.: Stanford University Press, 1989.

Stoler, Ann. *Race and the Education of Desire: Foucault's History of Sexuality and the Colonial Order of Things.* Durham, N.C.: Duke University Press, 1995.

Stone, Sandy. "The *Empire* Strikes Back: A Posttranssexual Manifesto." In *Body Guards:*

*The Cultural Politics of Gender Ambiguity,* ed. Julia Epstein and Kristina Straub, 280–304. New York: Routledge, 1991.

Stopes, Marie Carmichael. *Married Love.* London: Fifield, 1918; New York: Putnam's, 1931.

Strand, David. *Rickshaw Beijing: City People and Politics in the 1920s.* Berkeley and Los Angeles: University of California Press, 1989.

Stryker, Susan, ed. "The Transgender Issue." *GLQ,* vol. 4, no. 2 (1998). Special issue.

Su Yaping 蘇雅萍 et al. "Nü tongxinglianzhe xing'ai biantai da jiemi" 女同性戀者性愛變態大揭祕 (Revealing a hundred secrets in female homosexuals' sex and love). *Dujia baodao,* no. 139 (1991): 25–38.

"T de shenti" T 的身體 (Ts' bodies). *Nü pengyou,* no. 1 (1994): 4–14.

Taida Lambda 台大女同性戀文化研究社. *Women shi nü tongxinglian* 我們是女同性戀 (We are lesbians). Taipei: Shuoren chuban, 1995.

Tan, Chong Kee. "Re-Negotiating Transcultural Sexuality: The Deployment of Homosexual Eroticism and Prejudices in Taiwanese Fiction, 1960–1997." Ph.D. diss., Stanford University, 1998.

Tan Zhengbi 譚正璧 and Tan Xun 譚尋, eds. *Tanci xulu* 彈詞敘錄 (A catalog of *tanci* novels with summaries). Shanghai: Shanghai guji chubanshe, 1981.

Tang Fuling 唐富齡. "Lüe tan *Liaozhai zhiyi* zhong de aiqing xiaoshuo" 略談聊齋誌異中的愛情小說 (Love in *Liaozhai zhiyi*). *Pu Songling yanjiu jikan* 2 (1981): 99–122.

Tang, Xiaobing. *Global Space and the Nationalist Discourse of Modernity: The Historical Thinking of Liang Qichao.* Stanford, Calif.: Stanford University Press, 1996.

———. *Chinese Modern: The Heroic and the Quotidian.* Durham, N.C.: Duke University Press, 2000.

Tao Wu 檮杌. "Mo jing dang" 磨鏡黨 (The mirror-rubbing gang). In *Shanghai funü nie jingtai* 上海婦女孽鏡台 (A mirror of Shanghai women's sin), 4:65–70. Shanghai: Zhonghua tushu jicheng gongsi, 1918.

Telford, Ted. "Covariates of Men's Age at First Marriage: The Historical Demography of Chinese Lineages." *Population Studies* 46 (1992): 19–35.

Tompkins, Jane. *Sensational Designs: The Cultural Work of American Fiction, 1790–1860.* Oxford: Oxford University Press, 1985.

"Tongxinglian yu women tongzai" 同性戀與我們同在 (Gays and lesbians are with us). A special issue of *Xiandai wenming huabao* 現代文明畫報 (Modern civilization pictorial), no. 119 (2002).

Tongzhi gongzuofang 同志工作坊, ed. *Fan qishi zhi yue: Cujin tongxinglian renquan gongtinghui jishi* 反歧視之約: 促進同性戀人權公聽會記實 (An agreement against discrimination: A record of the public hearing to promote homosexual human rights). Taipei: Tongzhi gongzuofang, 1994.

"Tongzhi zhengjian da leitai: Chen Shuibian vs. Ma Yingjiu" 同志政見大擂台: 陳水扁 vs. 馬英九 (A duel about gay rights: Chen Shuibian vs. Ma Yingjiu). *G&L: Re'ai zazhi,* no. 15 (1998): 16–19.

Traub, Valerie. "The (In)Significance of 'Lesbian' Desire in Early Modern England." In *Erotic Politics: Desire on the Renaissance Stage,* ed. Susan Zimmerman, 150–69. New York: Routledge, 1992.

Trumbach, Randolph. *Sex and the Gender Revolution.* Vol. 1, *Heterosexuality and the Third Gender in Enlightenment London.* Chicago: University of Chicago Press, 1998.

Tsuzuki, Chushichi. *Edward Carpenter (1844–1929): Prophet of Human Fellowship.* Cambridge: Cambridge University Press, 1980.

van Gulik, Robert. *Sexual Life in Ancient China.* Leiden: E. J. Brill, 1961. Reprint, Leiden: E. J. Brill, 1974.

Vicinus, Martha. "Distance and Desire: English Boarding-School Friendships." *Signs* 9, no. 4 (1984): 600–622.

Vitiello, Giovanni. "The Dragon's Whim: Ming and Qing Homoerotic Tales from the Cut Sleeve." *T'oung Pao* 78 (1992): 341–72.

———. "Exemplary Sodomites: Male Homosexuality in Late Ming Fiction." Ph.D. diss., University of California, Berkeley, 1994.

———. "Exemplary Sodomites: Chivalry and Love in Late Ming Culture." *Nan nü* 2, no. 2 (2000): 207–57.

Volpp, Sophie. "The Male Queen: Boy Actors and Literati Libertines." Ph.D. diss., Harvard University, 1995.

Wakeman, Frederic. "The Civil Society and Public Sphere Debate: Western Reflections on Chinese Political Culture." *Modern China* 19, no. 2 (1993): 108–38.

Wakeman, Frederic, and Wen-hsin Yeh, eds. *Shanghai Sojourners.* Berkeley and Los Angeles: University of California Press, 1992.

Wan Yanhai 萬延海. "Fulu: Zhongguo dalu tongzhi de xiankuang" 中國大陸同志的現況 (Appendix: The current situation of mainland Chinese homosexuals). In *Beijing tongzhi gushi,* ed. Chou Wah-shan, 167–88. Hong Kong: Xianggang tongzhi yanjiushe, 1996.

Wang Anyi 王安憶. *Dixiongmen* 弟兄們 (Brothers). In *Zhulu zhong jie* 逐鹿中街 (Competing for dominance in the street), 123–203. Taipei: Maitian, 1992.

Wang Chengpin 汪誠品. *Qingchun de xing jiaoyu* 青春的性教育 (Sex education for youths). Shanghai: Xiongdi chubanshe, 1939.

Wang, David Der-wei 王德威. *Xiaoshuo Zhongguo: Wan Qing dao dangdai de zhongwen xiaoshuo* 小説中國：晚清到當代的中文小説 (Fiction China: Fiction in Chinese from the late Qing to the contemporary era). Taipei: Maitian, 1993.

———. *Fin-de-Siècle Splendor: Repressed Modernities of Late Qing Fiction, 1849–1911.* Stanford, Calif.: Stanford University Press, 1997.

———. "Gudude ren shi wuchide" 孤獨的人是無恥的 (The solitary ones are shameless). Introduction to *Siren shenghuo,* by Chen Ran, iii–viii. Taipei: Maitian, 1998.

———. *Ruhe xiandai, zenyang wenxue? Shijiu ershi shiji Zhongwen xiaoshuo xinlun* 如何現代，怎樣文學？十九・二十世紀中文小説新論 (The making of the modern, the making of a literature: New perspectives on nineteenth- and twentieth-century Chinese fiction). Taipei: Maitian, 1998.

Wang Haowei 王皓薇. "Buyao jiaochu yaokong qi: Tongzhi yao you 'xianshen' zizhu quan" 不要交出遙控器：同志要有「現身」自主權 (Don't hand out a remote control: Lesbians and gays should keep the initiative for coming out in their own hands). *Saodong,* no. 3 (1997): 52–57.

Wang Hui 汪暉. "The Fate of 'Mr. Science' in China: The Concept of Science and Its Application in Modern Chinese Thought." *Positions* 3, no. 1 (1995): 1–68.

Wang, Jing. *High Culture Fever.* Durham, N.C.: Duke University Press, 1996.

Wang Li'nuo 王麗娜. "*Liaozhai zhiyi* de minzu yuwen banben he waiwen yiben" 聊齋志異的民族語文版本和外文譯本 (The ethnic editions and foreign translations of *Liaozhai zhiyi*). In *Liaozhai zhiyi ziliao ji* 聊齋誌異資料集 (A collection of essays on *Liaozhai*), ed. Zhongguo xueshu ziliao she 中國學術資料社, 155–64. Hong Kong: The Sinological Bibliocenter, 1983.

Wang Meng 王蒙. "Mosheng de Chen Ran" 陌生的陳染 (The unfamiliar Chen Ran). In *Chen Ran wenji,* by Chen Ran, 1–4. Nanjing: Jiangsu wenyi chubanshe, 1996.

Wang Ping 王蘋, Ni Jiazhen 倪家珍, et al. "Xingbie zhengzhi yu tongzhi yundong" 性別政治與同志運動 (Gender politics and the lesbian/gay movement). In *Huaren tongzhi xin duben,* ed. Lu Jianxiong, 87–90. Hong Kong: Huasheng shudian, 1999.

Wang Qingning 王慶寧. "Qin'aide XXX" 親愛的 XXX (Dear XXX). In *Huaren tongzhi xin duben,* ed. Lu Jianxiong, 254–58. Hong Kong: Huasheng shudian, 1999.

Wang Xiaobo 王小波. "Yishu yu guanhuai ruoshi zuqun" 藝術與關懷弱勢族群 (Art and caring about minorities). *Zhonghua dushu bao,* 28 February 1996.

Wang Zheng. "Research on Women in Contemporary China." In *A Selected Guide to Women's Studies in China*, ed. Gail Hershatter et al., 1–43. Berkeley: University of California, Berkeley, Institute of East Asian Studies, 1998.

———. *Women in the Chinese Enlightenment: Oral and Textual Histories*. Berkeley and Los Angeles: University of California Press, 1999.

Weeks, Jeffrey. "Values in an Age of Uncertainty." In *Discourses of Sexuality*, ed. Domna Stanton, 389–411. Ann Arbor: University of Michigan Press, 1992.

Wei Hui 衛慧. *Shanghai baobei* 上海寶貝 (Shanghai baby). Shenyang: Chunfeng wenyi chubanshe, 1999.

Wei Sheng 薇生, trans. "Tongxing ai zai nüzi jiaoyu shang de xin yiyi" 同性愛在女子教育上的新意義 (The new meaning of same-sex love in women's education), by Furuya Toyoko 古屋登代子. *Funü zazhi* 1, no. 6 (1925): 1064–69.

Weixing shiguan zhaizhu 唯性史觀齋主. *Zhongguo tongxinglian mishi* 中國同性戀祕史 (The secret history of homosexuality in China). Hong Kong: Yuzhou chubanshe, 1964.

Wen Yiduo 聞一多. *Chuci yanjiu shizhong* 楚辭研究十種 (Ten studies of Chuci). Hong Kong: Weiya shuwu, n.d.

Wharton, Henry Thorton. *Sappho: Memoir, Text, Selected Renderings, and a Literal Translation*. 3d ed. London: Simpkin, Marshall, Hamilton, Kent, 1907.

Widmer, Ellen. "Xiaoqing's Literary Legacy and the Place of the Woman Writer in Late Imperial China." *Late Imperial China* 13, no. 1 (1992): 111–55.

Wilton, Tamsin. *Lesbian Studies: Setting an Agenda*. New York: Routledge, 1995.

Witke, Roxane Heather. "Transformation of Attitudes towards Women during the May Fourth Era of Modern China." Ph.D. diss., University of California, Berkeley, 1970.

Wittig, Monique. *The Straight Mind and Other Essays*. Boston: Beacon, 1992.

Wolf, Margery, and Roxane Witke, eds. *Women in Chinese Society*. Stanford, Calif.: Stanford University Press, 1975.

Women zhi jian 我們之間 et al. "Kangyi Huashi zhuanji" 抗議華視專輯 (Feature articles to protest against CTV [Chinese Television Co.]). *Nü pengyou*, no. 24 (1998): 35–43.

Wong Bik Wan (Huang Biyun) 黃碧雲. "Ta shi nüzi, wo ye shi nüzi" 她是女子, 我也是女子 (She is a woman, so am I). In *Ta shi nüzi, wo ye shi nüzi* 她是女子, 我也是女子 (She is a woman, so am I), 1–18. Taipei: Maitian, 1994.

Wu Zao 吳藻. *Qiao ying* 喬影 (The disguised image). In *Qingren zaju chu er ji* 清人雜劇初二集 (The first and second volumes of Qing *zaju* plays), ed. Zheng Zhenduo 鄭振鐸, 2:287–310. Reprint. Hong Kong: Longmen shudian, 1969.

*Xiandai hanyu cidian* 現代漢語詞典 (The dictionary of the modern Chinese language). Beijing: Shangwu, 1973.

Xiao Mao 小貓. "Jing, yin, ti, tou: 'Women zhijian' ba zhounian daogao ci" 精、淫、剔、透:「我們之間」八週年禱告詞 (A prayer on the eighth anniversary of *Between Us*). *Nü pengyou*, no. 21 (1998): 38.

———. "Zuozeide han zhuo zei" 作賊的喊捉賊 (The thief cries out against theft). *Nü pengyou*, no. 23 (1998): 10.

Xiao Mao 小貓 and Gou Gou 狗狗. "Guoxiao jiaoshi fang shilu" 國小教師訪實錄 (An interview with a primary school teacher). *Nü pengyou*, no. 23 (1998): 8–9.

Xiao Sui 小歲. "Menghuan rensheng—zai jingcheng mou jiuba caifang shilu" 夢幻人生——在京城某酒吧採訪實錄 (A dream-like life—a factual record of an interview in a bar in the capital). *Xiandai wenming huabao*, no. 119 (2002): 61–63.

Xiao Ying 肖鷹. "Jiushi niandai Zhongguo wenxue: Quanqiuhua yu ziwo rentong" 九十年代中國文學: 全球化與自我認同 (Chinese literature in the 1990s: Globalization and self identity). *Wenxue pinglun* 2000, no. 2 (March): 103–11.

Xiaomingxiong 小明雄 [Samshasha]. *Zhongguo tongxing'ai shilu* 中國同性愛史錄 (The history of homosexuality in China). Hong Kong: Fenhong sanjiao chubanshe, 1984. Rev. and enlarged ed. Hong Kong: Fenhong sanjiao chubanshe, 1997.

Xie Bingying 謝冰瑩. *Yige nübing de zizhuan* 一個女兵的自傳 (The autobiography of a woman soldier). Shanghai: Liangyou tushu, 1936.

Xie Jin 謝晉, dir. *Wutai jiemei* 舞台姐妹 (Stage sisters). Shanghai: Tianma Film Studio, 1965.

Xie Se 謝瑟, trans. "Nü xuesheng de tongxing ai" 女學生的同性愛 (Same-sex love among female students). *Xin wenhua* 1, no. 6 (1927): 57–74. A translation of Havelock Ellis's "The School Friendships of Girls," in *Studies in the Psychology of Sex* (3d ed.), vol. 2, *Sexual Inversion* (Philadelphia: F. A. Davis, 1920).

Xinzhi gongzuoshi 新知工作室. "Chai jie hunyin shenhua" 拆解婚姻神話 (Dismantle the marriage myth). *Funü xinzhi*, no. 158 (1995): 10–12.

Xu Ke 徐珂. *Qingbai leichao* 清稗類鈔 (Classified notes of Qing-dynasty unofficial historical material). 48 vols. Shanghai: Shangwu yinshuguan, 1917.

Xu Kun 徐坤. "Yinwei chenmo tai jiu" 因為沈默太久 (Because we have kept silent for too long). *Zhonghua dushu bao*, 10 January 1996.

———. *Shuangdiao yexingchuan: Jiushi niandai de nüxing xiezuo* 雙調夜行船: 九十年代的女性寫作 (Double tunes on a night boat: Female writing of the 1990s). Taiyuan: Shanxi jiaoyu chubanshe, 1999.

Xu Shan 徐珊. "Nuola: Hechu shi guicheng: Lun xin shiqi nüxing wenxue chuangzuo zhong nüxing yishi de fazhan liubian" 娜拉: 何處是歸程: 論新時期女性文學創作中女性意識的發展流變 (Nora: Where is the way home: On the transformation of female consciousness in women's literature of the new era). *Wenyi pinglun* 1999, no. 1 (January): 58–69; 1999, no. 2 (March): 40–54.

Xu She 許奢. "Huan ju shouji" 懽懼手記 (Notes on joy and fear). *Funü xinzhi*, no. 149 (1994): 4–5.

Xu Zhaoren 徐兆仁. *Daojiao zongheng* 道教縱橫 (Aspects of the Taoist religion). Tianjin: Tianjin jiaoyu chubanshe, 1993.

Xuan Xiaofo 玄小佛. *Yuan zhi wai* 圓之外 (Outside the perfect circle). 1976; reprint, Taipei: Wansheng chuban, 1990.

Xue Tang 薛糖. "Women shenshen xiang'ai, dan jue bushi 'zhenzhengde' tongxinglian?" 我們深深相愛, 但絕不是「真正的」同性戀 (We are deeply in love with each other, but we are definitely not "real" lesbians?). *Funü xinzhi*, no. 149 (1994): 7–8.

Xue Yi 薛毅. "Fuchu lishi dibiao zhi hou" 浮出歷史地表之後 (After emerging above the horizon of history). In "Jiushi niandai de nüxing: Geren xiezuo (bitan)" 九十年代的女性: 個人寫作 (筆談) (Female writing in the 1990s: Individualistic writing: A forum), by Wang Xiaoming 王曉明 et al. *Wenxue pinglun* 1999, no. 5 (September): 50–55.

Yan Shi 晏始. "Nannü de geli yu tongxing ai" 男女的隔離與同性愛 (The segregation between the sexes and same-sex love). *Funü zazhi* 9, no. 5 (1923): 14–15.

Yan Yunxiang. "The Politics of Consumerism in Chinese Society." In *China Briefing 2000: The Continuing Transformation,* ed. Tyrene White, 159–93. Armonk, N.Y.: M. E. Sharpe, 2000.

Yang, Mayfair Mei-hui. "From Gender Erasure to Gender Difference." In *Spaces of Their Own: Women's Public Sphere in Transnational China,* ed. Mayfair Yang, 35–67. Minneapolis: University of Minnesota Press, 1999.

———. Introduction to *Spaces of Their Own: Women's Public Sphere in Transnational China,* ed. Mayfair Yang, 1–31. Minneapolis: University of Minnesota Press, 1999.

———, ed. *Spaces of Their Own: Women's Public Sphere in Transnational China.* Minneapolis: University of Minnesota Press, 1999.

Yang Sheng 楊望. Preface to *Tamende shijie: Zhongguo nan tongxinglian qunluo toushi,* by Li Yinhe and Wang Xiaobo, i–ii. Hong Kong: Tiandi tushu gongsi, 1992.

Yang Zhensheng 楊振聲. "Ta weishenmo huran fafeng le" 她為甚麼忽然發瘋了 (Why did she suddenly go crazy?). *Chen bao fukan*, 11 January 1926, 13–14.

Yanping yingye gongsi 延平影業公司. "Nühuan" 女歡 (Female pleasures). *G&L: Re'ai zazhi*, no. 15 (1998): 142–47.

Ye Dingluo 葉鼎洛. *Nanyou* 男友 (Boyfriend). Shanghai: Liangyou tushu, [1920s]. Reprint. Shanghai: Shanghai shudian, 1989.

Ye Huiling 葉惠齡. *Liaozhai zhiyi zhong guihu gushi de tantao* 聊齋志異中鬼狐故事的探討 (Ghosts and foxes in *Liaozhai zhiyi*). Taipei: Wenhua daxue chubanbu, 1982.

Ye Shaojun 葉紹鈞 (Ye Shengtao). *Ye Shengtao ji* 葉聖陶集 (Works by Ye Shengtao). Edited by Ye Shishan 葉至善 et al. 4 vols. Nanjing: Jiangsu jiaoyu chubanshe, 1987.

Ye Zi 葉子. "Nü tongzhi de ziwei zhi dao" 女同志的自衛之道 (Lesbians' self-defense). *Nü pengyou*, no. 4 (1995): 16–17.

Yeh, Michelle. *Modern Chinese Poetry: Theory and Practice since 1917*. New Haven, Conn.: Yale University Press, 1991.

———. "International Theory and the Transnational Critic: China in the Age of Multiculturalism." In *Modern Chinese Literature and Cultural Studies in the Age of Theory: Reimagining a Field*, ed. Rey Chow, 251–80. Durham, N.C.: Duke University Press, 2000.

Yeh, Wen-hsin. *The Alienated Academy: Culture and Politics in Republican China, 1919–1937*. Cambridge, Mass.: Harvard University Press, 1990.

———, ed. *Becoming Chinese: Passages to Modernity and Beyond*. Berkeley and Los Angeles: University of California Press, 2000.

Yi Bi 一碧. *Xing dian* 性典 (A dictionary of sex). Shanghai: Qizhi shuju, 1930.

Yi Bin 益斌 et al. *Lao Shanghai guanggao* 老上海廣告 (Advertisements in old-time Shanghai). Shanghai: Shanghai huabao chubanshe, 1995.

Yidian 一點. "Jiannan de miandui" 艱難的面對 (To face it with difficulty). *Zhonghua dushu bao*, 24 January 1996.

Yu Dafu 郁達夫. *Ta shi yige ruo nüzi* 她是一個弱女子 (She is a weak woman). In *Ta shi yige ruo nüzi*, 101–89. Beijing: Renmin wenxue chubanshe, 1990.

Yu Youwei 魚幼薇. "Manman chang lu—leisibian dashi ji" 漫漫長路：蕾絲邊大事記 (A long journey—a chronicle of major events in lesbian history). *Ai bao*, no. 2 (1994): 7–9.

Yue, Ming-Bao. "Gendering the Origins of Modern Chinese Fiction." In *Gender and Sexuality in Twentieth-Century Chinese Literature and Society*, ed. Tonglin Lu, 47–65. Albany: State University of New York Press, 1993.

Yulong 魚龍, comp. "Tongzhi falü renquan zuotanhui" 同志法律人權座談會 (A forum on gay legal rights). *G&L: Re'ai zazhi*, no. 15 (1998): 162–63.

Yung, Bell. "Model Opera as Model." In *Popular Chinese Literature and Performing Arts in the People's Republic of China, 1949–1979*, ed. Bonnie S. McDougall, 144–64. Berkeley and Los Angeles: University of California Press, 1984.

Yuxuan Aji 魚玄阿璣. "Jiehun quan yu bu jiehun quan" 結婚權與不結婚權 (The right of marriage and the right not to marry). *Nü pengyou*, no. 3 (1995): 16–17.

———. "Xishou zhi qian, fenli, you qi biyao" 攜手之前, 分離, 有其必要 (Before holding hands, it is necessary to break up). *Funü xinzhi*, no. 161 (1995): 16–18.

Yuxuan Aji 魚玄阿璣 and Zheng Meili 鄭美里. "Fulu: Xingfu zheng zai bijin" 附錄：幸福正在逼近 (Appendix: Happiness is approaching). In *Nüer quan: Taiwan nü tongzhi de xingbie, jiating yu quannei shenghuo*, by Zheng Meili, 209–21. Taipei: Nüshu wenhua, 1997.

Yuxuan Aji 魚玄阿璣 et al. "Taibei tongwanjie zhuanti" 台北同玩節專題 (Feature articles on the Taipei lesbian and gay festival). *Nü pengyou*, no. 33 (2000): 6–23.

Zarrow, Peter. *Anarchism and Chinese Political Culture*. New York: Columbia University Press, 1991.

Zeitlin, Judith. *Historian of the Strange: Pu Songling and the Chinese Classical Tale.* Stanford, Calif.: Stanford University Press, 1993.

Zha, Jianying. *China Pop: How Soap Operas, Tabloids, and Bestsellers Are Transforming a Culture.* New York: New Press, 1995.

Zhang Dening 章德寧 and Yue Jianyi 岳建一, eds. *Zhongguo zhiqing qinglian baogao* 中國知青情戀報告 (Educated youths report on their love and romance). 3 vols. Beijing: Guangming ribao chubanshe, 1998.

Zhang Jie 張潔. "The Ark." In *Love Must Not Be Forgotten,* trans. Gladys Yang, 1–13. Beijing: Panda, 1986.

———. *Love Must Not Be Forgotten.* Translated by Gladys Yang. Beijing: Panda, 1986.

Zhang Jingsheng 張競生, ed. *Xing shi* 性史 (Sex histories). Shanghai: Meide shudian, 1926.

———. "Disanzhong shui yu luanzhu ji shengji he youzhong de guanxi" 第三種水與卵珠及生機和優種的關係 (The relationships between the third kind of water, the ovum, the vital moment, and eugenics). *Xin wenhua* 1, no. 1 (1927): 104–8.

———. "Xing mei" 性美 (Sexual beauty). In *Zhang Jingsheng wenji,* ed. Jiang Zhongxiao et al., 2:276–81 (Guangzhou: Guangzhou chubanshe, 1998). Originally published in *Xin wenhua* 1, no. 6 (1927): 1–12.

———, ed. *Aiqing dingze* 愛情定則 (The rules of love). Shanghai: Meide shudian, 1928.

———. *Sex Histories: China's First Modern Treatise on Sex Education.* Translated by Howard Levy. Yokohama, 1967.

———. *Zhang Jingsheng wenji* 張競生文集 (Selected works of Zhang Jingsheng). Edited by Jiang Zhongxiao 江中孝 et al. 2 vols. Guangzhou: Guangzhou chubanshe, 1998.

Zhang Jingyuan 張京媛, ed. *Dangdai nüxing zhuyi wenxue piping* 當代女性主義文學批評 (Contemporary feminist literary criticism). Beijing: Beijing daxue chubanshe, 1992.

———. *Psychoanalysis in China: Literary Transformations, 1919–1949.* Ithaca, N.Y.: Cornell University, Cornell East Asia Program, 1992.

Zhang Juanfen 張娟芬. *Jiemei xiqiang* 姊妹「戲」牆 (Sisters trespassing the wall). Taipei: Lianhe wenxue chubanshe, 1998.

———. "Nütong shequn de rentong yu zhanyan" 女同社群的認同與展演 (Identity and performance in the lesbian community). *Chengpin haodu,* no. 5 (2000): 12–15.

———. *Aide ziyou shi: Nü tongzhi gushi shu* 愛的自由式：女同志故事書 (Free-style love: Lesbian stories). Taipei: Shibao, 2001.

Zhang Junmei 張君玫, trans. "Nüren rentong nüren" 女人認同女人. *Funü xinzhi,* no. 158 (1995): 2–4. A translation of Radicalesbians' "The Woman Identified Woman."

Zhang Minyun 張敏筠. *Xing kexue* 性科學 (Sexual science). Shanghai: Shanghai wenyi chubanshe, 1988. Originally published as *Weiwulun xing kexue* 唯物論性科學 (The sexual science of materialism) (Shanghai: Shidai shuju, 1950).

Zhang Xichen 章錫琛, ed. *Xin xing daode taolun ji* 新性道德討論集 (Discussions on new sexual morality). Shanghai: Liangxi tushuguan, 1925.

———. "*Xin nüxing* yu xing de yanjiu" 新女性與性的研究 (*New Woman* and the study of sex). *Xin nüxing* 2, no. 3 (1927): 237–41.

Zhang, Xudong. *Chinese Modernism in the Era of Reforms: Cultural Fever, Avant-garde Fiction, and the New Chinese Cinema.* Durham, N.C.: Duke University Press, 1997.

Zhang Yanfeng 張燕風. *Lao yuefenpai guanggao hua* 老月份牌廣告畫 (The advertisement paintings on old calendar posters). 2 vols. Taipei: Yingwen hansheng, 1994.

Zhang, Yingjin. *The City in Modern Chinese Literature and Film: Configurations of Space, Time, and Gender.* Stanford, Calif.: Stanford University Press, 1996.

Zhang Yiping 章衣萍. *Qingshu yishu* 情書一束 (Love letters). Beijing: Beixin shuju, 1926.

Zhang Ziping 張資平. *Fei xu* 飛絮 (Flying catkin). Shanghai: Chuangzaoshe chubanbu, 1927.

Zhao Jingsheng 趙景深. "Tongxing lian'ai xiaoshuo de chajin" 同性戀愛小說的查禁 (The banning of a novel about same-sex love). *Xiaoshuo yuebao* 20, no. 3 (1929): 611–12.

———. *Wenxue jianghua* 文學講話 (Lectures on literature). 6th ed. Shanghai: Zhongguo wenhua fuwushe, 1936.

———. "Zhongguo xin wenyi yu jingshen fenxi" 中國新文藝與精神分析 (Chinese new literature and psychoanalysis). In *Wenxue jianghua*, 21–28. Shanghai: Zhongguo wenhua fuwushe, 1936.

Zheng Daqun 鄭大群. "Nüxing jinji yu hou xinshiqi nüxing xiezuo" 女性禁忌與後新時期女性寫作 (Female taboo and post-new era female writing). *Wenyi pinglun* 2000, no. 2 (March): 33–40.

Zheng Meili 鄭美里. *Nüer quan: Taiwan nü tongzhi de xingbie, jiating yu quannei shenghuo* 女兒圈：台灣女同志的性別、家庭與圈內生活 (A circle of women: Taiwanese lesbians' genders, family, and life in the lesbian community). Taipei: Nüshu wenhua, 1997.

Zhong, Xueping. *Masculinity Besieged? Issues of Modernity and Male Subjectivity in Chinese Literature of the Late Twentieth Century*. Durham, N.C.: Duke University Press, 2000.

"Zhongguo meiren zhi xianqing (xuyu) (daiyue) (dushi) (douzhuang)" 中國美人之閑情（絮語）（待月）（讀詩）（鬥妝）(Chinese beauties' activities of leisure: "A long uninterrupted chat," "Waiting for the moon," "Reading a poem," "A competition in makeup"). *Meiyu* 1, no. 1 (1914): 4.

Zhonghua jingshen kexue hui 中華精神科學會 (Chinese Psychiatric Association). *Zhongguo jingshen zhang'ai fenlei yu zhenduan biaozhun disanban* 中國精神障礙分類與診斷標準第三版 (The Chinese classification of mental disorders third revision). Beijing, 2001.

Zhou Jianren 周建人. "Xing jiaoyu yundong de weiji" 性教育運動的危機 (Crisis in the movement of sex education). *Xin nüxing* 2, no. 2 (1927): 135–39.

Zhou Ke 周柯. "Jiliao er bu anfen de wenxue tansuo" 寂寥而不安分的文學探索 (A lonely and restless literary exploration). In *Zuichunli de yangguang*, by Chen Ran, 311–20. Wuhan: Changjiang wenyi chubanshe, 1992.

Zhou Yizhao 周燨昭. "Ping Zhang Jingsheng boshi *Meide xingyu*" 評張競生博士美的性慾 (A review of Dr. Zhang Jingsheng's *The Sex Drive of Beauty*). *Xin nüxing* 2, no. 5 (1927): 543–52.

Zhou Zuoren 周作人 (Kai Ming 開明). "Ailisi de hua" 靄理思的話 (The words of Ellis). *Chen bao fukan*, 23 February 1924.

———, trans. "Zeng suo huan" 贈所歡 (To the beloved). *Yu si* 語絲 (Threads of talk), 30 March 1925, 165–66. A translation of Sappho's "Fis Eromenav."

———. "Guanyu zhuo tongxing lian'ai" 關於捉同性戀愛 (Regarding the arrests of homosexuals [in Germany]). *Huabei ribao* 華北日報 (North China daily), December 1934. Collected in *Kucha suibi* 苦茶隨筆 (Jottings in the Bitter Tea Studio) (Hubei: Yuelu shushe, 1989), 161–63.

Zhu Huixiang 諸晦香. *Mingzhai xiaoshi* 明齋小識 (Notes from a bright studio). In *Biji xiaoshuo daguan* 筆記小說大觀 (A collection of the reprints of notation books) (50 vols.), 13:3271–3366. Taipei: Xinxing shuju, 1960.

Zhu Tianxin 朱天心. *Jirang ge* 擊壤歌 (Singing and drumming on the ground). 1977. Taipei: Yuanliu, 1994.

———. *Xiang wo juancun de xiongdimen* 想我眷村的兄弟們 (Missing my brothers in the military compounds). Taipei: Maitian, 1992.

———. *Gudu* 古都 (The old capital). Taipei: Maitian, 1997.

Zhu Yixuan 朱一玄, ed. *Liaozhai zhiyi ziliao huibian* 聊齋誌異資料彙編 (Collected materiel concerning *Liaozhai zhiyi*). Henan: Zhongzhou guji chubanshe, 1984.

Zi Yin 子昕. "Xiang ai rongyi xiang shou nan—zou jin lesbian" 相愛容易相守難——走近 lesbian (To love is easy; to stay together is difficult—approaching lesbians). *Xiandai wenming huabao,* no. 119 (2002): 59–60.

Zimet, Jaye. *Strange Sisters: The Art of Lesbian Pulp Fiction, 1949–1969.* New York: Viking Studio, 1999.

Zito, Angela. *Of Body and Brush: Grand Sacrifice as Text/Performance in Eighteenth-Century China.* Chicago: University of Chicago Press, 1997.

Zito, Angela, and Tani E. Barlow, eds. *Body, Subject, and Power in China.* Chicago: University of Chicago Press, 1994.

# INDEX

emotion. See *qing*

Enzensberger, Hans, 248

epistemology, 17, 43, 94, 99

erotica, Ming and Qing, 17. *See also* pornography

essentialism, 28, 198, 266, 272–73

Evans, Harriet, 8, 103, 180, 183

*Eyu shouji. See* Qiu Miaojin

Faderman, Lillian, 136

Fang Gang, 169, 170

female chastity, 21, 93

female consciousness. See *nüxing yishi*

female friendship, 3, 5, 17, 42, 53, 76, 135–37; *guizhong niyou* (intimate friends in the female quarters), 20, 47

female homoeroticism, use of term, 34. *See also* female-female relations

female homosexuality, use of term in post-Mao literary discussion, 185. *See also* female same-sex love; female-female relations; homosexuality

female narcissism, 180–81, 185, 201, 324 n. 25

female same-sex activity, as transhistorical term, 32–33. *See also* female-female relations

female same-sex desire, use of term, 34. *See also* female-female relations

female same-sex love: and formal education, Republican period, 102–5, 108–9, 111–12, 121–22, 129, 135–41; and social anxiety, Republican period, 106–9, 112–18, 122; use of term, 34. *See also* same-sex love

female same-sex unions, 53, 63, 78, 89

female-female relations: affectivity, 5, 17, 20, 26, 67, 74, 86; carnality, 1–3, 17, 20–21, 24–26, 32, 42, 47, 67, 78–81, 130–33, 303 n. 63; commitment, 21, 64, 81; conceptions of proper, 3; and Confucian teachings, 44; demonization of, 65, 133; desire, 5, 15, 21, 24–25, 32–33, 80; and discourse of female jealousy, 50; and gender subordination, 42; insignificance of, 21, 23, 48, 63–65, 93, 132–33; as isolated from male-male eroticism, late-imperial period, 5, 21; and law, 44, 93; as linked to male-male eroticism, late-imperial period, 59, 295 n. 59; in literati's writing, late-imperial period, 21–22, 49–51, 58–60, 63; long-term partnerships, 130–31; and marriage systems (*see* delayed-transfer marriage; free-choice monogamy; marriage imperative;

polygamy); May Fourth fiction of, 132–55; May Fourth studies of, 6, 52–53, 121–22; medicalization of (*see* sexology); preference, 21–22, 44, 46–47, 67, 86, 91, 238–46; and religion, 52, 58, 72–73, 84–86, 90; and schools, 25, 102–5, 108–9, 111–12, 121–22, 129, 135–41, 233, 269–70; and social institutions, 41–42, 232–35; and specters, 15, 81; and state, 193–94, 209–10, 220–21, 234–35, 332 n. 32; and substitution, 47, 81, 141–48, 192, 199, 209, 213–15; terms for, 15, 17, 33–34; topography of, 42; and traditional medicine, 44; and women's socioeconomic status, 7, 23, 53, 64, 94, 102, 122–23, 130, 234; in women's writing, late-imperial period, 22, 39–40, 45–46, 60–63, 300 n. 28. *See also* female friendship; female same-sex love; homosexuality; lesbian identities; sisterhood

femininity: as consistent with female-female attraction, 44; and discipline, 23; essentialist notions of, 8, 28, 185, 188–89

feminism: and lesbian movement in Taiwan, 29–30, 229, 237–46; and lesbian studies, 7–8; in post-Mao China, 27, 245, 297 n. 77

"Feng Sanniang." *See* Pu Songling

Foucault, Michel, 7, 14–15, 17, 20, 30, 180, 227, 275–76, 312 n. 57, 313 n. 65

free-choice monogamy, 183, 193

Freud, Sigmund, 68, 69, 79, 100, 141, 324 n. 25

*Funü shibao* (Women's times), 106–9

*Funü xinzhi* (Women's awakening), 238–42

*Funü zazhi* (Lady's journal), 111–13

Furth, Charlotte, 32, 44, 64

*G&L: Re'ai zazhi* (G&L: Love magazine), 3, 249–53

Garber, Marjorie, 181, 329 n. 21

gay identities: as construct, 30; and invocations of Chinese culture, 45–46, 64, 302 n. 54; postsocialist cosmopolitan, 10–11, 39; *tongzhi*, 235–36. *See also* lesbian identities

gay male activism, 10, 236. *See also* lesbian activism

"Gebi e lian" (A nightmarish affair in the Gobi), 165

gender: analysis, 7–8; asymmetry, 125; binarism, 6, 15, 33; hierarchy, 8, 27–28; reversals, 16 (*see also* transgenderism); system, 47

gender-transcendent consciousness, 28, 202–7, 217

New Woman (cont.)
316 n. 37; use of term (capitalization versus lowercase), 295–96 n. 63, 299 n. 22; writers, May Fourth period, 133–53
Newton, Esther, 136, 334 n. 58
Ni Jiazhen, 244
Nietzsche, Friedrich, 41
*Nü pengyou* (Girlfriend), 229, 234, 239, 247
*nü tongxinglian* (female homosexuality, female homosexual), as term, 32. *See also* lesbian identities
*nü tongzhi* (lesbian), as term, 32, 235–36. *See also* lesbian identities
Nü tongzhi huiyi (Convention of lesbians), 171
*nüxing si xiaoshuo* (novels of women's privacy), 179–80, 323 n. 19
*nüxing xiezuo* (female writing), 201
*nüxing yishi* (female consciousness), 27, 188, 195, 228, 297 n. 77
*nüxing zixuzhuan* (women's autobiographies), 179

odd woman, 21; and masochism, 72; and nonconformity, 22; and performative deprivation, 82–83; and religious practice, 22, 84–86. *See also* woman-preferring woman
*Old Acquaintances by the Seaside. See* Lu Yin
*One Person's War. See* Lin Bai

Pan Guangdan: on eugenics, 298 n. 2; on female homosexuality in premodern China, 47–48, 53, 58–59, 193; on male homosexuality in premodern China, 56, 120; and sexology, 6, 20, 25, 38, 48, 120, 121–22, 168, 298 n. 2, 312 n. 56
passing, 69, 219
patriarchy, 7, 24, 93, 182, 195; and diffused form of control, 16; state as, 27; in Taiwan, 232–33
Peng, Hsiao-yen, 114, 133–34
performance traditions: Beijing theater, 3; Taiwanese opera, 54, 302 n. 52
performativity: deprivation of, 82–83; and gender identities, 199; and sexual identities, 199; speech acts, 32, 305 n. 33
Pflugfelder, Gregory M., 42, 308 n. 9
phallocentrism, 24, 47, 72, 79, 81, 115–16, 305 n. 31
polygamy, 21, 46, 48, 49–52, 304 n. 6
Pontalis, Jean-Bertrand and Jean Laplanche, 80
pornography, 21, 67, 91, 176, 250, 253, 304 n. 3, 336 n. 2

Poster, Mark, 247
Povinelli, Elizabeth, 8, 11
*Private Life. See* Chen Ran
prostitution: courtesans, 290 n. 4; Lu Yin's encounter with, 143–46; and performance of same-sex acts, 291 n. 11
psychopathology. *See* sexology
Pu Songling: admonition against female-female love that excludes marriage, 67; "Aying," (Aying the parrot woman), 87; "Chang'e" (The fairy Chang'e), 306 n. 45; "Feng Sanniang" (The third female child of the Feng family), 69–86, 281–87; "Ji nü" (The weaving girl), 88; *Liaozhai zhiyi* (Liaozhai's records of the strange), 50, 67–89, 93, 306 nn. 45, 46; Qing commentaries on "Feng Sanniang," 71; reinscription of the *zhiguai* (recording the strange) tradition, 88; "Shao nü" (Miss Shao), 50
public sphere: bourgeois, as utopian ideal, 13, 15; cultural constitution of, in post-Mao China, 14; in late Qing and Republican China, 13–14, 26, 129; in Taiwan, 29, 229–30, 254, 271, 273–74; transnational Chinese women's, 159–60

*qing* (affect, emotion, feeling, sentiment), 3, 5, 17, 20, 21, 26, 67, 74, 86
*Qing shi* (The anatomy of love), 21
Qiu Miaojin, 28–29, 159, 256, 257, 261–74; on ambivalence, 265; *Eyu shouji* (The crocodile's journal), 262–74; masculinity, 266, 268; *Mengmate yishu* (Last letters from Montmartre), 262
Qiu Xinru, *Bi sheng hua* (Flowers generated from the writing brush), 89–91
Qiu Yuan, 118–20
Qu Yuan, 236
queer activism. *See* lesbian activism
queer theory: and postcolonial theory, 9, 46; and theories of postmodernism, 260; in transnational China, 8, 28, 38–39, 186, 225, 258–61
queerness, 9, 31, 183

racialization, of sexuality: in sexology, 123, 312 n. 57; in Zhang Jingsheng, 16, 115, 132
Rich, Adrienne, 92, 297 n. 76
Rofel, Lisa, 10–11, 39, 170
Rubin, Gayle, 334 n. 58
Rust, Paula, 205

same-sex activity, during Maoist period, 164–67

same-sex love, Republican period: alternative modernity, 122–25; in autobiographies, 156–58; and class, 101–2; concern for female (see female same-sex love); difference between terms for, 102–3, 308 n. 10; as discursive construct, 24, 100–126; and friendship, 104–5, 112–13; and homosexual orientation, 108, 119, 123; as intersubjective situational practice, 108–9, 117, 118, 123–25; Japanese examples, 108–9; in May Fourth fiction, 129, 132–55; as means to define cross-sex love, 101, 130–32; and schools, 101–2, 108–18, 129, 135–41; as translingual practice, 102; use of terms for, in book, 309 n. 10. *See also* homosexuality

Sappho, 54, 108, 128

scopophilia, 178, 271, 323 n. 17

separate spheres, the ideal of, 46, 48, 62, 294 n. 56

sex education, 6, 24, 26–27, 99

sex, illicit, 21, 39, 46, 164–67

sexology: and abnormalization of same-sex desire, 7, 16, 23–25, 37, 94, 99–100, 105–9, 112, 115–17, 119, 122; Chinese translation of, Republican period, 12, 15, 20, 23–25, 48, 94, 105–25; comeback of, in post-Mao China, 26–27, 28, 168; competition between May Fourth fiction and, 127–32; early Japanese translation of, 102, 308 n. 9; suppression of, Maoist period, 163–64; in Taiwan, 28–29, 232–24, 258, 268

sexual difference, 15, 27

sexual inversion, 24, 100, 102, 149, 153, 268

sexual psychology. *See* sexology

sexual science. *See* sexology

sexuality: deployment of, 7; May Fourth intellectuals' interest in, 15; rise of, 7, 275; as technology of gender, 8, 239; transnational, 8–12

Shan Zai, 106–9

Shen Fu, 49, 50

Shen Zemin, 109–11

Shi Tou, 171, 172–73, 321 n. 27, 328 n. 8, 334 n. 62

Silverman, Kaja, 179

sisterhood: *jiemei* (sisters), 3, 5, 17, 42, 286, 294 n. 52; Jiemei tongzhi (Queer Sisters), 336 n. 2; *jinlan hui* (union of sisters), 53

Siu, Helen, 53

sodomy. *See jijian*

Sommer, Matthew, 39, 54–55, 93, 298 n. 7, 299 n. 25

Stockard, Janice, 53

Stoler, Ann, 312 n. 57

Stonewall riot, 334–5

Stopes, Marie, 131

subaltern, 182

suicide, as motif, 58–59, 262, 265

Taida Lambda, 232, 243

*tanci* (narratives in verse), women's literary, 22, 40, 45, 50, 62–63, 89–91

Tao, women's cultivation of, 84–86, 90–91

Telford, Ted, 92–93

third space, of female homoerotic fiction in post-Mao China, 173–74, 181–84, 200, 259, 321 n. 31

*Tiankong* (Sky), 54, 171, 202, 205

tolerance, as containment, 44, 46–48, 51, 63–65, 122–23

tomboy/girl communities: TB/G, in Hong Kong, 292 n. 32; TB/G, in 1970s Taiwan, 258, 336 n. 7; T-po, in 1990s Taiwan, 226, 235, 244, 269, 331 n. 5. *See also* lesbian identities

*tongnü* (lesbian), as term, 32, 236. *See also* lesbian identities

Tongwanjie (Lesbian and Gay Festival), 246

*tongxing ai* (*tongxing'ai*), as term, 102–3, 308 n. 10. *See also* same-sex love

*tongxing lian* (*tongxing'lian*), as term, 102–3, 308 n. 10. *See also* same-sex love

*tongxing lian'ai,* as term, 102–3, 308 n. 10. *See also* same-sex love

*tongzhi* (lesbian, gay, bisexual, transgender, queer), as term, 235–36, 320 n. 24

transgenderism: compared with gender-transcendent consciousness, 206–7; debate in Taiwan, 261; in late-imperial literature, 22, 33, 40, 62–63, 78, 89–90, 298 n. 12; *Zhongguo bianxingren xianxiang* (The phenomenon of Chinese transsexuals; Fang Gang), 169

translation: of cultures, 31; between discourses, 20; and hypothetical equivalence, 20, 31–32; and modernity, 9, 31; of sexology (*see* sexology); across time, across space, 30–34; translator's agency, 101

transvestitism, 38. *See also* transgenderism

*Tugo* (Together), 3

*tuzi* (rabbit), 165

Ulrichs, Karl Heinrich, 30

uncanny, 68–69. *See also* woman-preferring woman

"Under the Pine Hill." *See* Zhang Yiping